Viz Graphic Novel

FLAME OF RECCA™

Vol. 14

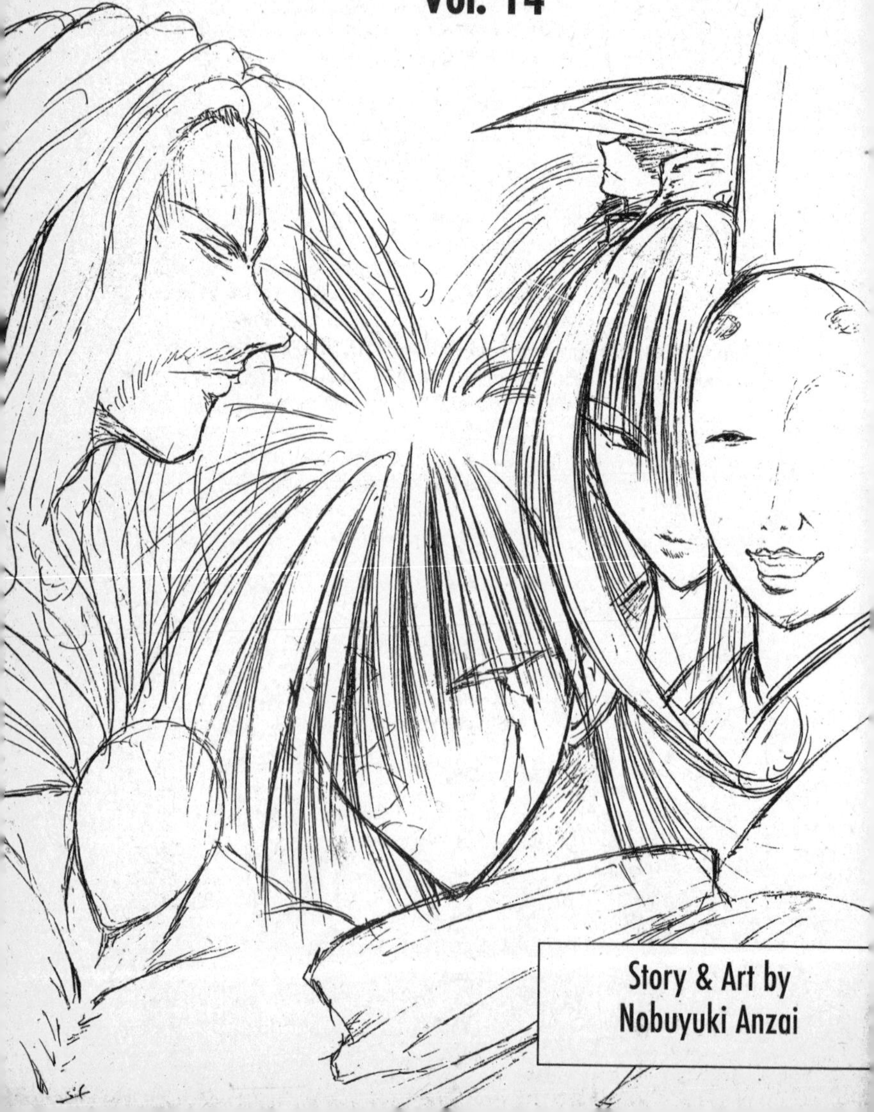

Story & Art by
Nobuyuki Anzai

Contents

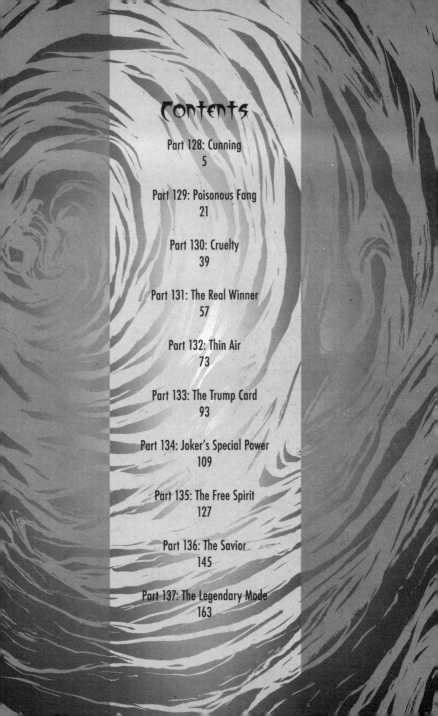

PART 128: CUNNING

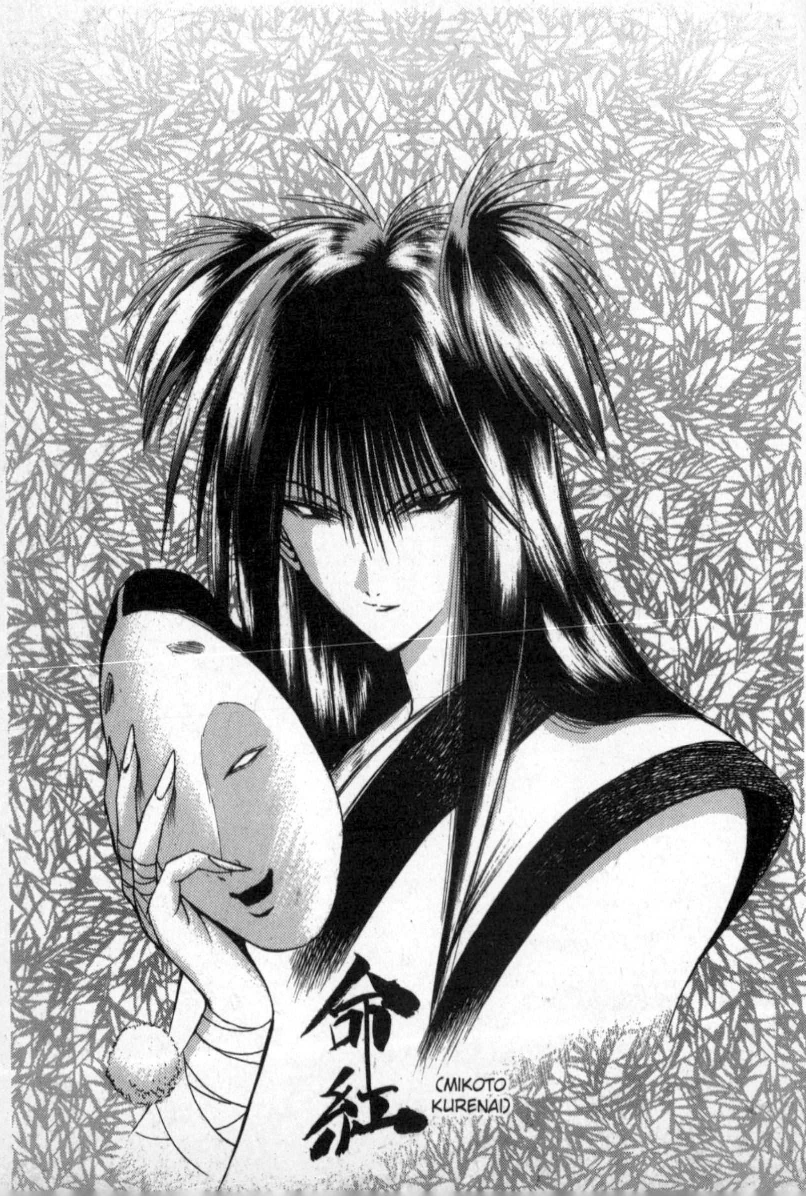
命紅
(MIKOTO KURENAI)

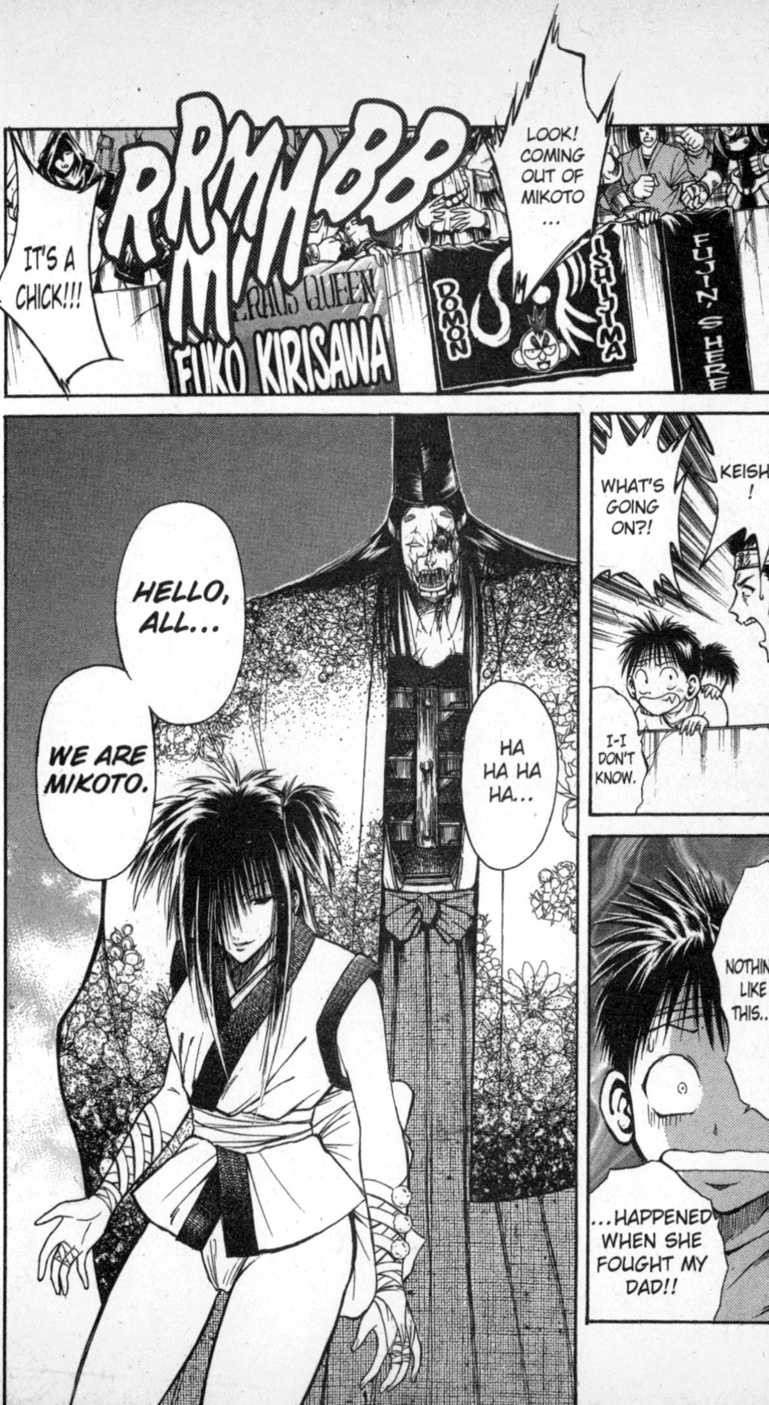
LOOK! COMING OUT OF MIKOTO...
FUJIN'S HERE
DOMON ISHIJIMA
FUKO KIRISAWA
IT'S A CHICK!!!
KEISHU!
WHAT'S GOING ON?!
I-I DON'T KNOW.
NOTHING LIKE THIS...
...HAPPENED WHEN SHE FOUGHT MY DAD!!
HA HA HA HA...
HELLO, ALL...
WE ARE MIKOTO.

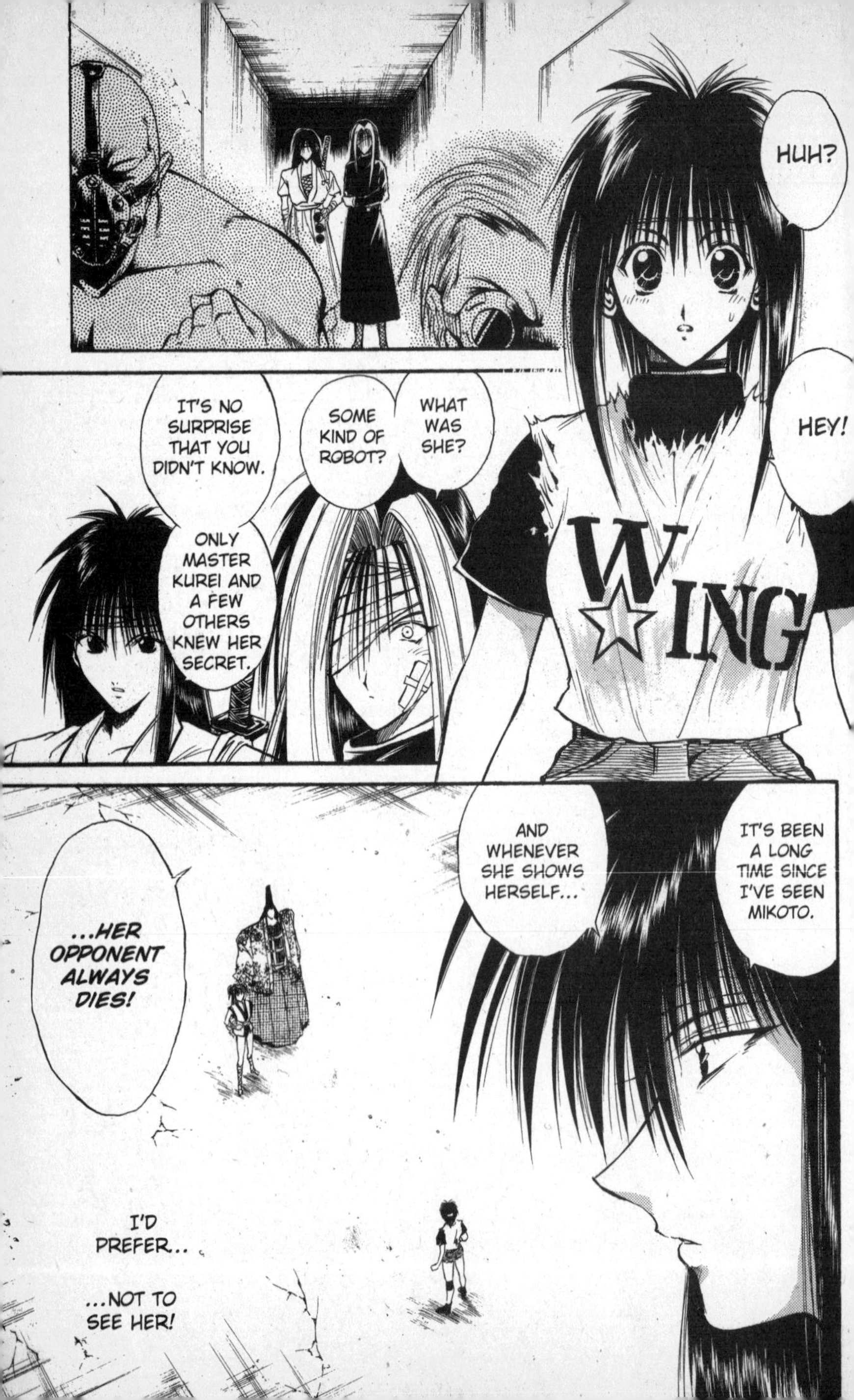
HUH?
HEY!
WHAT WAS SHE?
SOME KIND OF ROBOT?
IT'S NO SURPRISE THAT YOU DIDN'T KNOW.
ONLY MASTER KUREI AND A FEW OTHERS KNEW HER SECRET.
IT'S BEEN A LONG TIME SINCE I'VE SEEN MIKOTO.
AND WHENEVER SHE SHOWS HERSELF...
...HER OPPONENT ALWAYS DIES!
I'D PREFER...
...NOT TO SEE HER!

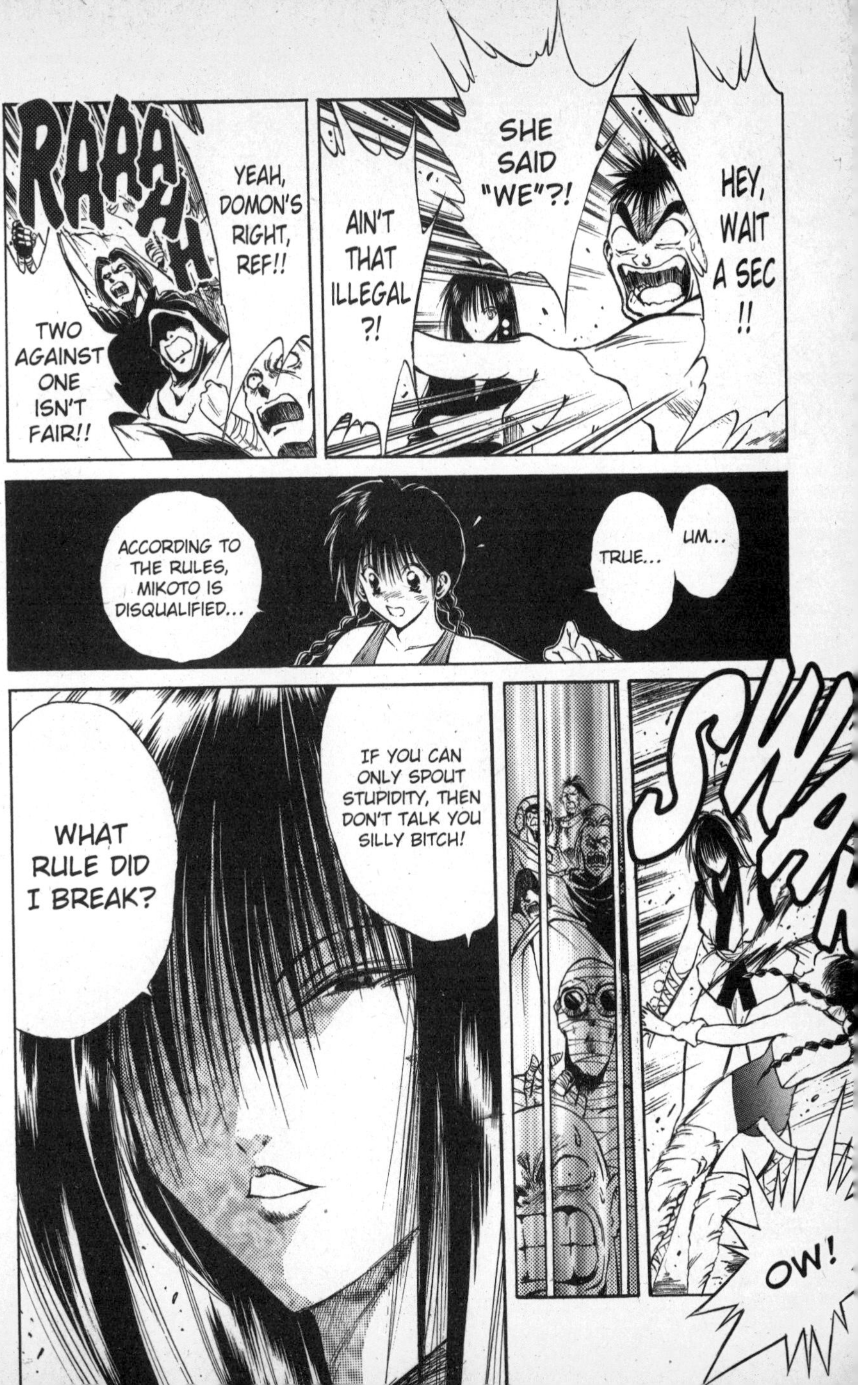
HEY, WAIT A SEC!!
SHE SAID "WE"?!
AIN'T THAT ILLEGAL?!
RAAAAH
YEAH, DOMON'S RIGHT, REF!!
TWO AGAINST ONE ISN'T FAIR!!
UM...
TRUE...
ACCORDING TO THE RULES, MIKOTO IS DISQUALIFIED...
OW!
IF YOU CAN ONLY SPOUT STUPIDITY, THEN DON'T TALK YOU SILLY BITCH!
WHAT RULE DID I BREAK?

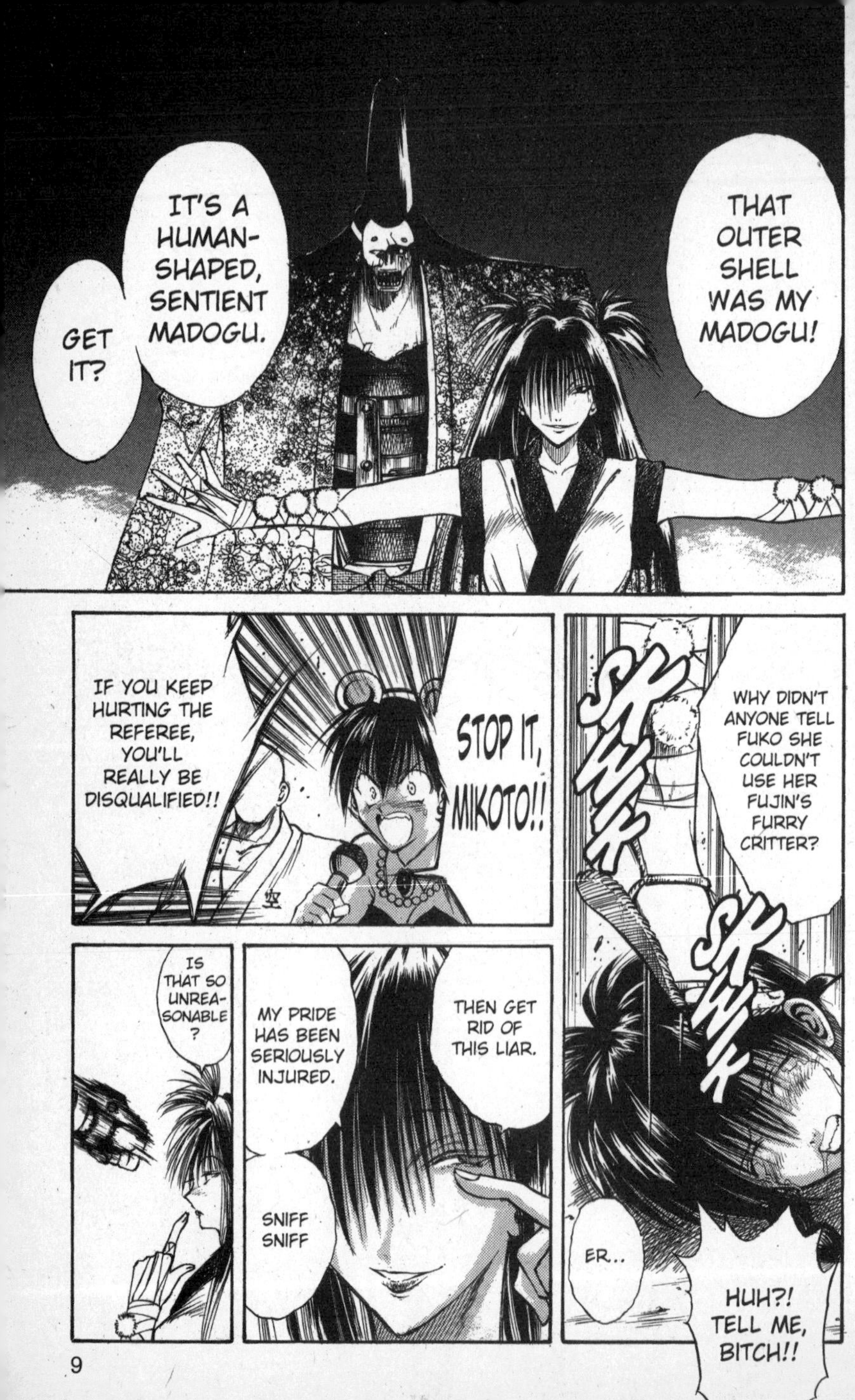
THAT OUTER SHELL WAS MY MADOGU!
IT'S A HUMAN-SHAPED, SENTIENT MADOGU.
GET IT?
SHNIK
WHY DIDN'T ANYONE TELL FUKO SHE COULDN'T USE HER FUJIN'S FURRY CRITTER?
SHNIK
ER...
HUH?! TELL ME, BITCH!!
STOP IT, MIKOTO!!
IF YOU KEEP HURTING THE REFEREE, YOU'LL REALLY BE DISQUALIFIED!!
THEN GET RID OF THIS LIAR.
MY PRIDE HAS BEEN SERIOUSLY INJURED.
SNIFF SNIFF
IS THAT SO UNREA-SONABLE?

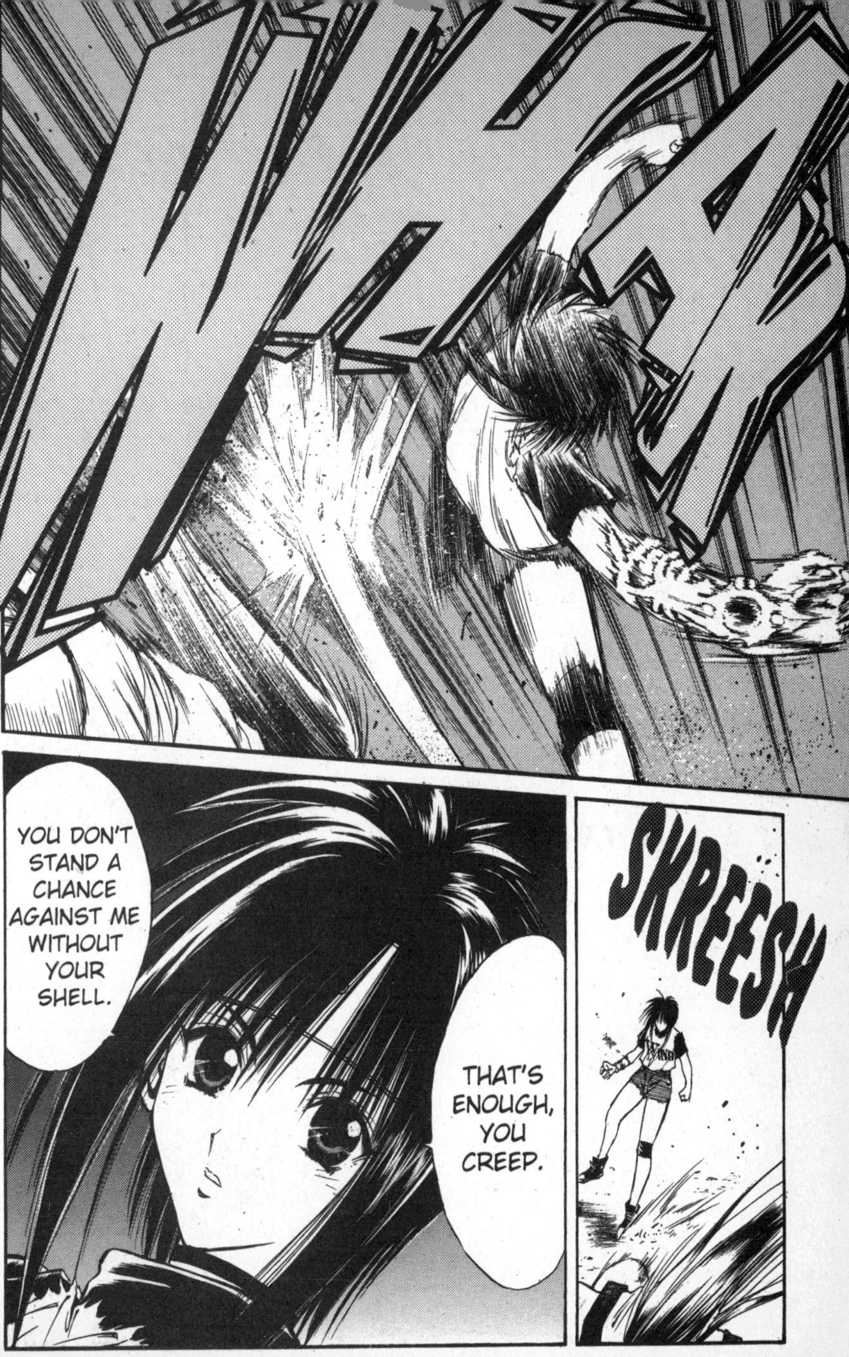
SKREESH
YOU DON'T STAND A CHANCE AGAINST ME WITHOUT YOUR SHELL.
THAT'S ENOUGH, YOU CREEP.

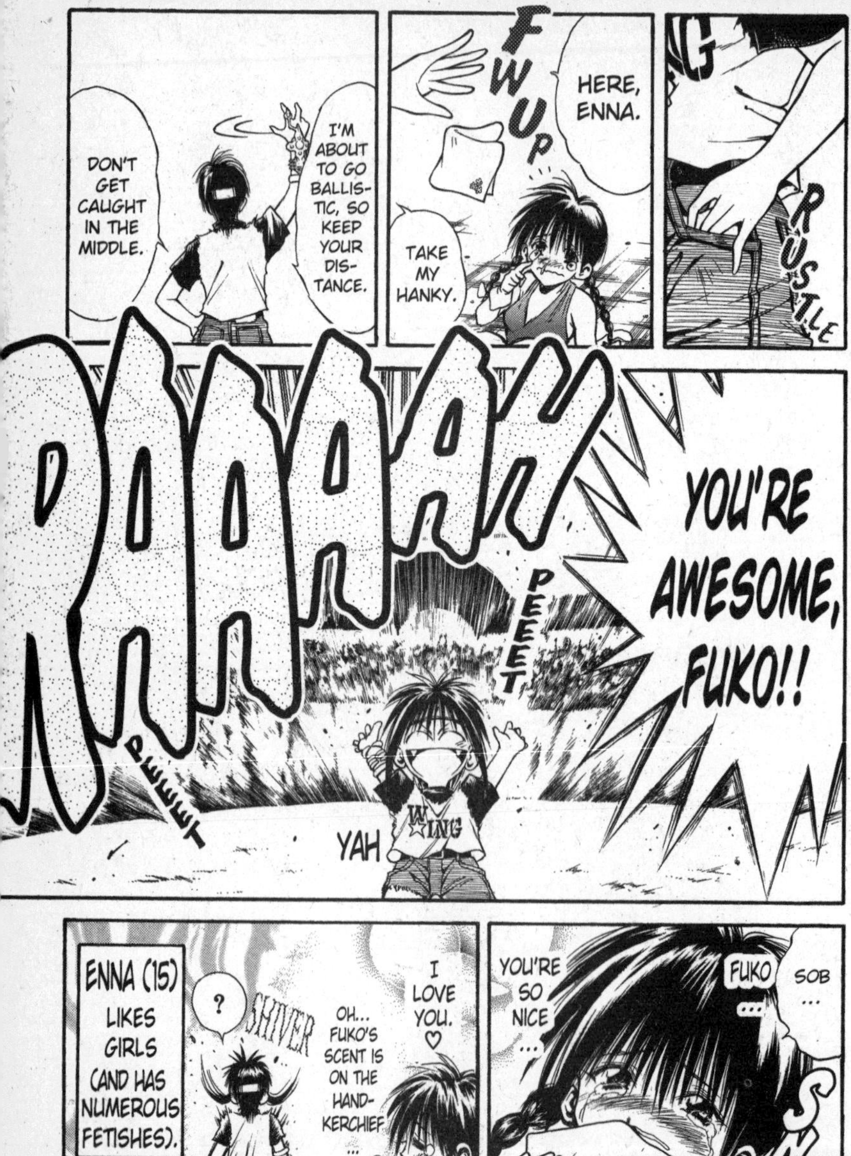
RUSTLE
FWUP
HERE, ENNA.
TAKE MY HANKY.
I'M ABOUT TO GO BALLIS-TIC, SO KEEP YOUR DIS-TANCE.
DON'T GET CAUGHT IN THE MIDDLE.
YOU'RE AWESOME, FUKO!!
RAAAAY
PEEEET
PWEET
YAH
FUKO...
SOB...
YOU'RE SO NICE...
SNIFF
I LOVE YOU. ♡
OH... FUKO'S SCENT IS ON THE HAND-KERCHIEF...
SHIVER
?
ENNA (15)
LIKES GIRLS (AND HAS NUMEROUS FETISHES).

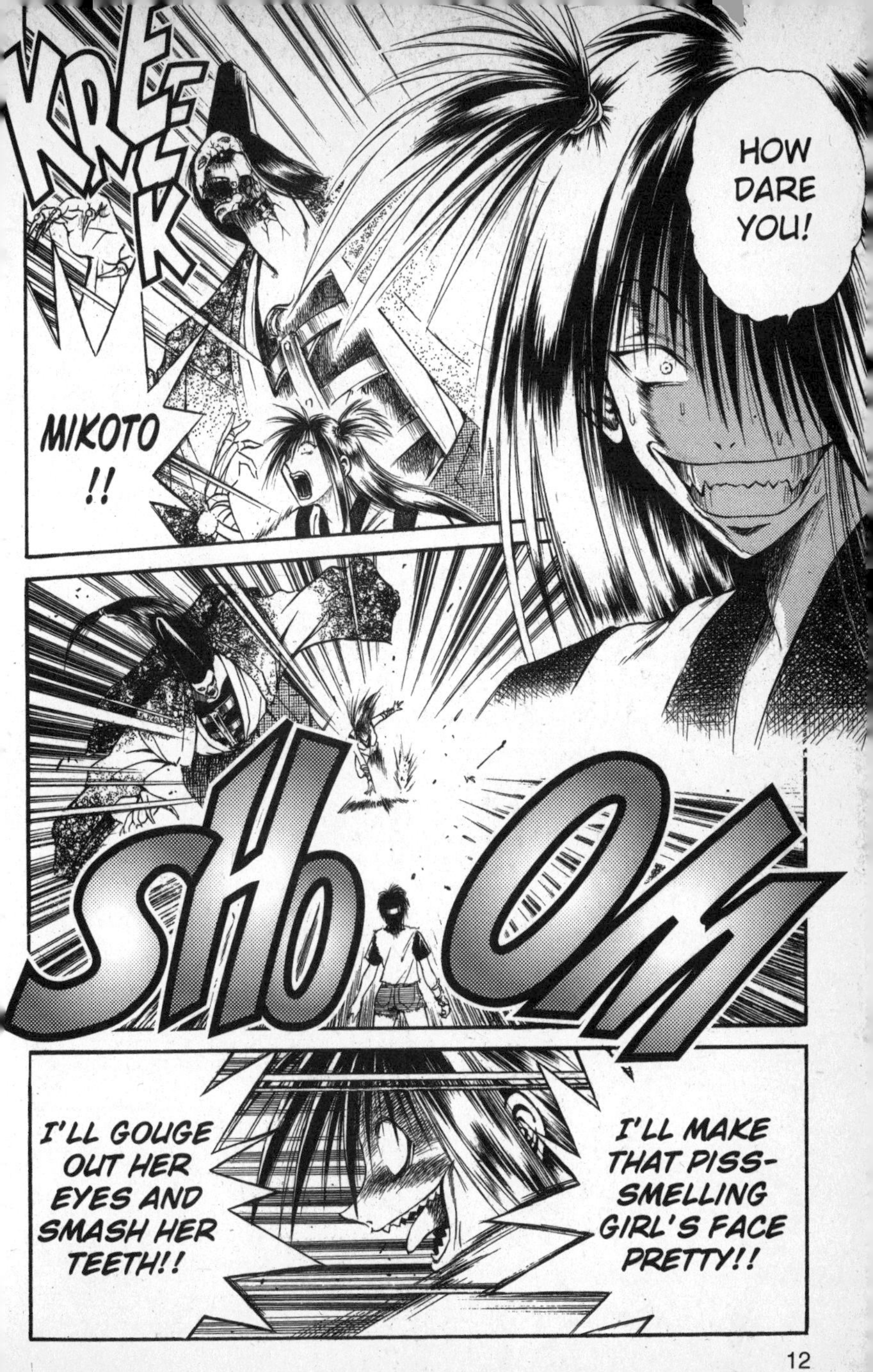
HOW DARE YOU!
KREEEK
MIKOTO !!
SHOOM
I'LL MAKE THAT PISS-SMELLING GIRL'S FACE PRETTY!!
I'LL GOUGE OUT HER EYES AND SMASH HER TEETH!!

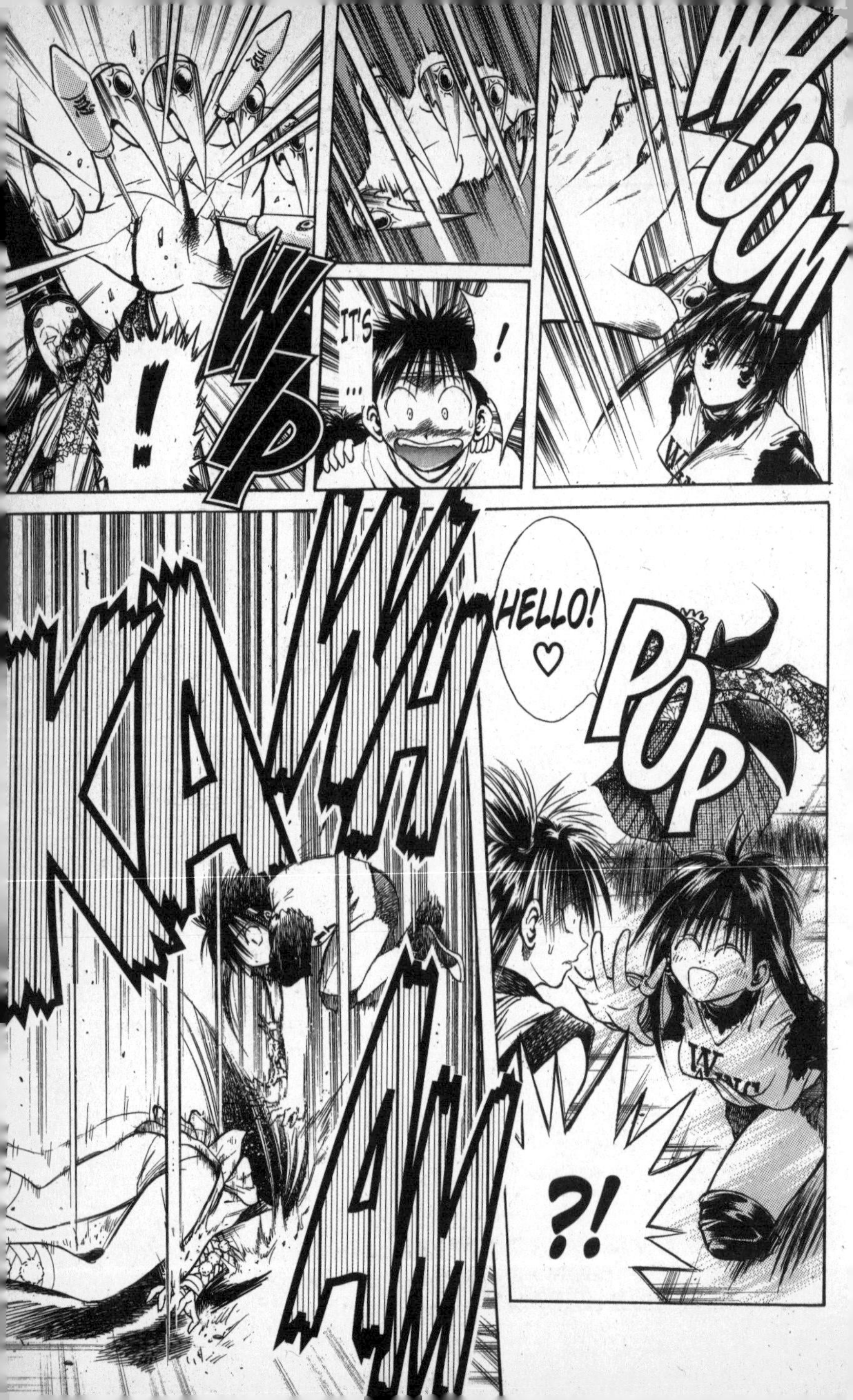
WHOOM
IT'S ...
!
WHIP
!
HELLO! ♡
POP
?!

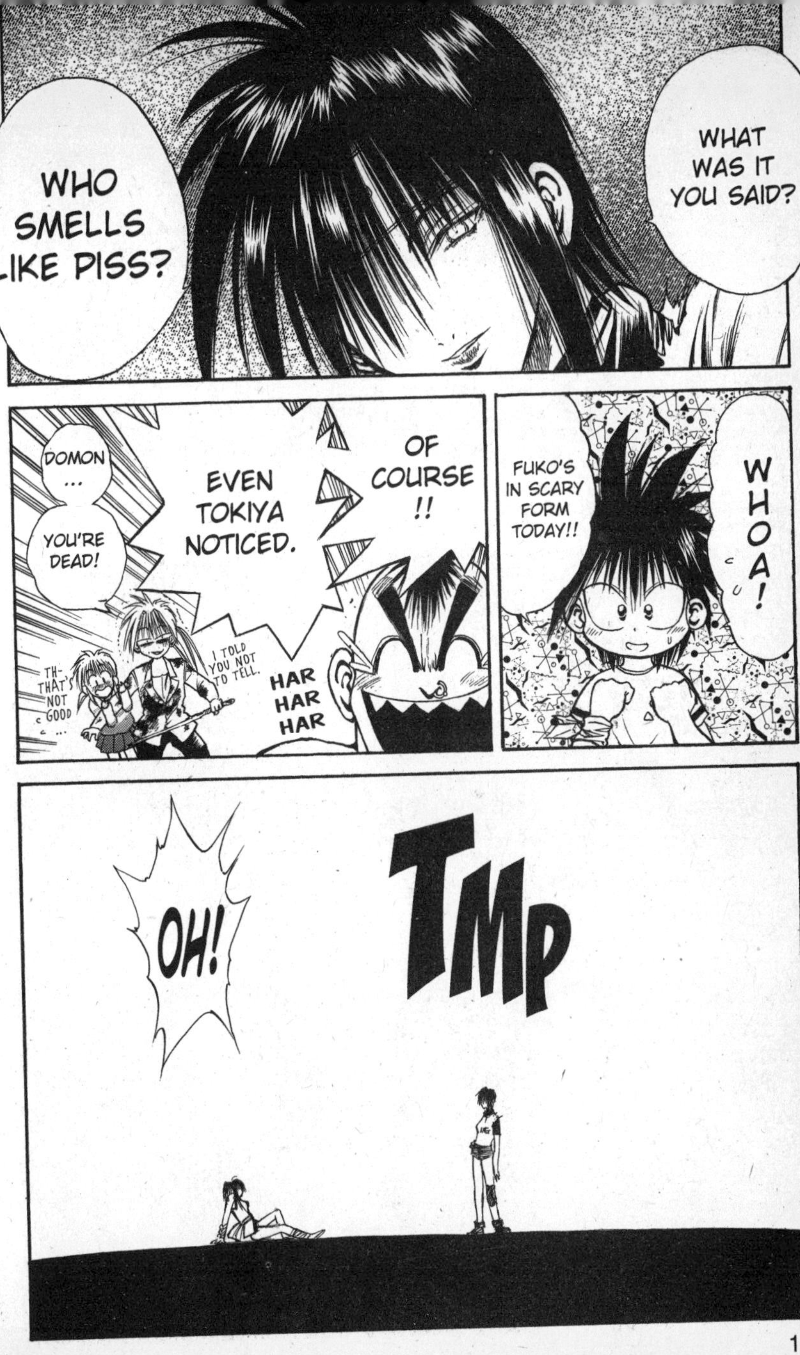
WHAT WAS IT YOU SAID?
WHO SMELLS LIKE PISS?
WHOA!
FUKO'S IN SCARY FORM TODAY!!
OF COURSE!!
EVEN TOKIYA NOTICED.
DOMON...
YOU'RE DEAD!
I TOLD YOU NOT TO TELL.
HAR HAR HAR
TH-THAT'S NOT GOOD...
TMP
OH!

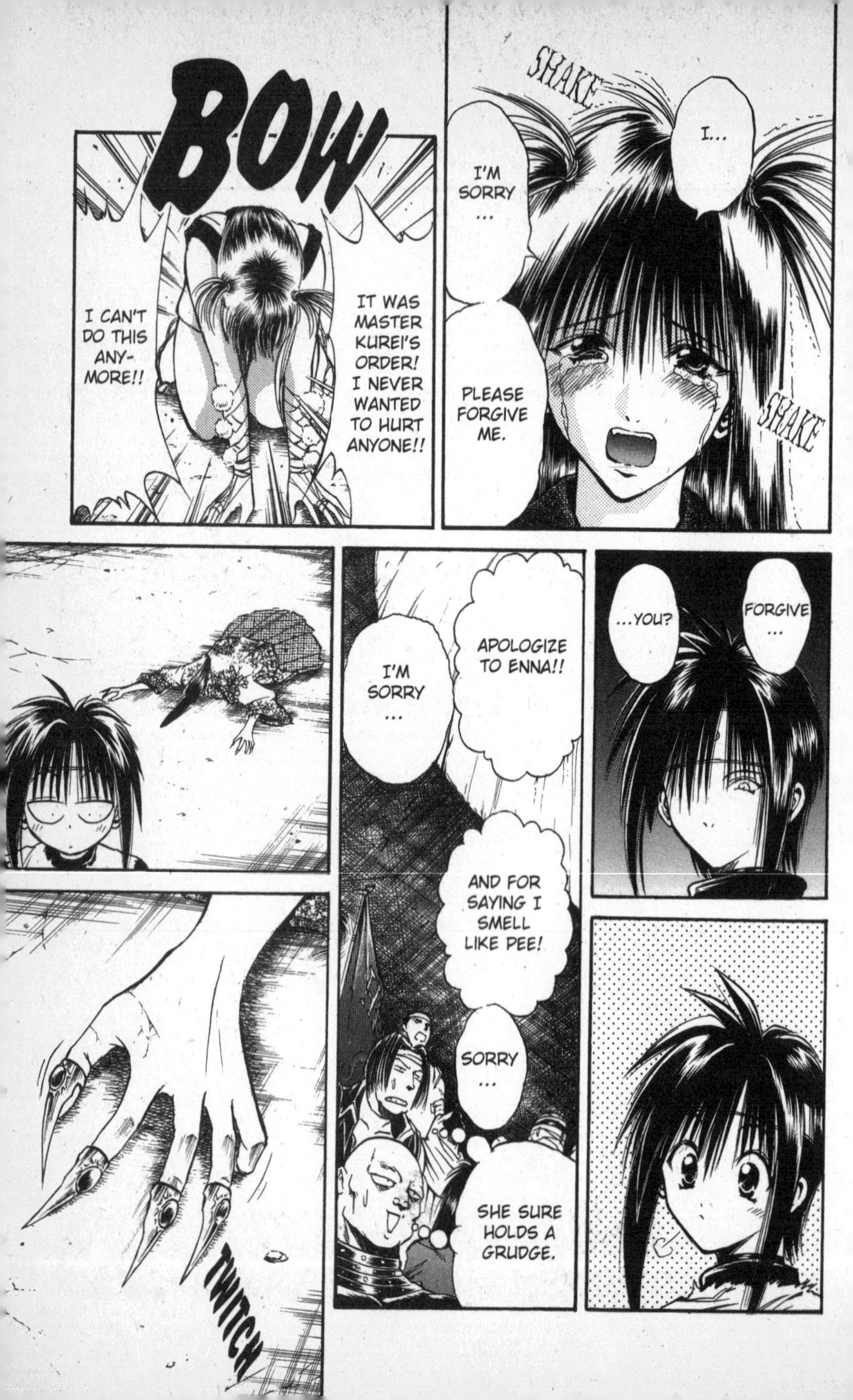
SHAKE
I...
I'M SORRY ...
SHAKE
PLEASE FORGIVE ME.
BOW
IT WAS MASTER KUREI'S ORDER! I NEVER WANTED TO HURT ANYONE!!
I CAN'T DO THIS ANY-MORE!!
FORGIVE ...
...YOU?
APOLOGIZE TO ENNA!!
I'M SORRY ...
AND FOR SAYING I SMELL LIKE PEE!
SORRY ...
SHE SURE HOLDS A GRUDGE.
TWITCH

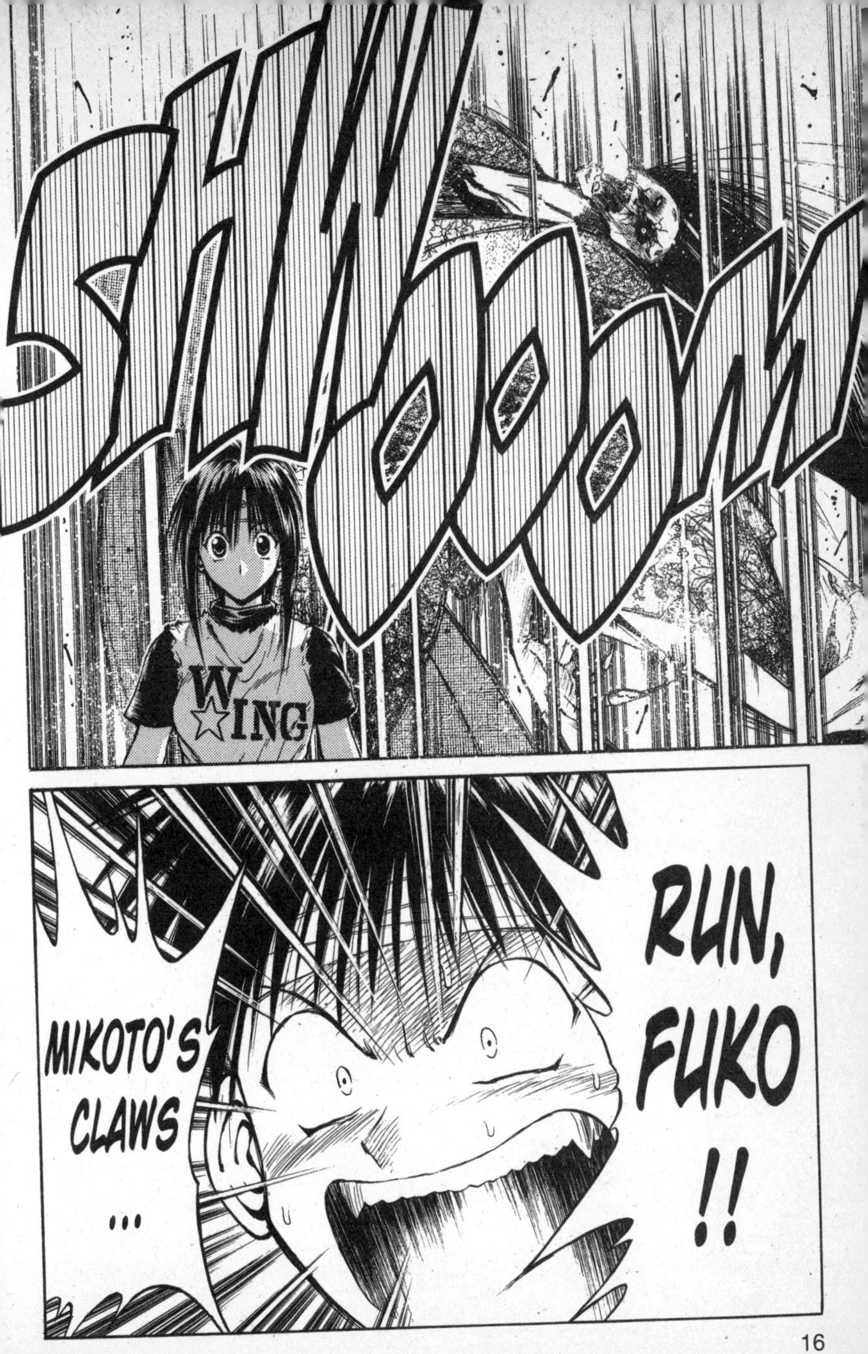
RUN, FUKO !!
MIKOTO'S CLAWS ...

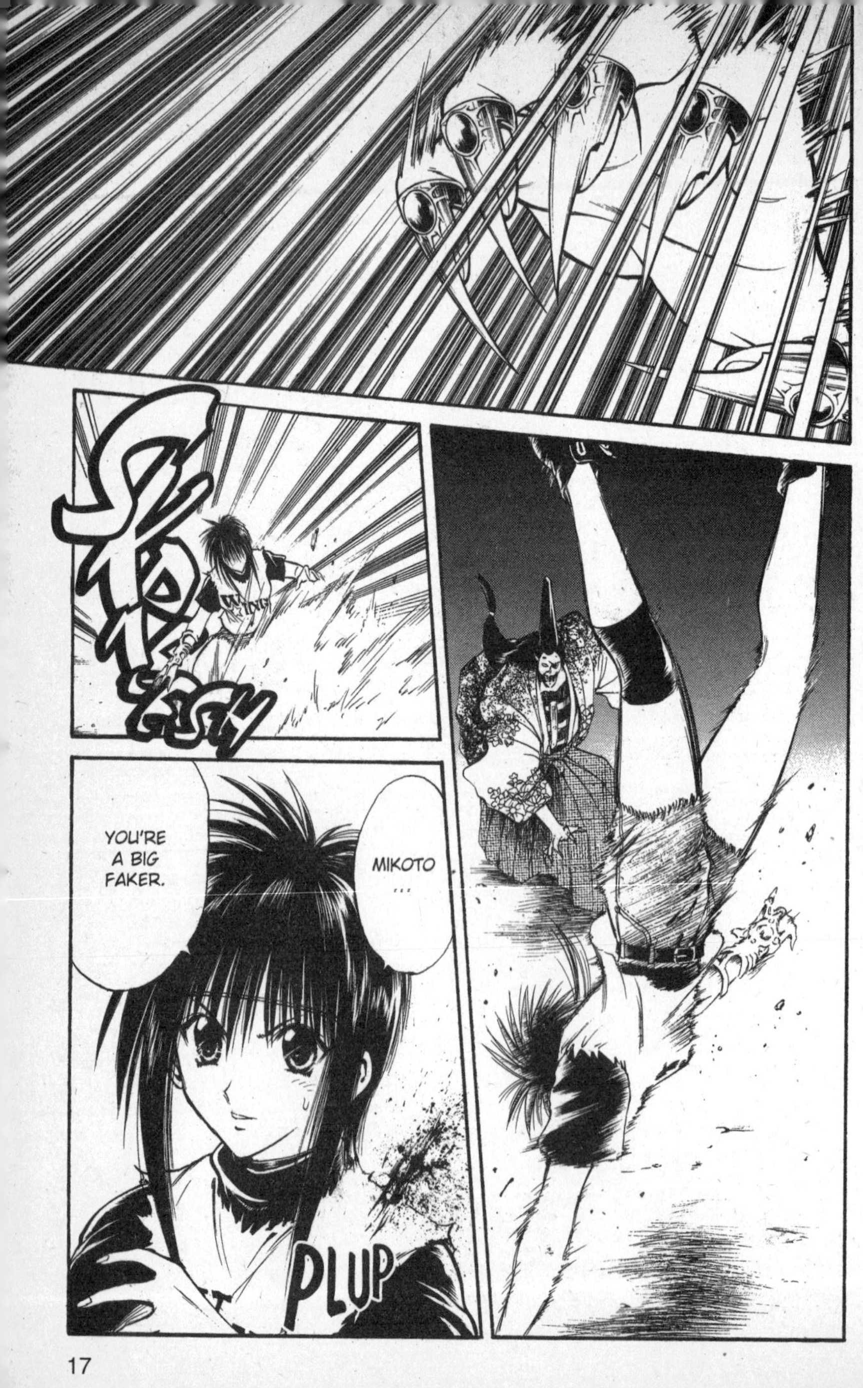
SWISH
MIKOTO...
YOU'RE A BIG FAKER.
PLUP

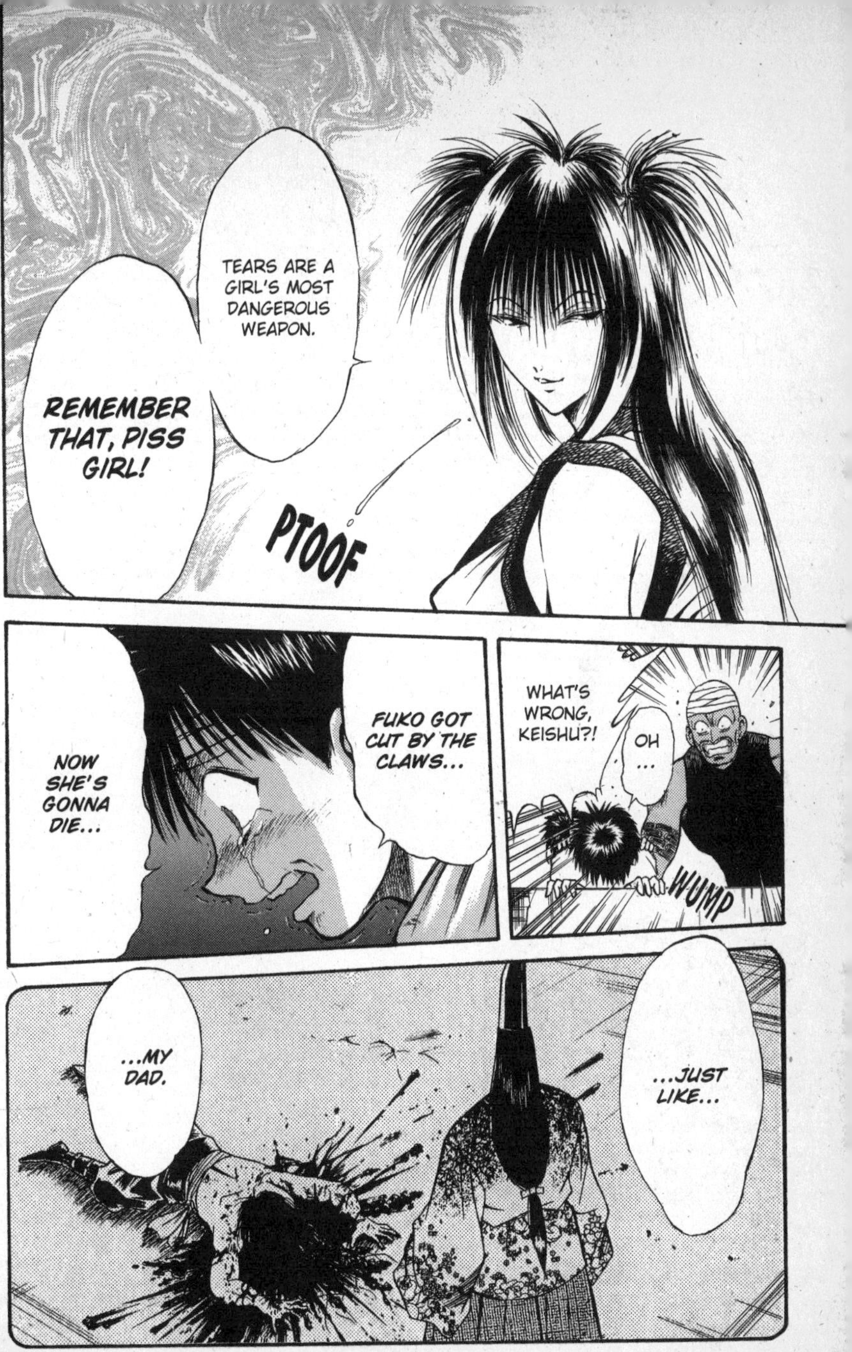
TEARS ARE A GIRL'S MOST DANGEROUS WEAPON.
REMEMBER THAT, PISS GIRL!
PTOOF
WHAT'S WRONG, KEISHU?!
OH ...
WUMP
FUKO GOT CUT BY THE CLAWS...
NOW SHE'S GONNA DIE...
...JUST LIKE...
...MY DAD.

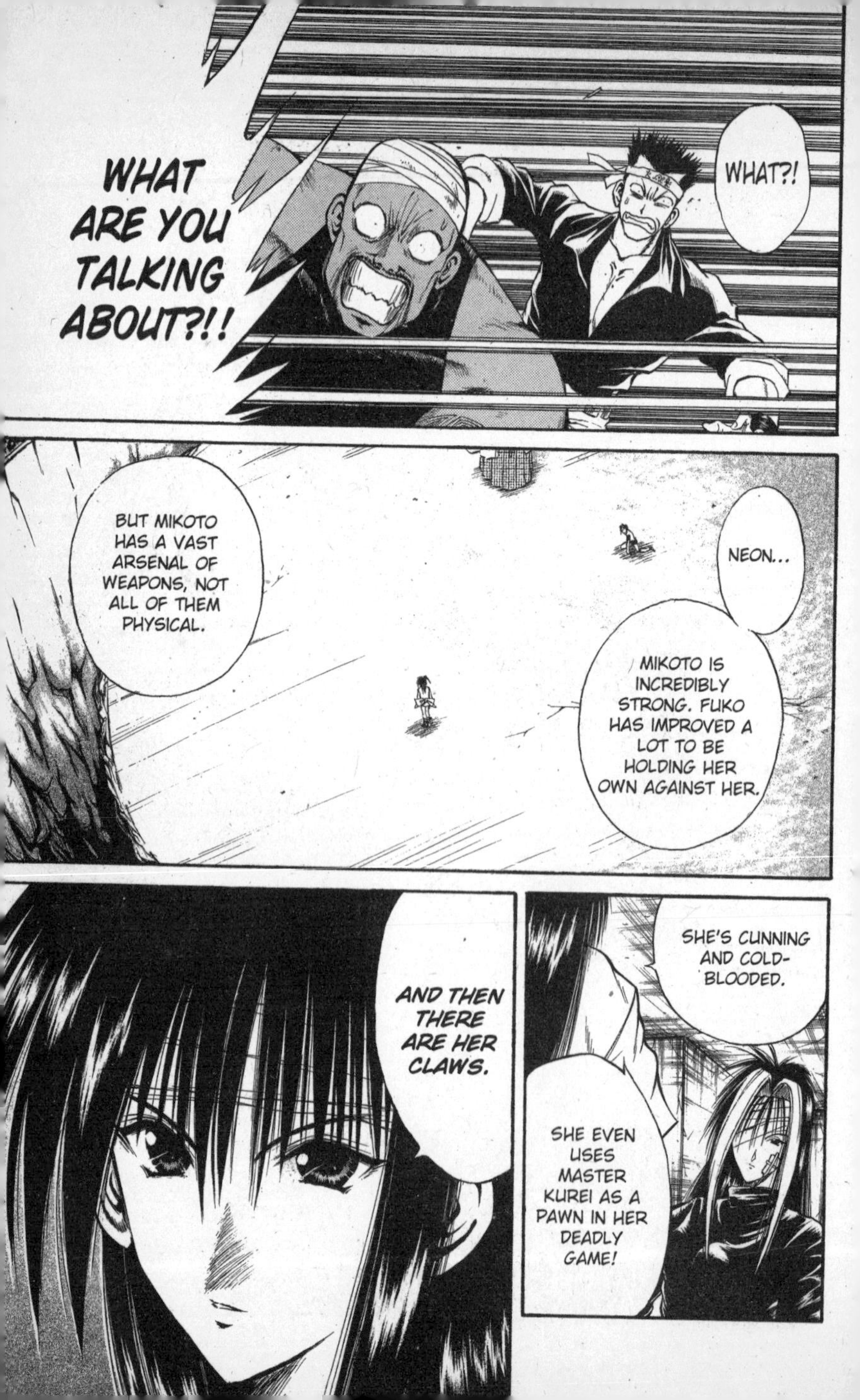
WHAT?!
WHAT ARE YOU TALKING ABOUT?!!
NEON...
MIKOTO IS INCREDIBLY STRONG. FUKO HAS IMPROVED A LOT TO BE HOLDING HER OWN AGAINST HER.
BUT MIKOTO HAS A VAST ARSENAL OF WEAPONS, NOT ALL OF THEM PHYSICAL.
SHE'S CUNNING AND COLD-BLOODED.
SHE EVEN USES MASTER KUREI AS A PAWN IN HER DEADLY GAME!
AND THEN THERE ARE HER CLAWS.

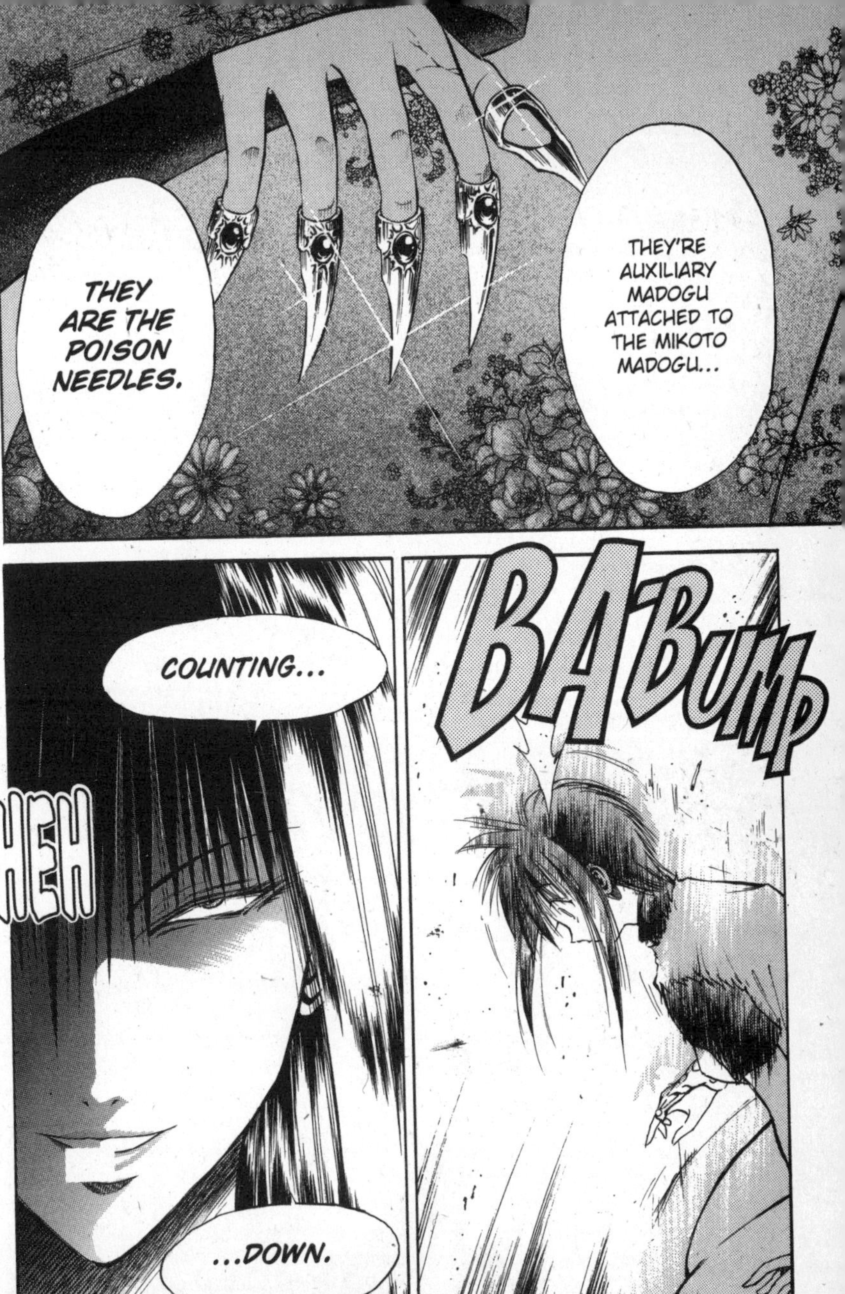
THEY'RE AUXILIARY MADOGU ATTACHED TO THE MIKOTO MADOGU...
THEY ARE THE POISON NEEDLES.
BA-BUMP
COUNTING...
HEH
...DOWN.

Part 129: Poisonous Fang

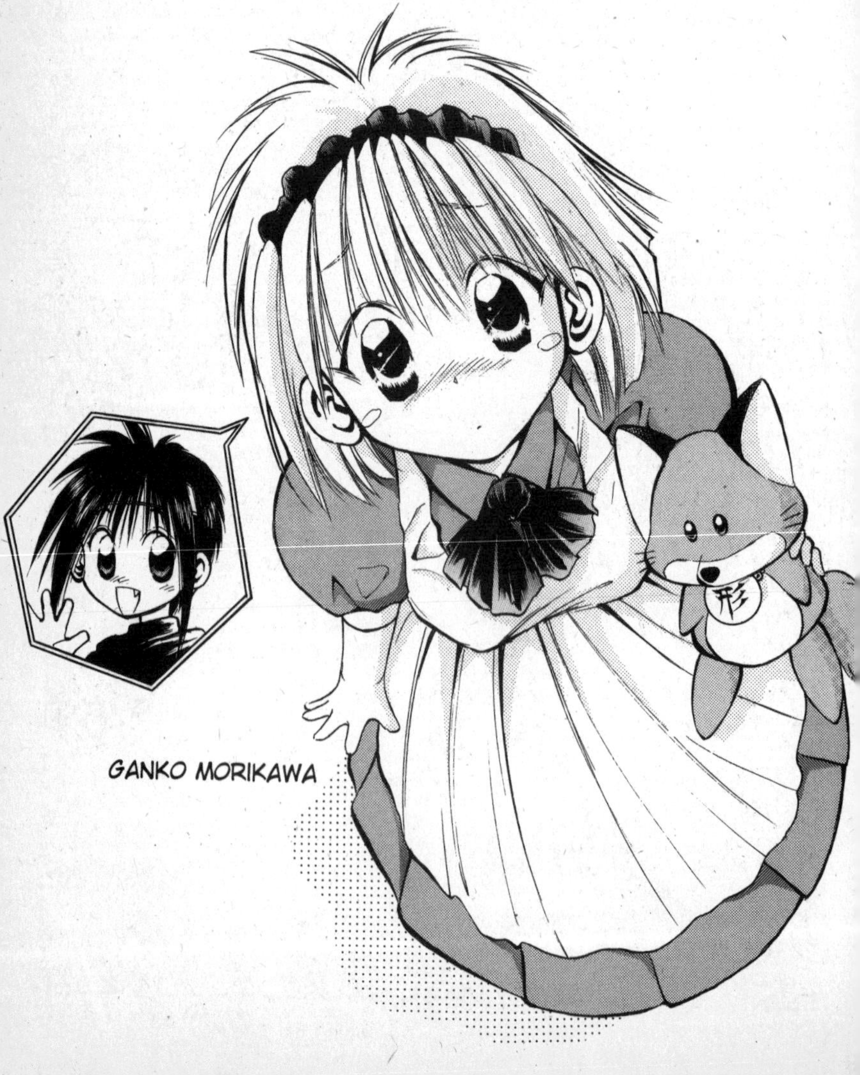
GANKO MORIKAWA

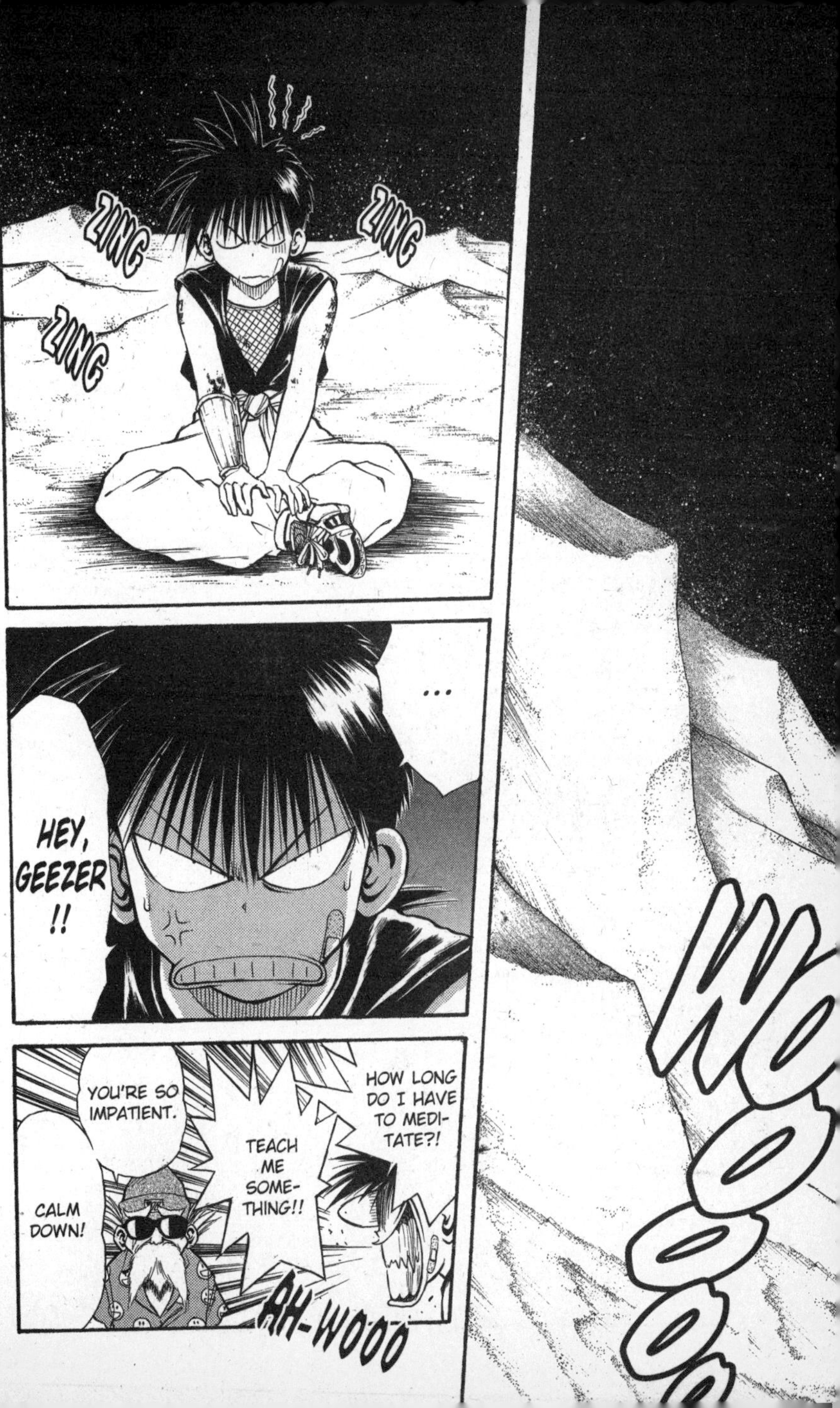
WOOOOOO
ZING
ZING
ZING
...
HEY, GEEZER!!
HOW LONG DO I HAVE TO MEDI-TATE?!
TEACH ME SOME-THING!!
YOU'RE SO IMPATIENT.
CALM DOWN!
AH-WOOO

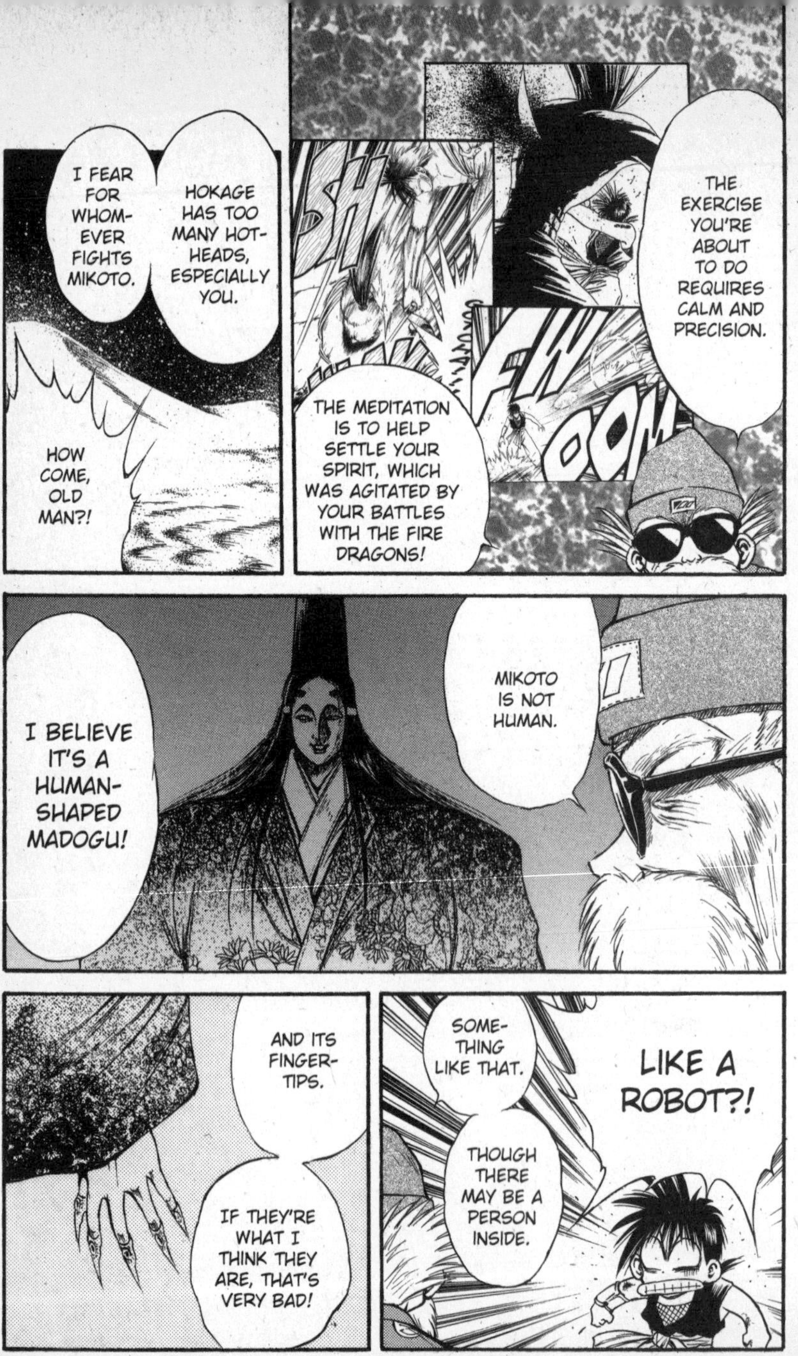
THE EXERCISE YOU'RE ABOUT TO DO REQUIRES CALM AND PRECISION.
SH
FWOOM
THE MEDITATION IS TO HELP SETTLE YOUR SPIRIT, WHICH WAS AGITATED BY YOUR BATTLES WITH THE FIRE DRAGONS!
HOKAGE HAS TOO MANY HOT-HEADS, ESPECIALLY YOU.
I FEAR FOR WHOM-EVER FIGHTS MIKOTO.
HOW COME, OLD MAN?!
MIKOTO IS NOT HUMAN.
I BELIEVE IT'S A HUMAN-SHAPED MADOGU!
LIKE A ROBOT?!
SOME-THING LIKE THAT.
THOUGH THERE MAY BE A PERSON INSIDE.
AND ITS FINGER-TIPS.
IF THEY'RE WHAT I THINK THEY ARE, THAT'S VERY BAD!

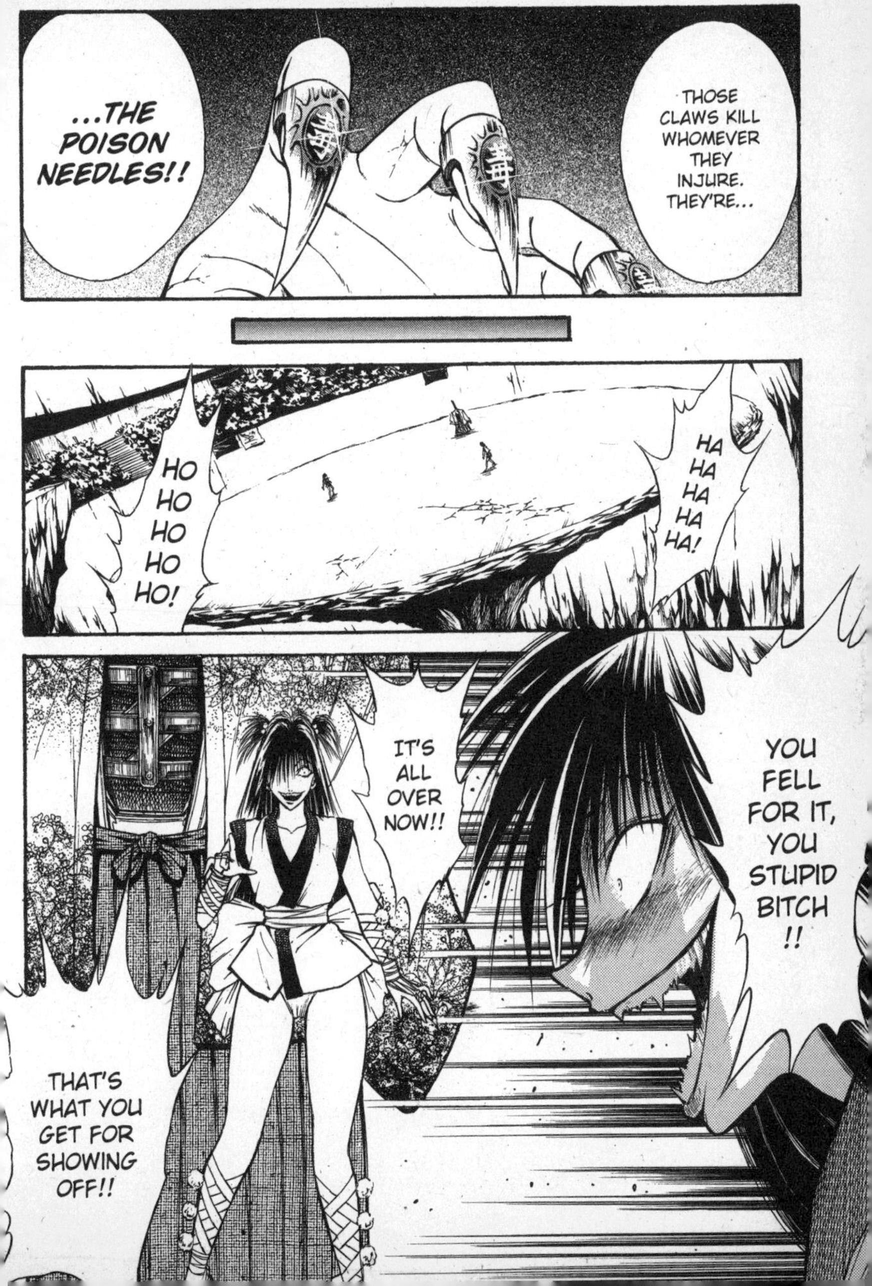
THOSE CLAWS KILL WHOMEVER THEY INJURE. THEY'RE...
...THE POISON NEEDLES!!
HA HA HA HA HA!
HO HO HO HO HO!
YOU FELL FOR IT, YOU STUPID BITCH!!
IT'S ALL OVER NOW!!
THAT'S WHAT YOU GET FOR SHOWING OFF!!

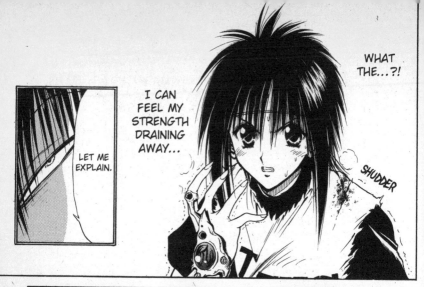

WHAT THE...?!

I CAN FEEL MY STRENGTH DRAINING AWAY...

LET ME EXPLAIN.

SHUDDER

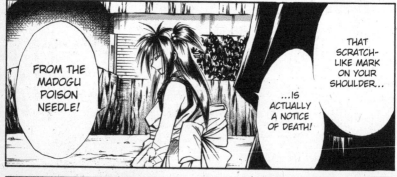

THAT SCRATCH-LIKE MARK ON YOUR SHOULDER..

...IS ACTUALLY A NOTICE OF DEATH!

FROM THE MADOGU POISON NEEDLE!

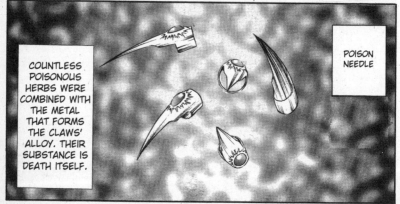

POISON NEEDLE

COUNTLESS POISONOUS HERBS WERE COMBINED WITH THE METAL THAT FORMS THE CLAWS' ALLOY. THEIR SUBSTANCE IS DEATH ITSELF.

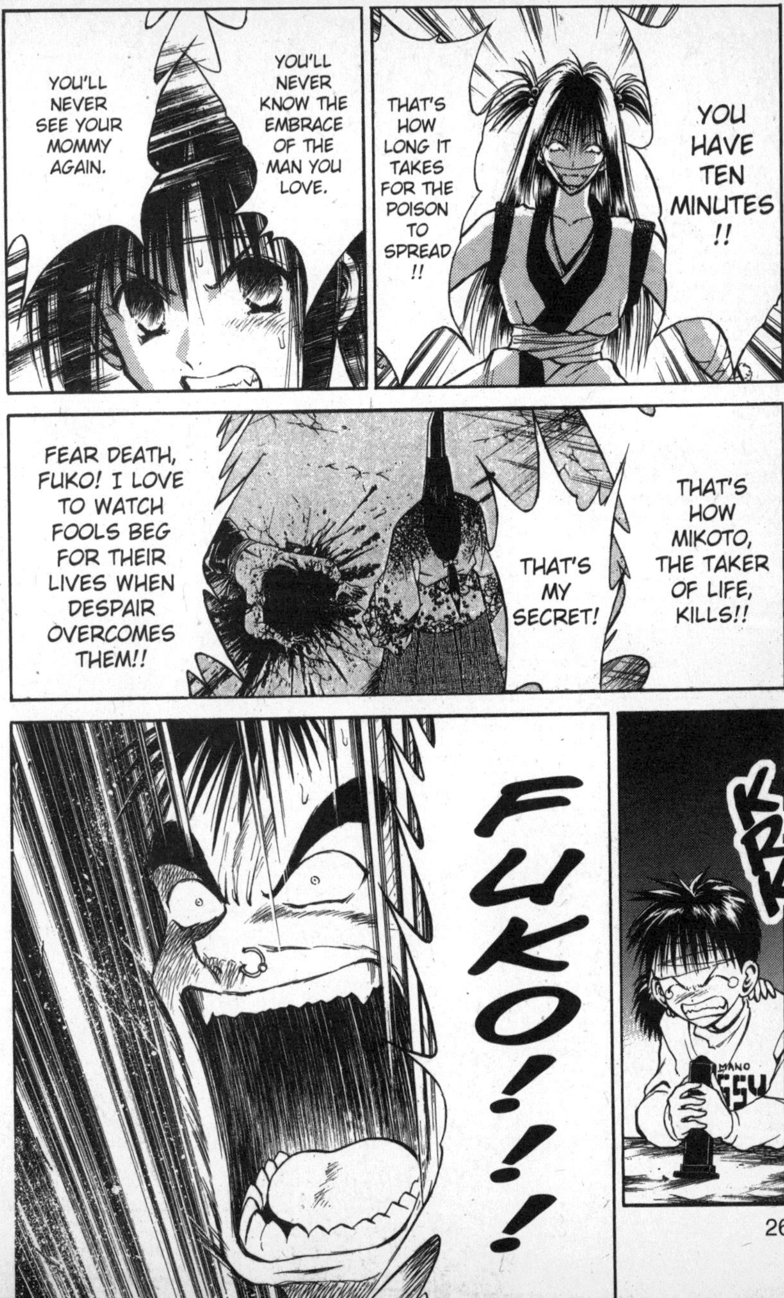
YOU HAVE TEN MINUTES!!
THAT'S HOW LONG IT TAKES FOR THE POISON TO SPREAD!!
YOU'LL NEVER KNOW THE EMBRACE OF THE MAN YOU LOVE.
YOU'LL NEVER SEE YOUR MOMMY AGAIN.
THAT'S HOW MIKOTO, THE TAKER OF LIFE, KILLS!!
THAT'S MY SECRET!
FEAR DEATH, FUKO! I LOVE TO WATCH FOOLS BEG FOR THEIR LIVES WHEN DESPAIR OVERCOMES THEM!!
KRRK
FUKO!!!!

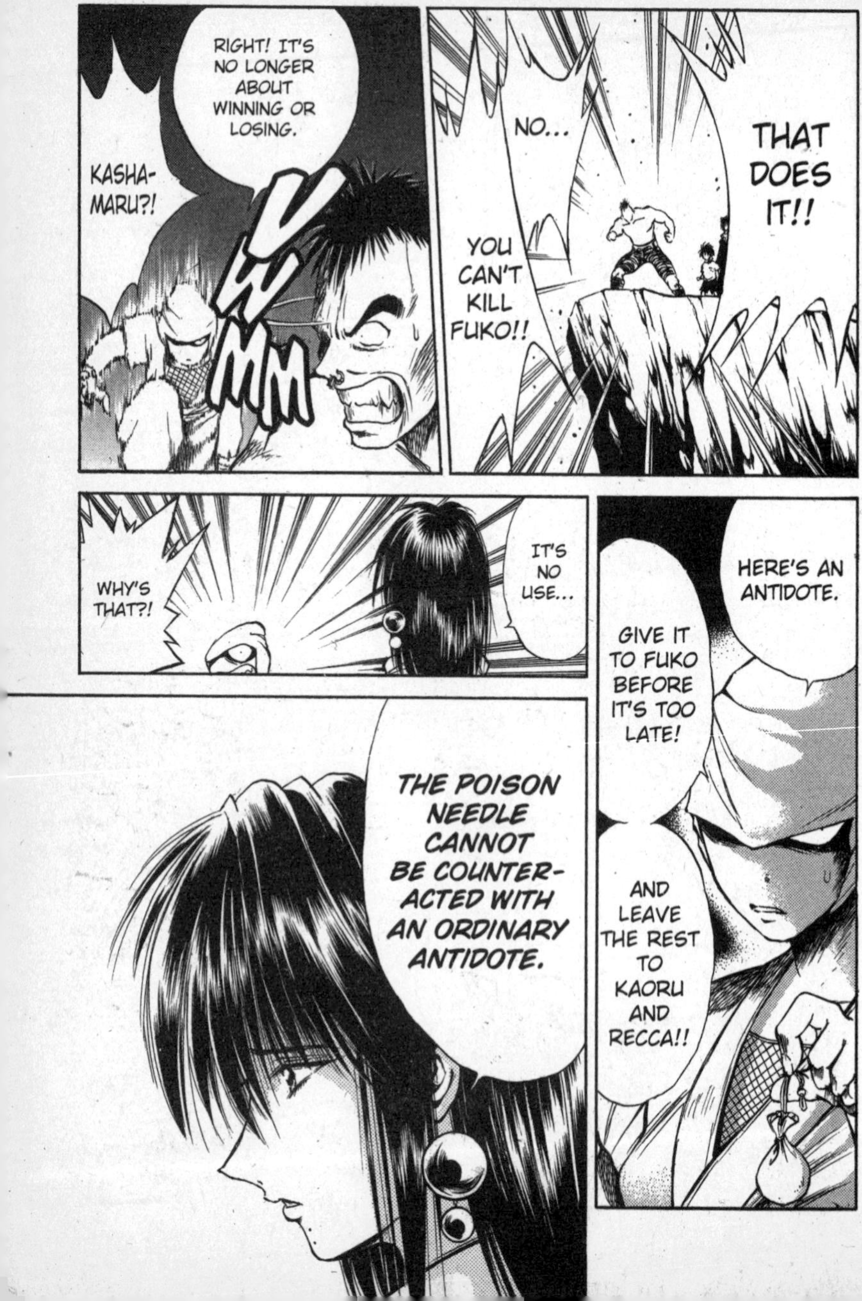
THAT DOES IT!!
NO...
YOU CAN'T KILL FUKO!!
RIGHT! IT'S NO LONGER ABOUT WINNING OR LOSING.
VWMM
KASHA-MARU?!
HERE'S AN ANTIDOTE.
GIVE IT TO FUKO BEFORE IT'S TOO LATE!
AND LEAVE THE REST TO KAORU AND RECCA!!
IT'S NO USE...
WHY'S THAT?!
THE POISON NEEDLE CANNOT BE COUNTER-ACTED WITH AN ORDINARY ANTIDOTE.

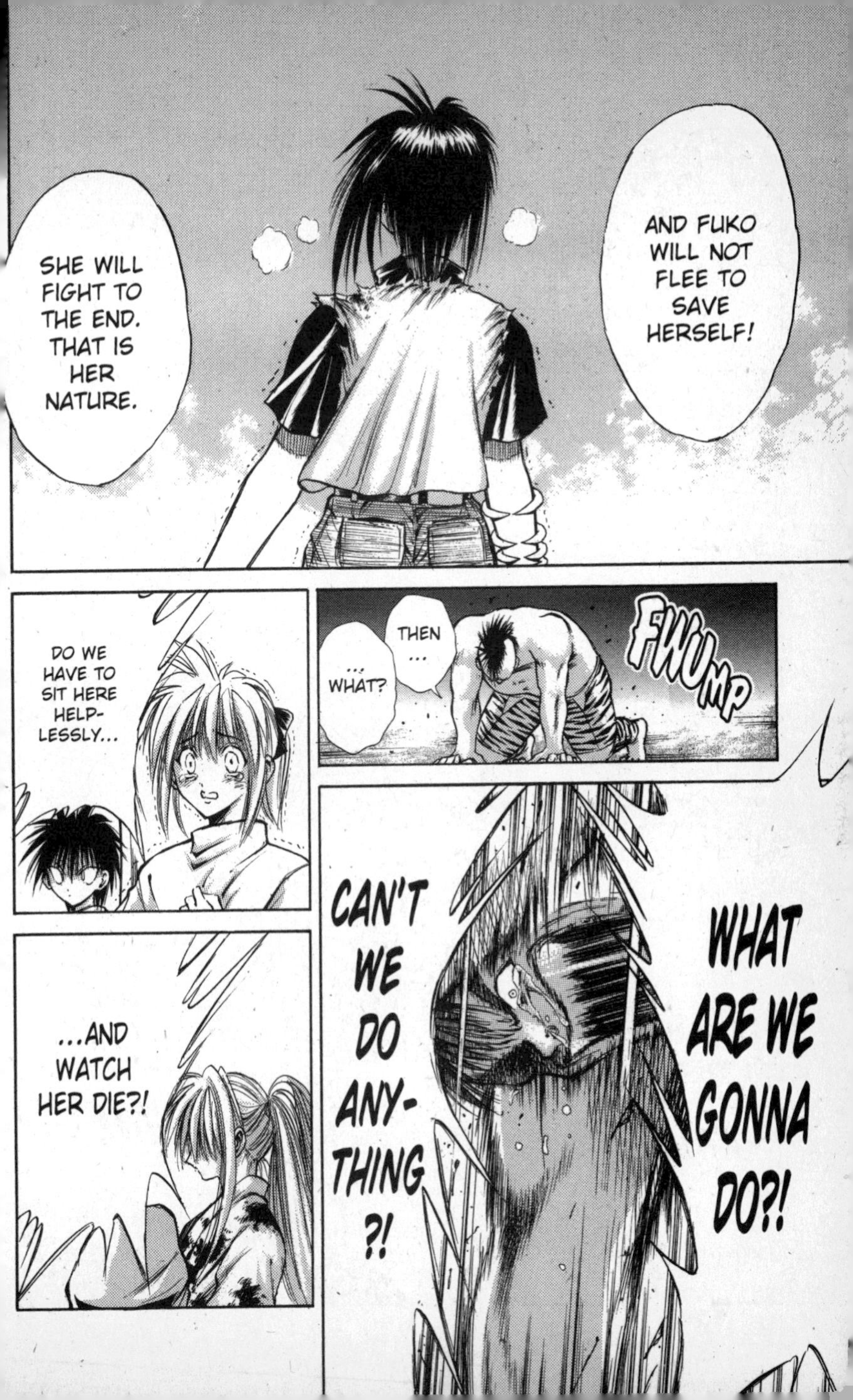
AND FUKO WILL NOT FLEE TO SAVE HERSELF!
SHE WILL FIGHT TO THE END. THAT IS HER NATURE.
FWUMP
THEN ...
... WHAT?
DO WE HAVE TO SIT HERE HELPLESSLY...
...AND WATCH HER DIE?!
WHAT ARE WE GONNA DO?!
CAN'T WE DO ANYTHING?!

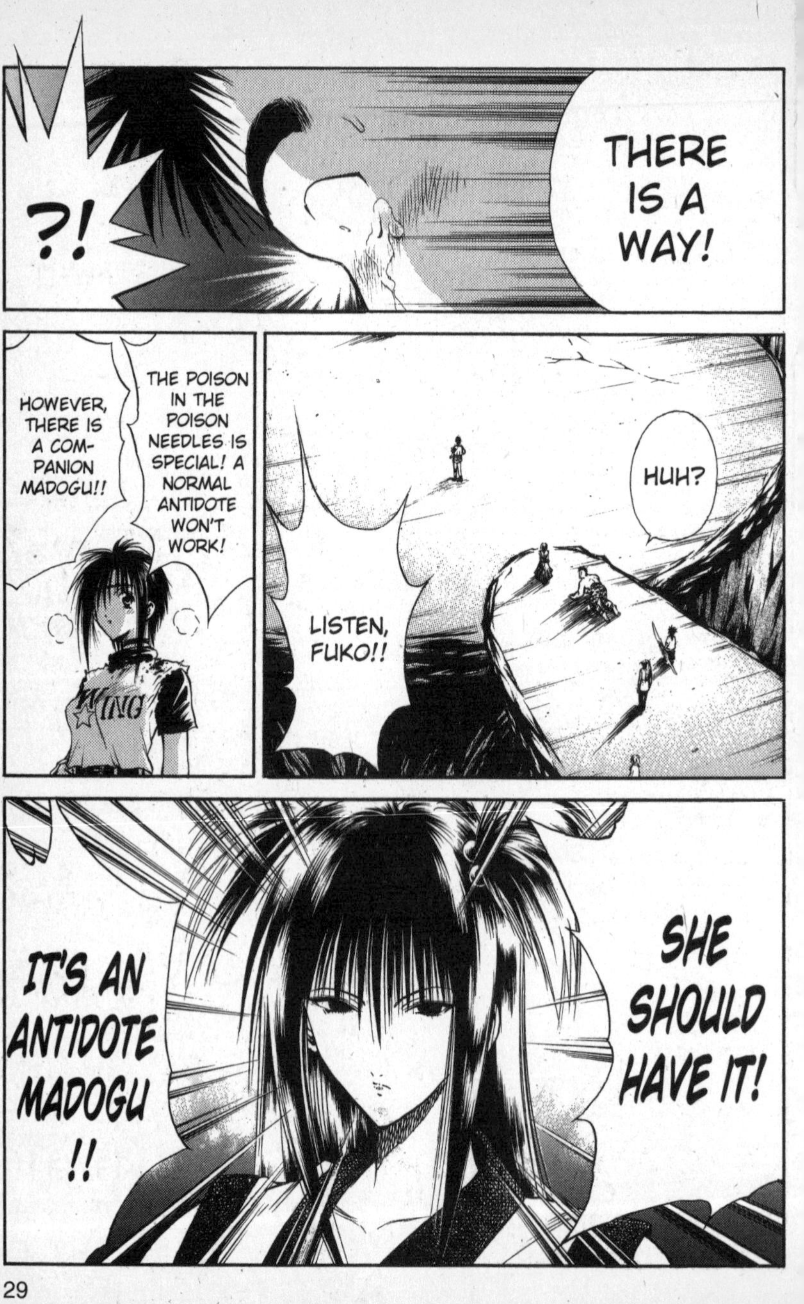
THERE IS A WAY!
?!
HUH?
LISTEN, FUKO!!
THE POISON IN THE POISON NEEDLES IS SPECIAL! A NORMAL ANTIDOTE WON'T WORK!
HOWEVER, THERE IS A COM-PANION MADOGU!!
SHE SHOULD HAVE IT!
IT'S AN ANTIDOTE MADOGU !!

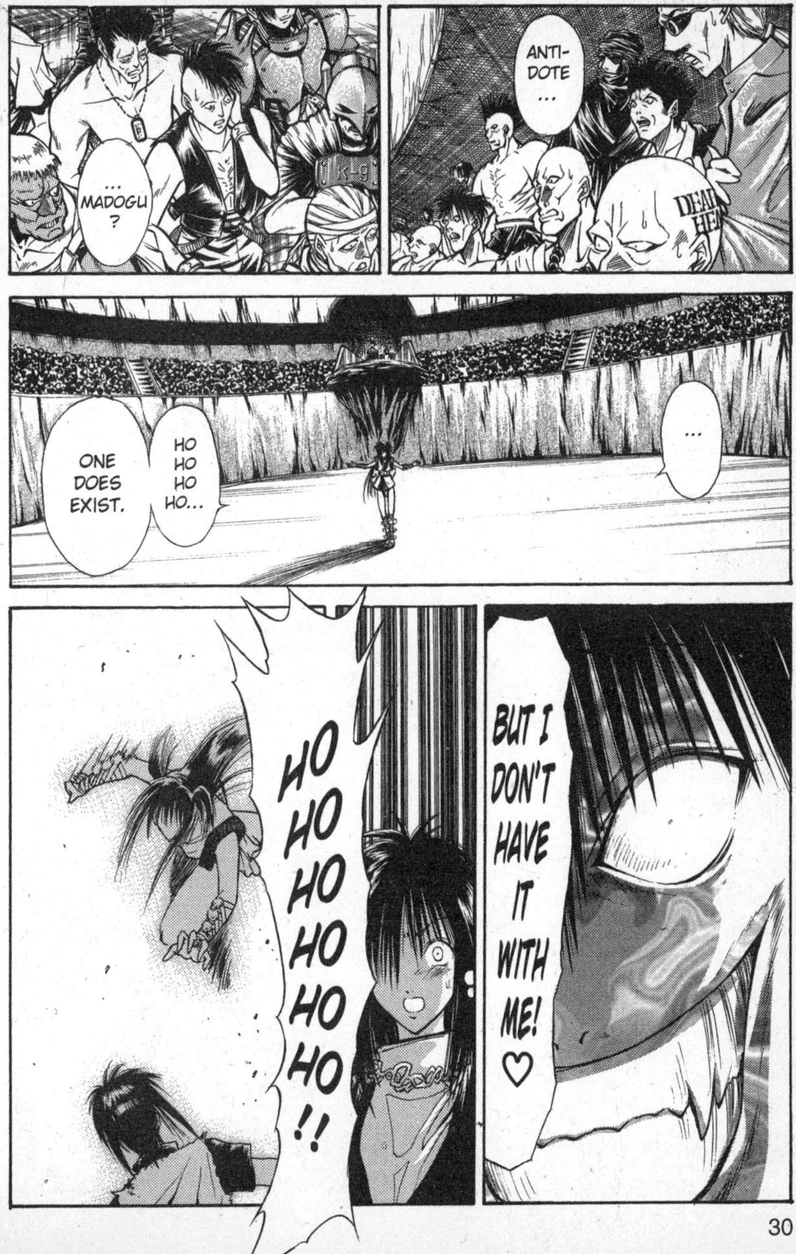
ANTI-DOTE ...
... MADOGU ?
...
HO HO HO HO...
ONE DOES EXIST.
BUT I DON'T HAVE IT WITH ME! ♡
HO HO HO HO HO HO HO HO!!

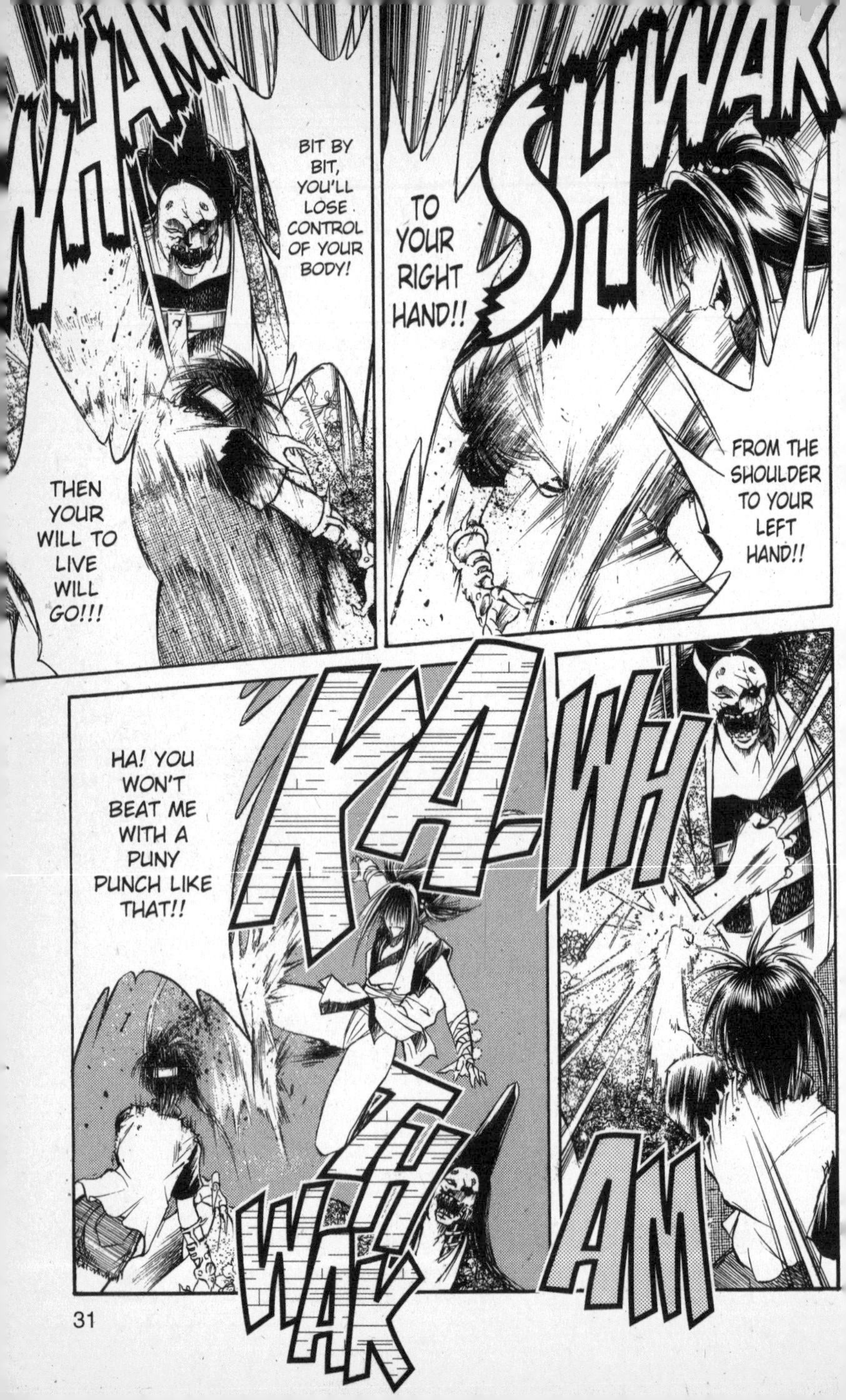
SHWAK
TO YOUR RIGHT HAND!!
FROM THE SHOULDER TO YOUR LEFT HAND!!
WHAM
BIT BY BIT, YOU'LL LOSE CONTROL OF YOUR BODY!
THEN YOUR WILL TO LIVE WILL GO!!!
WHAM
KA-THWAK
HA! YOU WON'T BEAT ME WITH A PUNY PUNCH LIKE THAT!!

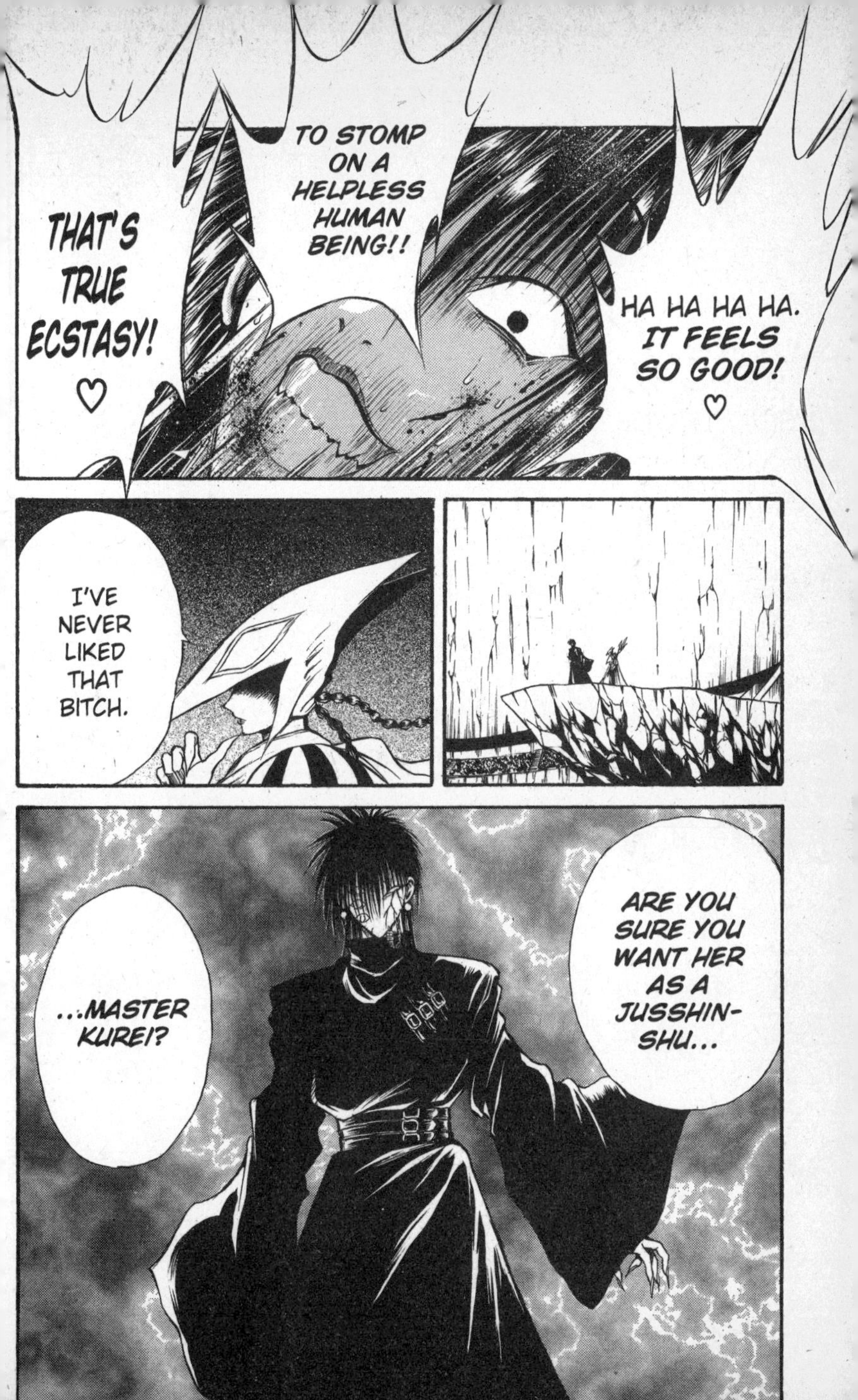
HA HA HA HA. IT FEELS SO GOOD! ♡
TO STOMP ON A HELPLESS HUMAN BEING!!
THAT'S TRUE ECSTASY! ♡
I'VE NEVER LIKED THAT BITCH.
ARE YOU SURE YOU WANT HER AS A JUSSHIN-SHU...
...MASTER KUREI?

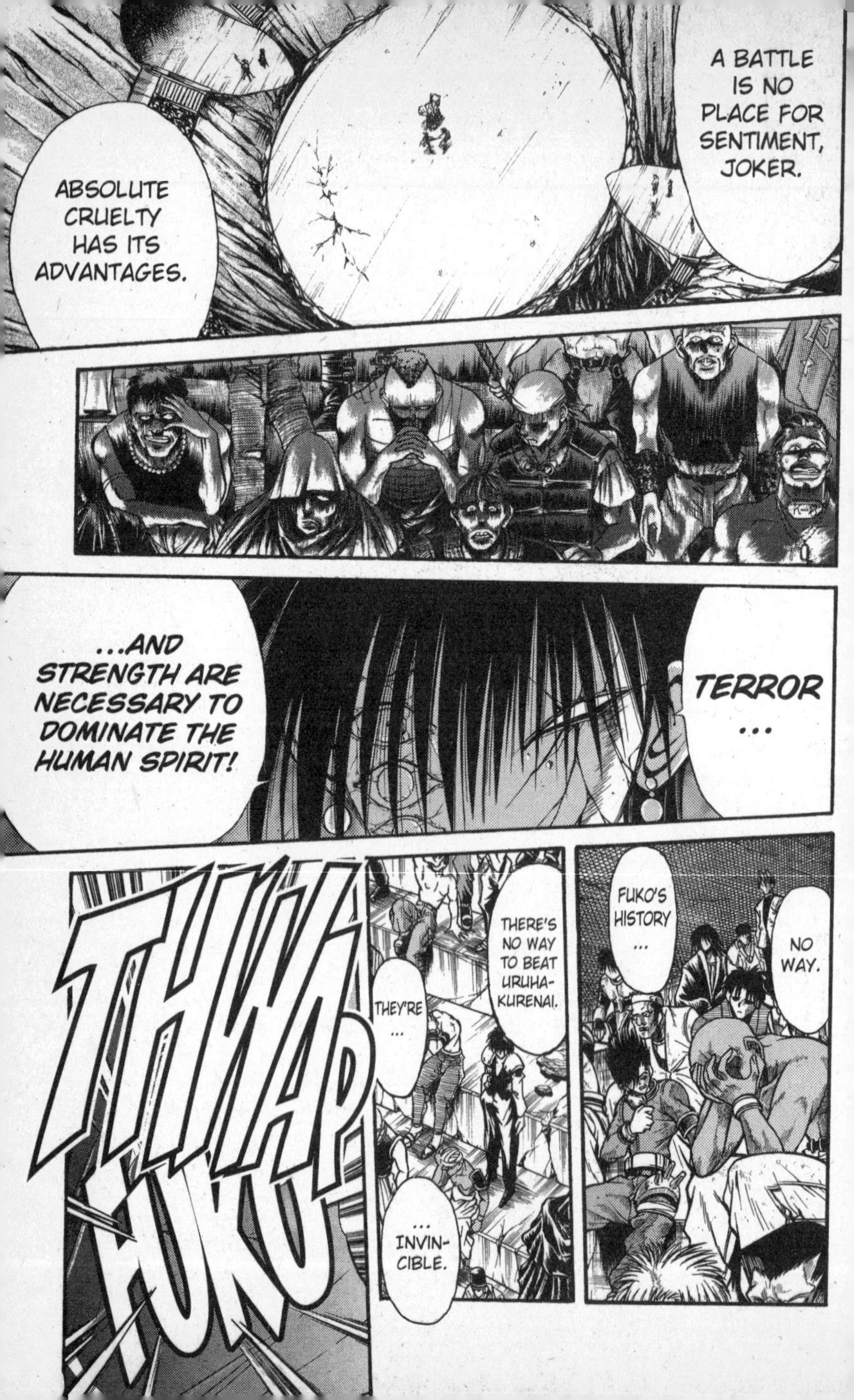
A BATTLE IS NO PLACE FOR SENTIMENT, JOKER.
ABSOLUTE CRUELTY HAS ITS ADVANTAGES.
TERROR ...
...AND STRENGTH ARE NECESSARY TO DOMINATE THE HUMAN SPIRIT!
NO WAY.
FUKO'S HISTORY ...
THERE'S NO WAY TO BEAT URUHA-KURENAI.
THEY'RE ...
... INVINCIBLE.
THWAP
FUKO

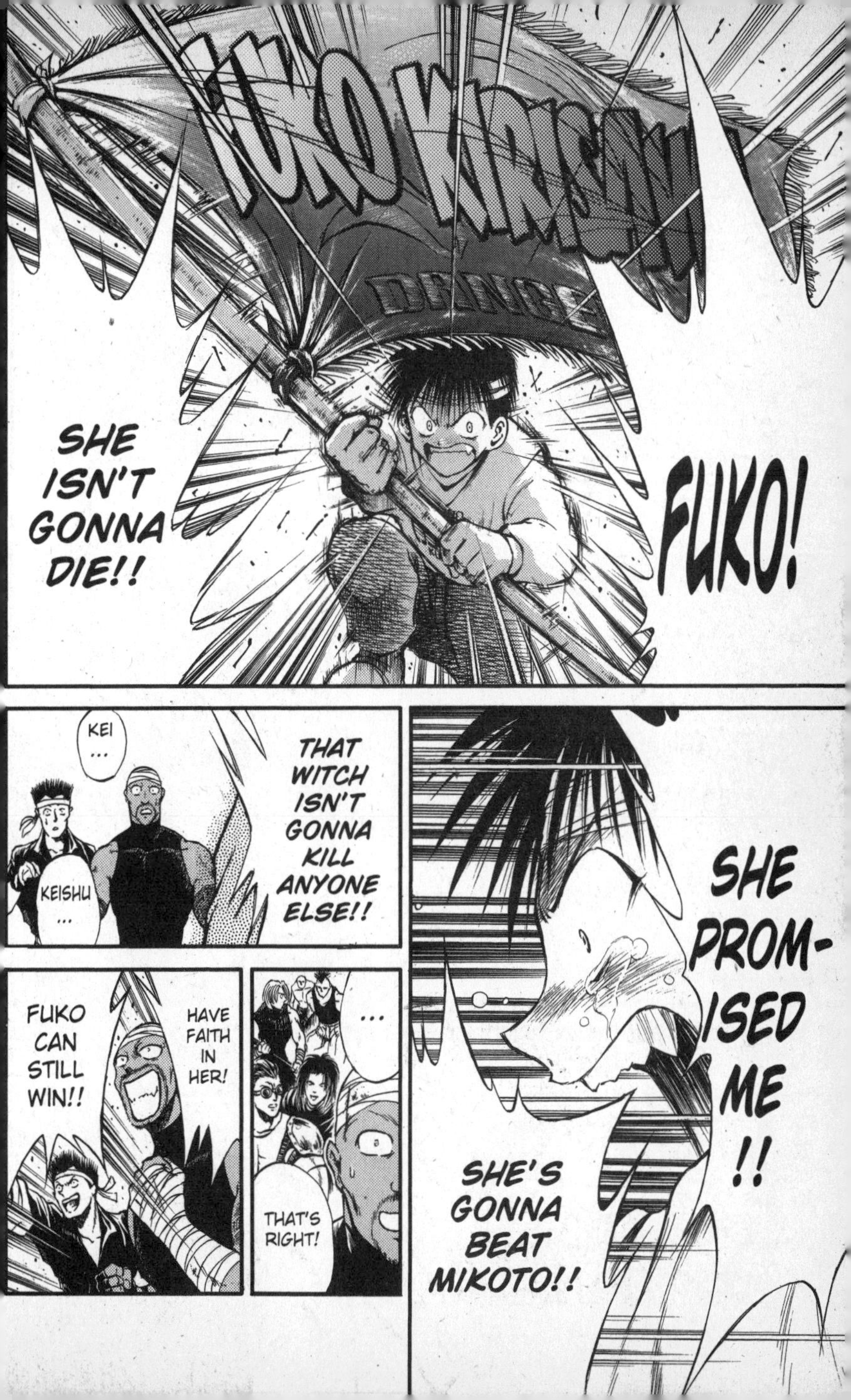
FUKO!
SHE ISN'T GONNA DIE!!
SHE PROMISED ME!!
SHE'S GONNA BEAT MIKOTO!!
THAT WITCH ISN'T GONNA KILL ANYONE ELSE!!
KEI...
KEISHU...
...
THAT'S RIGHT!
HAVE FAITH IN HER!
FUKO CAN STILL WIN!!

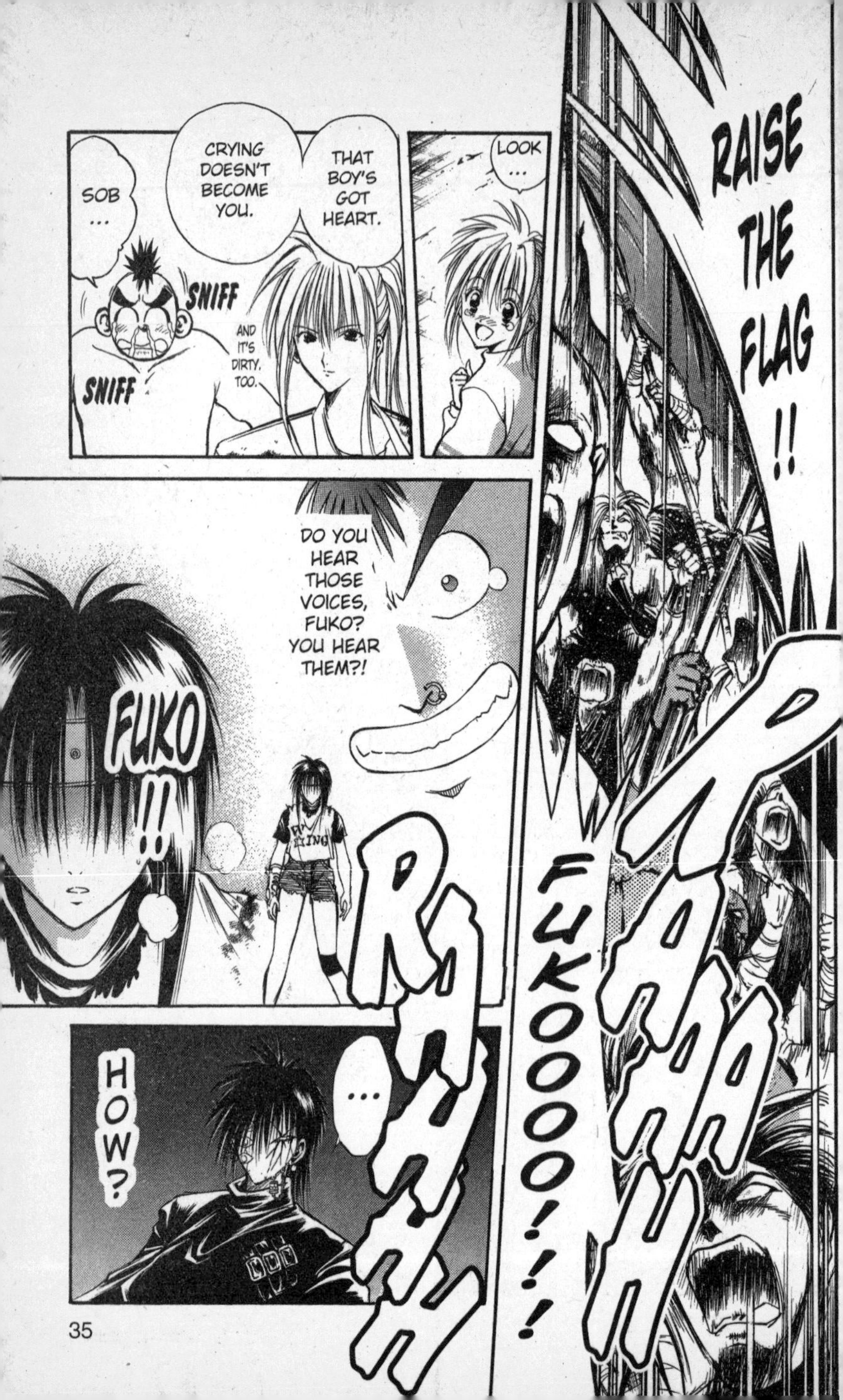
RAISE THE FLAG!!
FUKOOOOO!!!
LOOK...
THAT BOY'S GOT HEART.
CRYING DOESN'T BECOME YOU.
AND IT'S DIRTY, TOO.
SOB...
SNIFF
SNIFF
DO YOU HEAR THOSE VOICES, FUKO? YOU HEAR THEM?!
FUKO!!!
...
HOW?

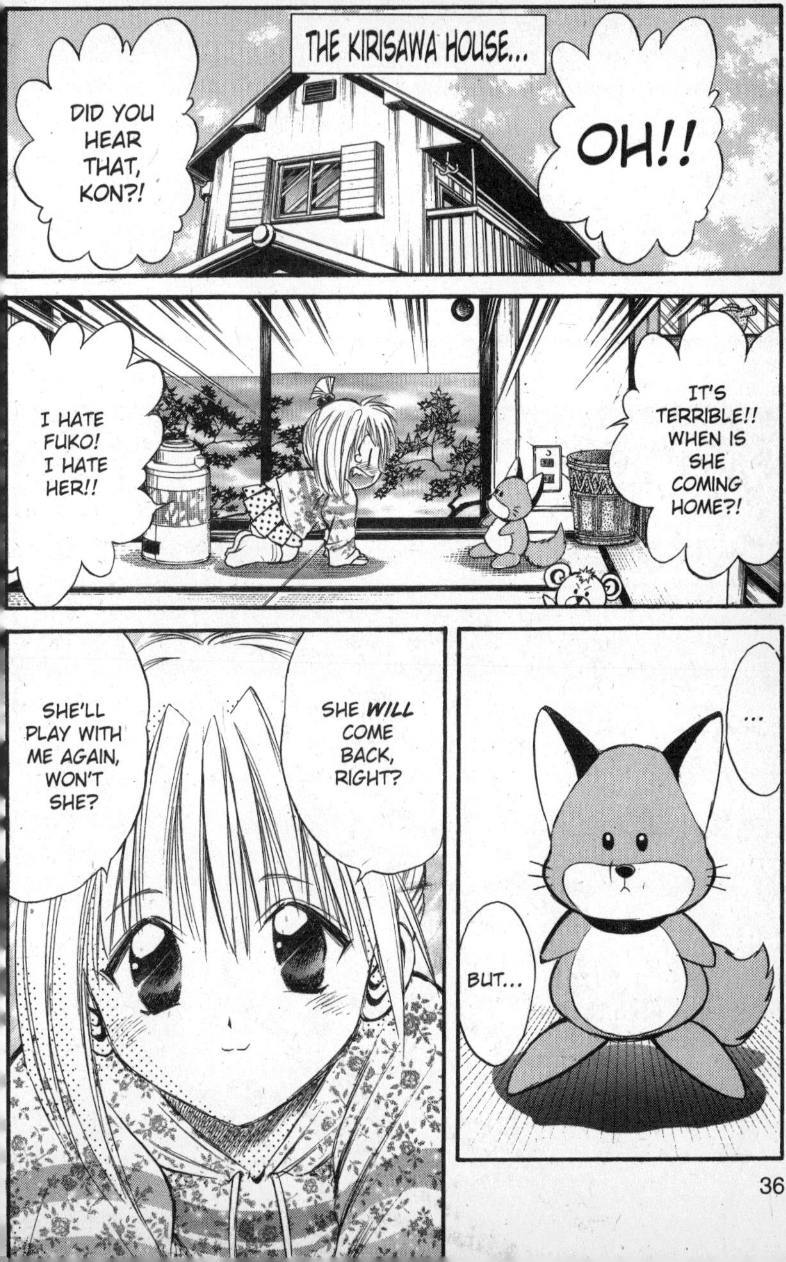
THE KIRISAWA HOUSE...
OH!!
DID YOU HEAR THAT, KON?!
IT'S TERRIBLE!! WHEN IS SHE COMING HOME?!
I HATE FUKO! I HATE HER!!
...
BUT...
SHE WILL COME BACK, RIGHT?
SHE'LL PLAY WITH ME AGAIN, WON'T SHE?

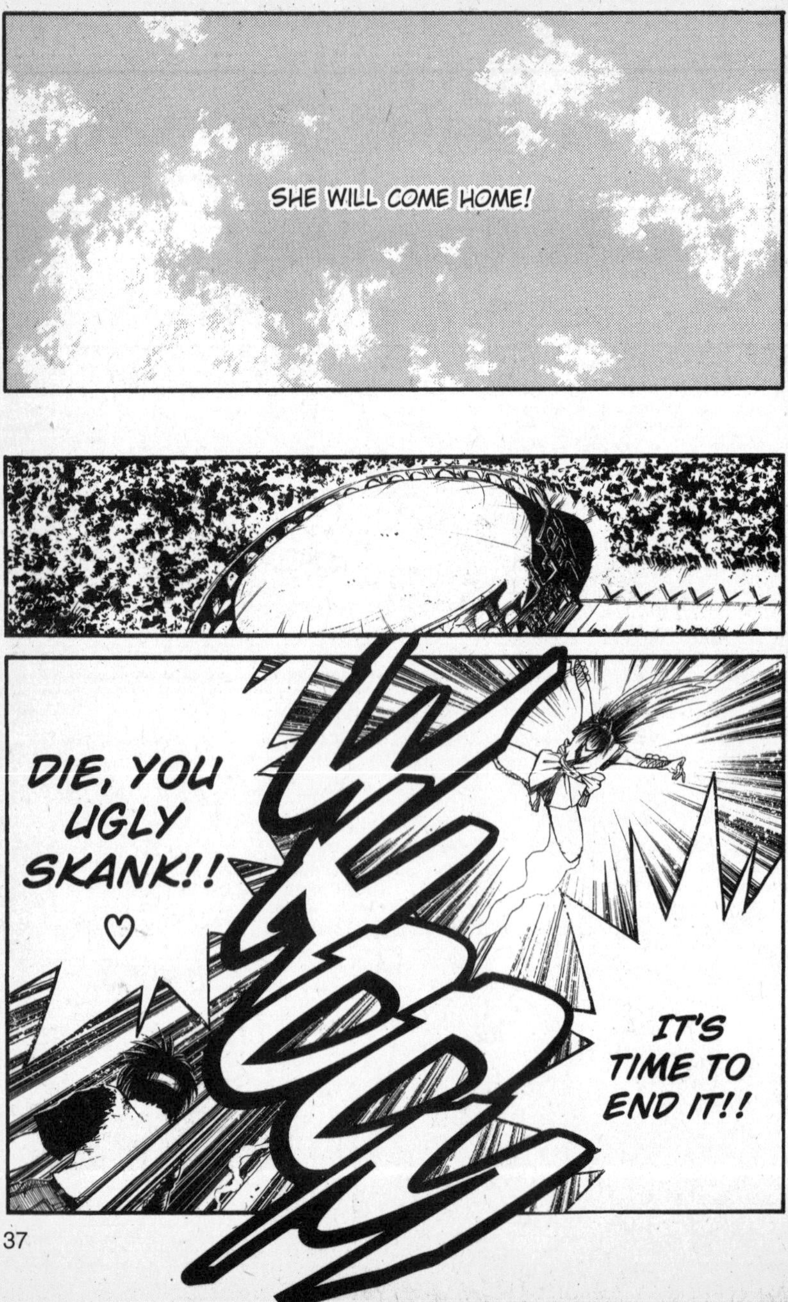
SHE WILL COME HOME!
DIE, YOU UGLY SKANK!! ♡
IT'S TIME TO END IT!!

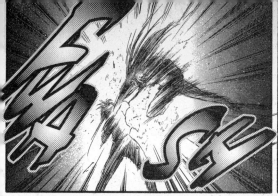
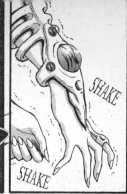

SHAKE

SHAKE

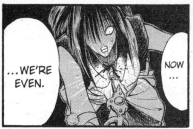

...WE'RE EVEN.

NOW...

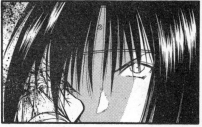

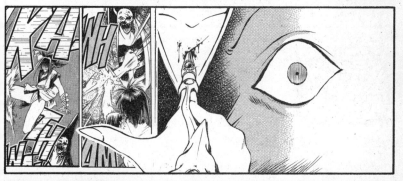

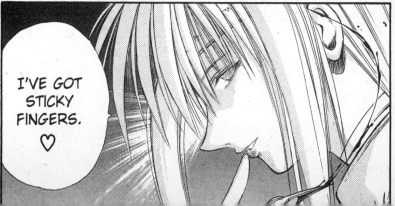

I'VE GOT STICKY FINGERS.

♡

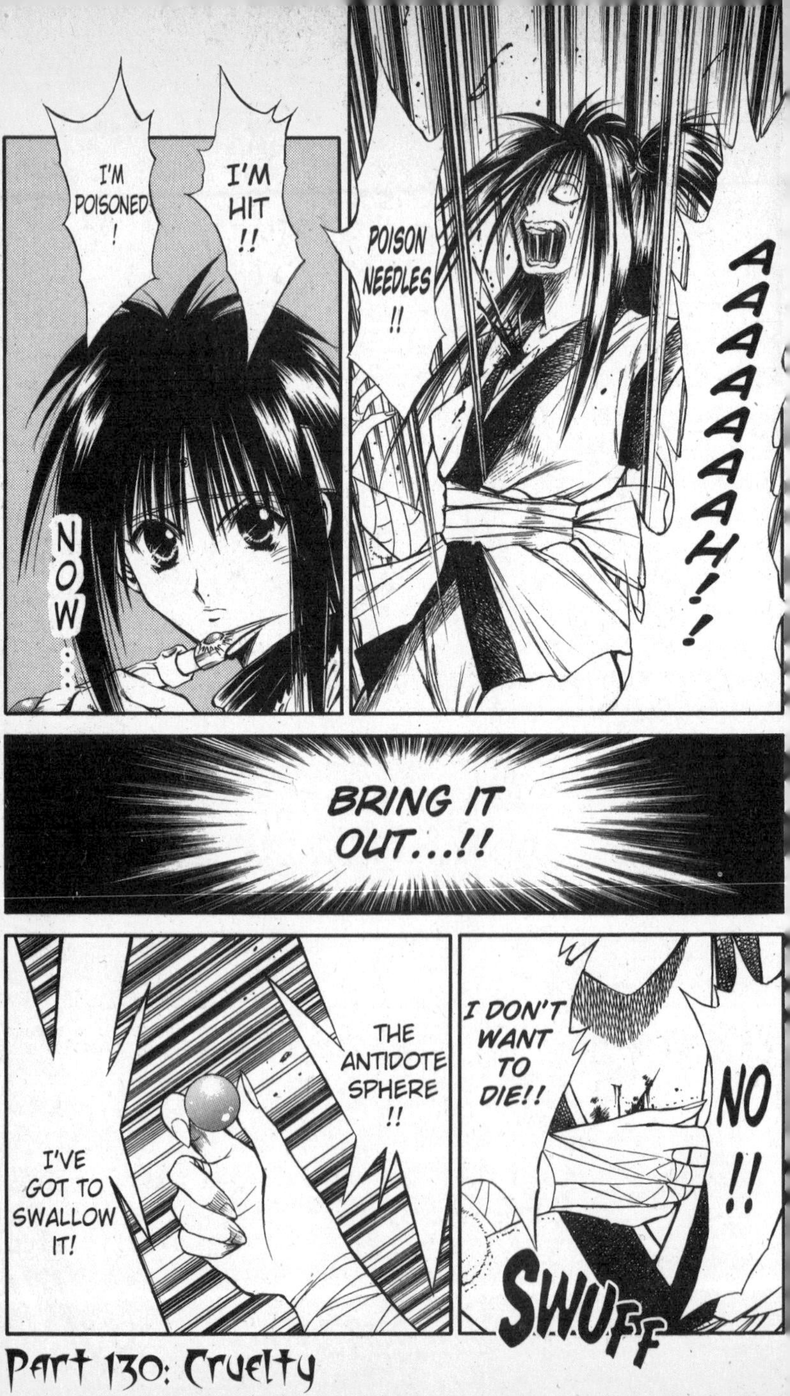
AAAAAAAAH!!!
POISON NEEDLES!!
I'M HIT!!
I'M POISONED!
NOW...
BRING IT OUT...!!
NO!!
I DON'T WANT TO DIE!!
SWUFF
THE ANTIDOTE SPHERE!!
I'VE GOT TO SWALLOW IT!

Part 130: Cruelty

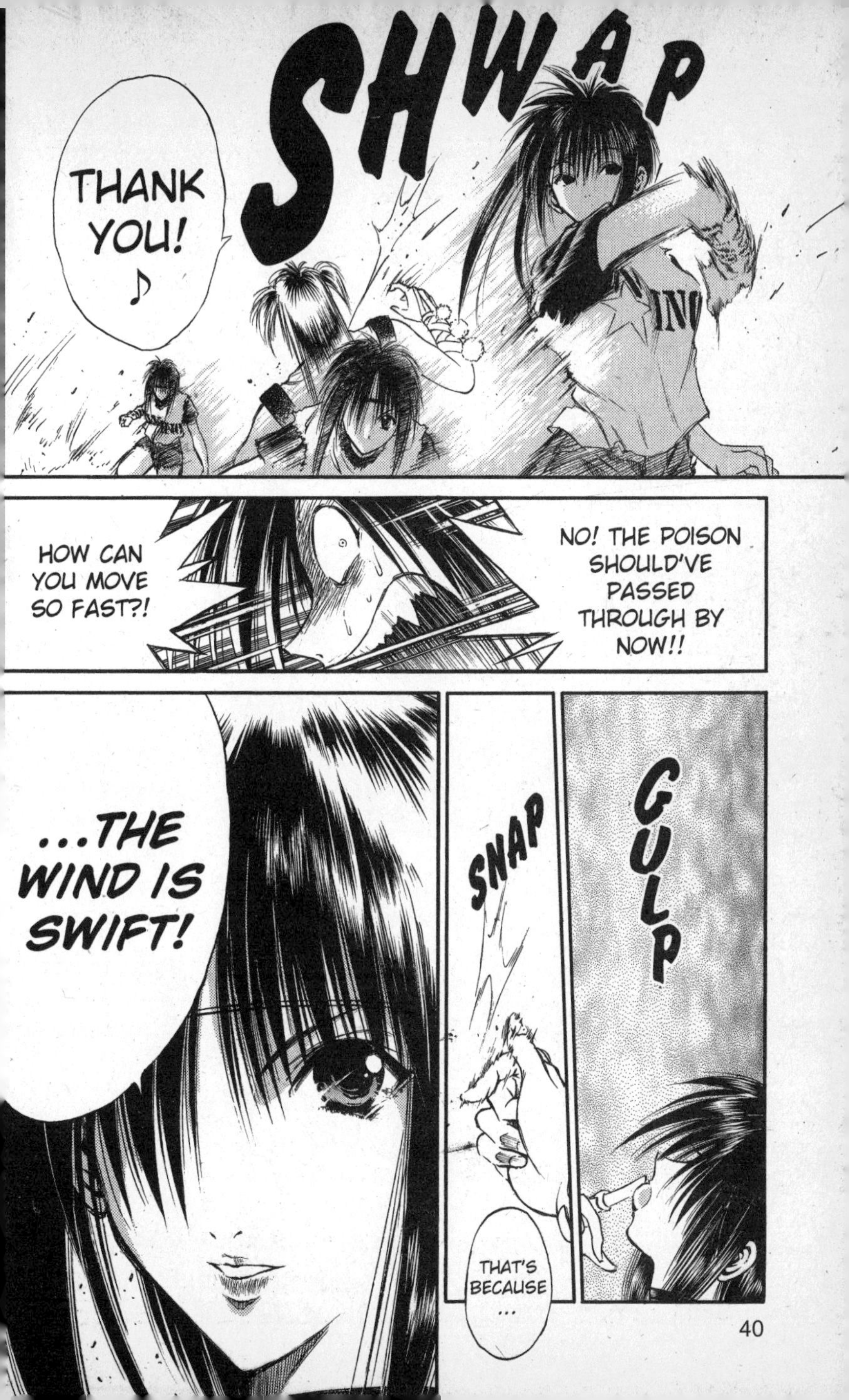
SHWAP
THANK YOU! ♪
NO! THE POISON SHOULD'VE PASSED THROUGH BY NOW!!
HOW CAN YOU MOVE SO FAST?!
GULP
SNAP
THAT'S BECAUSE ...
...THE WIND IS SWIFT!

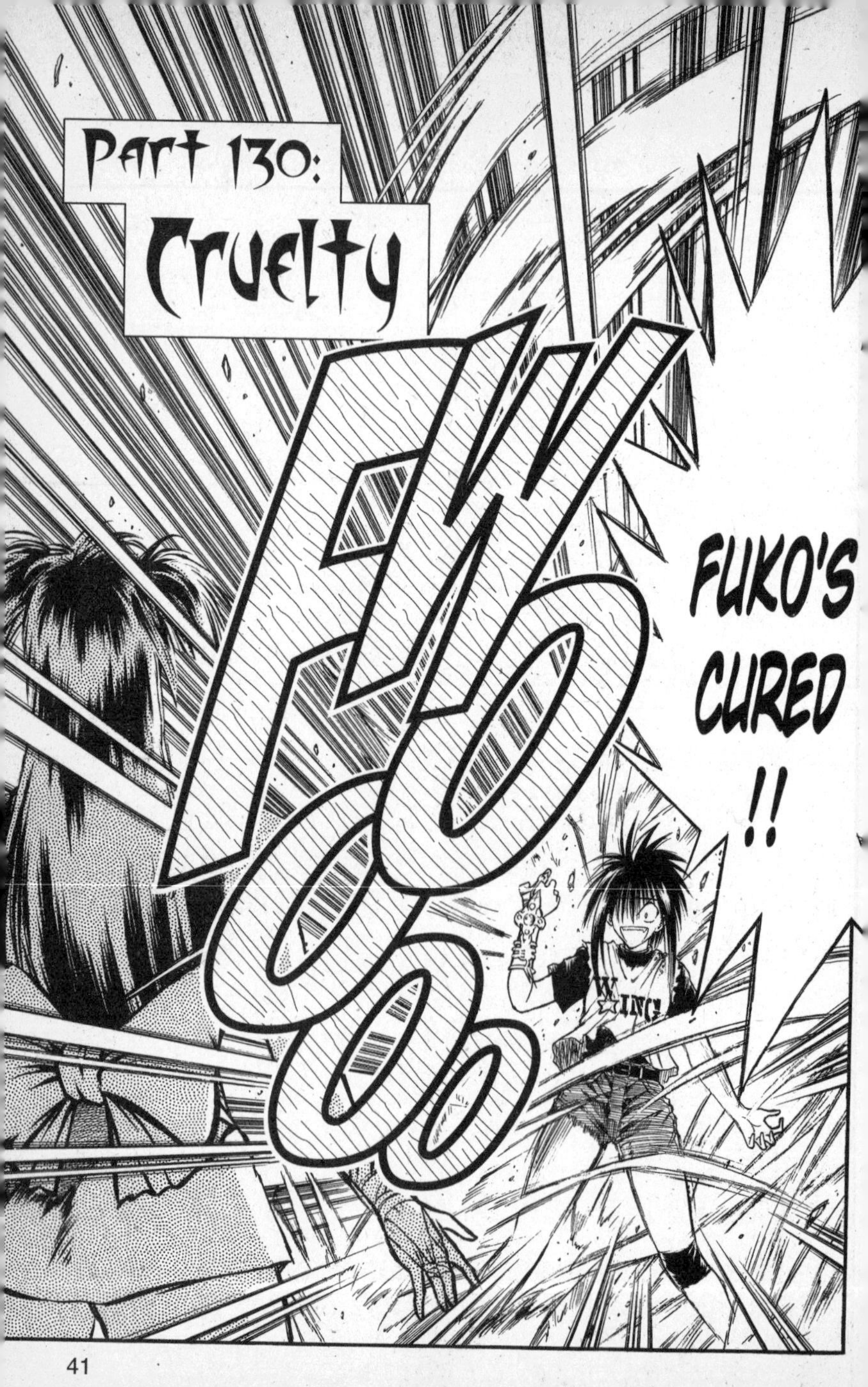

Part 130:
Cruelty
FUKO'S CURED !!

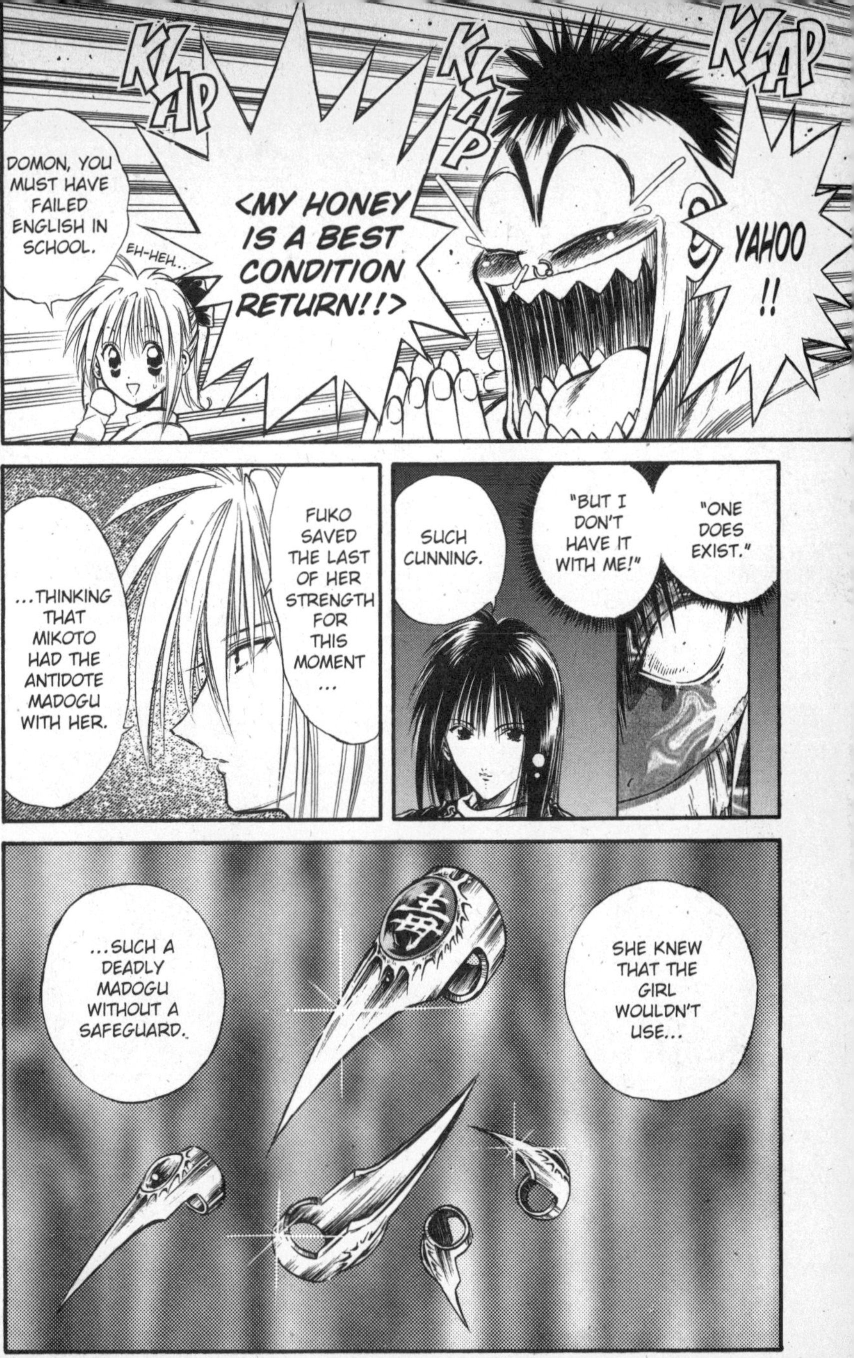
KLAP
YAHOO !!
KLAP KLAP
<MY HONEY IS A BEST CONDITION RETURN!!>
KLAP
EH-HEH...
DOMON, YOU MUST HAVE FAILED ENGLISH IN SCHOOL.
"ONE DOES EXIST."
"BUT I DON'T HAVE IT WITH ME!"
SUCH CUNNING.
FUKO SAVED THE LAST OF HER STRENGTH FOR THIS MOMENT ...
...THINKING THAT MIKOTO HAD THE ANTIDOTE MADOGU WITH HER.
SHE KNEW THAT THE GIRL WOULDN'T USE...
...SUCH A DEADLY MADOGU WITHOUT A SAFEGUARD.

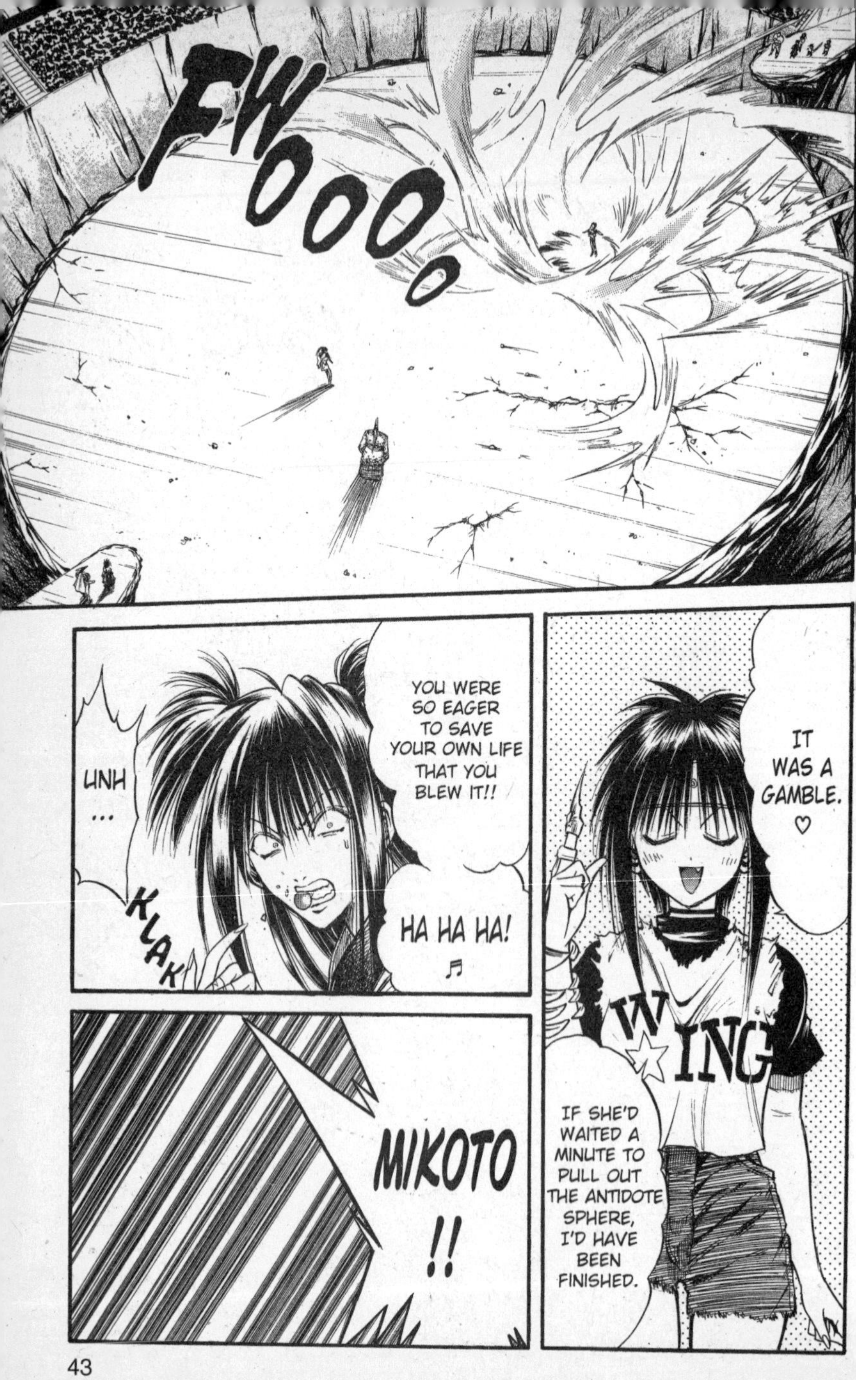
FWOOOOo
IT WAS A GAMBLE. ♡
IF SHE'D WAITED A MINUTE TO PULL OUT THE ANTIDOTE SPHERE, I'D HAVE BEEN FINISHED.
YOU WERE SO EAGER TO SAVE YOUR OWN LIFE THAT YOU BLEW IT!!
HA HA HA! ♫
UNH ...
KLAK
MIKOTO !!

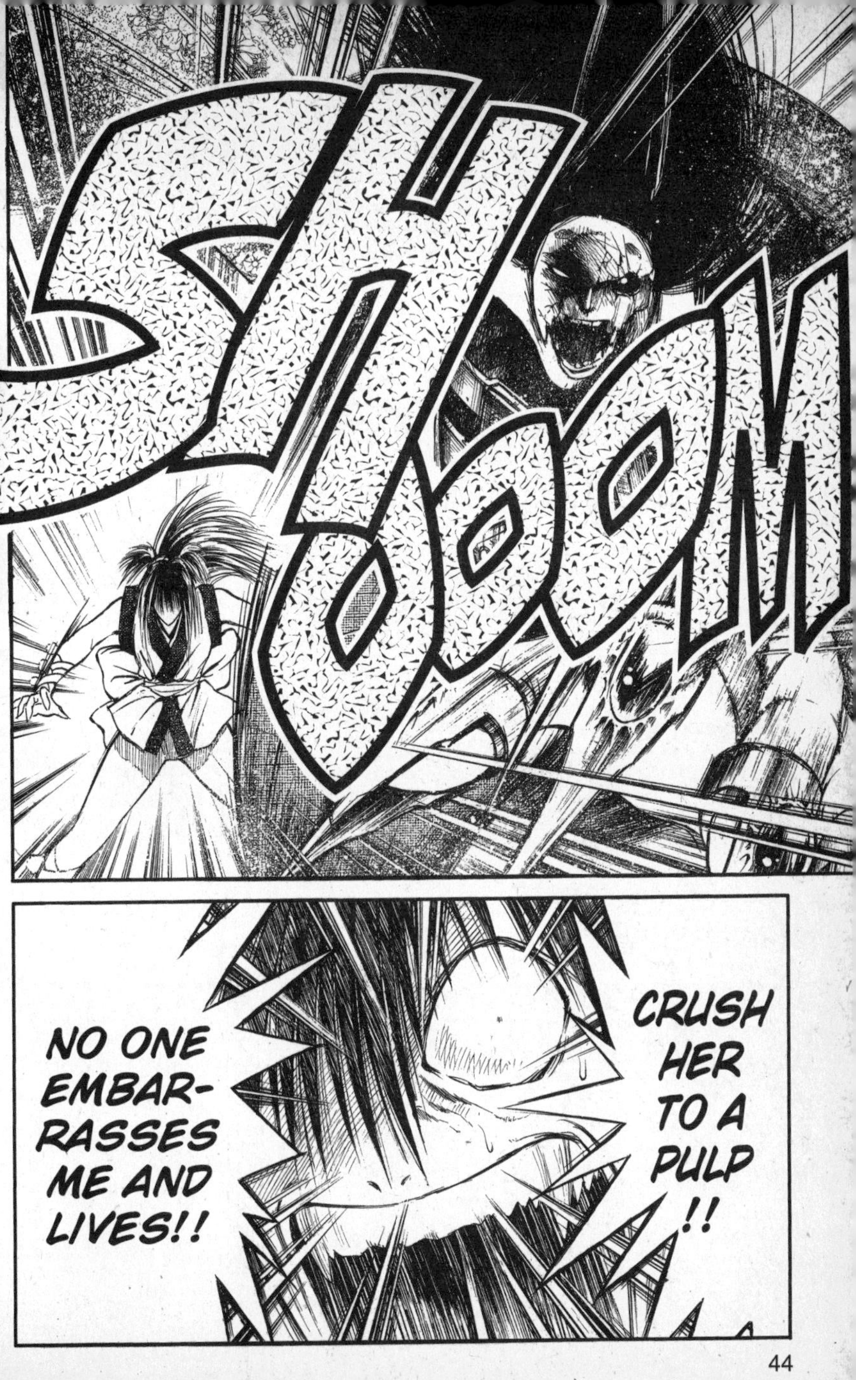
SHOOM
CRUSH HER TO A PULP!!
NO ONE EMBARRASSES ME AND LIVES!!

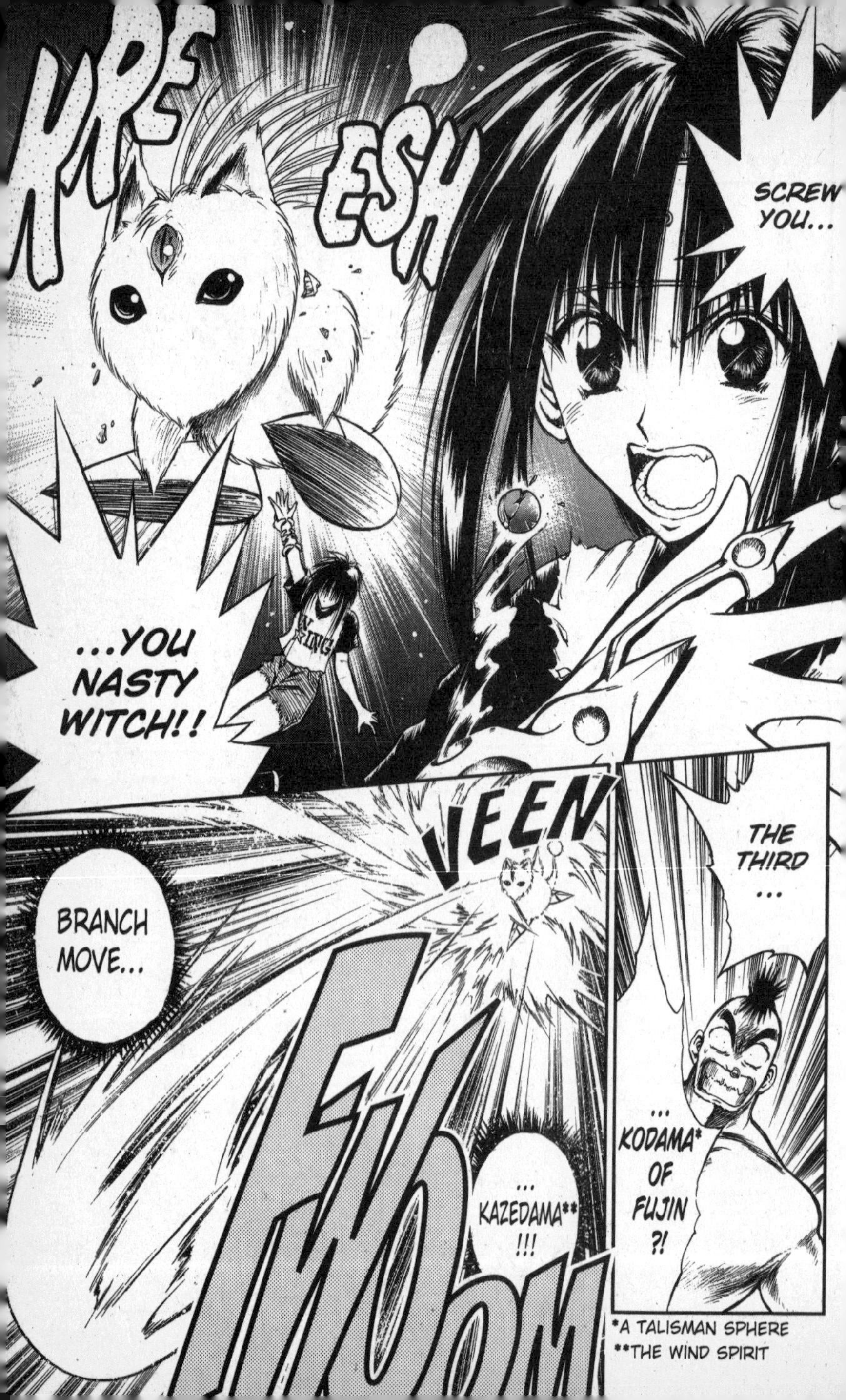
SCREW YOU...
KRE
ESH
...YOU NASTY WITCH!!
THE THIRD ...
... KODAMA* OF FUJIN ?!
VEEN
BRANCH MOVE...
... KAZEDAMA** !!!
FWOOM

*A TALISMAN SPHERE

**THE WIND SPIRIT

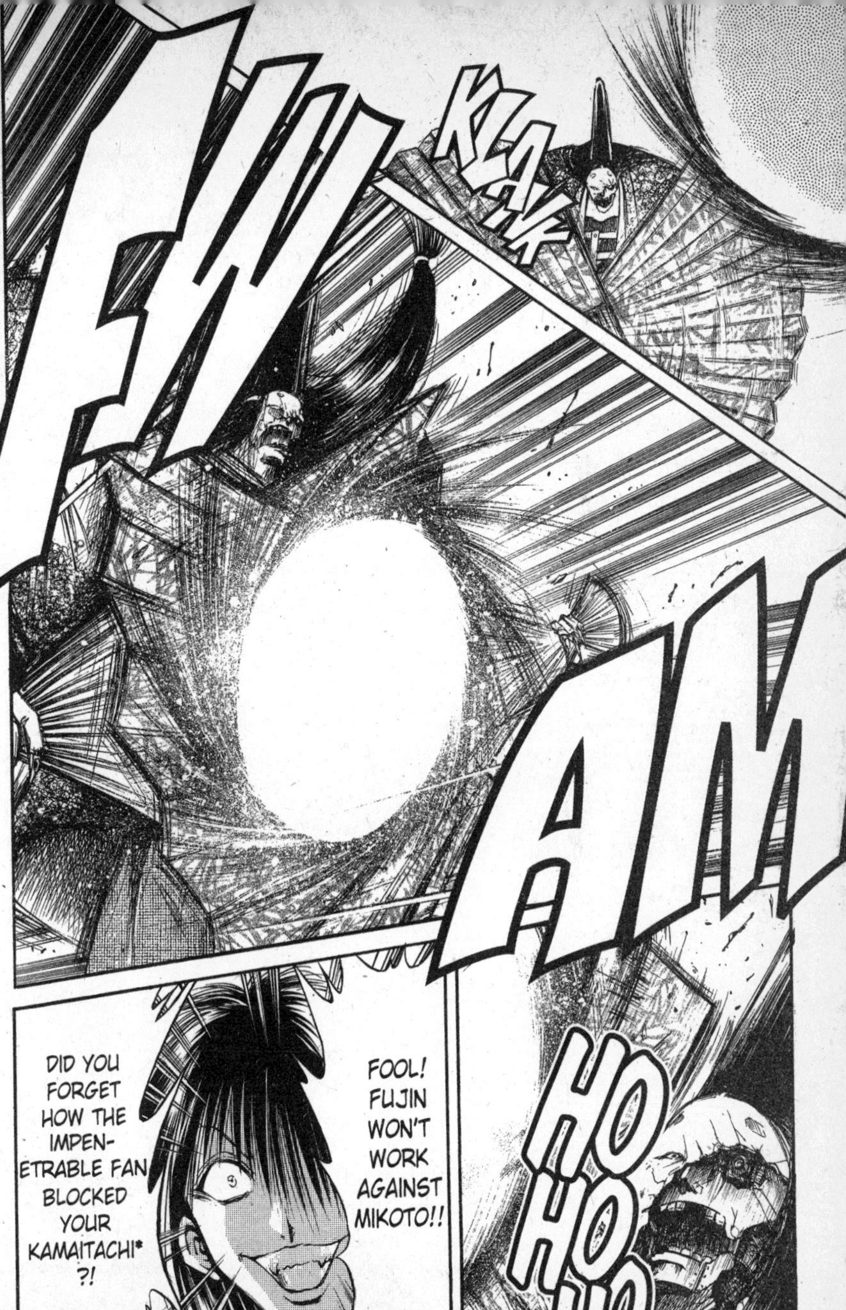
KLAK
HO HO HO HO
FOOL! FUJIN WON'T WORK AGAINST MIKOTO!!
DID YOU FORGET HOW THE IMPENETRABLE FAN BLOCKED YOUR KAMAITACHI* ?!

*FUKO'S WIND-SLICING TECHNIQUE

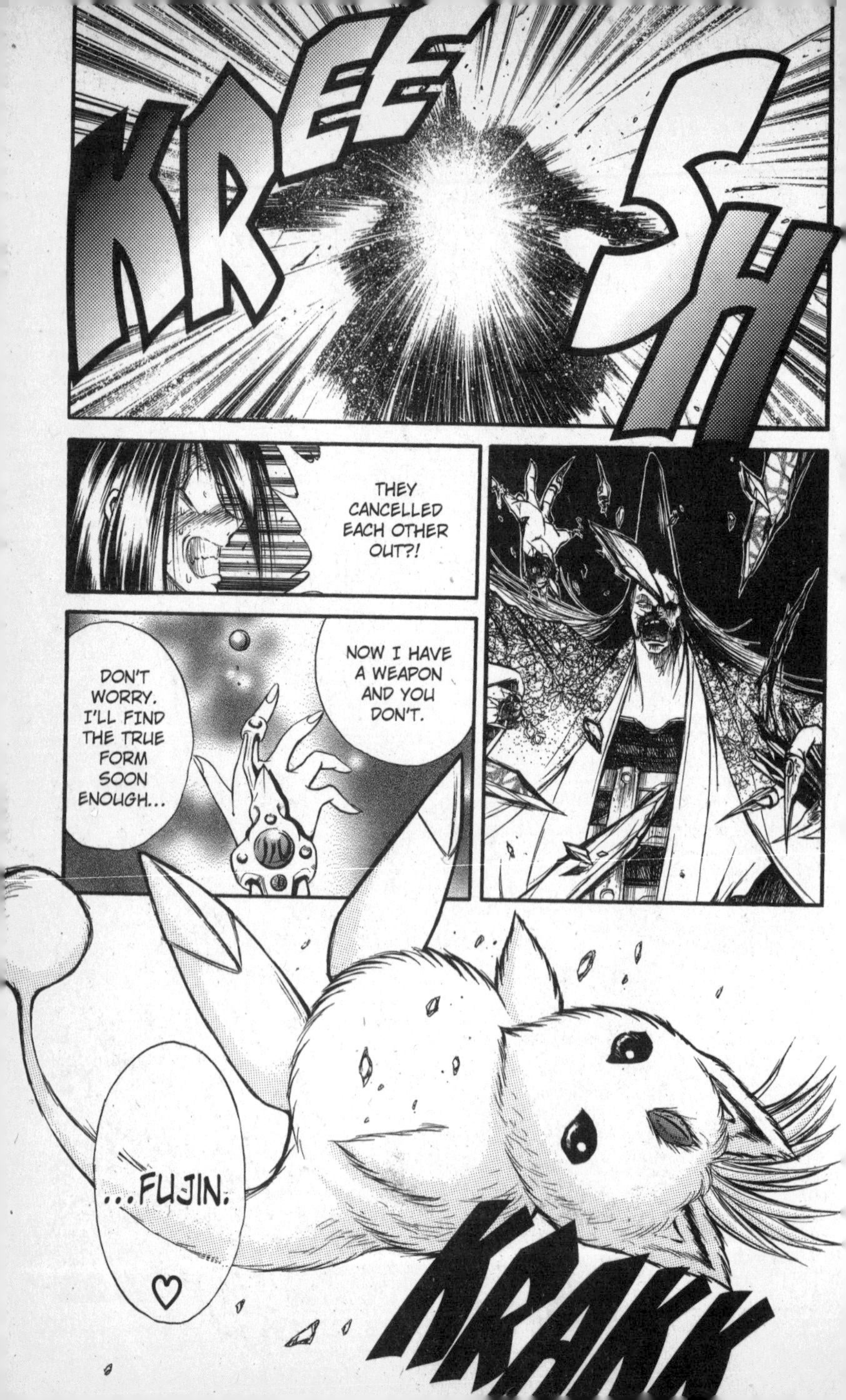
KREESH
THEY CANCELLED EACH OTHER OUT?!
NOW I HAVE A WEAPON AND YOU DON'T.
DON'T WORRY. I'LL FIND THE TRUE FORM SOON ENOUGH...
...FUJIN. ♡
KRAKK

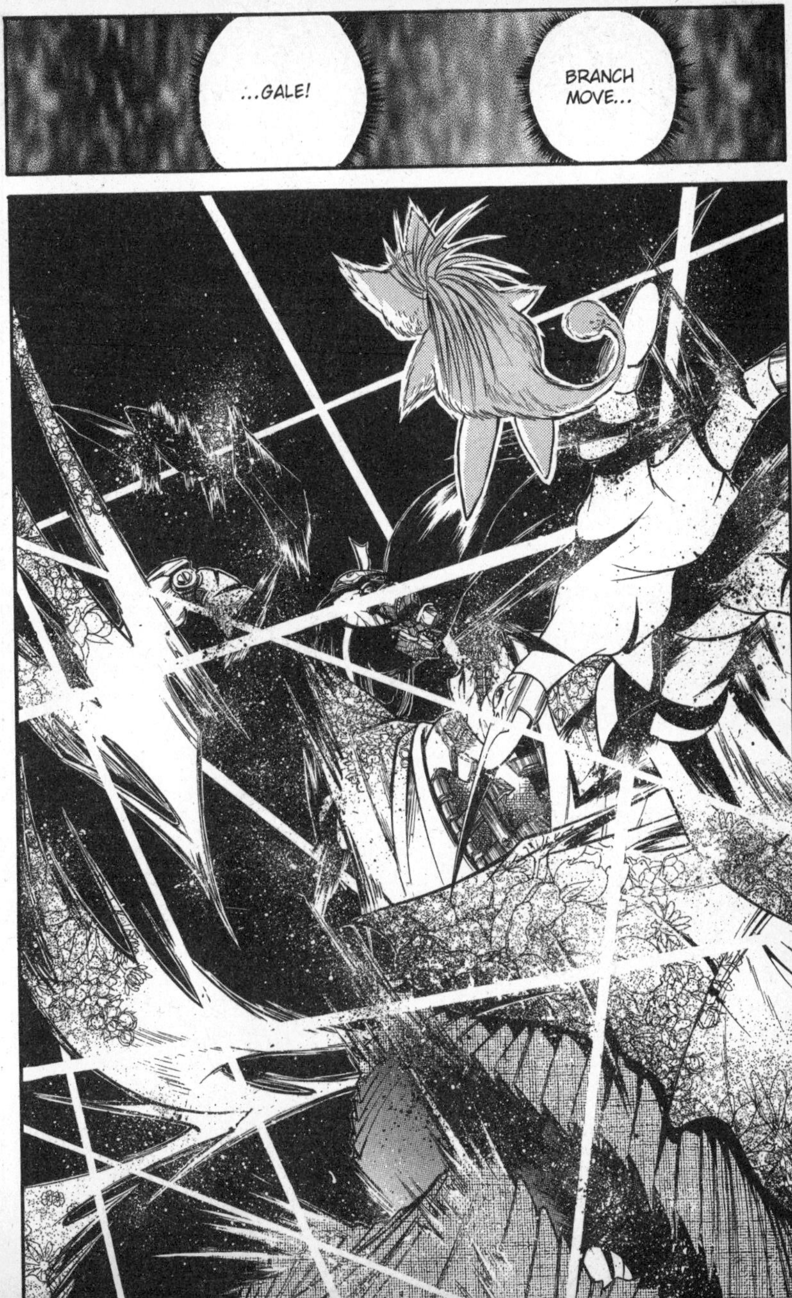
BRANCH MOVE...
...GALE!

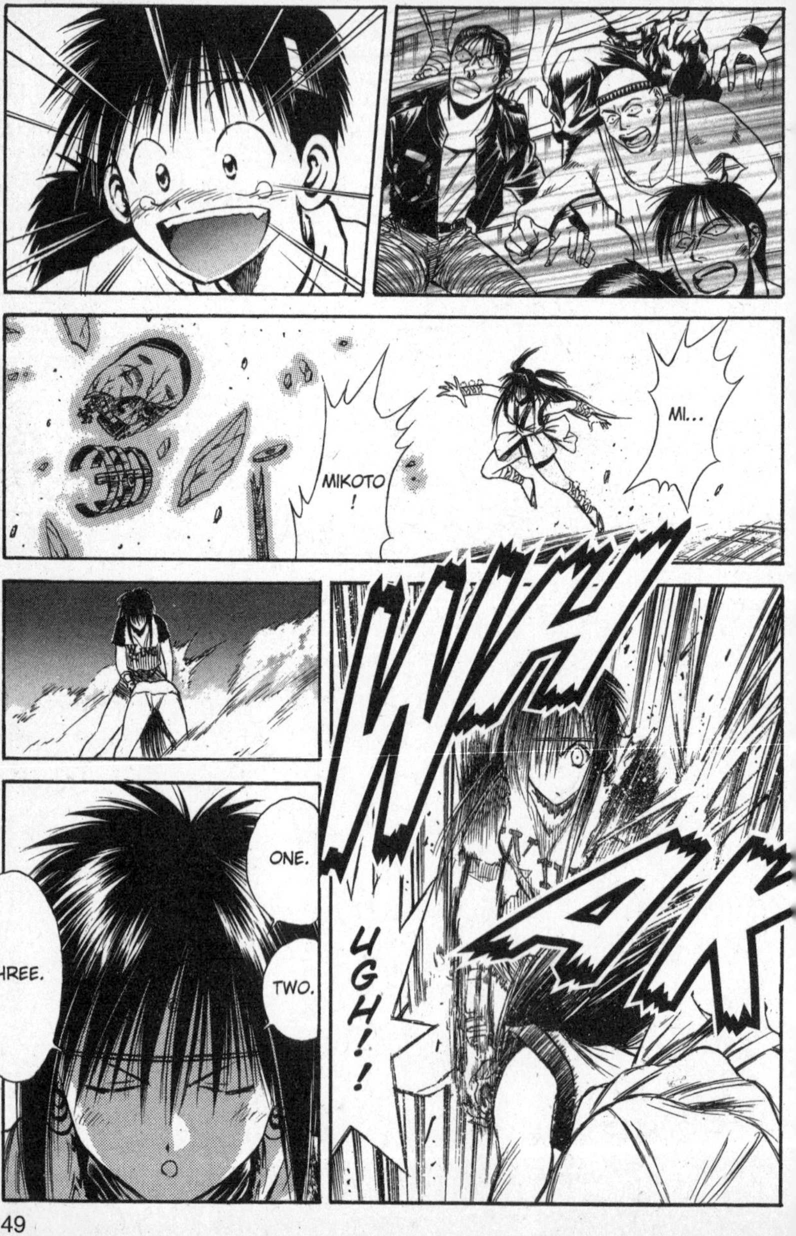
MI...
MIKOTO!
WHAK
UGH!!
ONE.
TWO.
THREE.

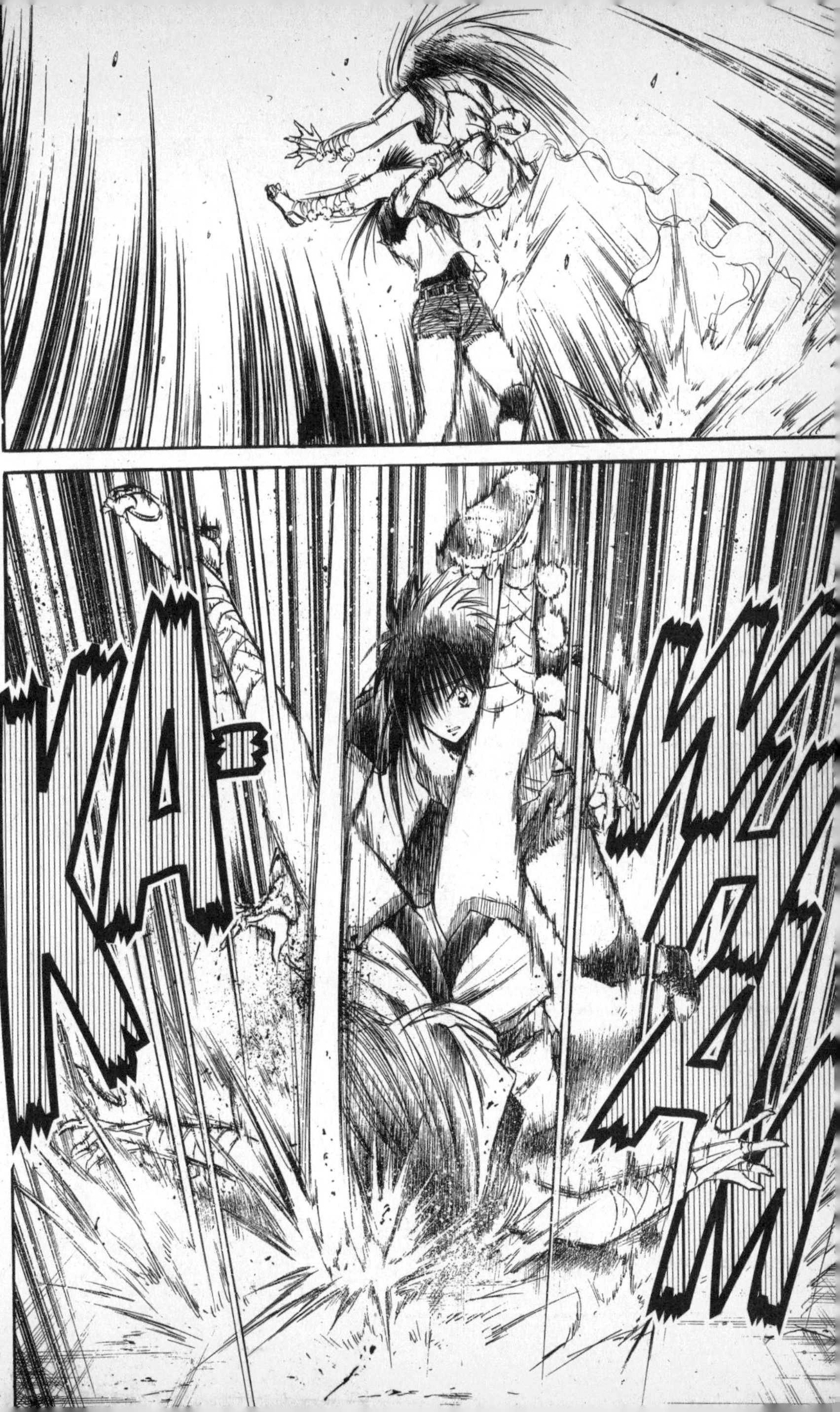

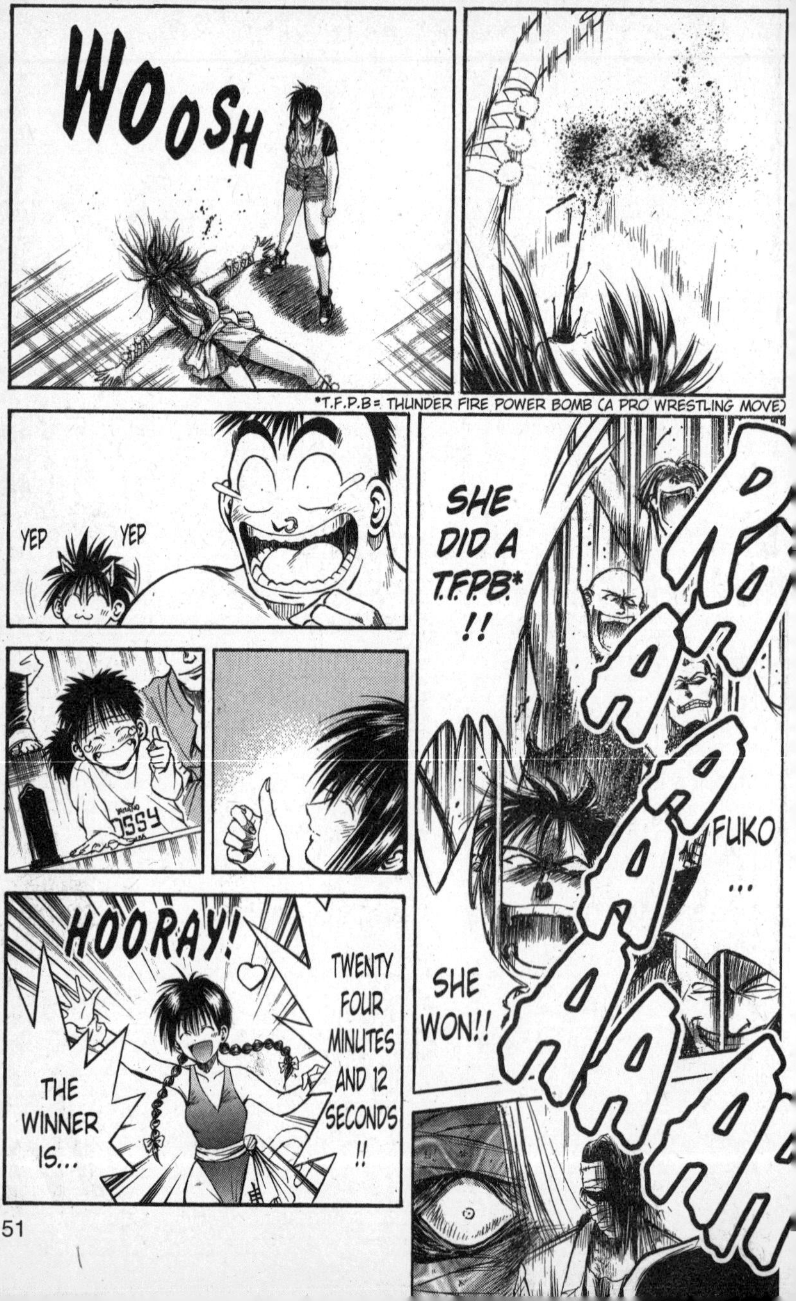
WOOSH
*T.F.P.B = THUNDER FIRE POWER BOMB (A PRO WRESTLING MOVE)
RAAAAAAAA
SHE DID A T.F.P.B.* !!
FUKO ...
SHE WON!!
YEP YEP
HOORAY!
TWENTY FOUR MINUTES AND 12 SECONDS !!
THE WINNER IS...

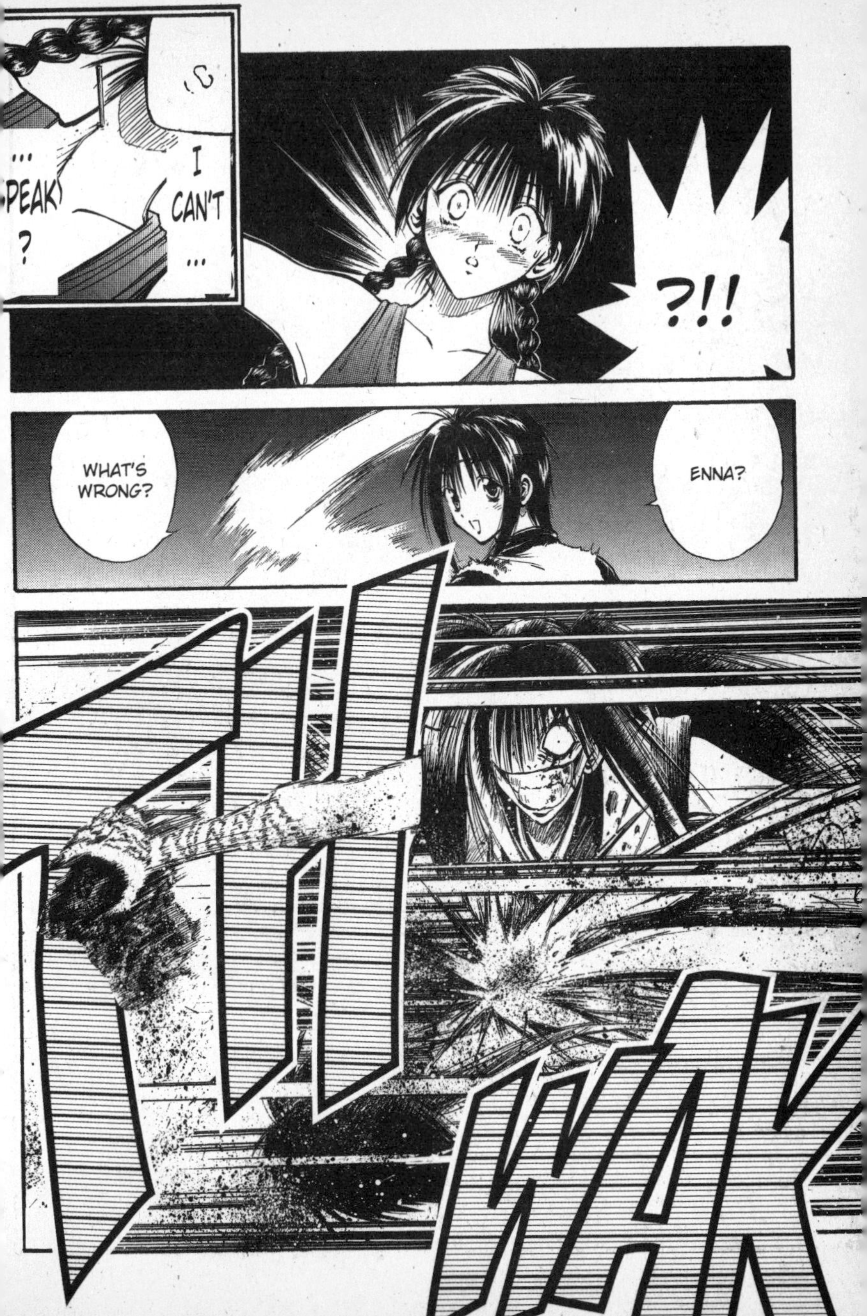
?!!
I CAN'T ...
... PEAK ?
ENNA?
WHAT'S WRONG?
WAK

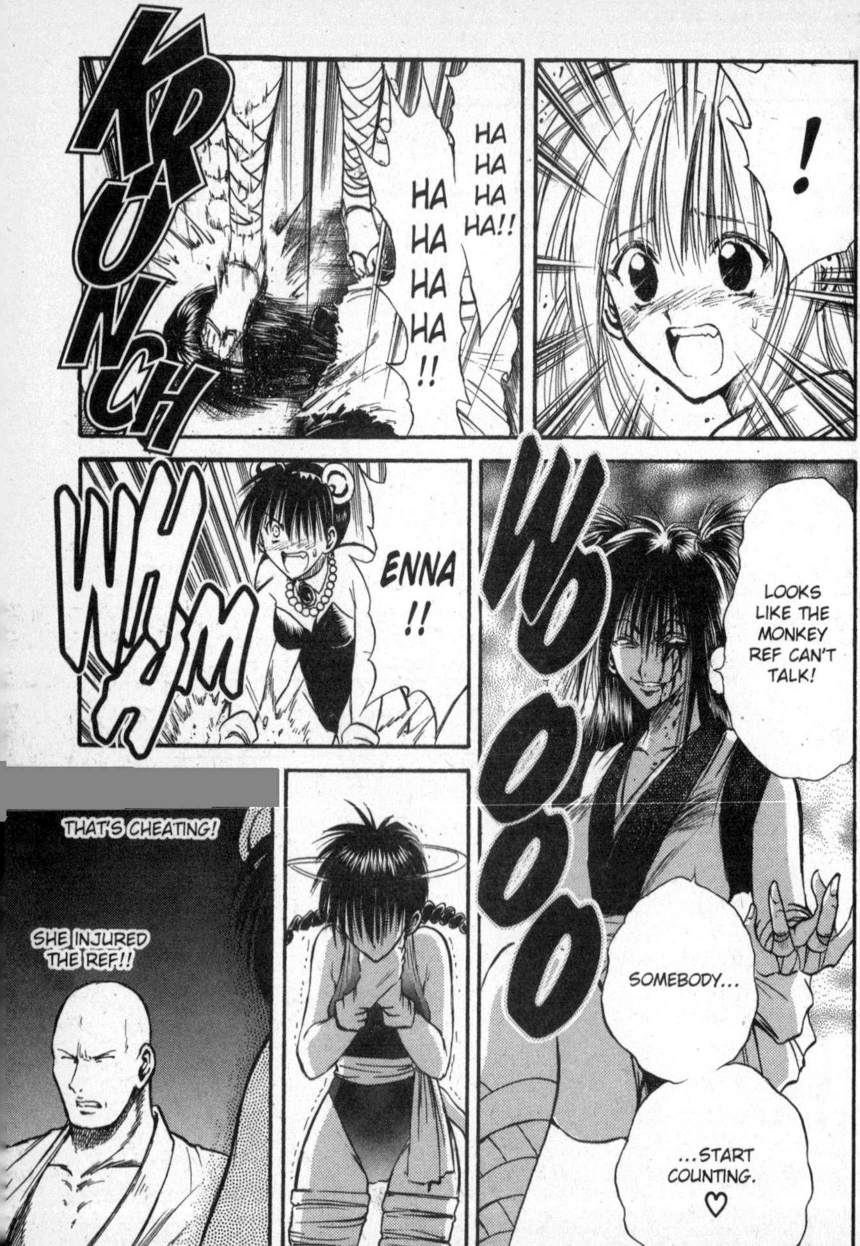
!
KRUNCH
HA HA HA HA!!
HA HA HA HA !!
WOOO
LOOKS LIKE THE MONKEY REF CAN'T TALK!
SOMEBODY...
...START COUNTING. ♡
ENNA !!
WHAM
THAT'S CHEATING!
SHE INJURED THE REF!!

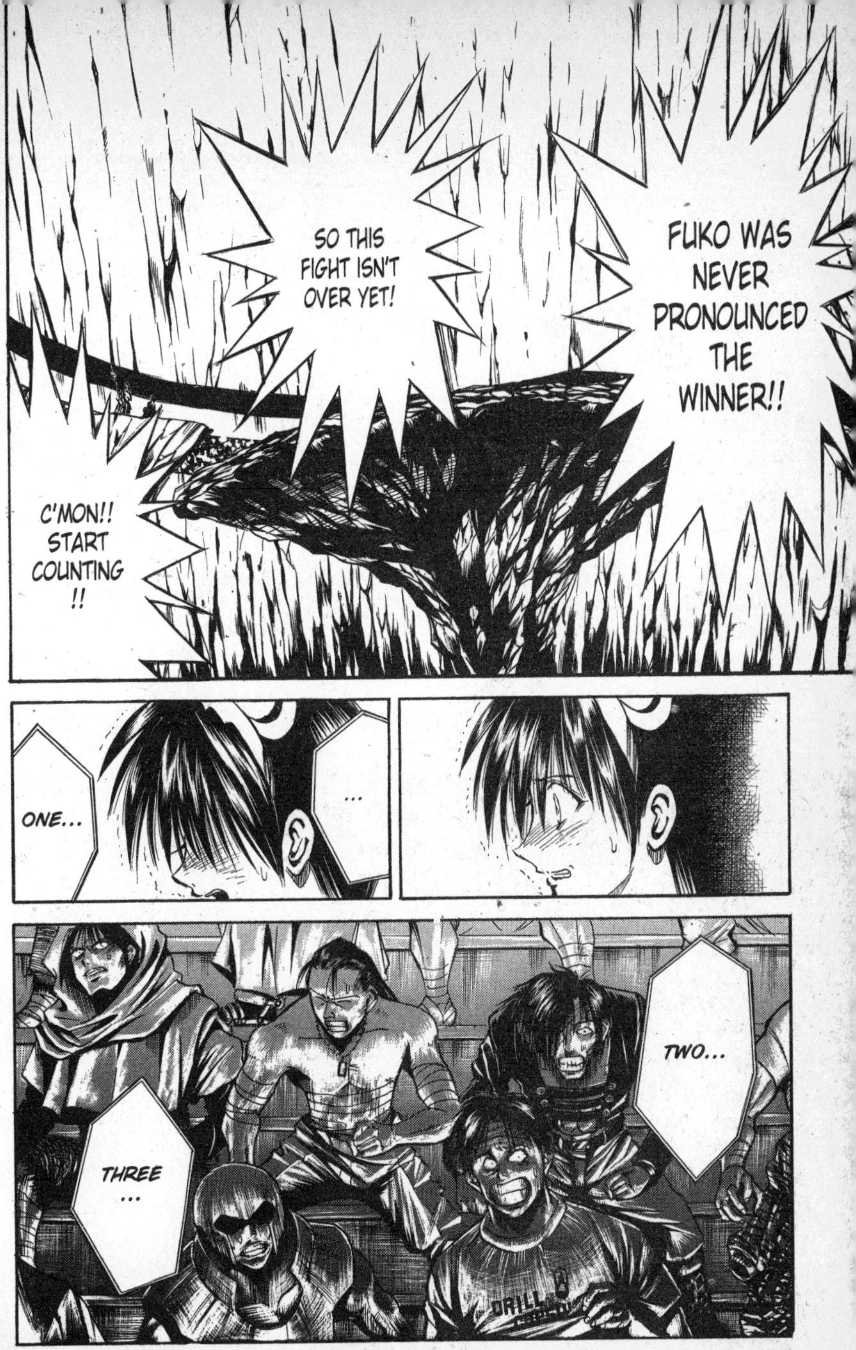
FUKO WAS NEVER PRONOUNCED THE WINNER!!
SO THIS FIGHT ISN'T OVER YET!
C'MON!! START COUNTING !!
...
ONE...
TWO...
THREE ...

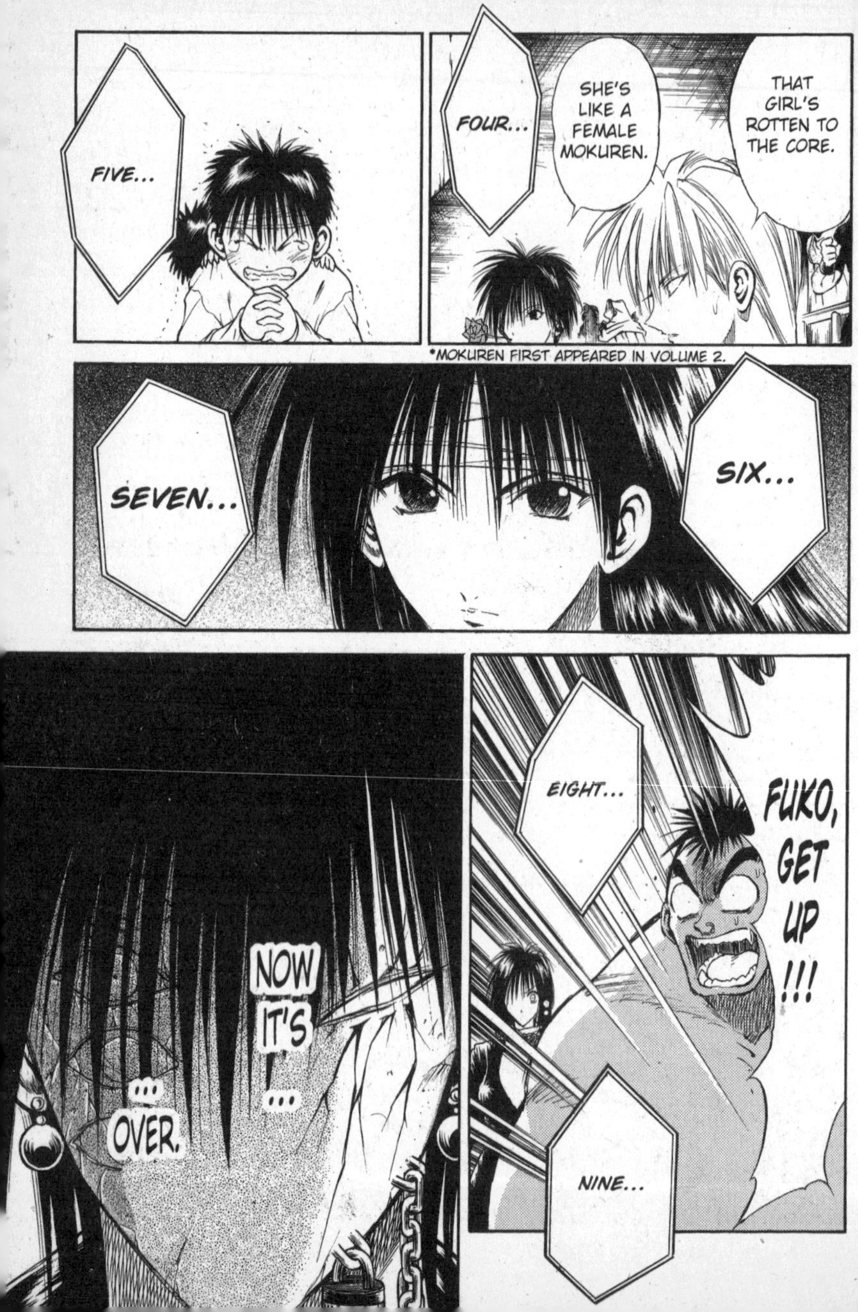
THAT GIRL'S ROTTEN TO THE CORE.
SHE'S LIKE A FEMALE MOKUREN.
FOUR...
FIVE...
SIX...
SEVEN...
FUKO, GET UP!!!
EIGHT...
NINE...
NOW IT'S ...
... OVER.
*MOKUREN FIRST APPEARED IN VOLUME 2.

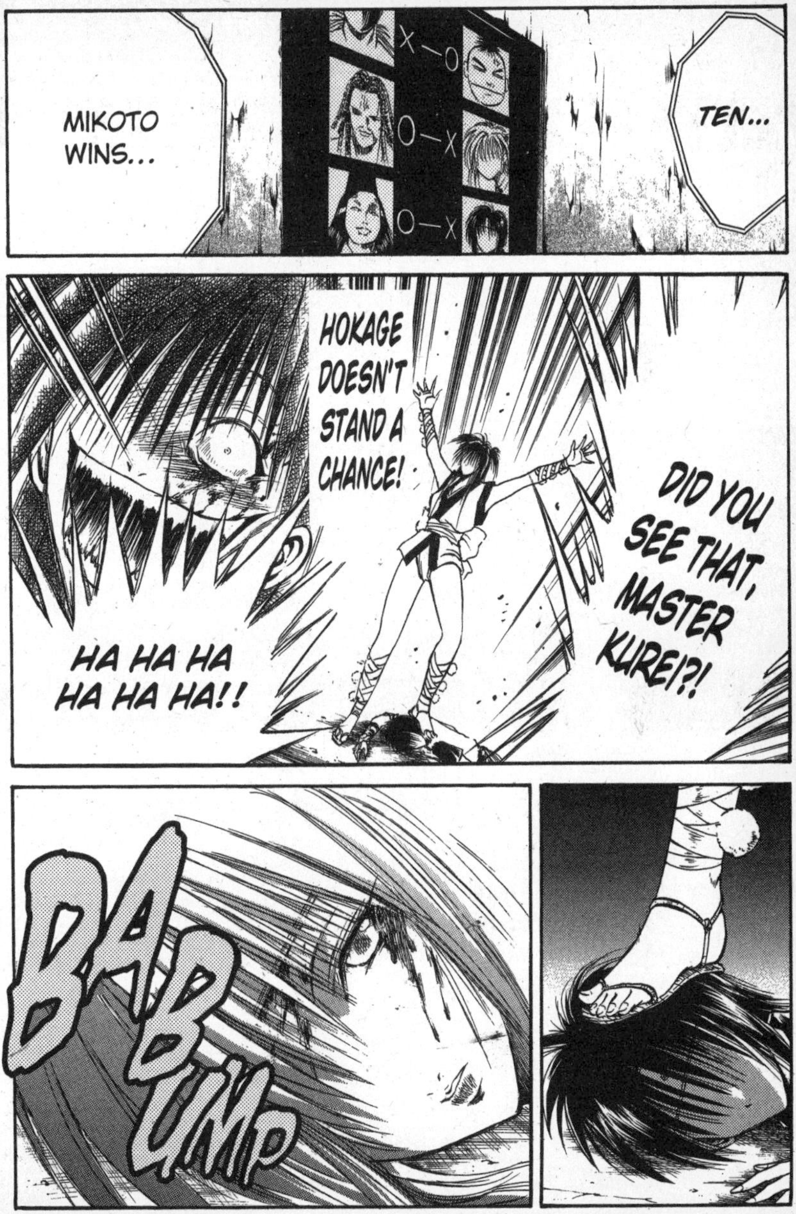
TEN...
MIKOTO WINS...
DID YOU SEE THAT, MASTER KUREI!?!
HOKAGE DOESN'T STAND A CHANCE!
HA HA HA HA HA HA!!
BABUMP

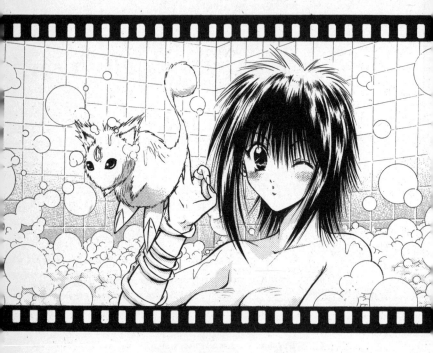

Part 131:
The Real Winner

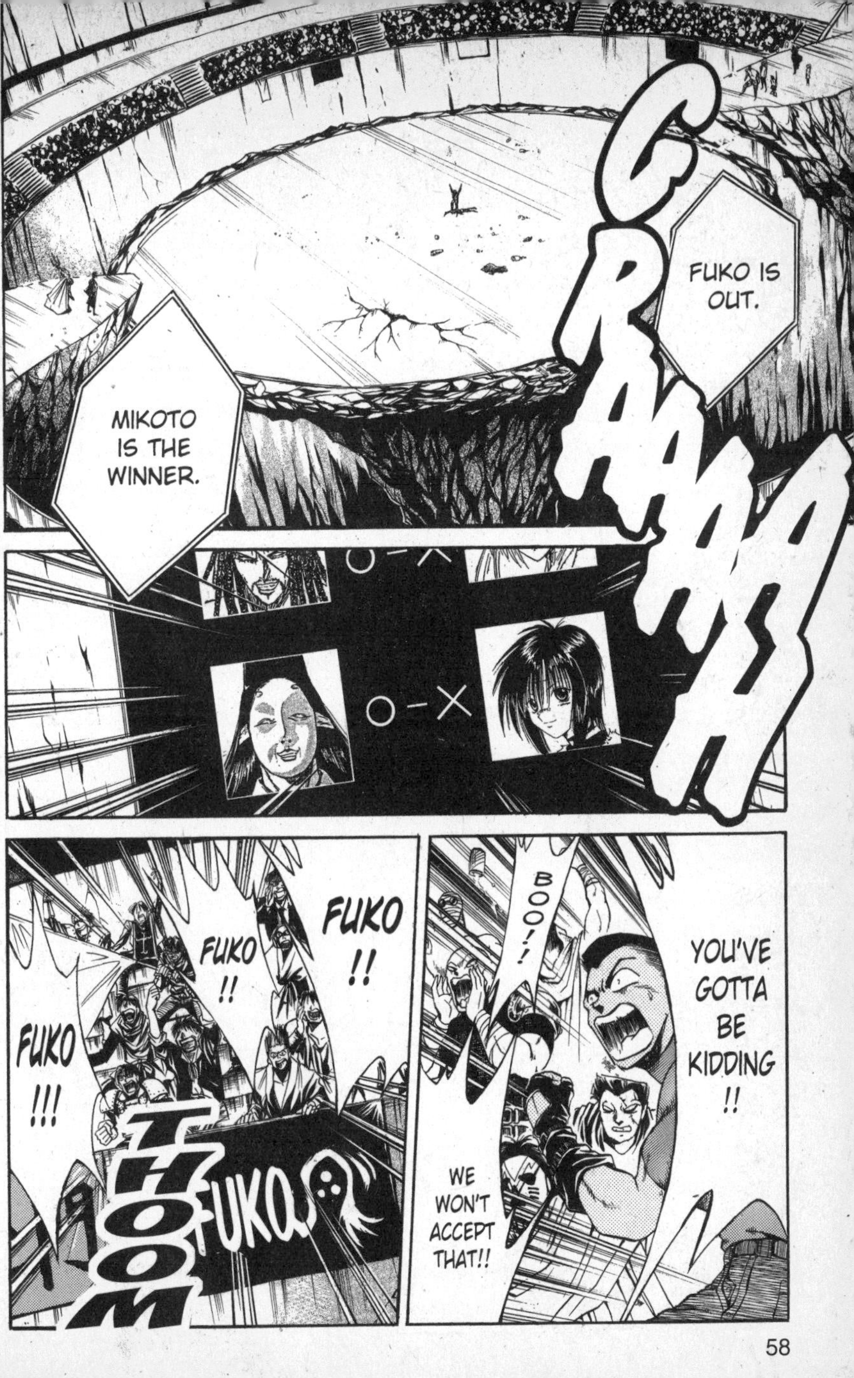
CRAAASH
FUKO IS OUT.
MIKOTO IS THE WINNER.
YOU'VE GOTTA BE KIDDING!!
BOO!!
WE WON'T ACCEPT THAT!!
FUKO!!
FUKO!!
FUKO!!!
FUKO
THOOM

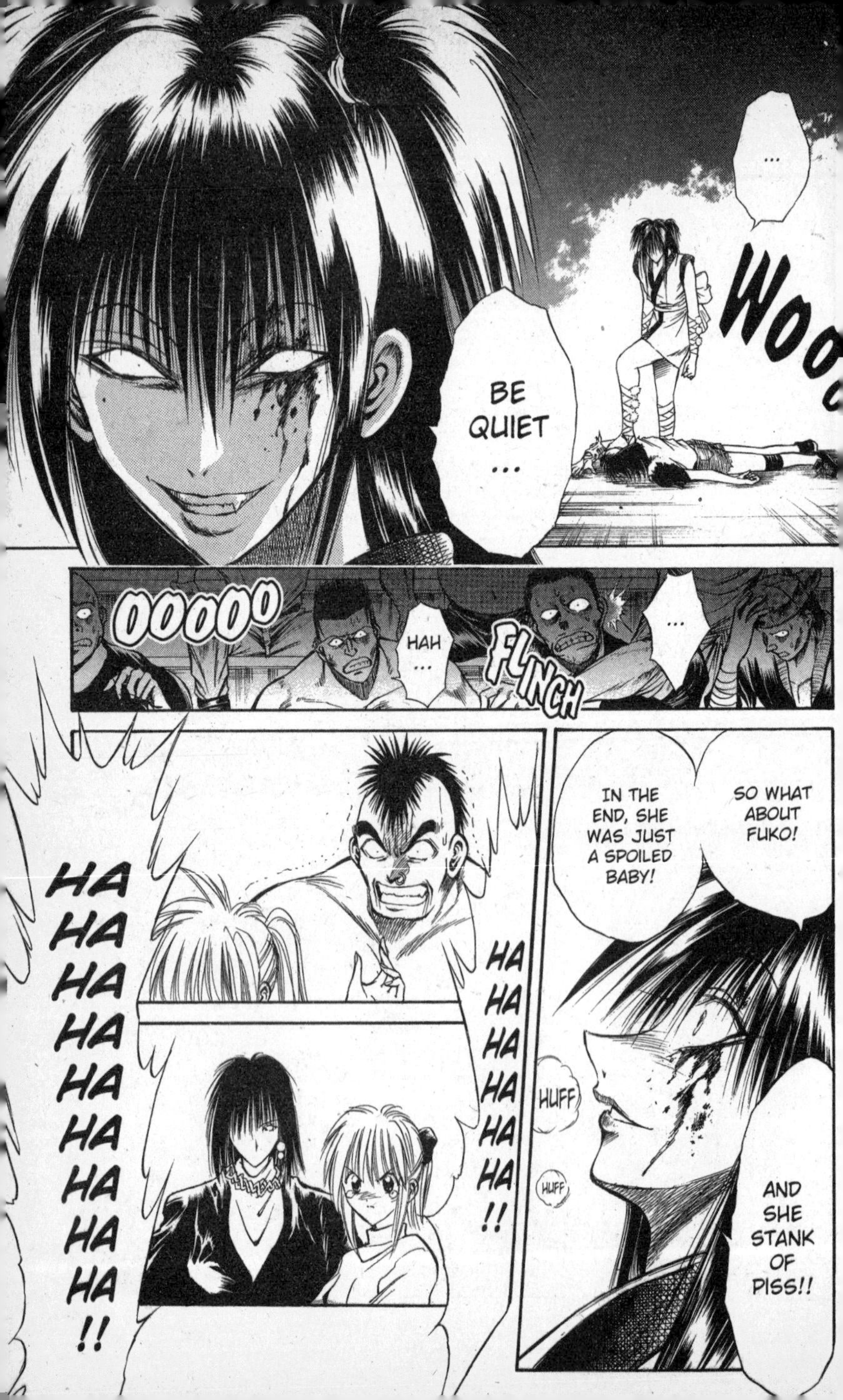
...
WOOO
BE QUIET ...
...
FLINCH
HAH ...
OOOOO
SO WHAT ABOUT FUKO!
IN THE END, SHE WAS JUST A SPOILED BABY!
HUFF
HUFF
AND SHE STANK OF PISS!!
HA HA HA HA HA HA HA HA !!
HA HA HA HA HA HA HA HA HA HA HA !!

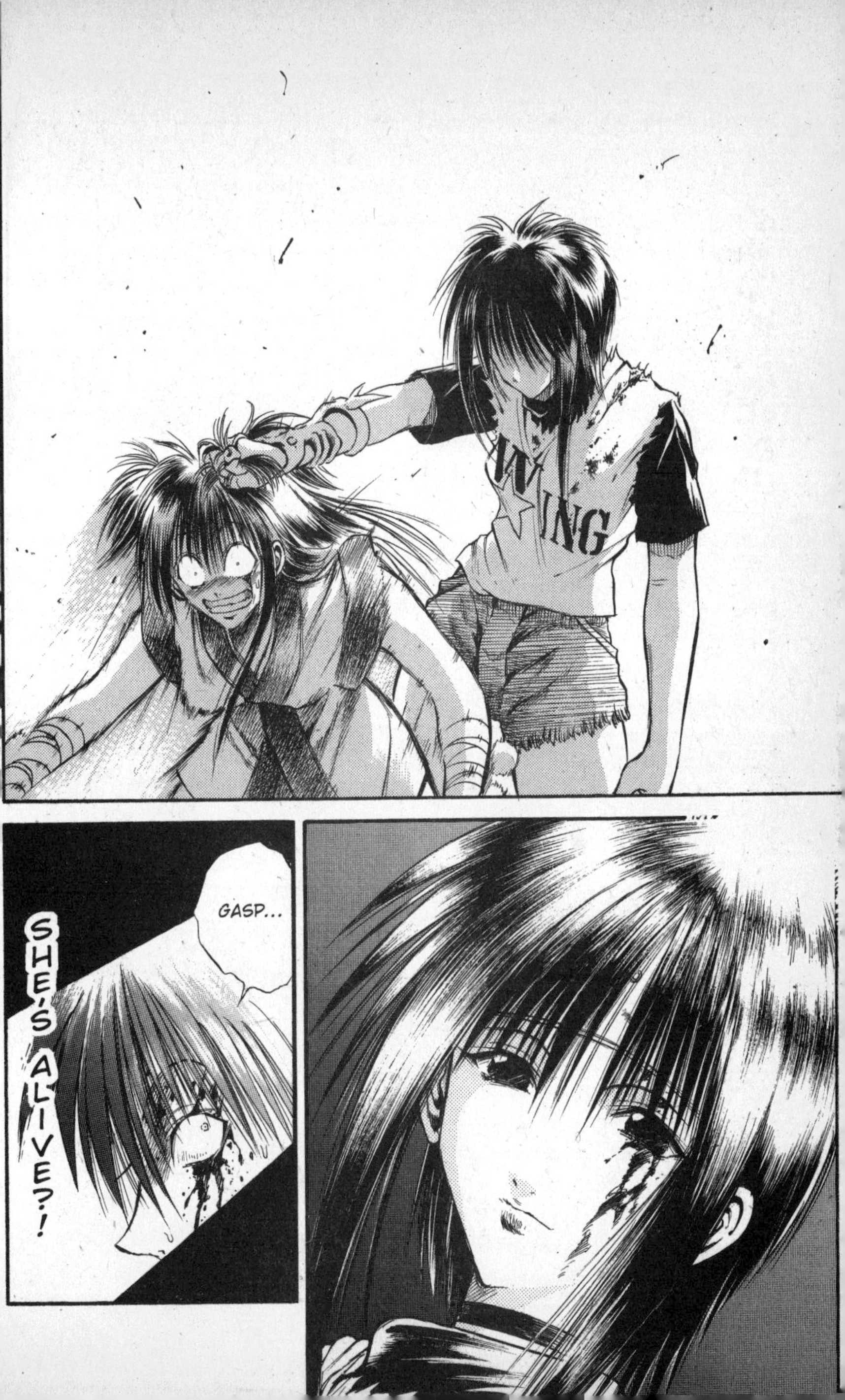
GASP...
SHE'S ALIVE?!

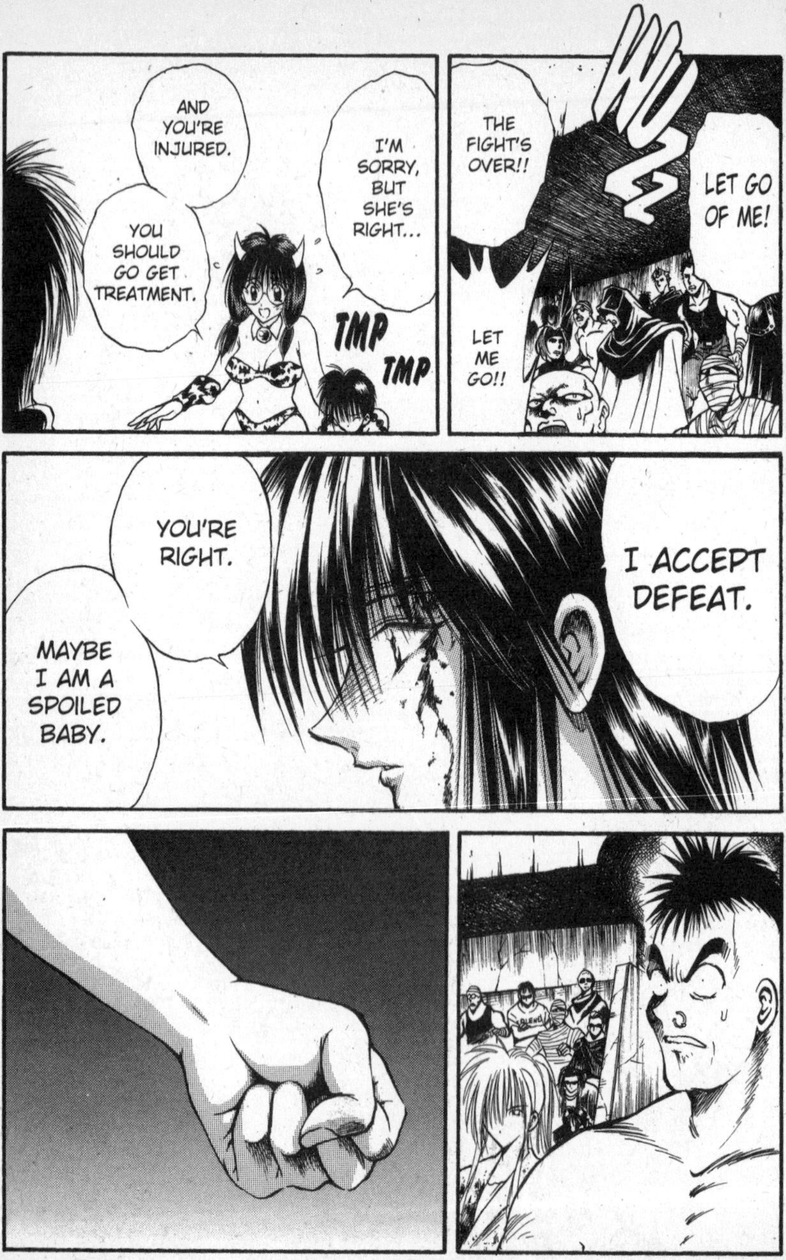
WHUZZ
LET GO OF ME!
THE FIGHT'S OVER!!
LET ME GO!!
I'M SORRY, BUT SHE'S RIGHT...
AND YOU'RE INJURED.
YOU SHOULD GO GET TREATMENT.
TMP
TMP
I ACCEPT DEFEAT.
YOU'RE RIGHT.
MAYBE I AM A SPOILED BABY.

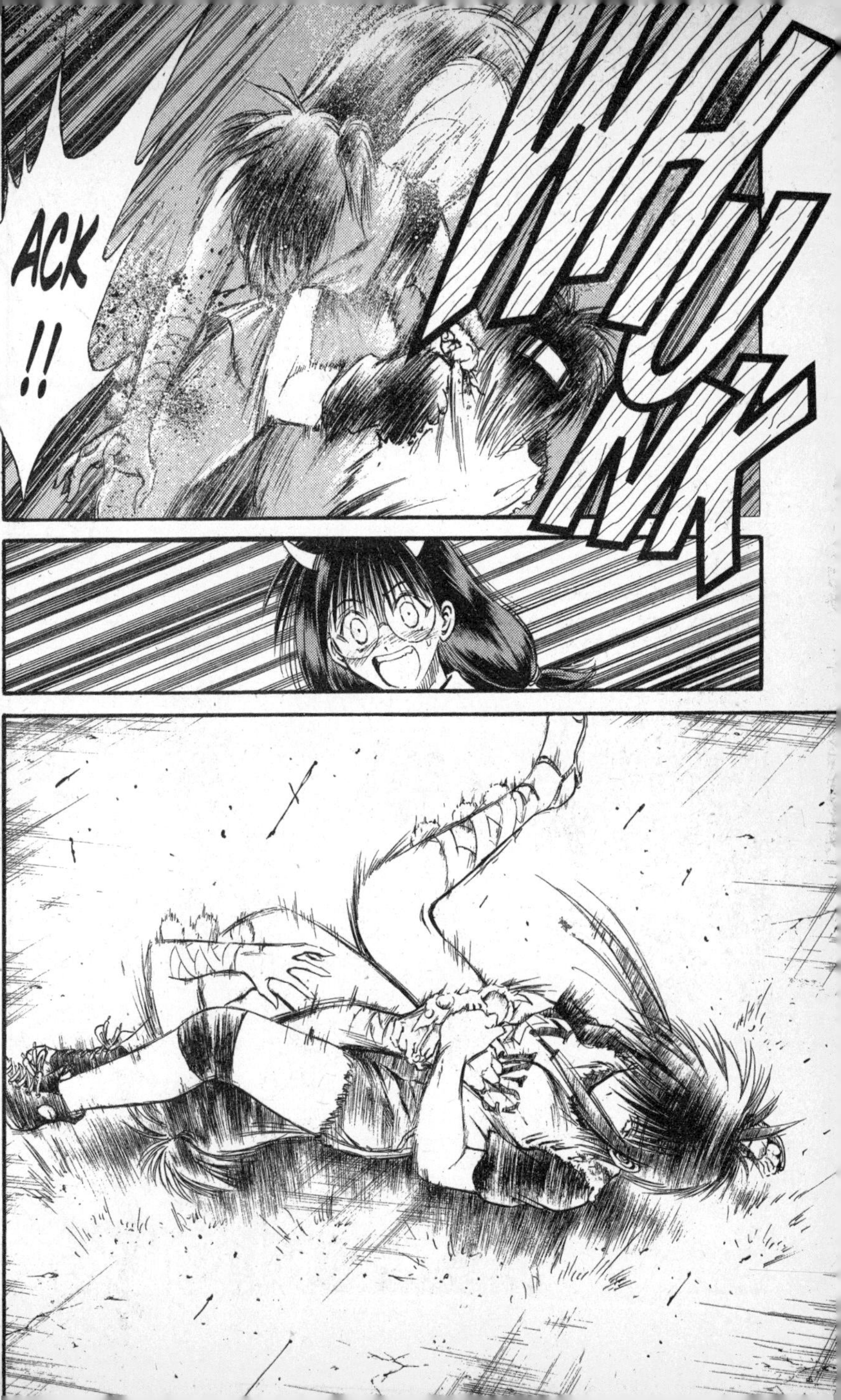
WHUNK
ACK !!

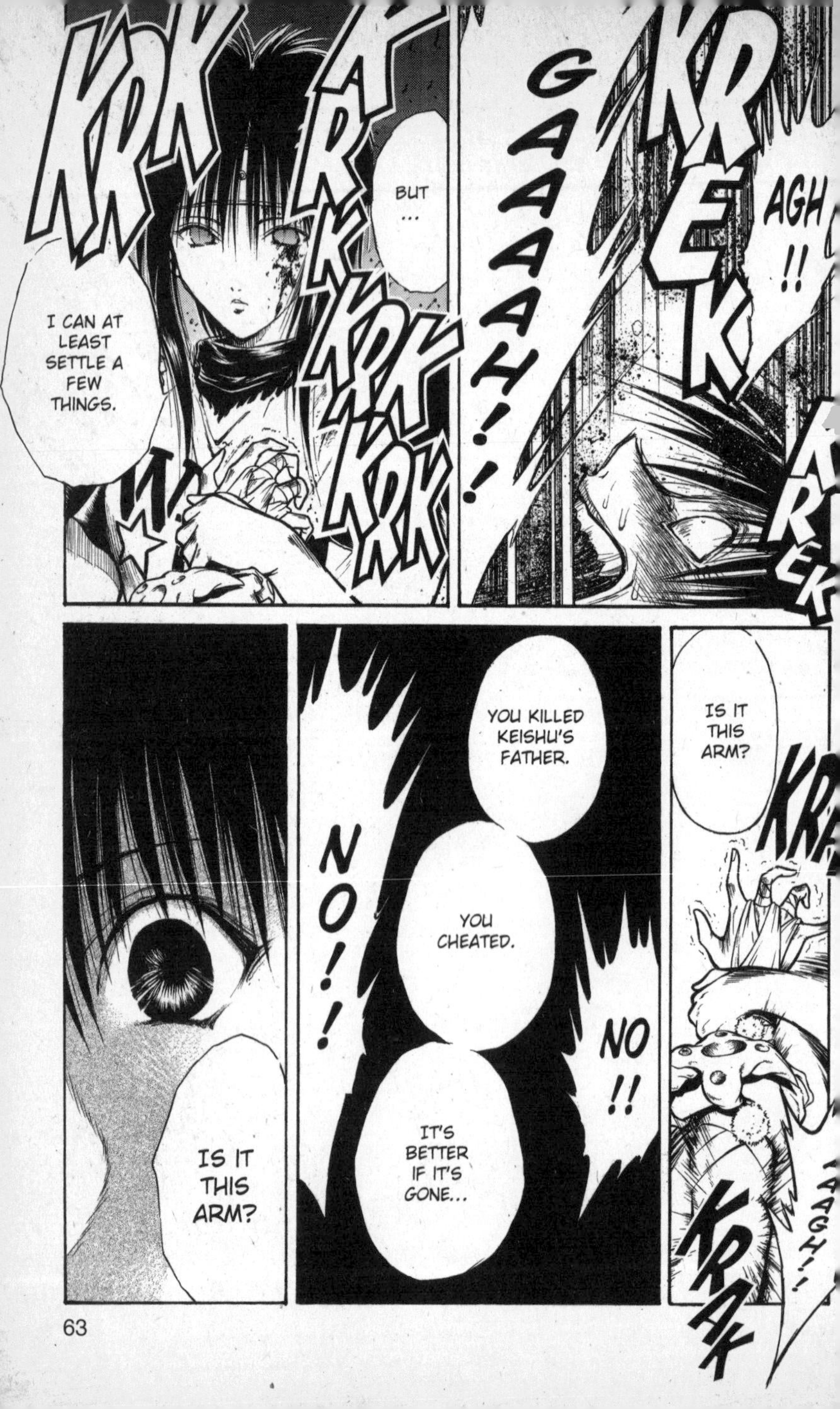

KREK
AGH!!
KREK
GAAAAAH!!
BUT...
KRK
KRK
KRK
I CAN AT LEAST SETTLE A FEW THINGS.
IS IT THIS ARM?
KRAK
AGH!!
YOU KILLED KEISHU'S FATHER.
YOU CHEATED.
IT'S BETTER IF IT'S GONE...
NO!!
NO!!
IS IT THIS ARM?

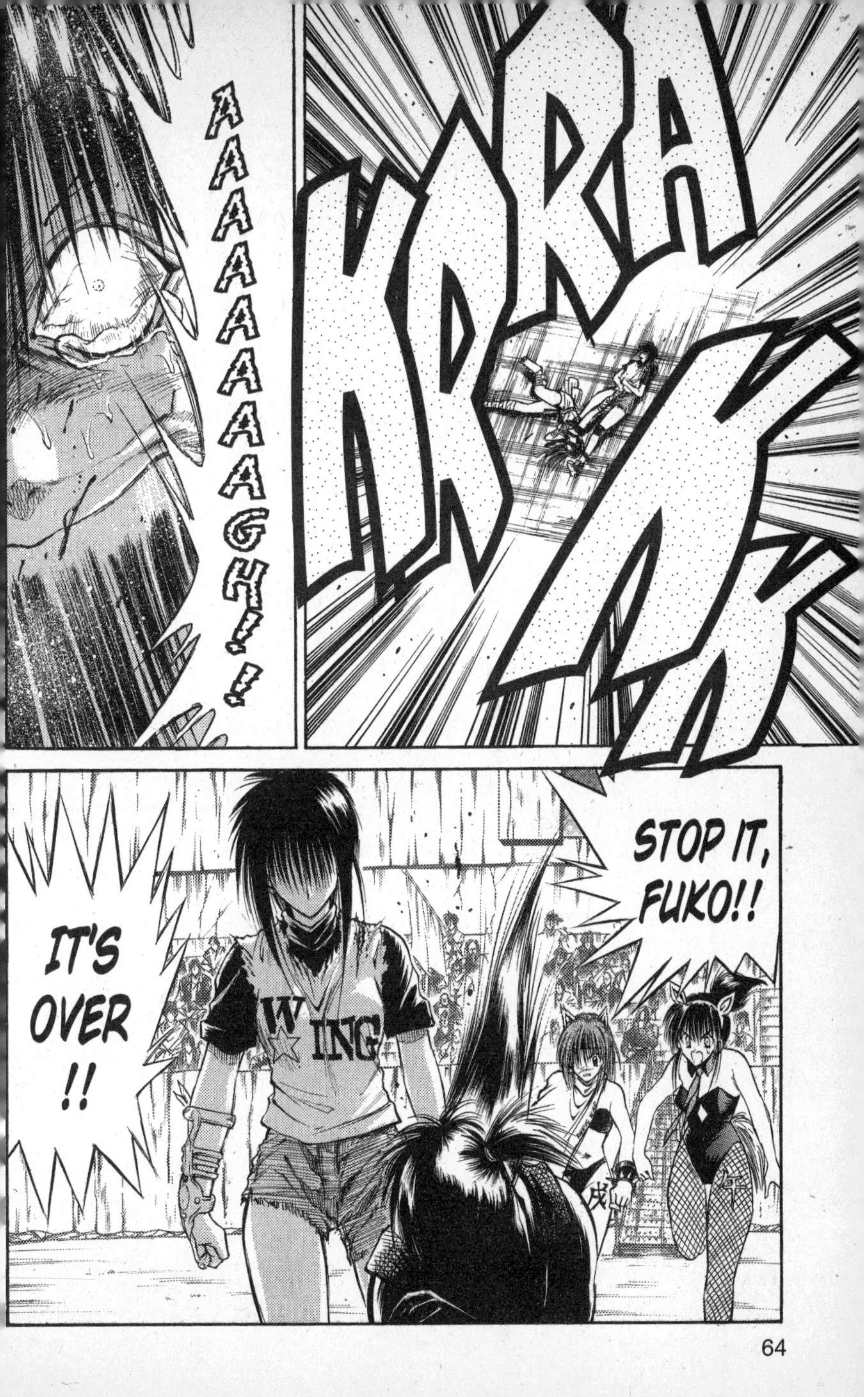
AAAAAAAAAGH!!!
STOP IT, FUKO!!
IT'S OVER!!

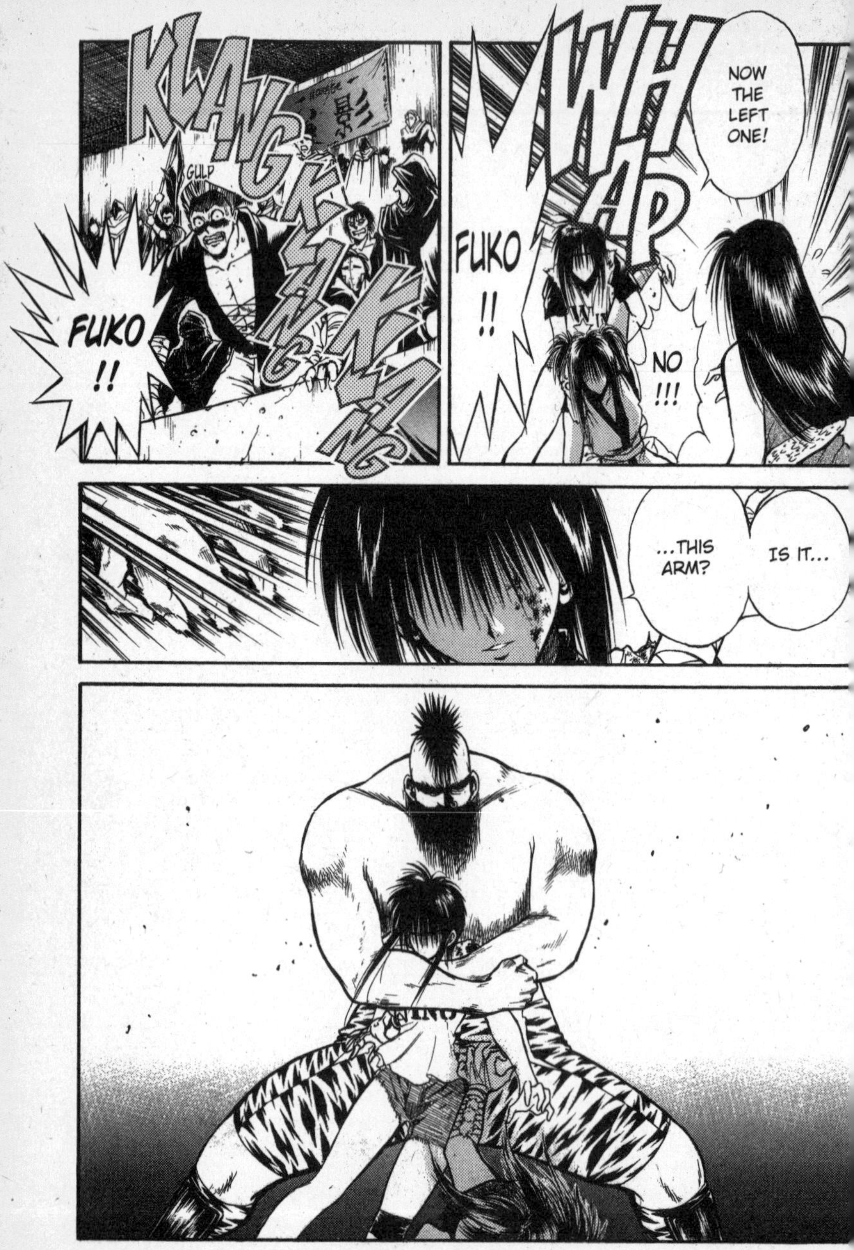

NOW THE LEFT ONE!
WHAP
FUKO !!
NO !!!
KLANGK
GULP
FUKO !!
IS IT...
...THIS ARM?

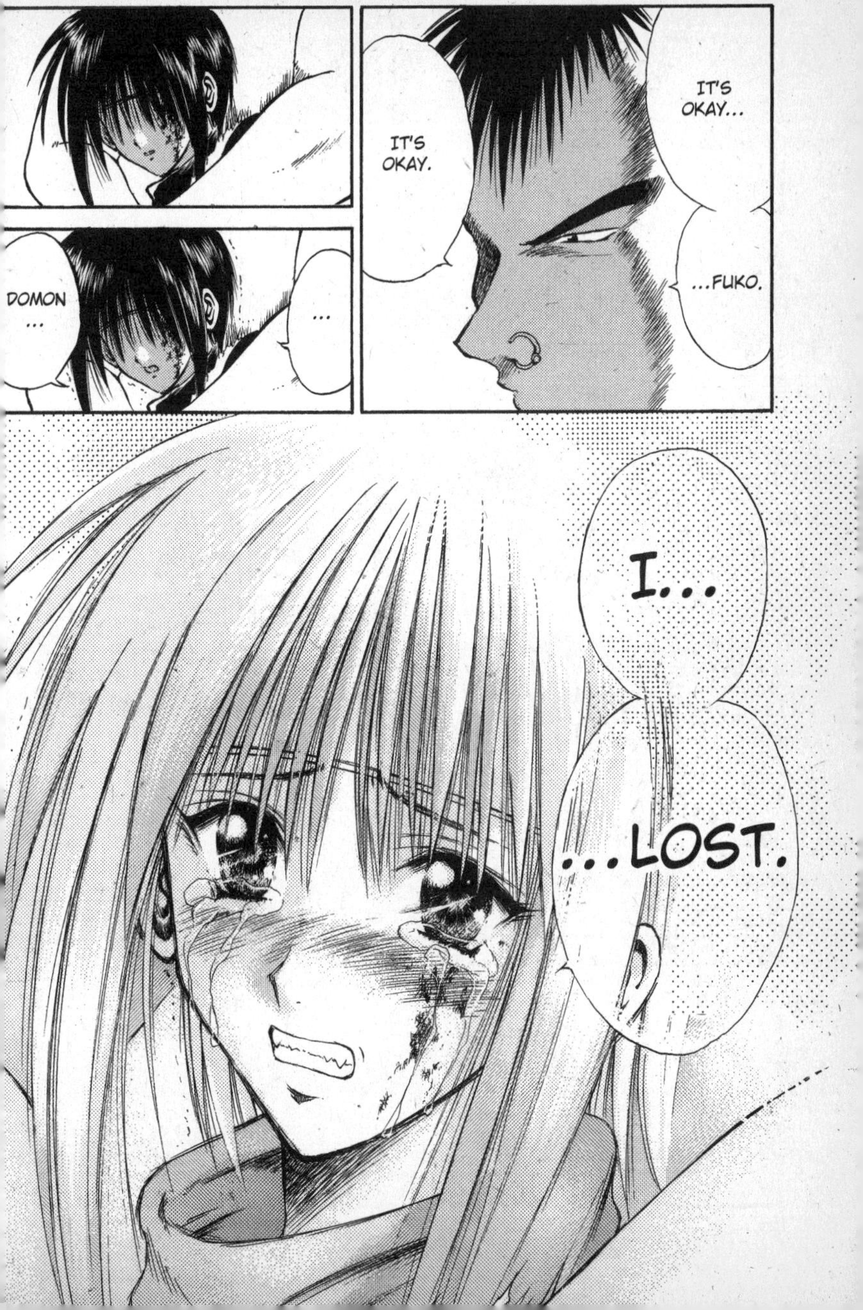
IT'S OKAY...
...FUKO.
IT'S OKAY.
...
DOMON ...
I...
...LOST.

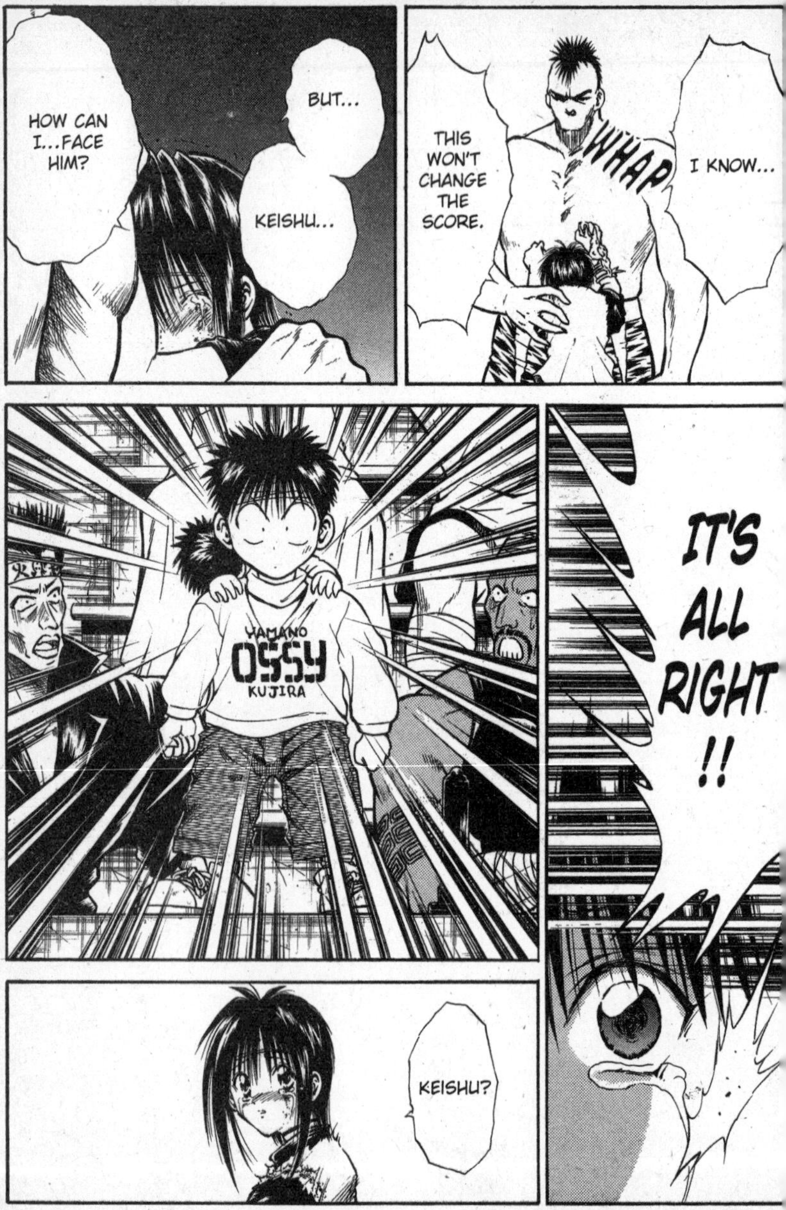
I KNOW...
WHAP
THIS WON'T CHANGE THE SCORE.
BUT...
KEISHU...
HOW CAN I...FACE HIM?
IT'S ALL RIGHT!!
YAMANO
OSSY
KUJIRA
KEISHU?

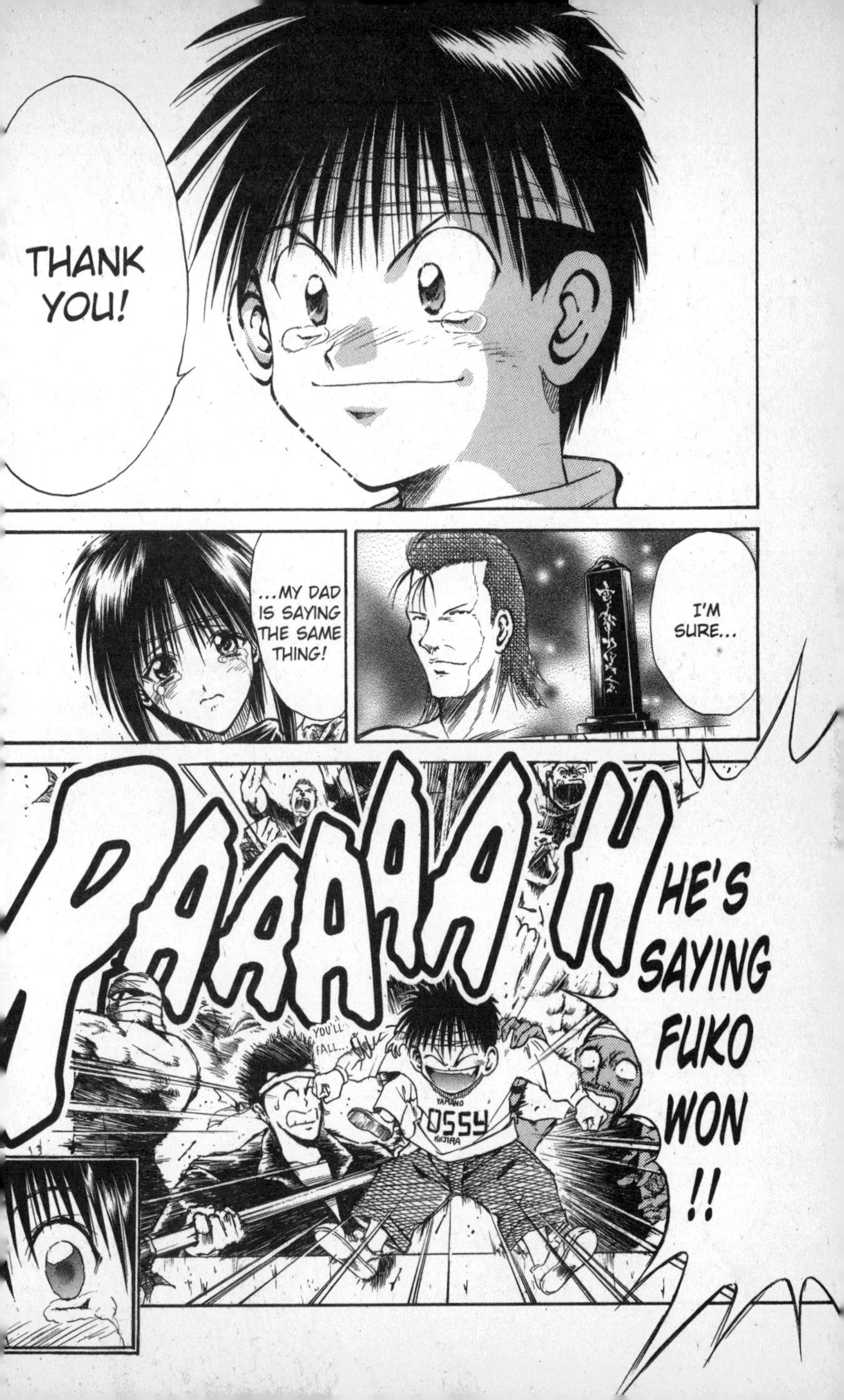
THANK YOU!
I'M SURE...
...MY DAD IS SAYING THE SAME THING!
HE'S SAYING FUKO WON!!
RAAAAH
YOU'LL FALL...

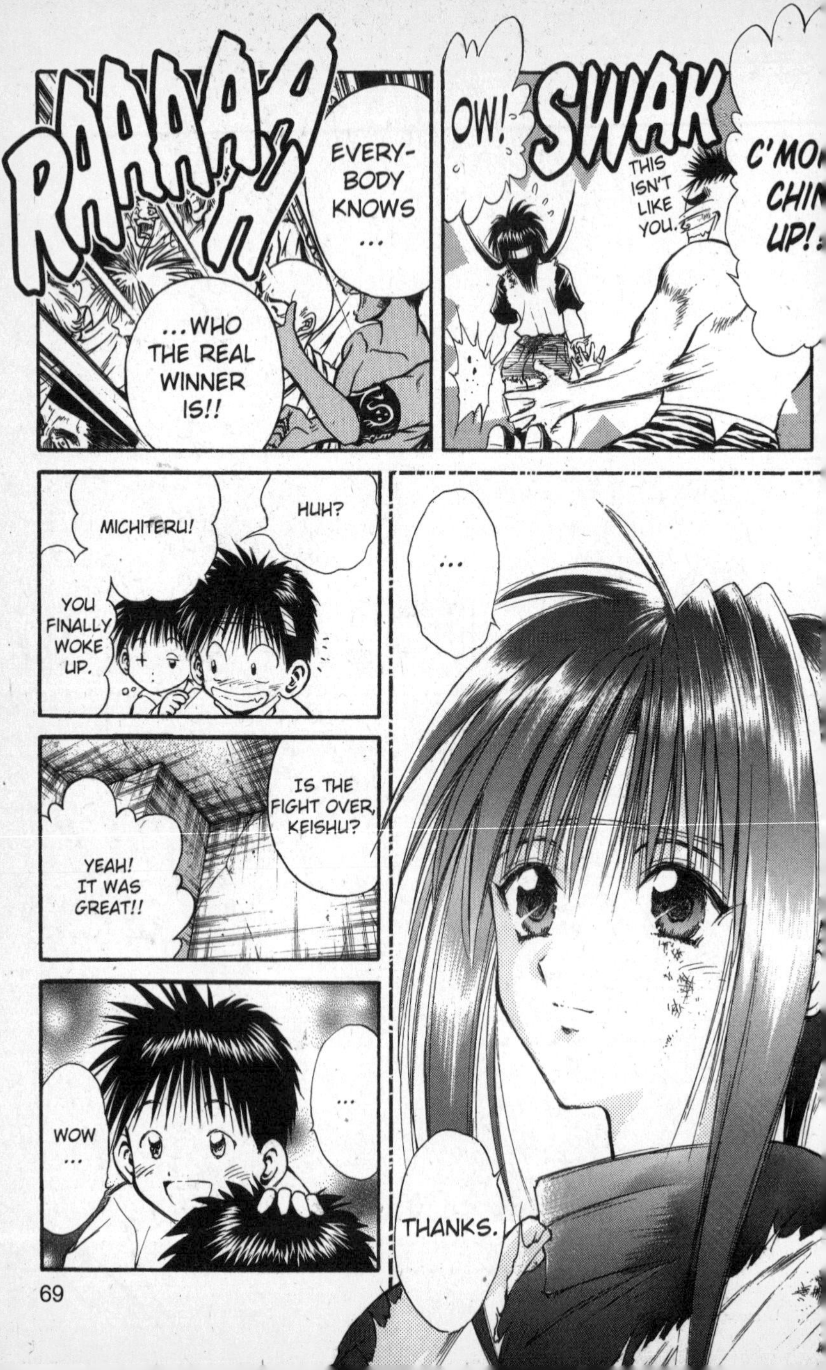

C'MO CHIN UP!..
SWAK
THIS ISN'T LIKE YOU..
OW!
RAAAAAH
EVERY-BODY KNOWS ...
...WHO THE REAL WINNER IS!!
...
THANKS.
HUH?
MICHITERU!
YOU FINALLY WOKE UP.
IS THE FIGHT OVER, KEISHU?
YEAH! IT WAS GREAT!!
...
WOW ...

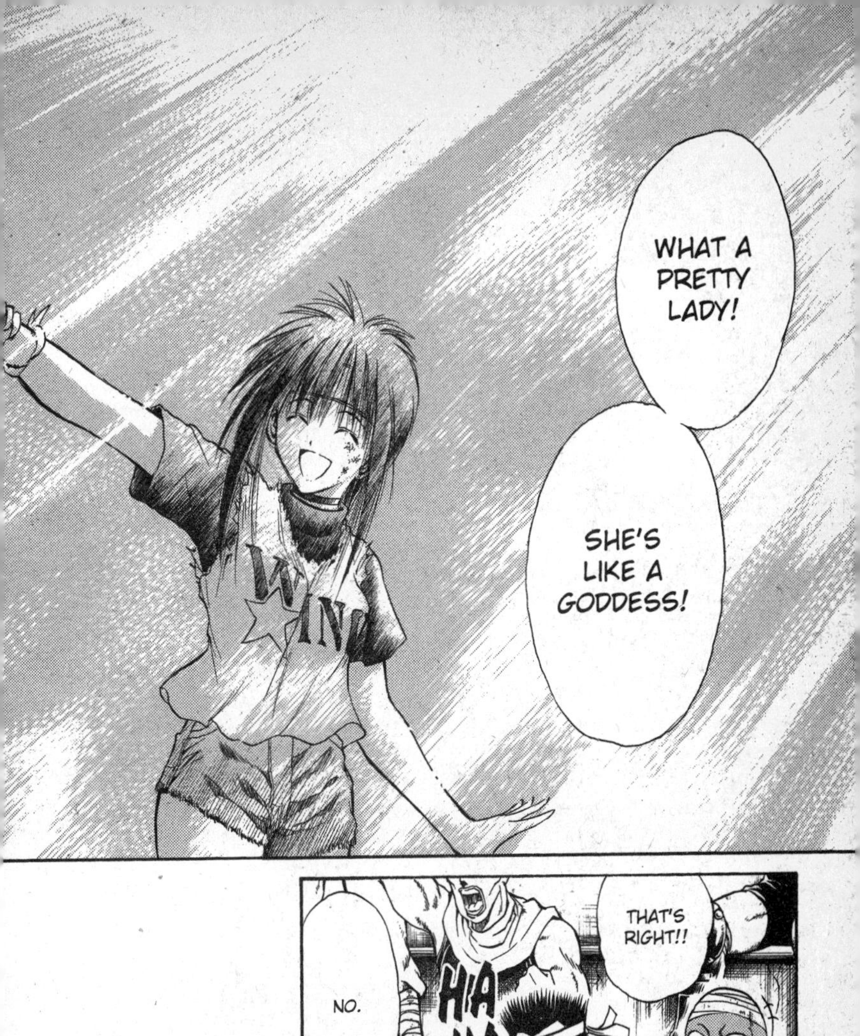
WHAT A PRETTY LADY!
SHE'S LIKE A GODDESS!

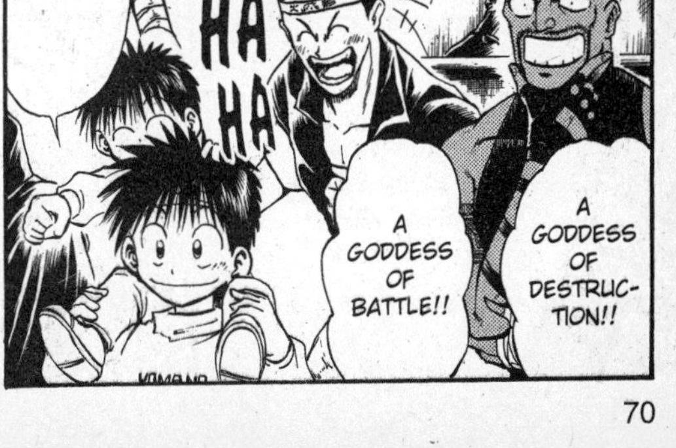
THAT'S RIGHT!!
HA HA HA HA
NO.
A GODDESS OF DESTRUCTION!!
A GODDESS OF BATTLE!!

A GODDESS OF...

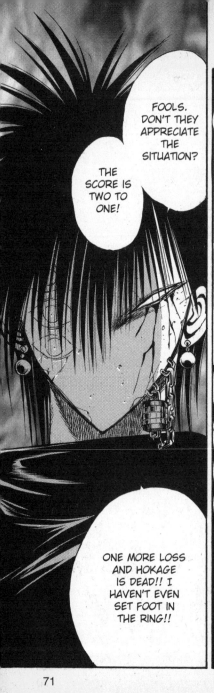

FOOLS. DON'T THEY APPRECIATE THE SITUATION?

THE SCORE IS TWO TO ONE!

ONE MORE LOSS AND HOKAGE IS DEAD!! I HAVEN'T EVEN SET FOOT IN THE RING!!

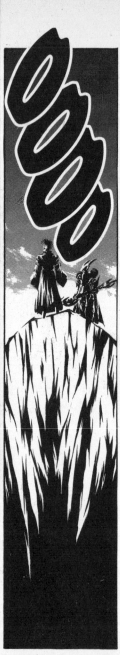

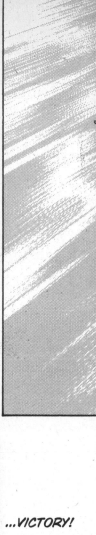

...VICTORY!

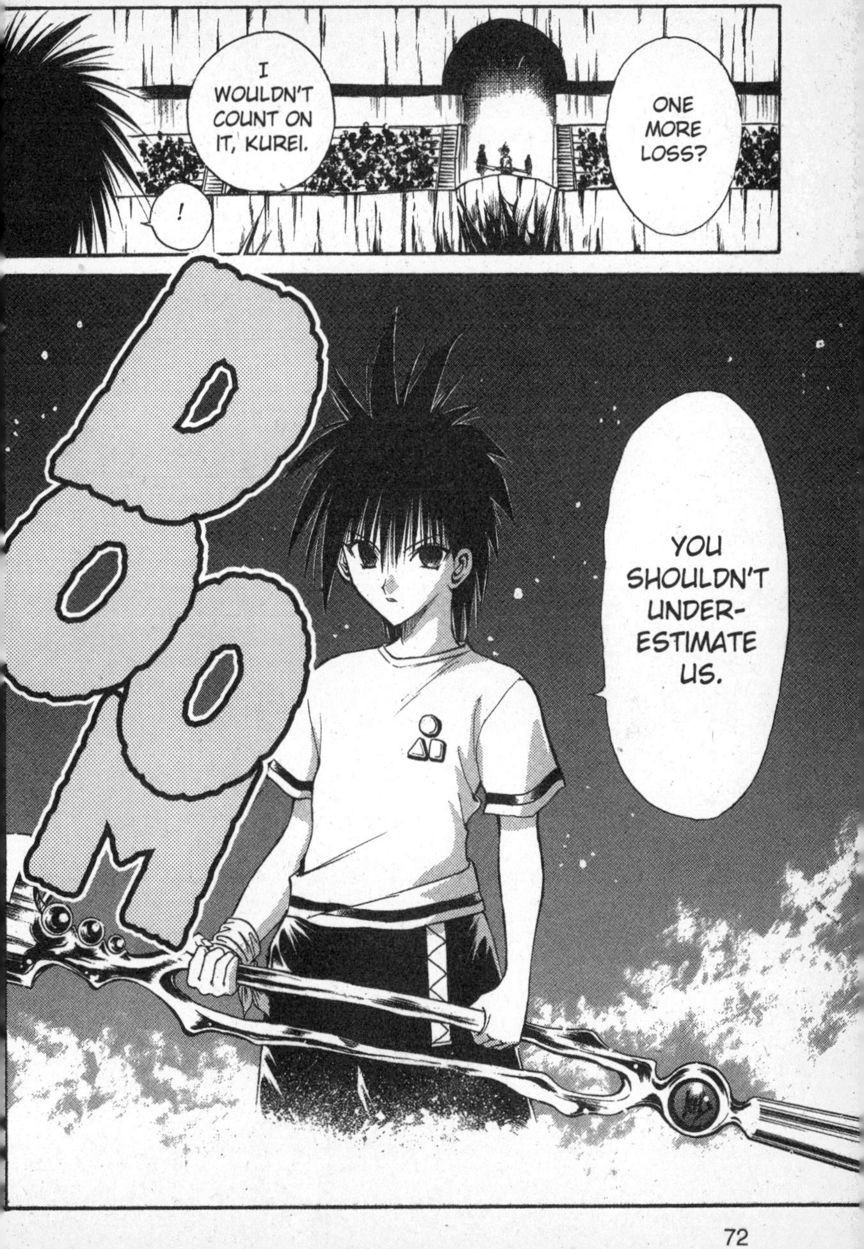
ONE MORE LOSS?
I WOULDN'T COUNT ON IT, KUREI.
!
YOU SHOULDN'T UNDER-ESTIMATE US.
DOOM

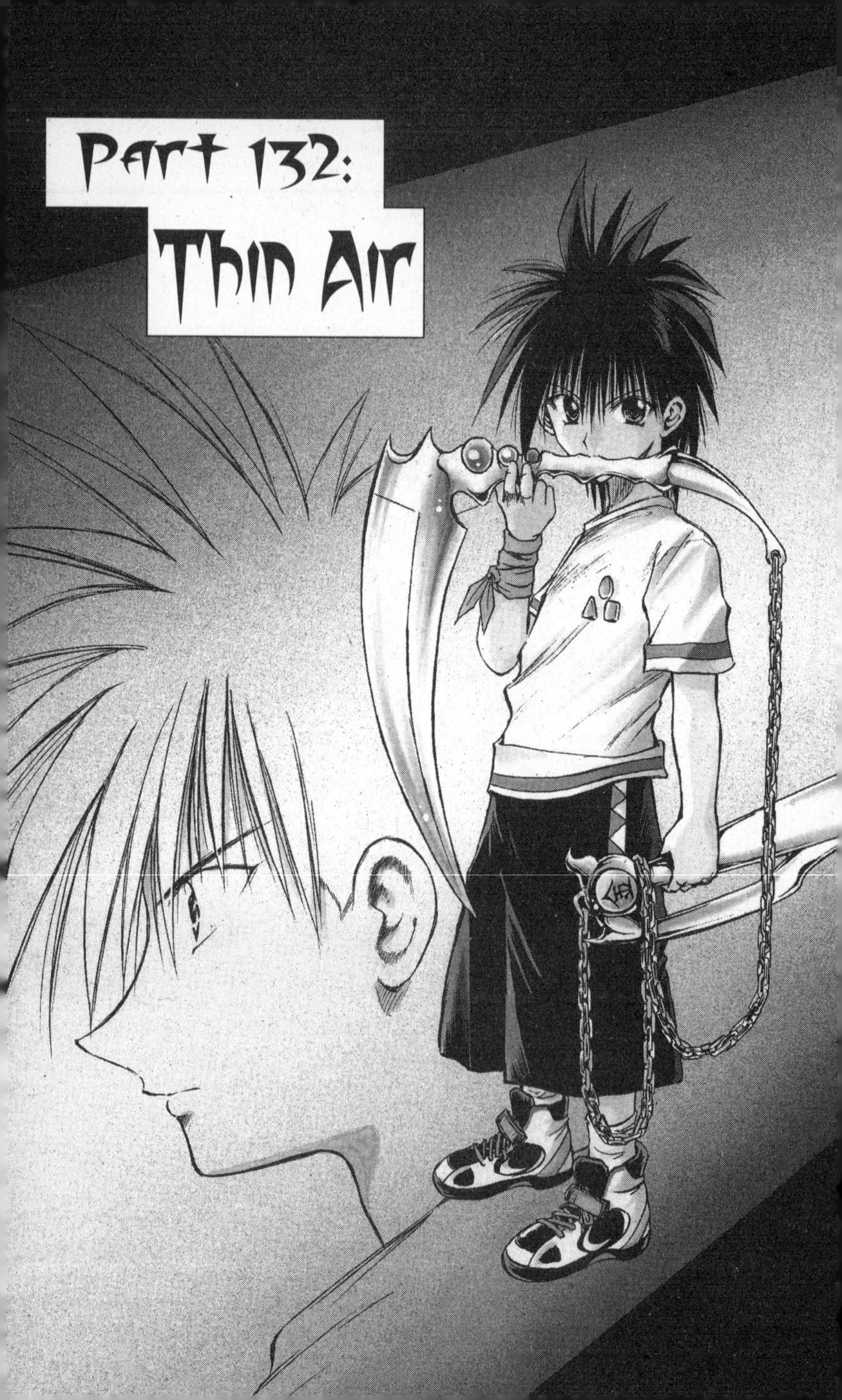
Part 132:
Thin Air

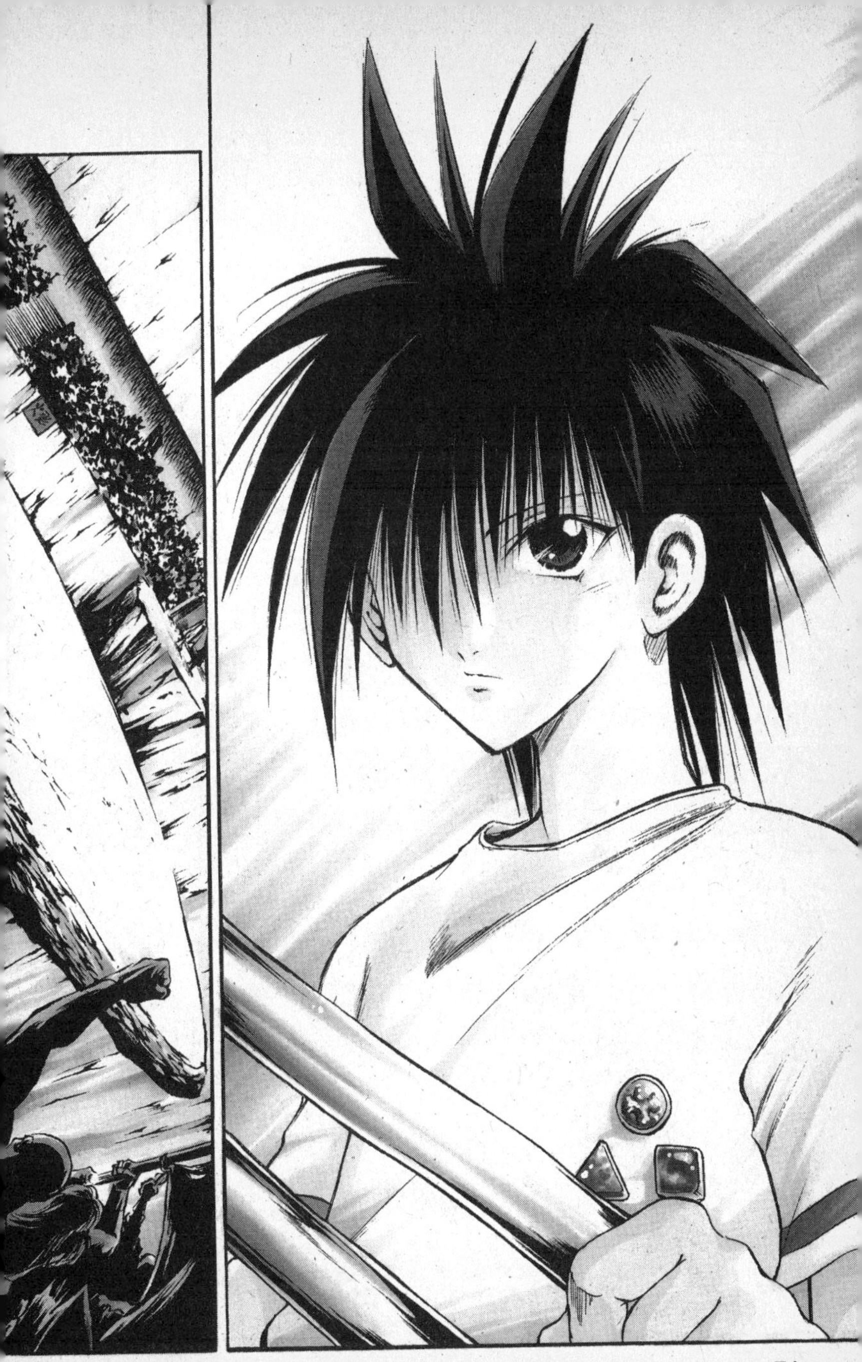

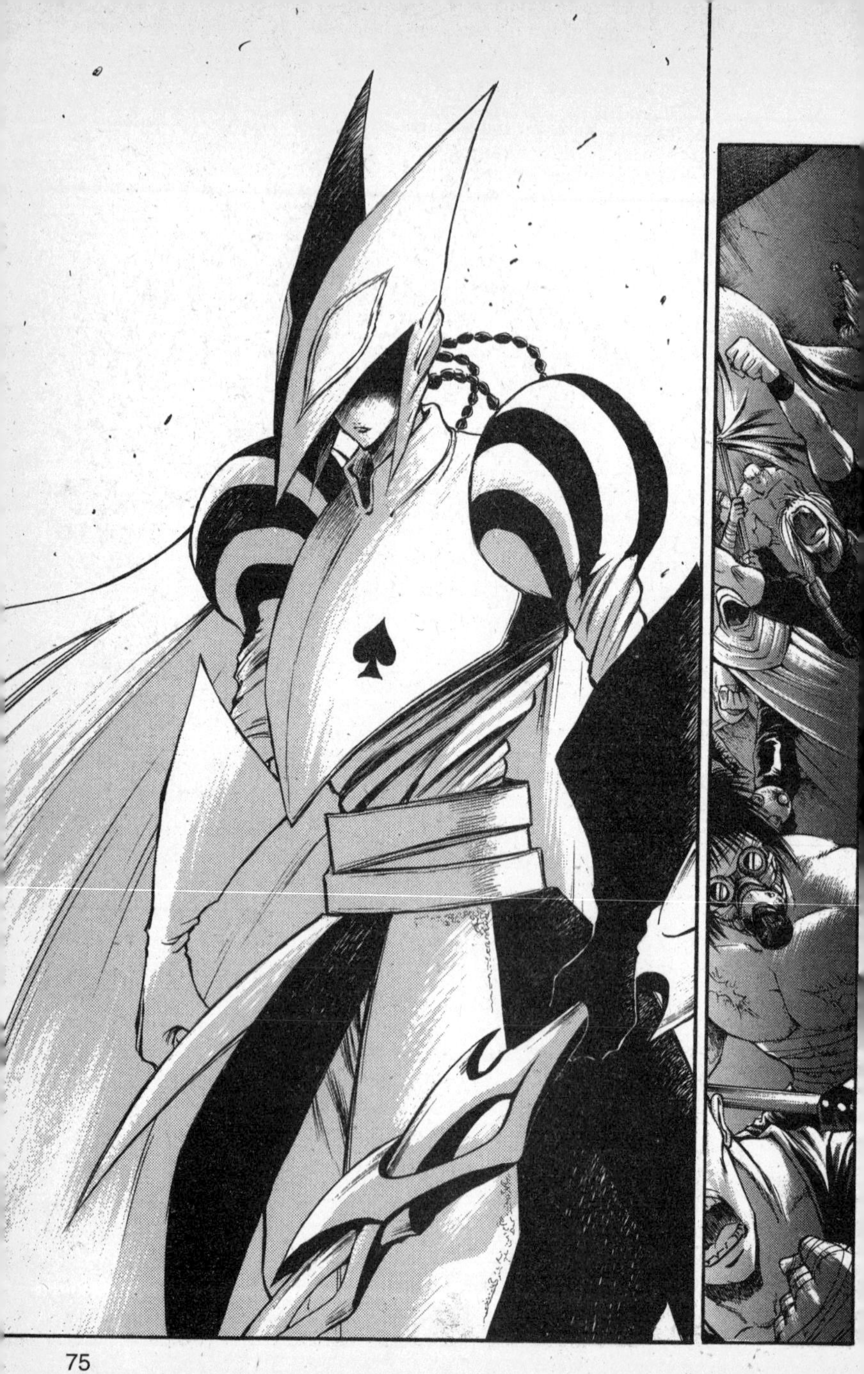

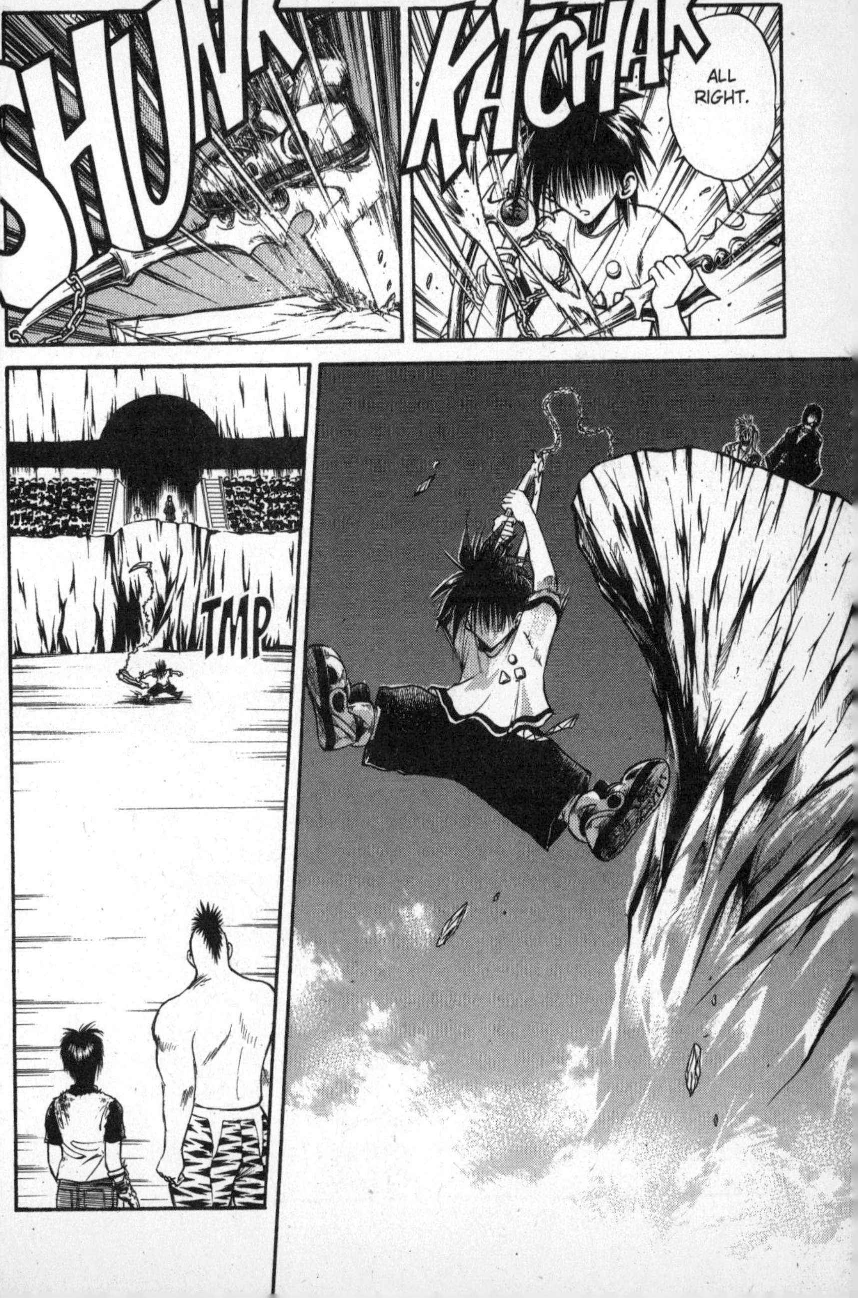
KACHAK
ALL RIGHT.
SHUNK
TMP

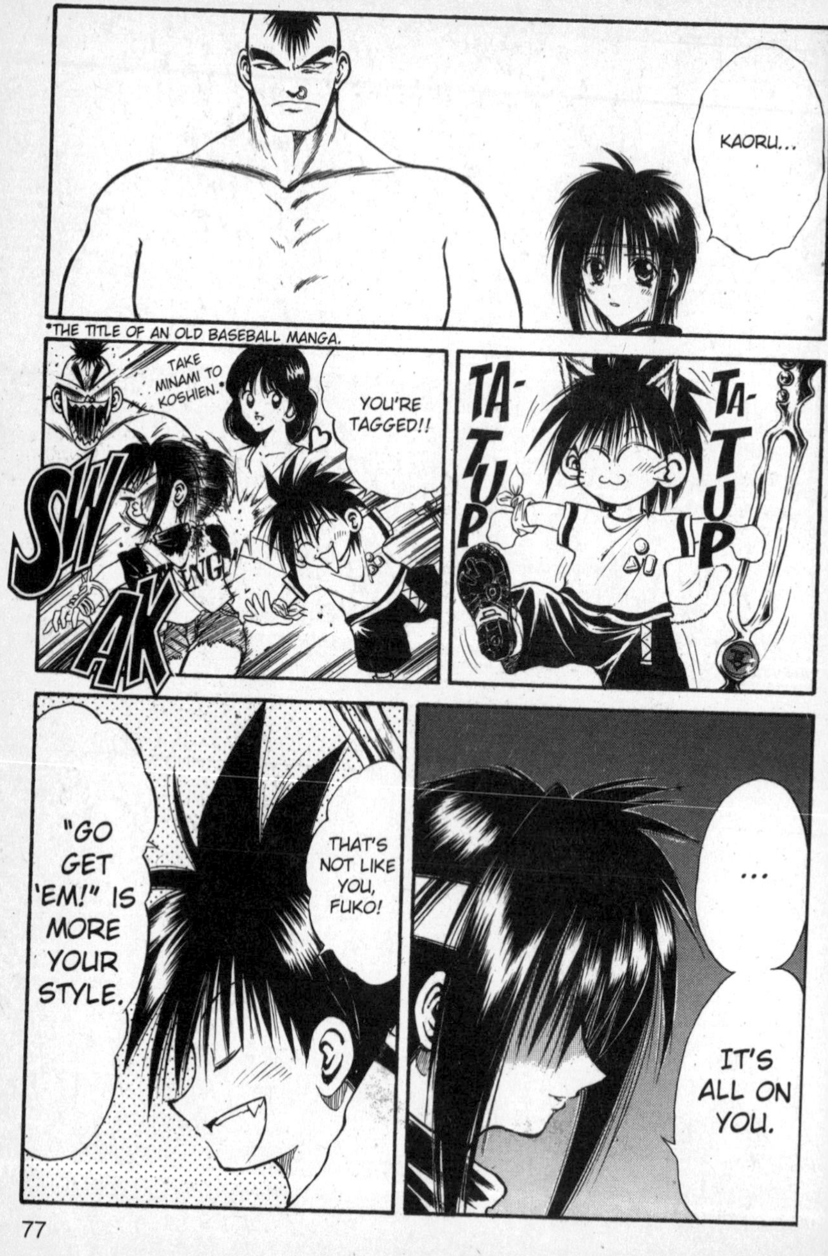
KAORU...
TA-TUP
TA-TUP
YOU'RE TAGGED!!
TAKE MINAMI TO KOSHIEN.*
SWAK
...
IT'S ALL ON YOU.
THAT'S NOT LIKE YOU, FUKO!
"GO GET 'EM!" IS MORE YOUR STYLE.

*THE TITLE OF AN OLD BASEBALL MANGA.

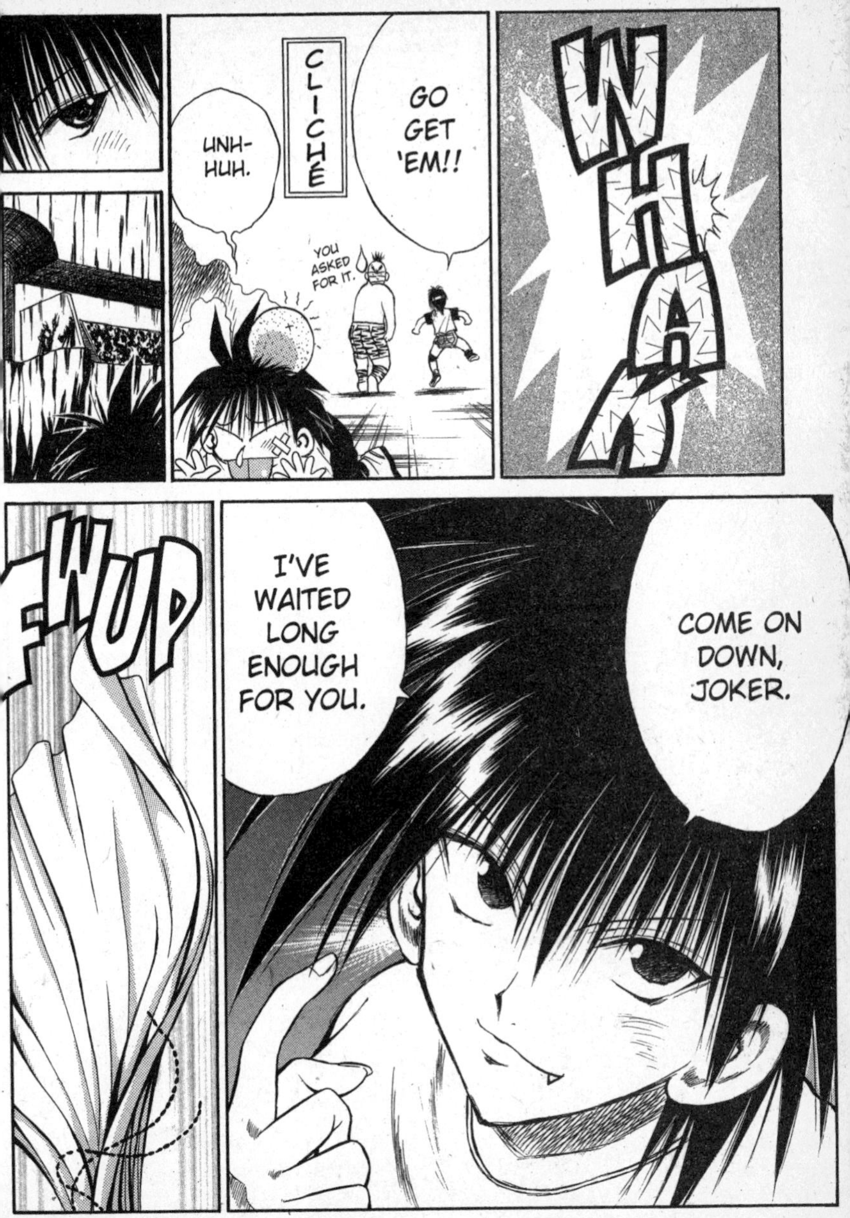
WHAA
GO GET 'EM!!
CLICHÉ
UNH-HUH.
YOU ASKED FOR IT.
COME ON DOWN, JOKER.
I'VE WAITED LONG ENOUGH FOR YOU.
FWUP

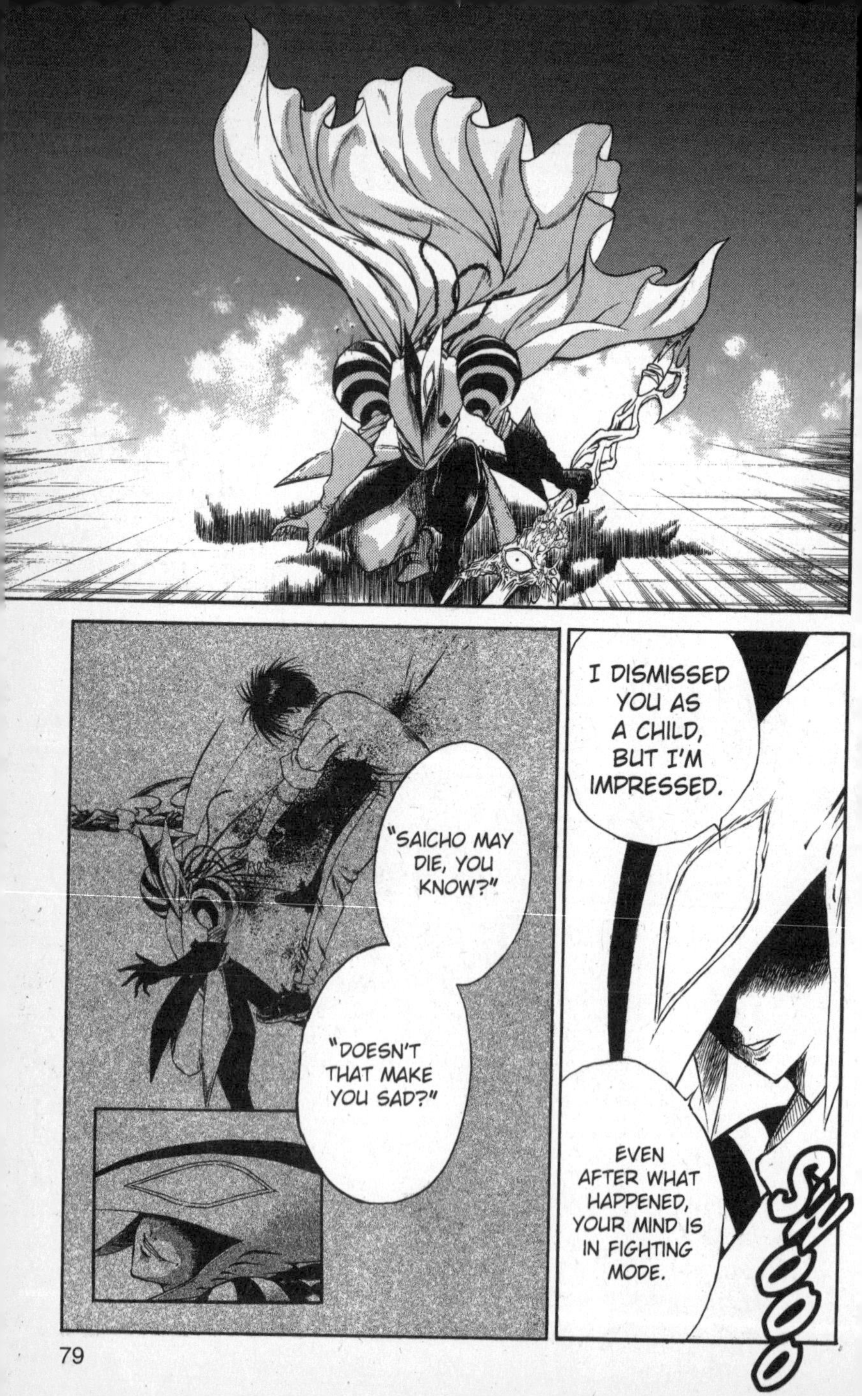
I DISMISSED YOU AS A CHILD, BUT I'M IMPRESSED.
EVEN AFTER WHAT HAPPENED, YOUR MIND IS IN FIGHTING MODE.
SHOOOO
"SAICHO MAY DIE, YOU KNOW?"
"DOESN'T THAT MAKE YOU SAD?"

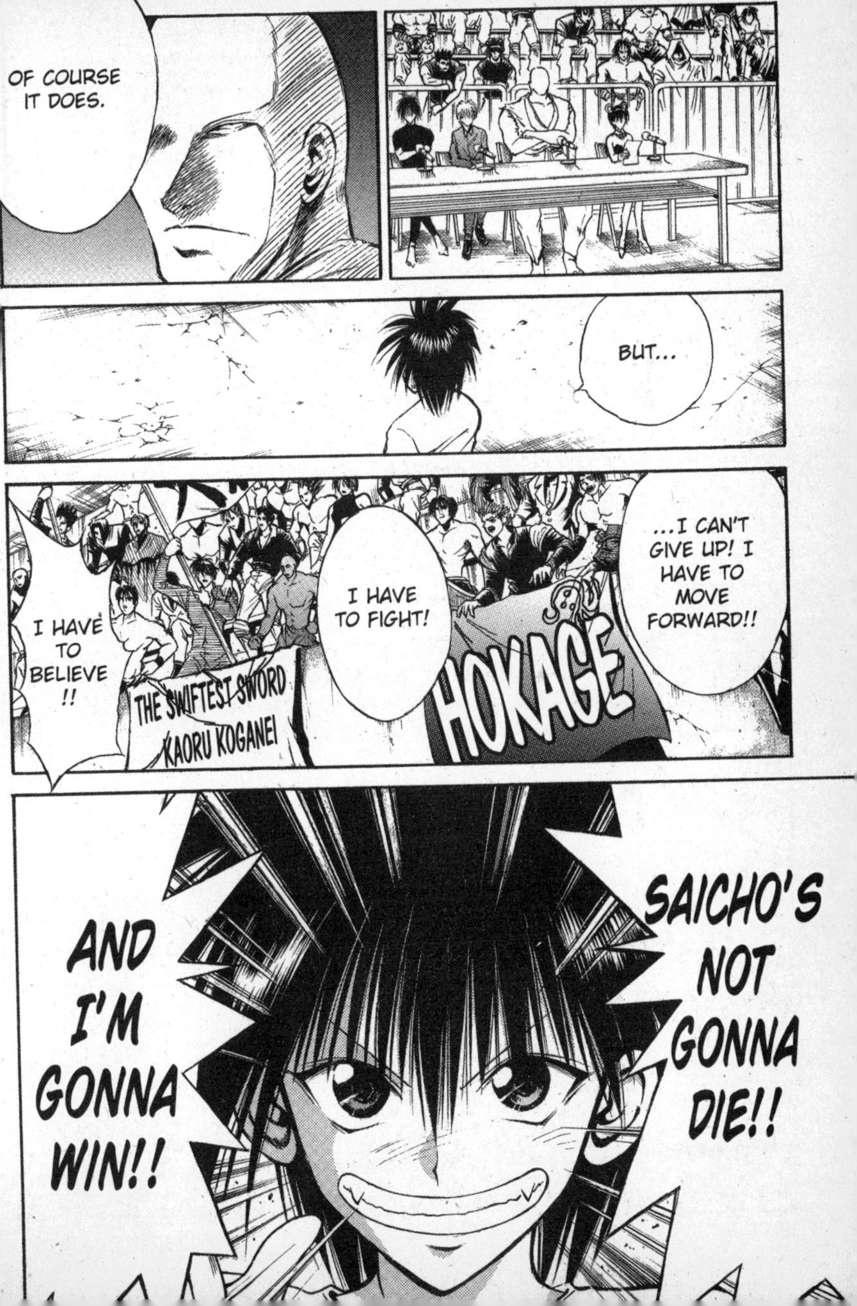
OF COURSE IT DOES.
BUT...
...I CAN'T GIVE UP! I HAVE TO MOVE FORWARD!!
HOKAGE
I HAVE TO FIGHT!
THE SWIFTEST SWORD KAORU KOGANEI
I HAVE TO BELIEVE!!
SAICHO'S NOT GONNA DIE!!
AND I'M GONNA WIN!!

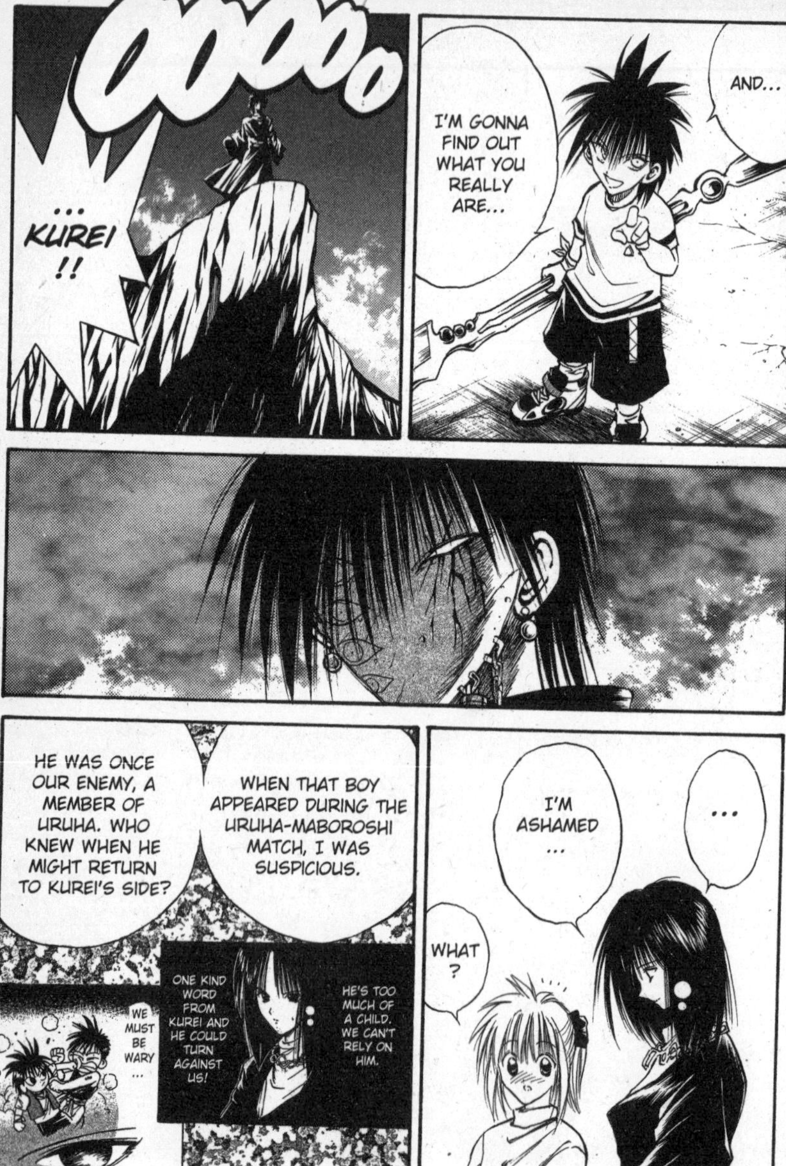

AND...
I'M GONNA FIND OUT WHAT YOU REALLY ARE...
OOOOO
...KUREI!!
...
I'M ASHAMED...
WHAT?
WHEN THAT BOY APPEARED DURING THE URUHA-MABOROSHI MATCH, I WAS SUSPICIOUS.
HE WAS ONCE OUR ENEMY, A MEMBER OF URUHA. WHO KNEW WHEN HE MIGHT RETURN TO KUREI'S SIDE?
HE'S TOO MUCH OF A CHILD. WE CAN'T RELY ON HIM.
ONE KIND WORD FROM KUREI AND HE COULD TURN AGAINST US!
WE MUST BE WARY...

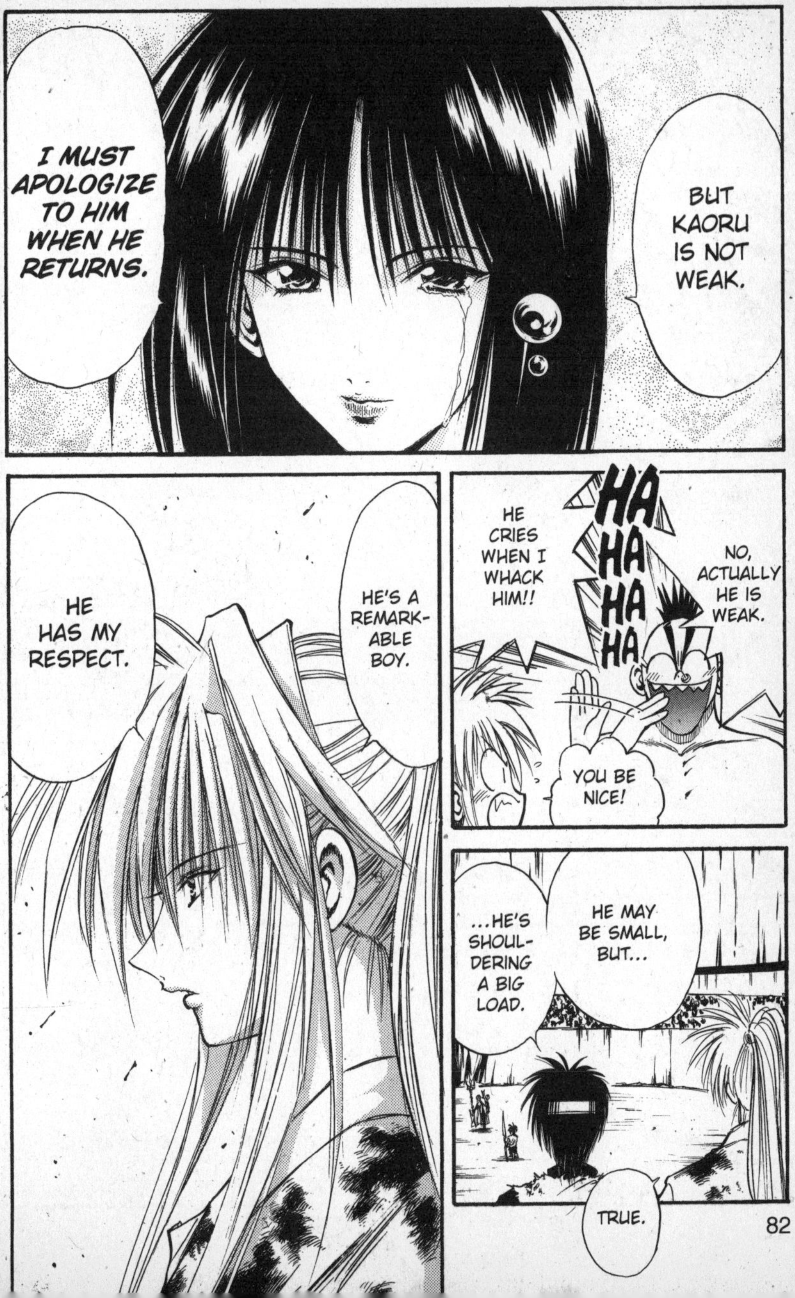
BUT KAORU IS NOT WEAK.
I MUST APOLOGIZE TO HIM WHEN HE RETURNS.
NO, ACTUALLY HE IS WEAK.
HA HA HA HA HA
HE CRIES WHEN I WHACK HIM!!
YOU BE NICE!
HE MAY BE SMALL, BUT...
...HE'S SHOUL-DERING A BIG LOAD.
TRUE.
HE'S A REMARK-ABLE BOY.
HE HAS MY RESPECT.

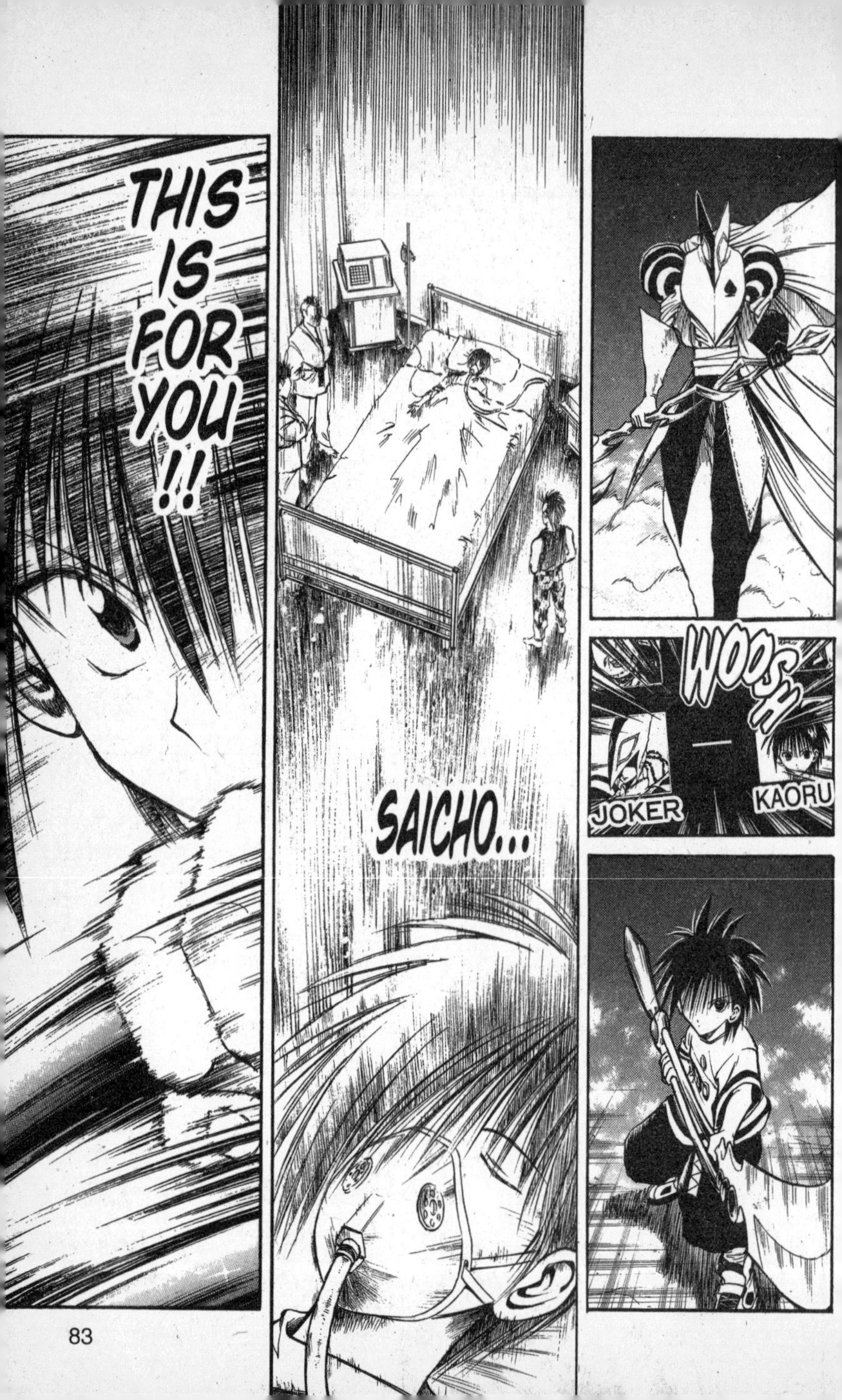
WOOSH
KAORU
JOKER
SAICHO...
THIS IS FOR YOU!!

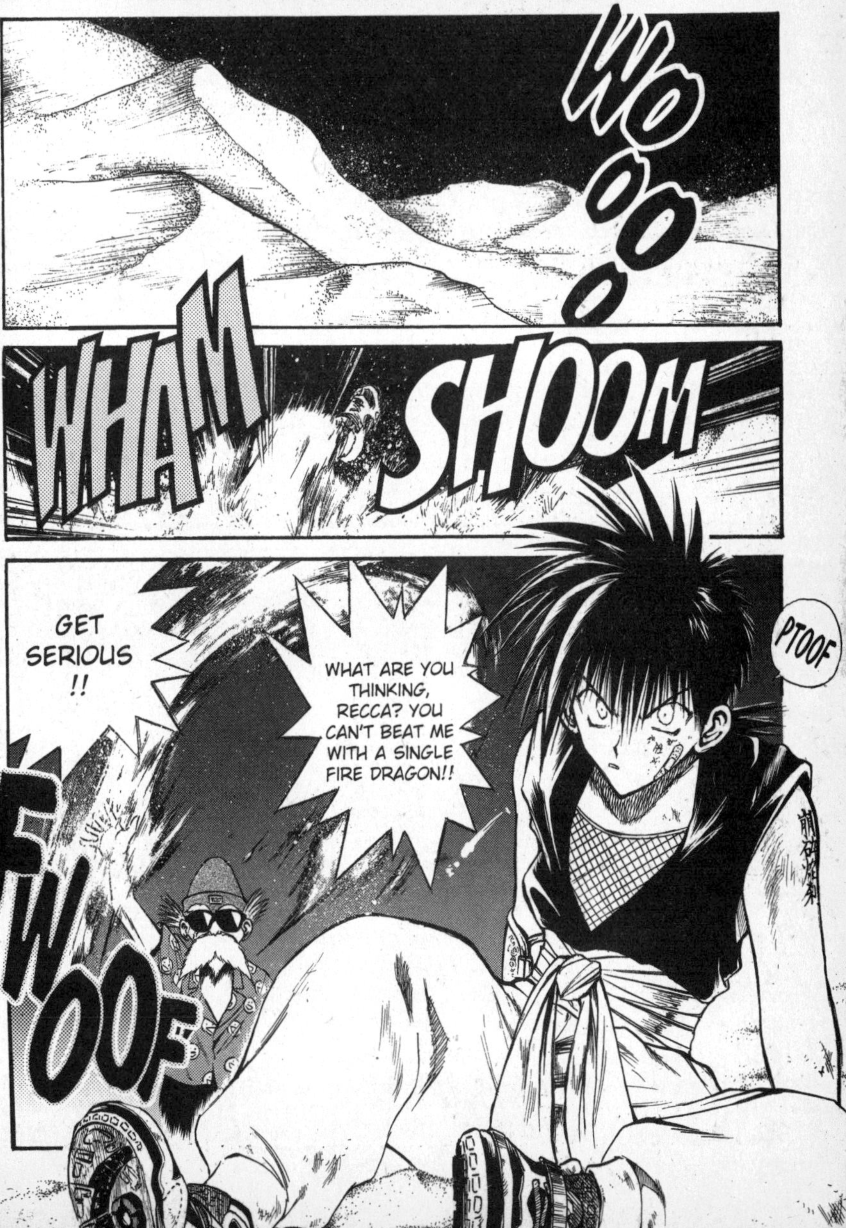
WOOOO
SHOOM
WHAM
PTOOF
WHAT ARE YOU THINKING, RECCA? YOU CAN'T BEAT ME WITH A SINGLE FIRE DRAGON!!
GET SERIOUS!!
FWOOF

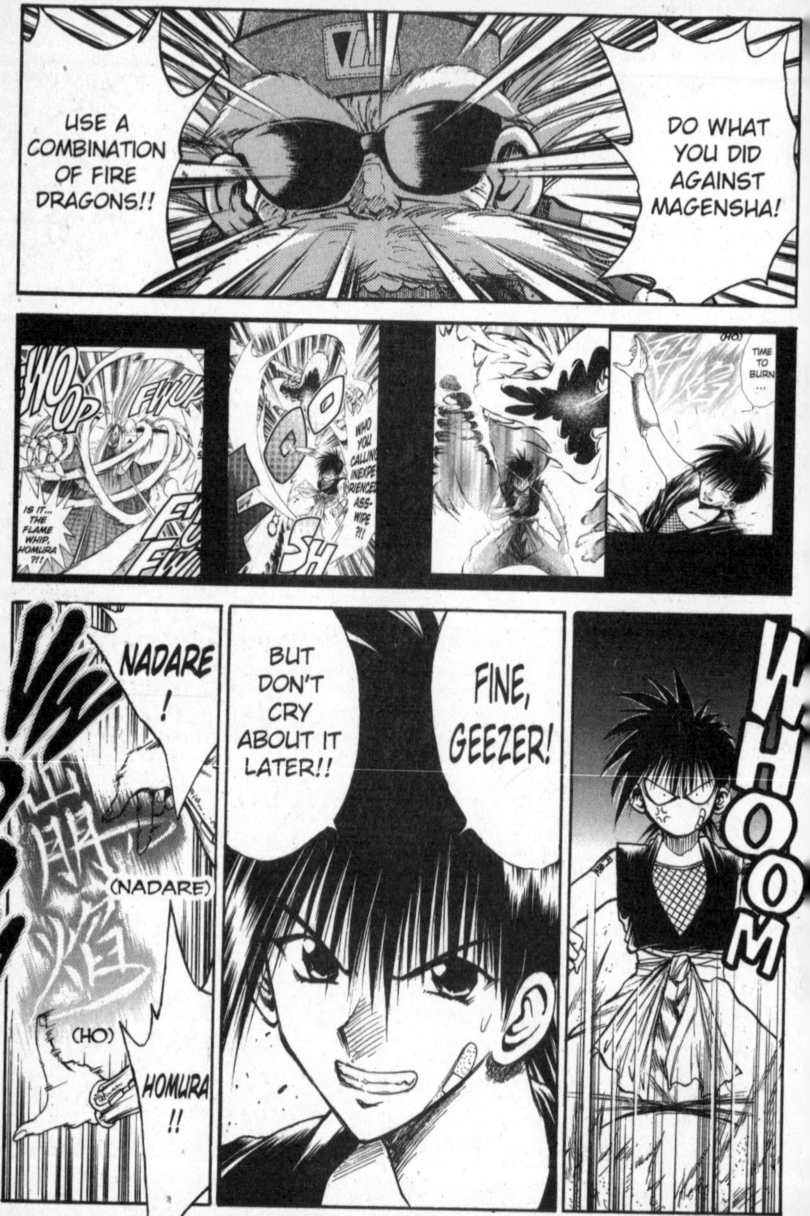
DO WHAT YOU DID AGAINST MAGENSHA!
USE A COMBINATION OF FIRE DRAGONS!!
(HO)
TIME TO BURN...
OO
WHO YOU CALLING INEXPERIENCED ASS-WIPE?!!
SH
WOOP
FWUP
IS IT... THE FLAME WHIP, HOMURA?!!
FWU FWU
WHOOM
FINE, GEEZER!
BUT DON'T CRY ABOUT IT LATER!!
NADARE!
(NADARE)
(HO)
HOMURA!!
WOOOM

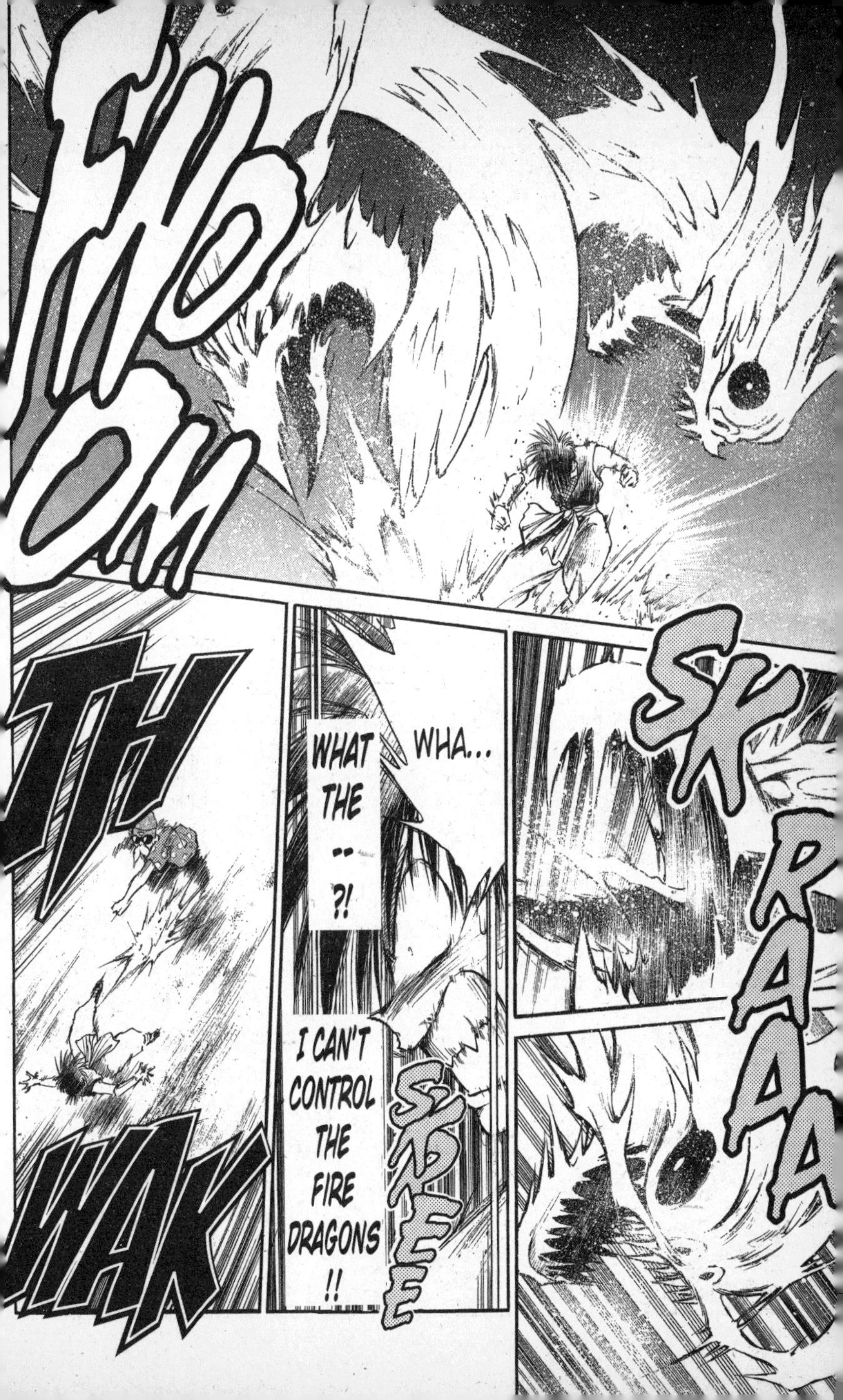
FWOOM
SKRAAA
WHA...
WHAT THE --?!
I CAN'T CONTROL THE FIRE DRAGONS!!
SKREEE
THWAK

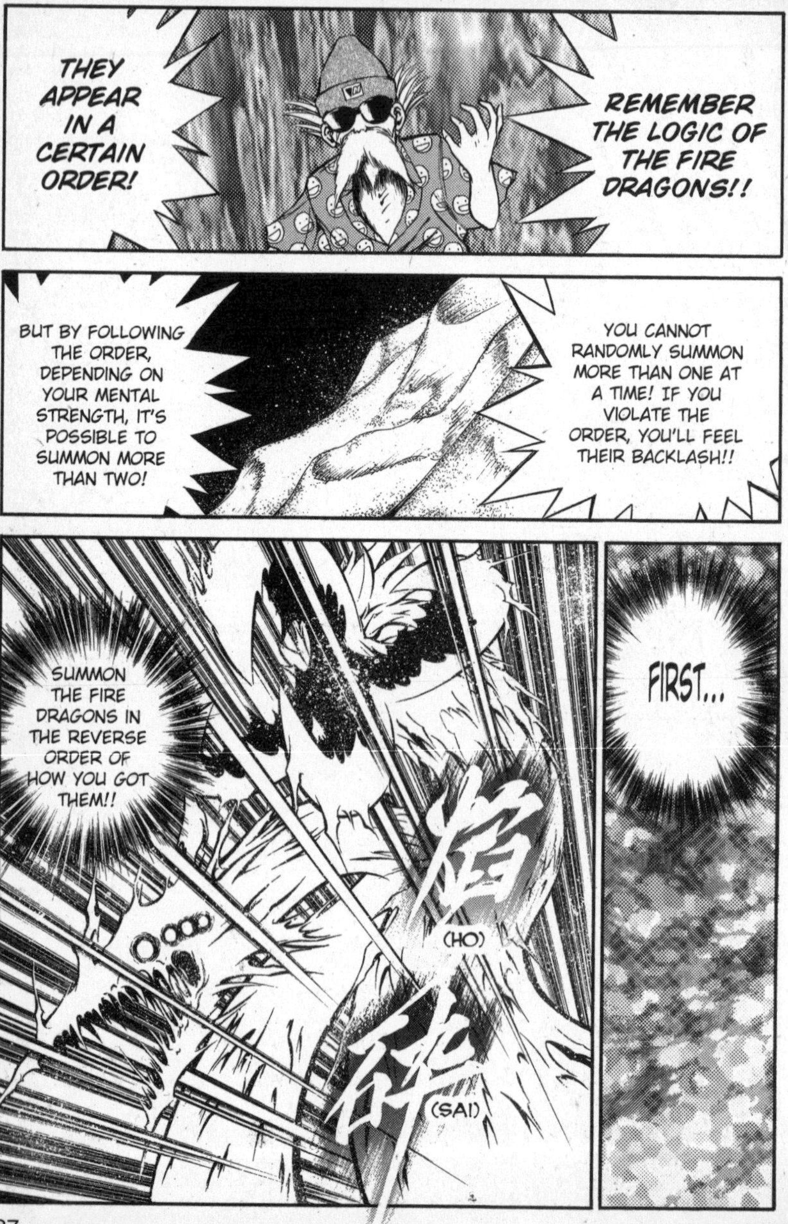
REMEMBER THE LOGIC OF THE FIRE DRAGONS!!
THEY APPEAR IN A CERTAIN ORDER!
YOU CANNOT RANDOMLY SUMMON MORE THAN ONE AT A TIME! IF YOU VIOLATE THE ORDER, YOU'LL FEEL THEIR BACKLASH!!
BUT BY FOLLOWING THE ORDER, DEPENDING ON YOUR MENTAL STRENGTH, IT'S POSSIBLE TO SUMMON MORE THAN TWO!
FIRST...
SUMMON THE FIRE DRAGONS IN THE REVERSE ORDER OF HOW YOU GOT THEM!!
(HO)
(SAI)

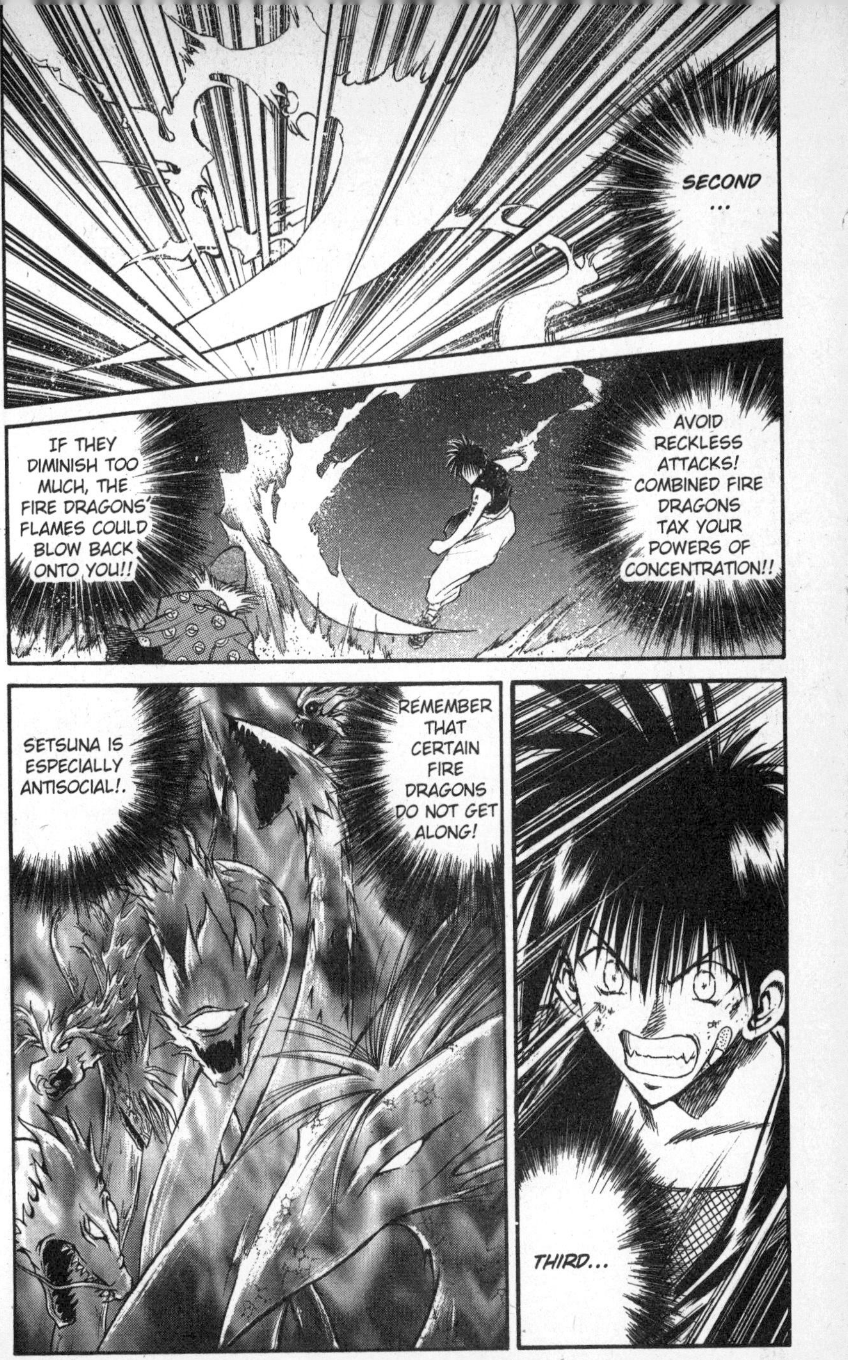
SECOND ...
AVOID RECKLESS ATTACKS! COMBINED FIRE DRAGONS TAX YOUR POWERS OF CONCENTRATION!!
IF THEY DIMINISH TOO MUCH, THE FIRE DRAGONS' FLAMES COULD BLOW BACK ONTO YOU!!
THIRD...
REMEMBER THAT CERTAIN FIRE DRAGONS DO NOT GET ALONG!
SETSUNA IS ESPECIALLY ANTISOCIAL!.

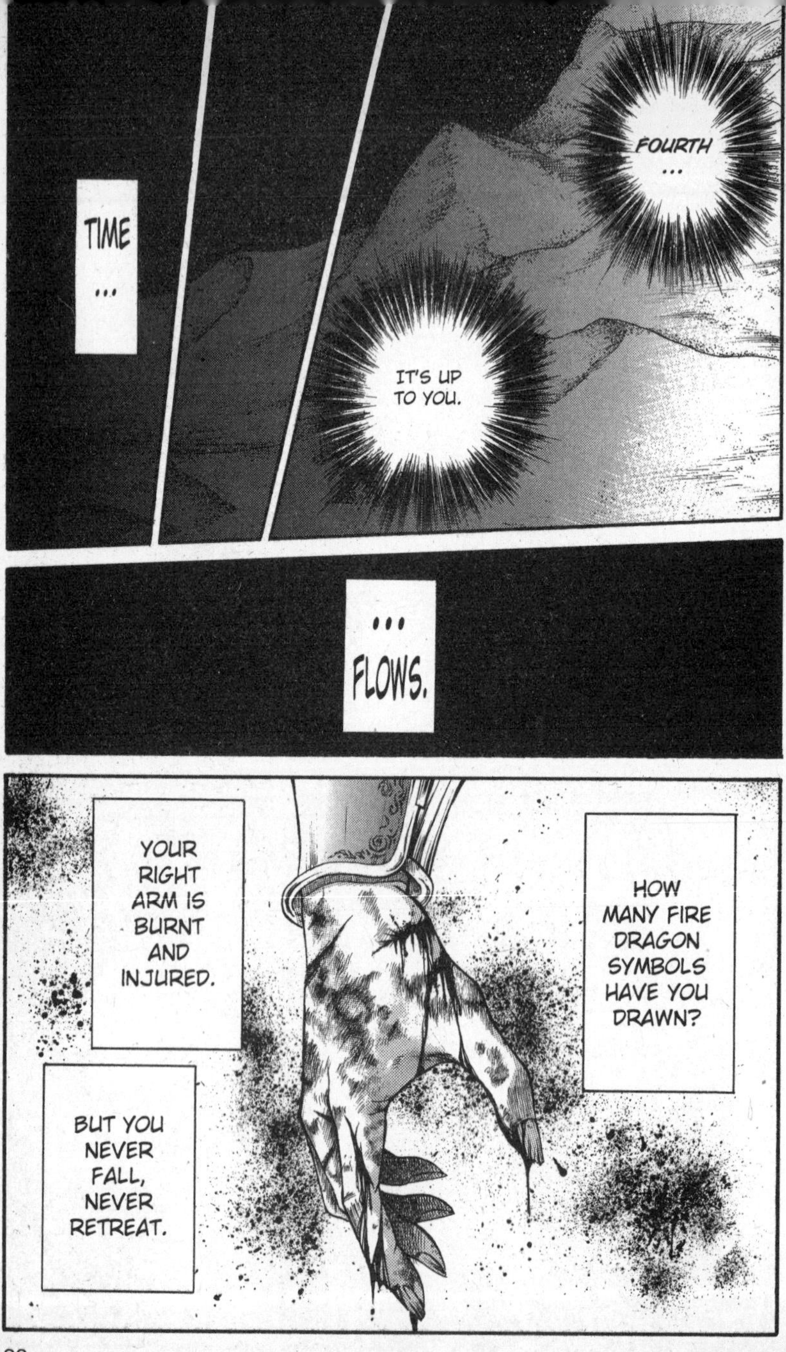
FOURTH ...
IT'S UP TO YOU.
TIME ...
... FLOWS.
HOW MANY FIRE DRAGON SYMBOLS HAVE YOU DRAWN?
YOUR RIGHT ARM IS BURNT AND INJURED.
BUT YOU NEVER FALL, NEVER RETREAT.

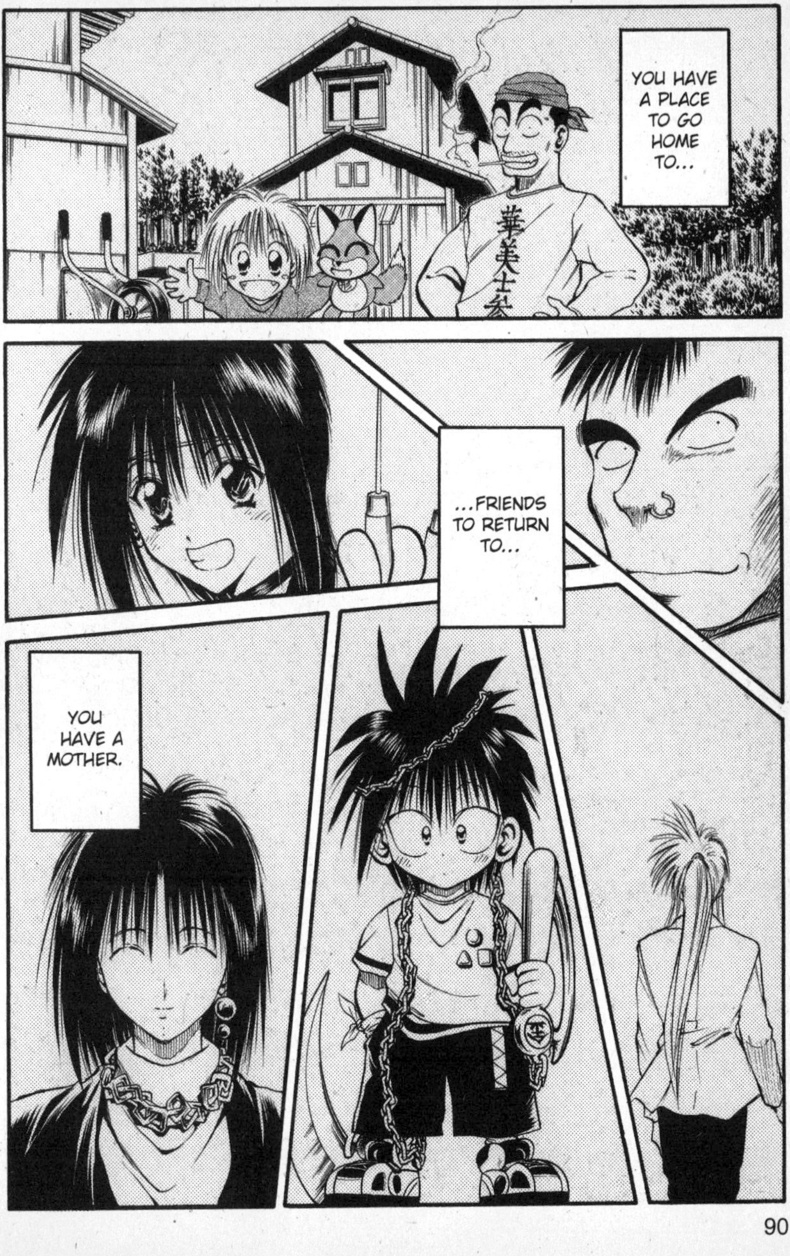
YOU HAVE A PLACE TO GO HOME TO...
...FRIENDS TO RETURN TO...
YOU HAVE A MOTHER.

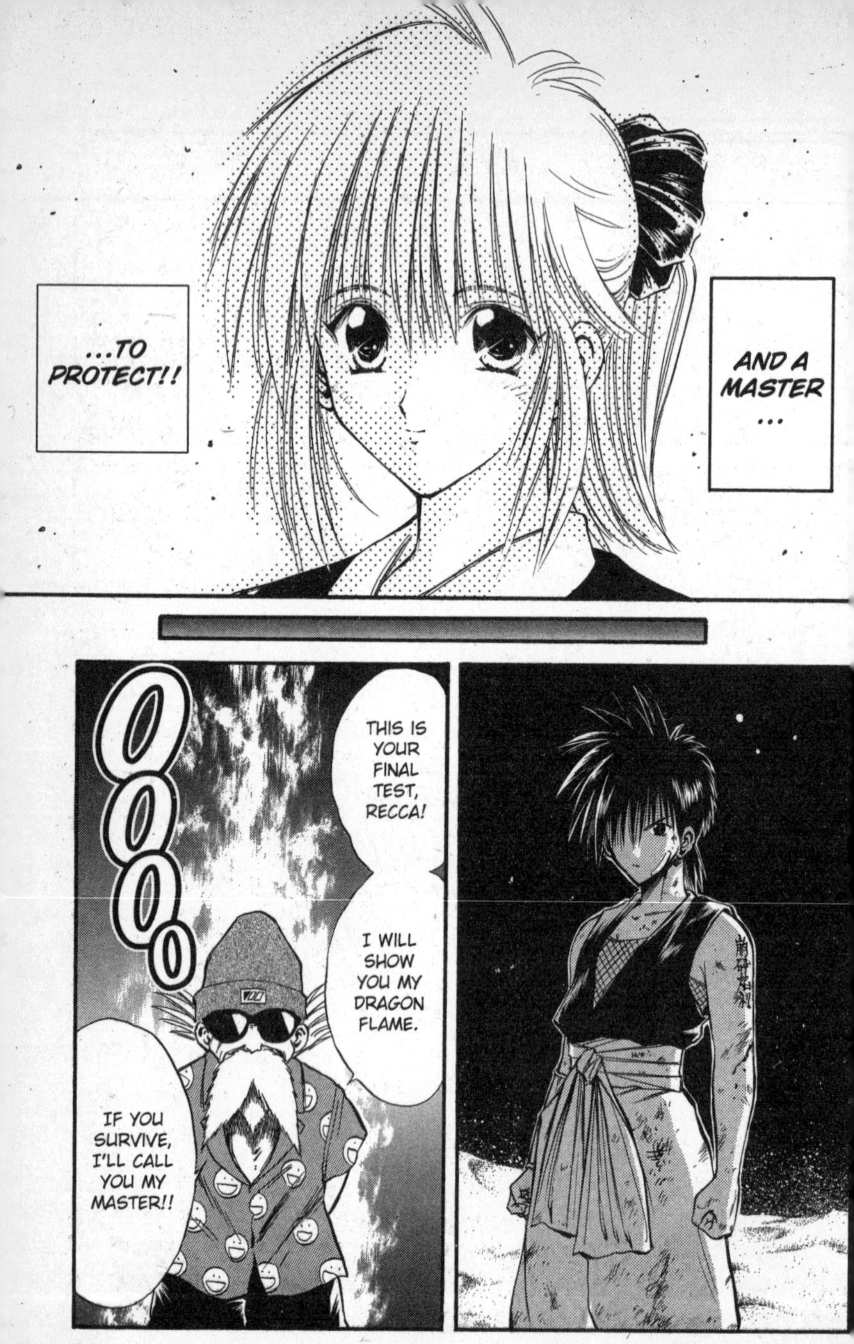
AND A MASTER ...
...TO PROTECT!!
THIS IS YOUR FINAL TEST, RECCA!
OOOO
I WILL SHOW YOU MY DRAGON FLAME.
IF YOU SURVIVE, I'LL CALL YOU MY MASTER!!

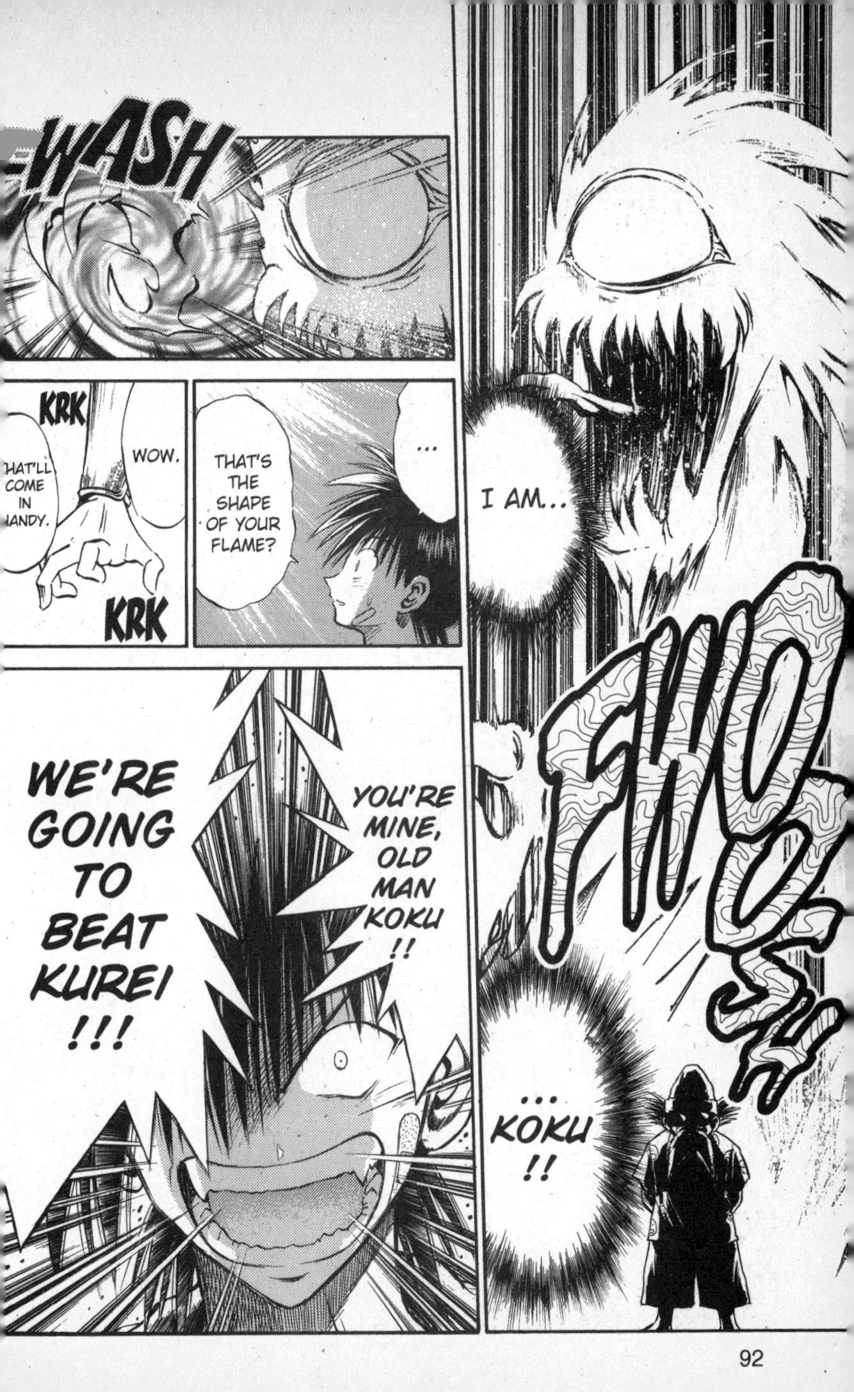
I AM...
FWOOSH
...KOKU!!
WASH
...
THAT'S THE SHAPE OF YOUR FLAME?
KRK
WOW.
THAT'LL COME IN HANDY.
KRK
YOU'RE MINE, OLD MAN KOKU!!
WE'RE GOING TO BEAT KUREI!!!

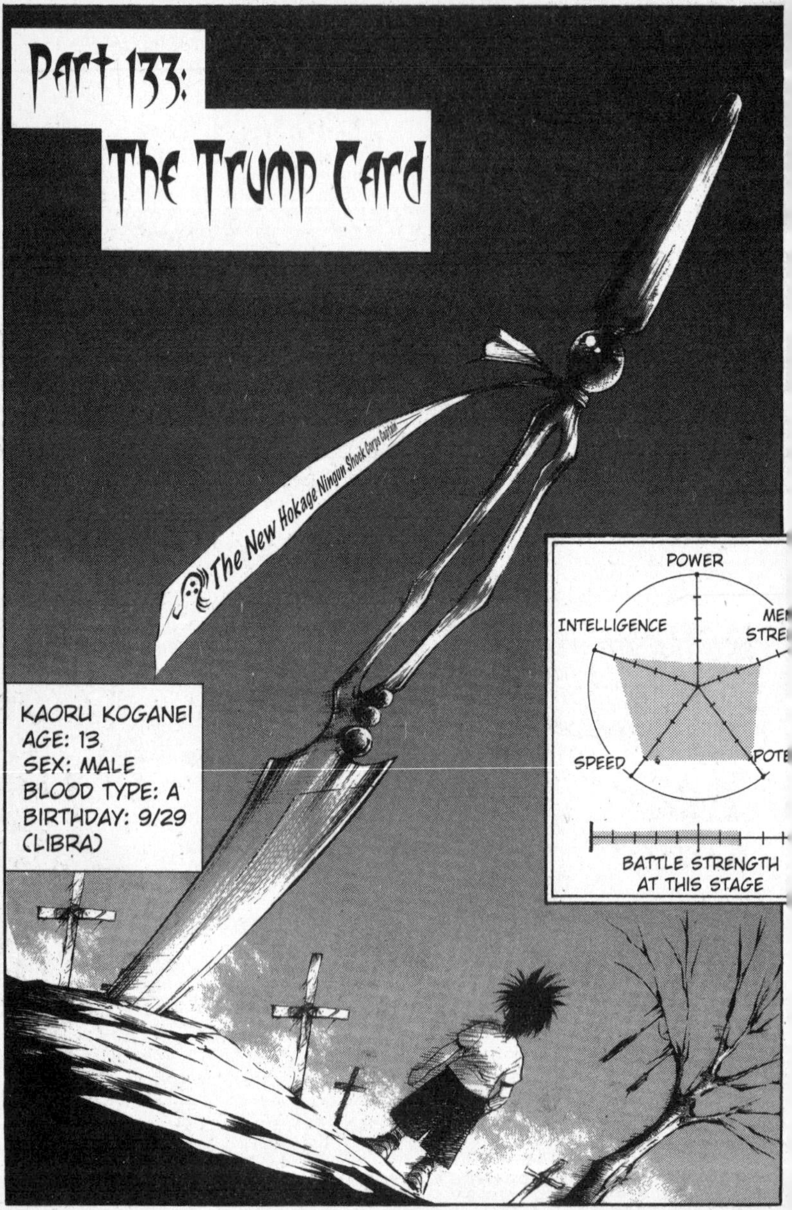

Part 133:
The Trump Card
The New Hokage Ningun Shock Corps Captain
POWER
INTELLIGENCE
SPEED
BATTLE STRENGTH AT THIS STAGE
KAORU KOGANEI
AGE: 13
SEX: MALE
BLOOD TYPE: A
BIRTHDAY: 9/29 (LIBRA)

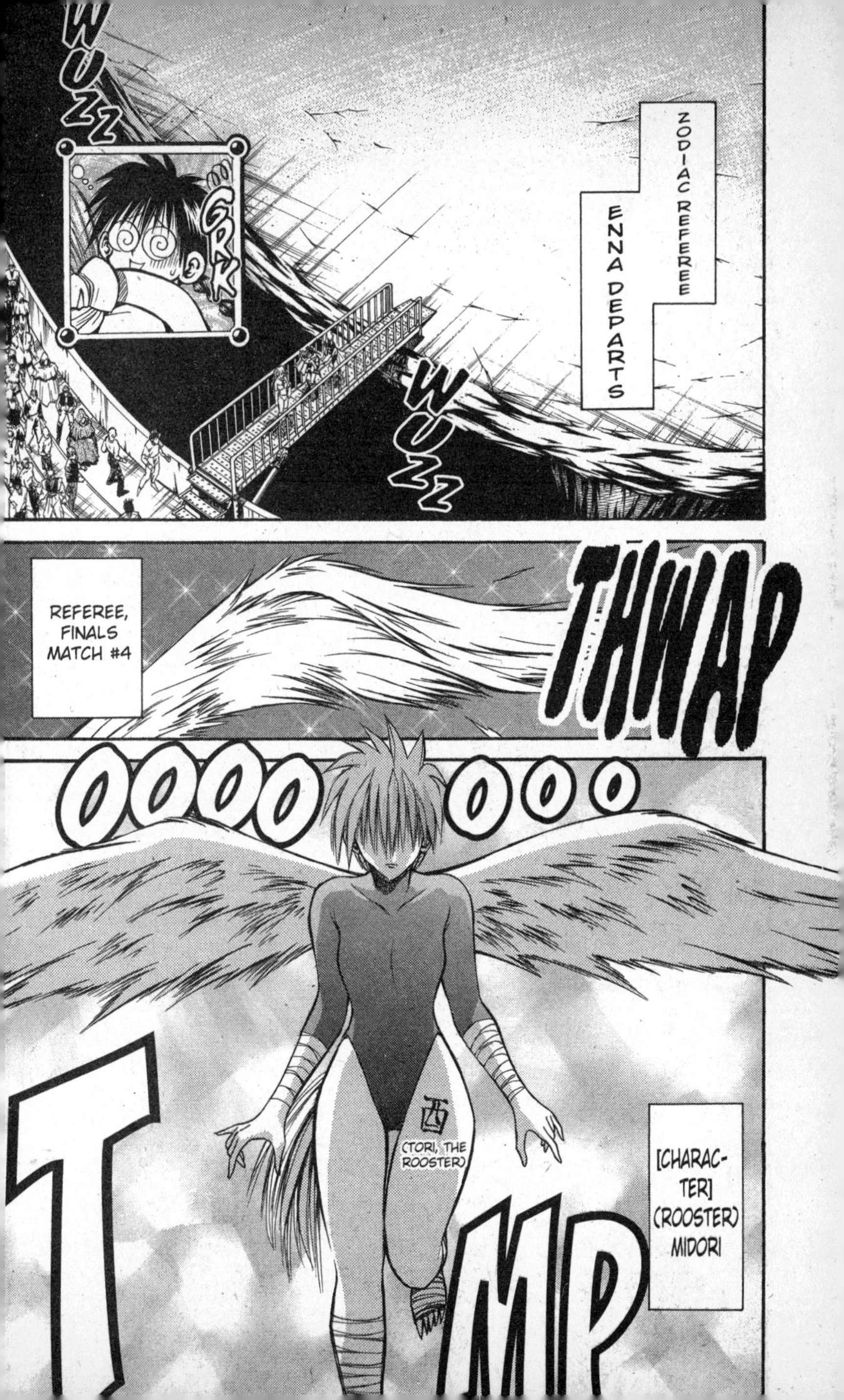
ZODIAC REFEREE
ENNA DEPARTS
WUZZ
GRK
WUZZ
THWAP
REFEREE, FINALS MATCH #4
OOOO OOO
[CHARAC-TER] (ROOSTER) MIDORI
(TORI, THE ROOSTER)
T MP

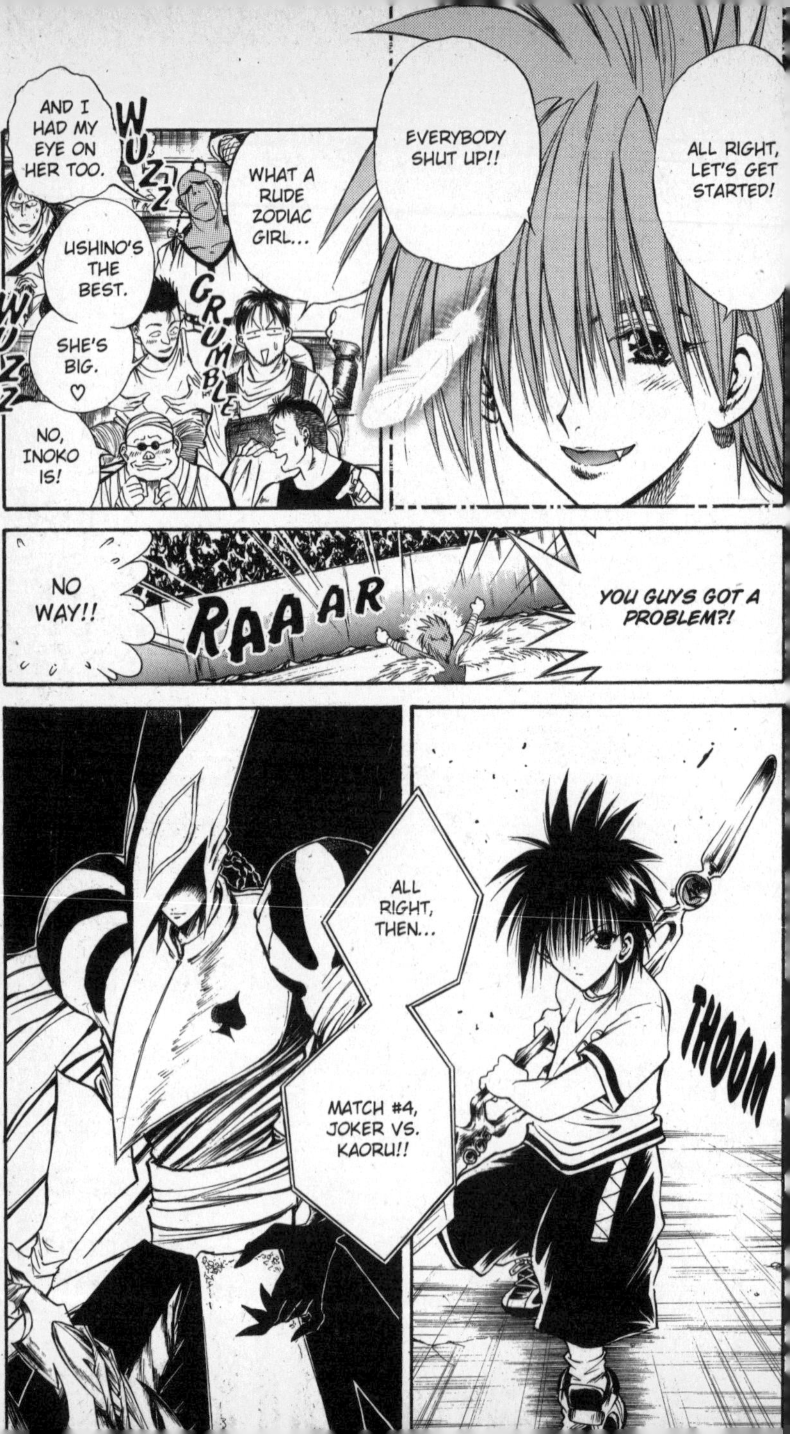
ALL RIGHT, LET'S GET STARTED!
EVERYBODY SHUT UP!!
WHAT A RUDE ZODIAC GIRL...
GRUMBLE
WUZZ
AND I HAD MY EYE ON HER TOO.
USHINO'S THE BEST.
WUZZ
SHE'S BIG. ♡
NO, INOKO IS!
YOU GUYS GOT A PROBLEM?!
RAAAR
NO WAY!!
THOOM
ALL RIGHT, THEN...
MATCH #4, JOKER VS. KAORU!!

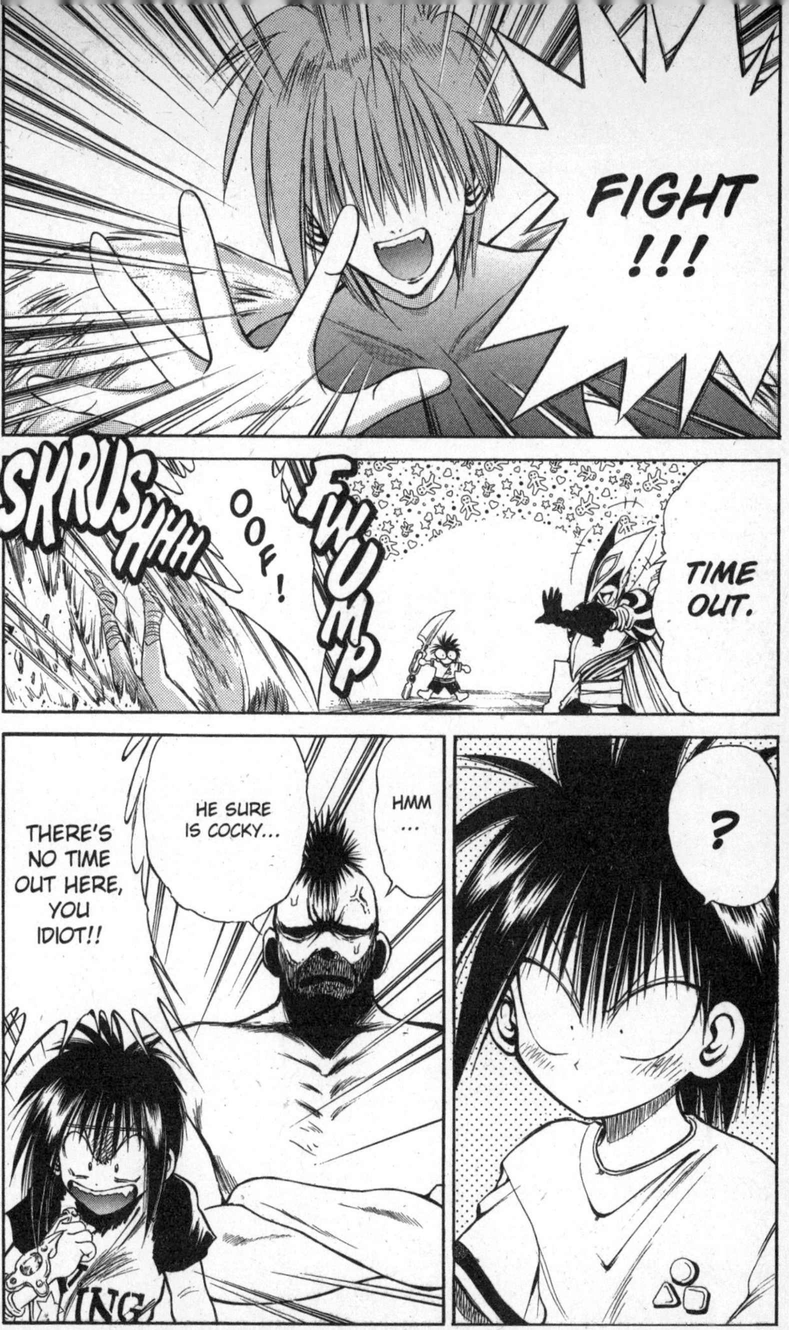
FIGHT!!!
TIME OUT.
FWUMP
OOF!
SKRUSHHH
?
HMM...
HE SURE IS COCKY...
THERE'S NO TIME OUT HERE, YOU IDIOT!!

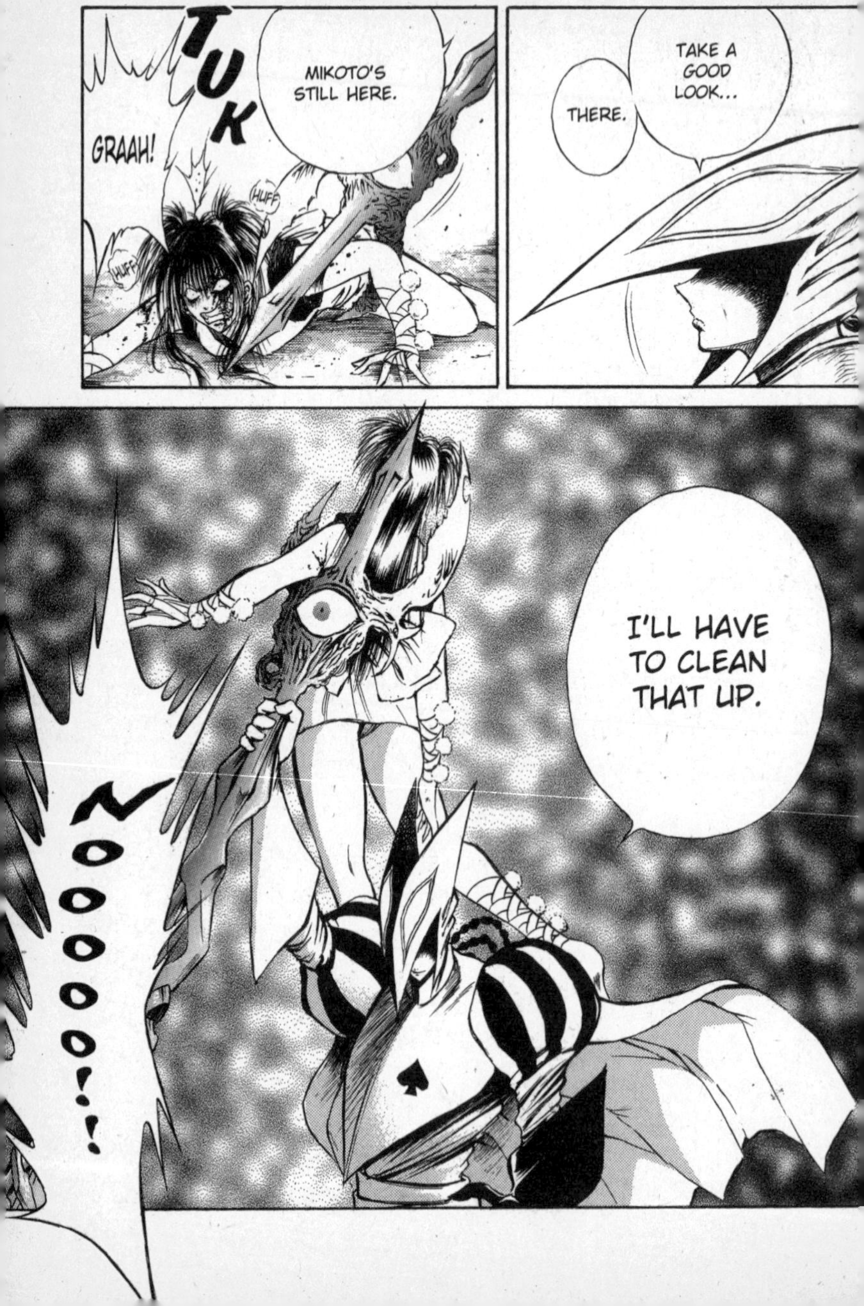
TAKE A GOOD LOOK...
THERE.
MIKOTO'S STILL HERE.
TUK
GRAAH!
HUFF
HUFF
I'LL HAVE TO CLEAN THAT UP.
NOOOOO!!

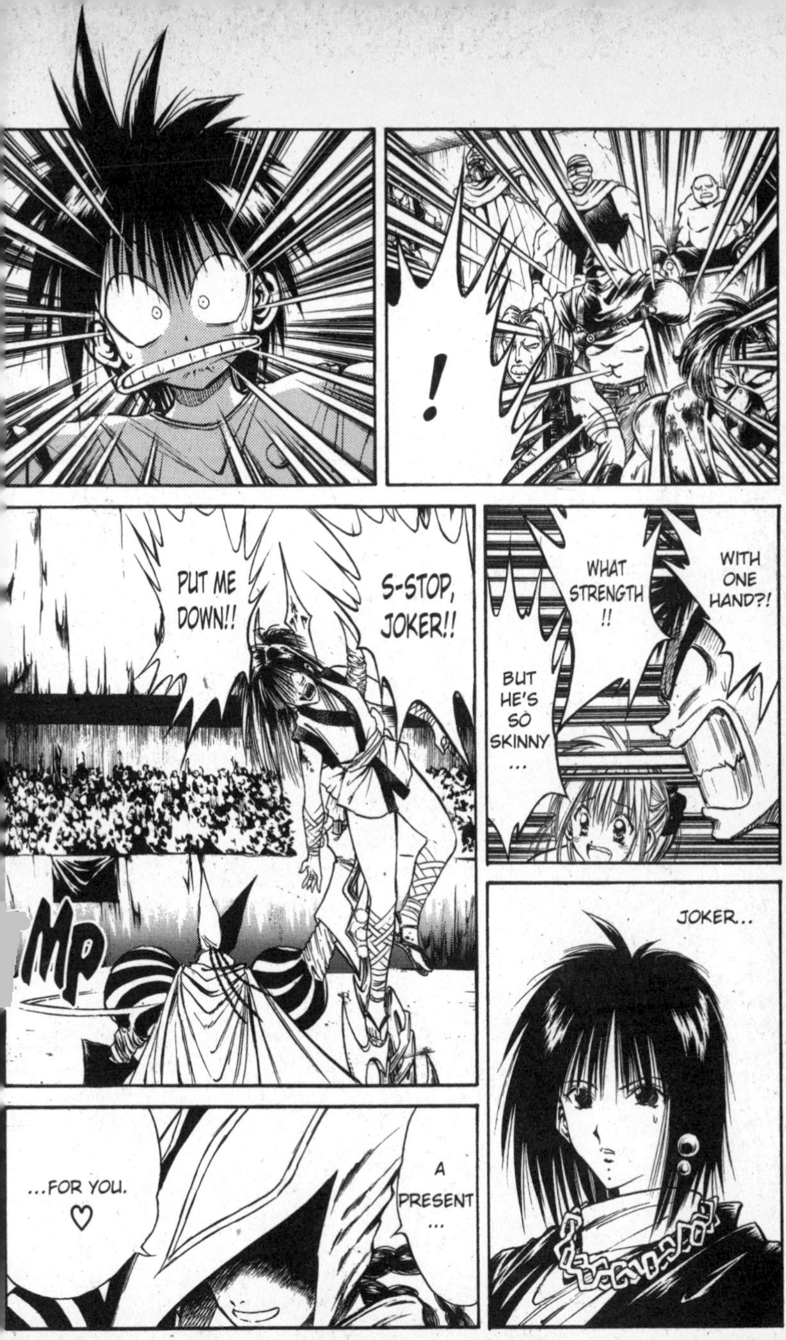
!
WITH ONE HAND?!
WHAT STRENGTH!!
BUT HE'S SO SKINNY...
S-STOP, JOKER!!
PUT ME DOWN!!
MP
JOKER...
A PRESENT...
...FOR YOU. ♡

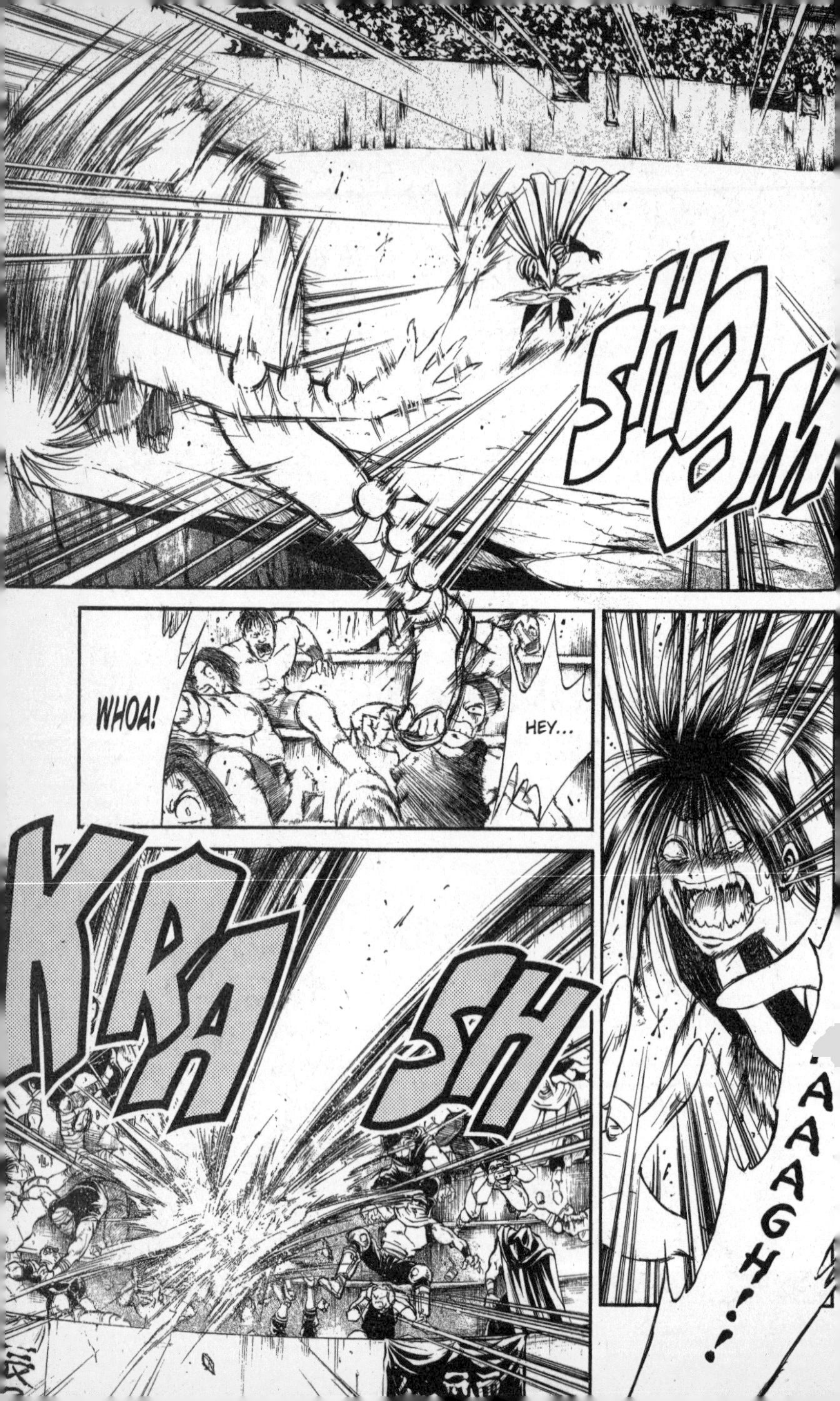
SHOOM
AAAAGH!!!
HEY...
WHOA!
KRASH

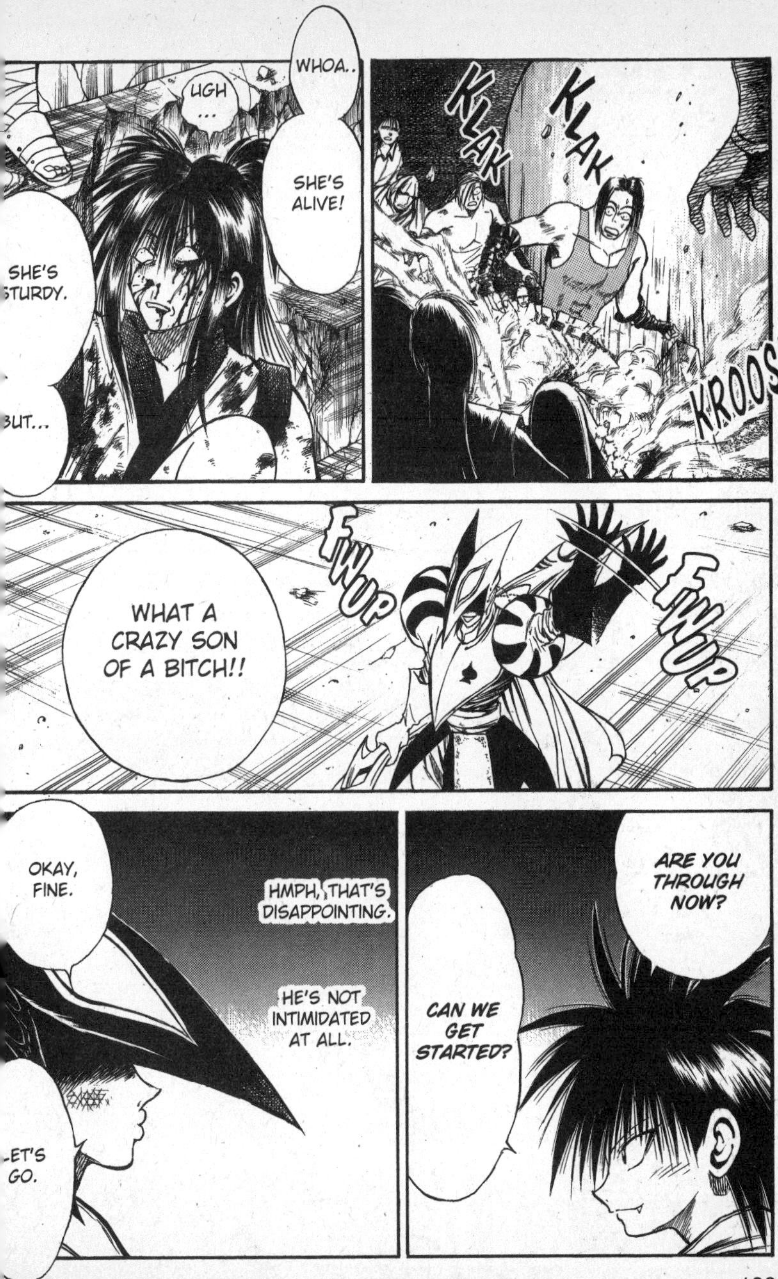
KLAK
KLAK
KROOSH
WHOA..
SHE'S ALIVE!
UGH ...
SHE'S STURDY.
BUT...
FWUP
FWUP
WHAT A CRAZY SON OF A BITCH!!
ARE YOU THROUGH NOW?
CAN WE GET STARTED?
HMPH, THAT'S DISAPPOINTING.
HE'S NOT INTIMIDATED AT ALL.
OKAY, FINE.
LET'S GO.

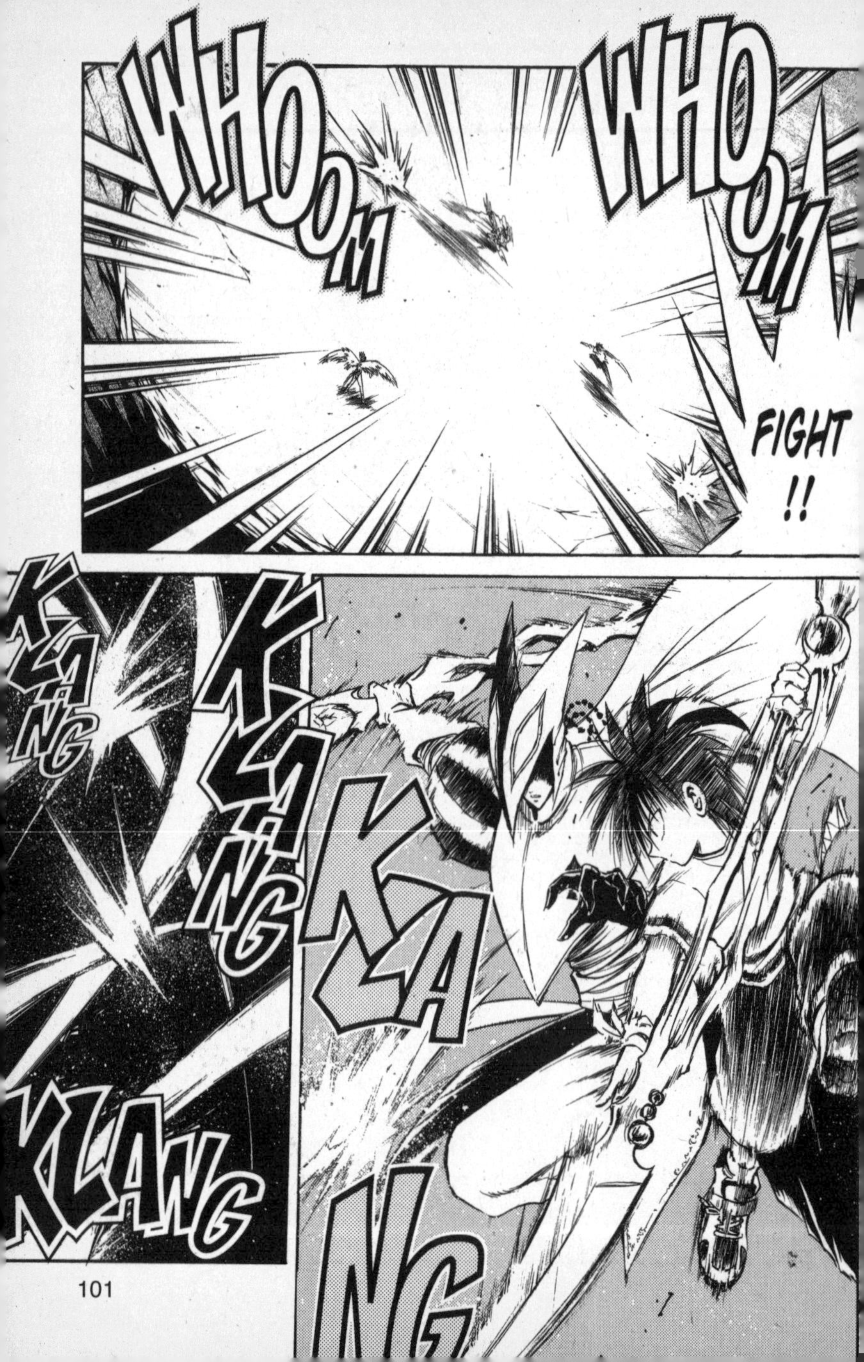
WHOOOM
WHOOOM
FIGHT !!
KALANG
KLANG
KLANG
KLANG

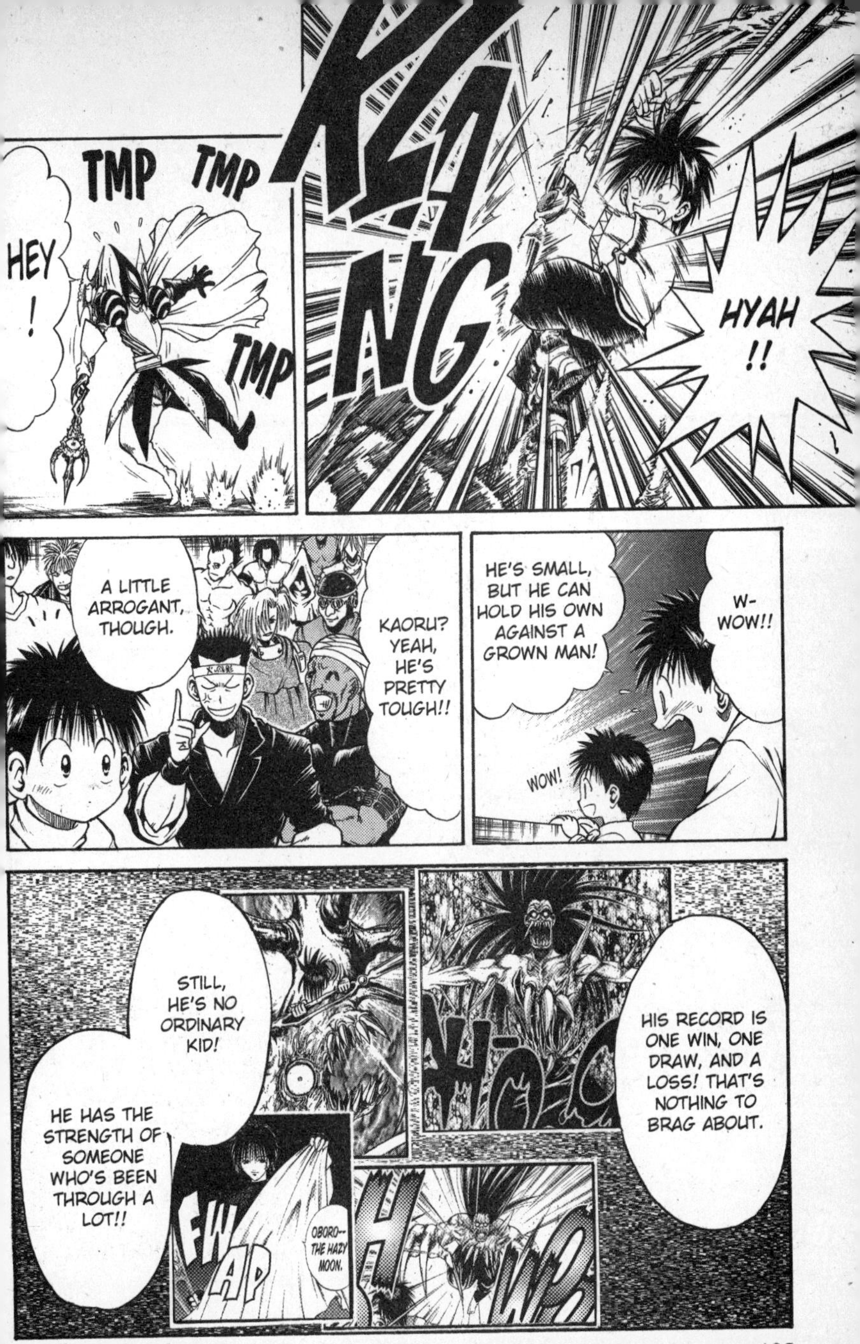
KA-NG
HYAH!!
HEY!
TMP TMP
TMP
W-WOW!!
HE'S SMALL, BUT HE CAN HOLD HIS OWN AGAINST A GROWN MAN!
WOW!
KAORU? YEAH, HE'S PRETTY TOUGH!!
A LITTLE ARROGANT, THOUGH.
HIS RECORD IS ONE WIN, ONE DRAW, AND A LOSS! THAT'S NOTHING TO BRAG ABOUT.
STILL, HE'S NO ORDINARY KID!
HE HAS THE STRENGTH OF SOMEONE WHO'S BEEN THROUGH A LOT!!
FWAP
OBORO-- THE HAZY MOON.

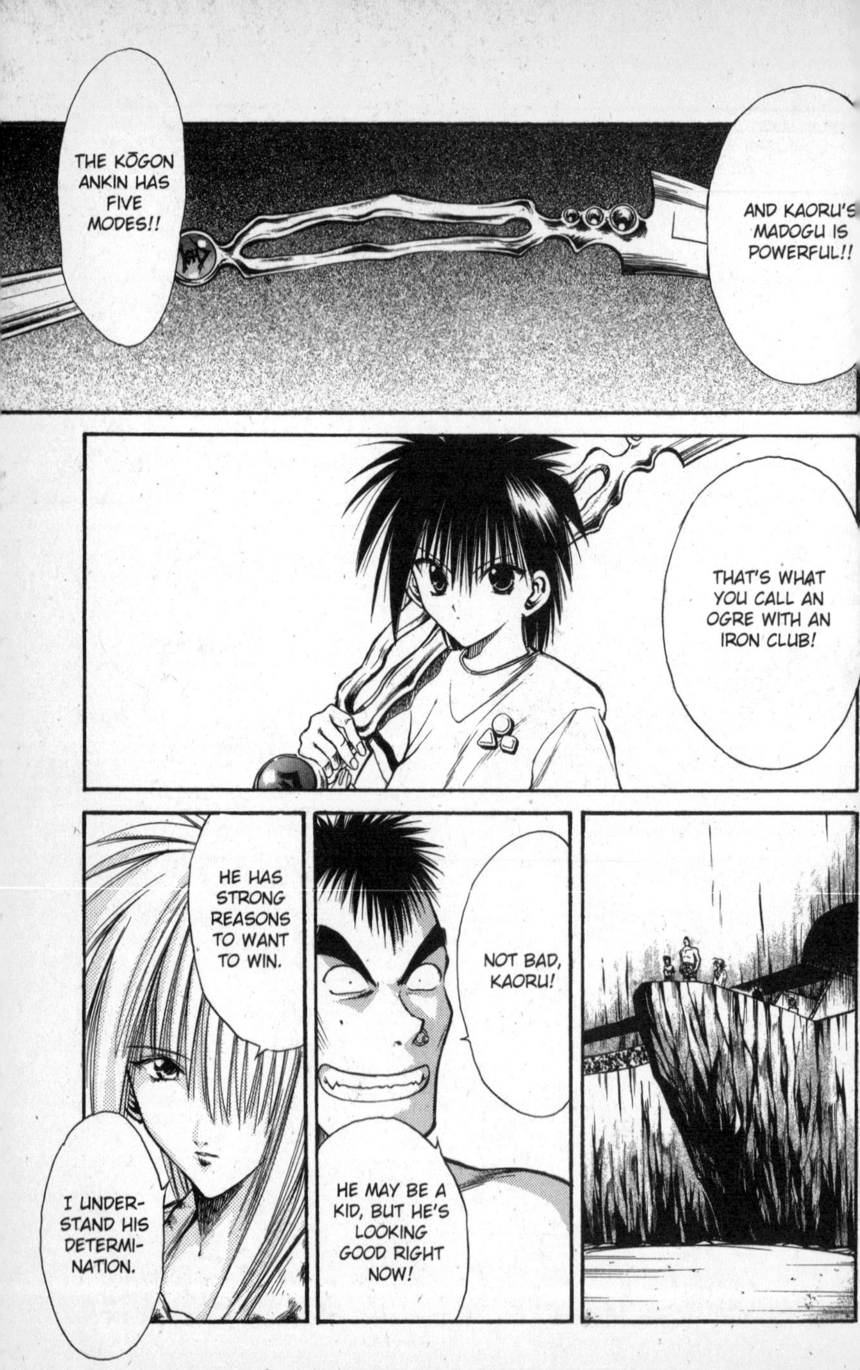
THE KŌGON ANKIN HAS FIVE MODES!!
AND KAORU'S MADOGU IS POWERFUL!!
THAT'S WHAT YOU CALL AN OGRE WITH AN IRON CLUB!
NOT BAD, KAORU!
HE MAY BE A KID, BUT HE'S LOOKING GOOD RIGHT NOW!
HE HAS STRONG REASONS TO WANT TO WIN.
I UNDERSTAND HIS DETERMINATION.

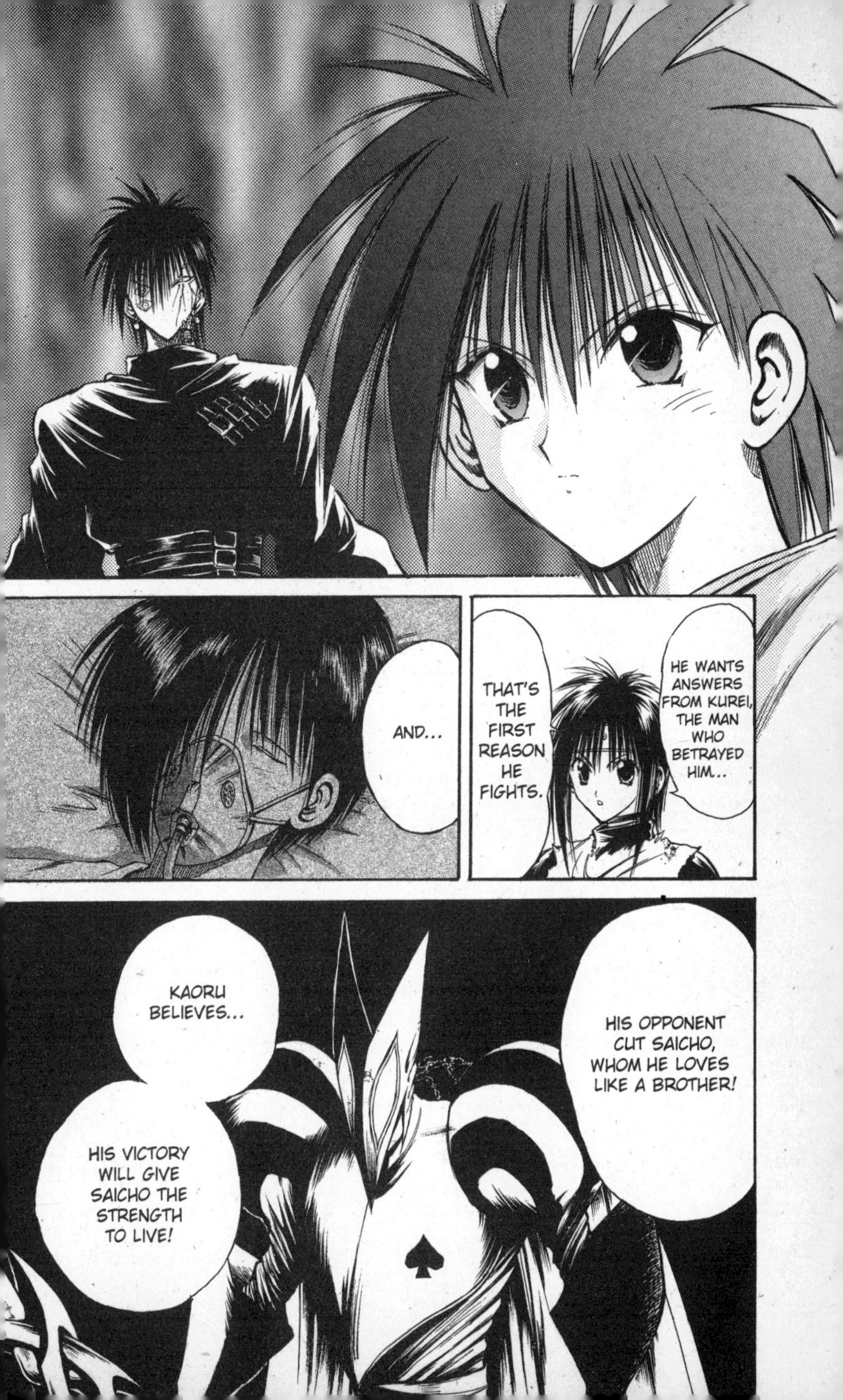
HE WANTS ANSWERS FROM KUREI, THE MAN WHO BETRAYED HIM..
THAT'S THE FIRST REASON HE FIGHTS.
AND...
HIS OPPONENT CUT SAICHO, WHOM HE LOVES LIKE A BROTHER!
KAORU BELIEVES...
HIS VICTORY WILL GIVE SAICHO THE STRENGTH TO LIVE!

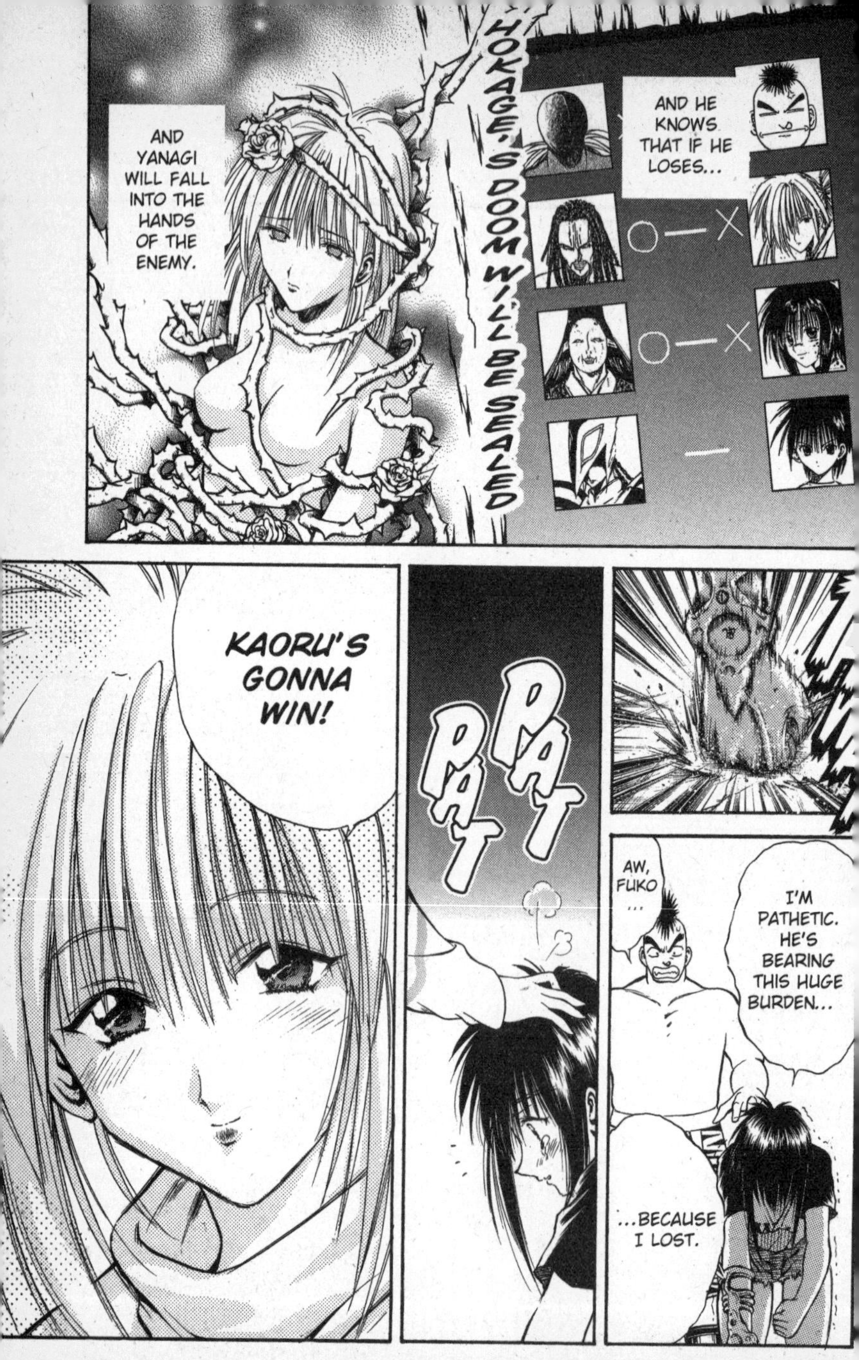
AND HE KNOWS THAT IF HE LOSES...
HOKAGE'S DOOM WILL BE SEALED
AND YANAGI WILL FALL INTO THE HANDS OF THE ENEMY.
AW, FUKO...
I'M PATHETIC. HE'S BEARING THIS HUGE BURDEN...
...BECAUSE I LOST.
PAT PAT
KAORU'S GONNA WIN!

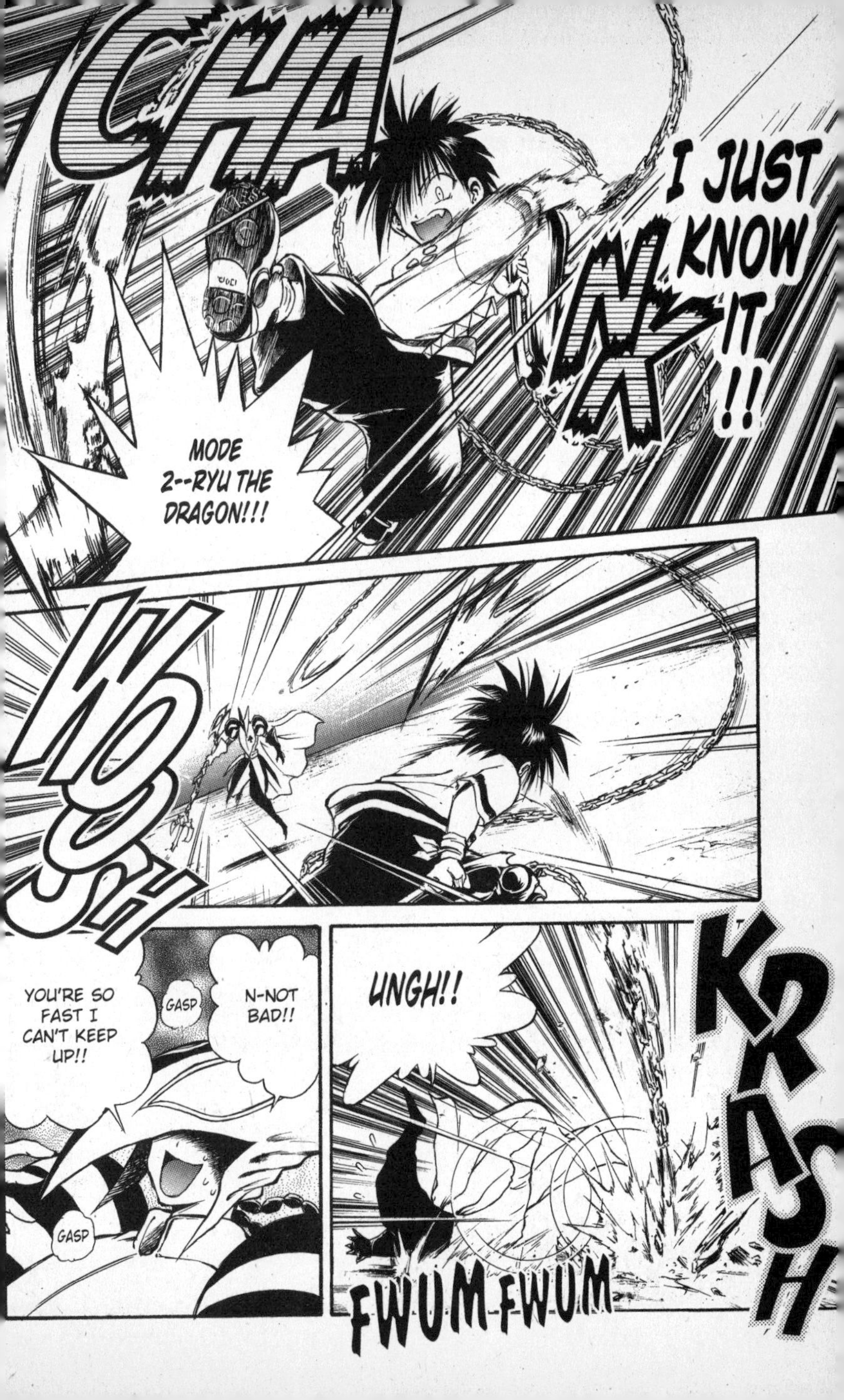
I JUST KNOW IT!!
CHA
NK
MODE 2--RYU THE DRAGON!!!
WHOOSH
KRASH
UNGH!!
FWUM FWUM
N-NOT BAD!!
GASP
YOU'RE SO FAST I CAN'T KEEP UP!!
GASP

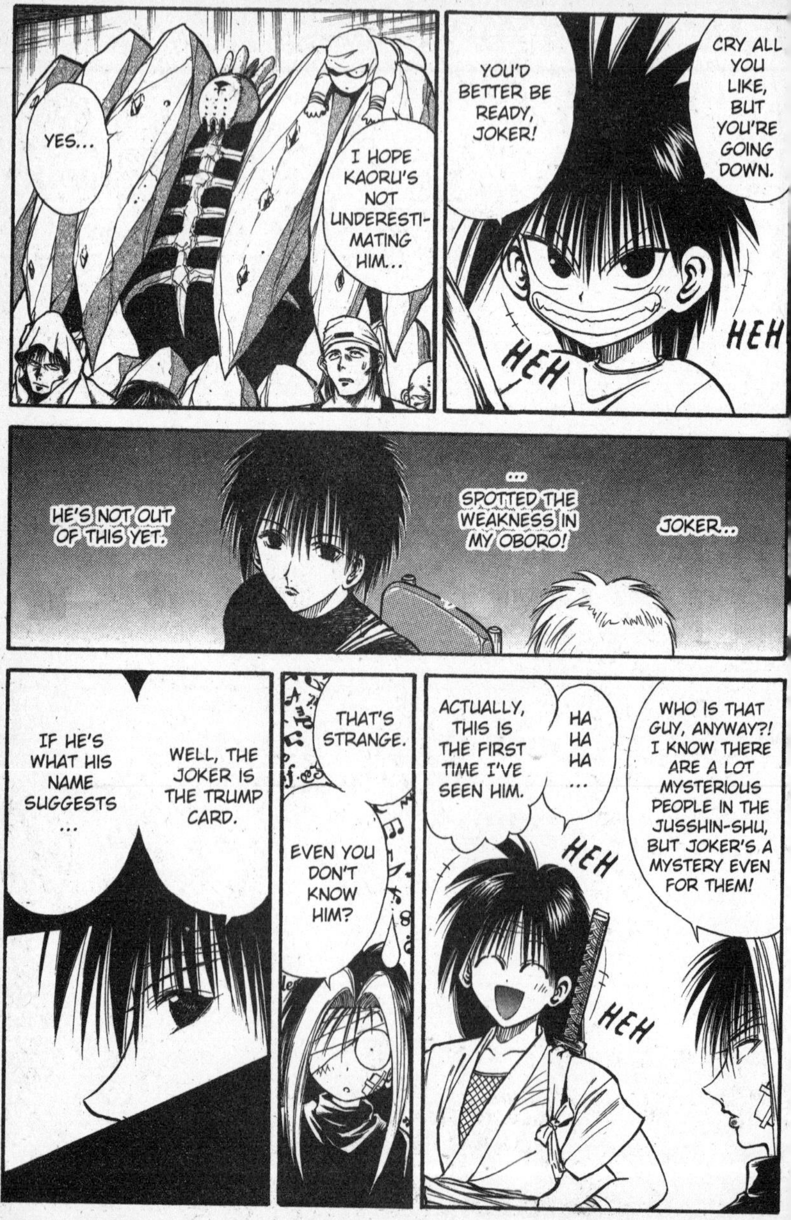

CRY ALL YOU LIKE, BUT YOU'RE GOING DOWN.
YOU'D BETTER BE READY, JOKER!
HEH
HEH
I HOPE KAORU'S NOT UNDERESTI-MATING HIM...
YES...
JOKER...
... SPOTTED THE WEAKNESS IN MY OBORO!
HE'S NOT OUT OF THIS YET.
WHO IS THAT GUY, ANYWAY?! I KNOW THERE ARE A LOT MYSTERIOUS PEOPLE IN THE JUSSHIN-SHU, BUT JOKER'S A MYSTERY EVEN FOR THEM!
HA HA HA ...
ACTUALLY, THIS IS THE FIRST TIME I'VE SEEN HIM.
HEH
HEH
THAT'S STRANGE.
EVEN YOU DON'T KNOW HIM?
WELL, THE JOKER IS THE TRUMP CARD.
IF HE'S WHAT HIS NAME SUGGESTS ...

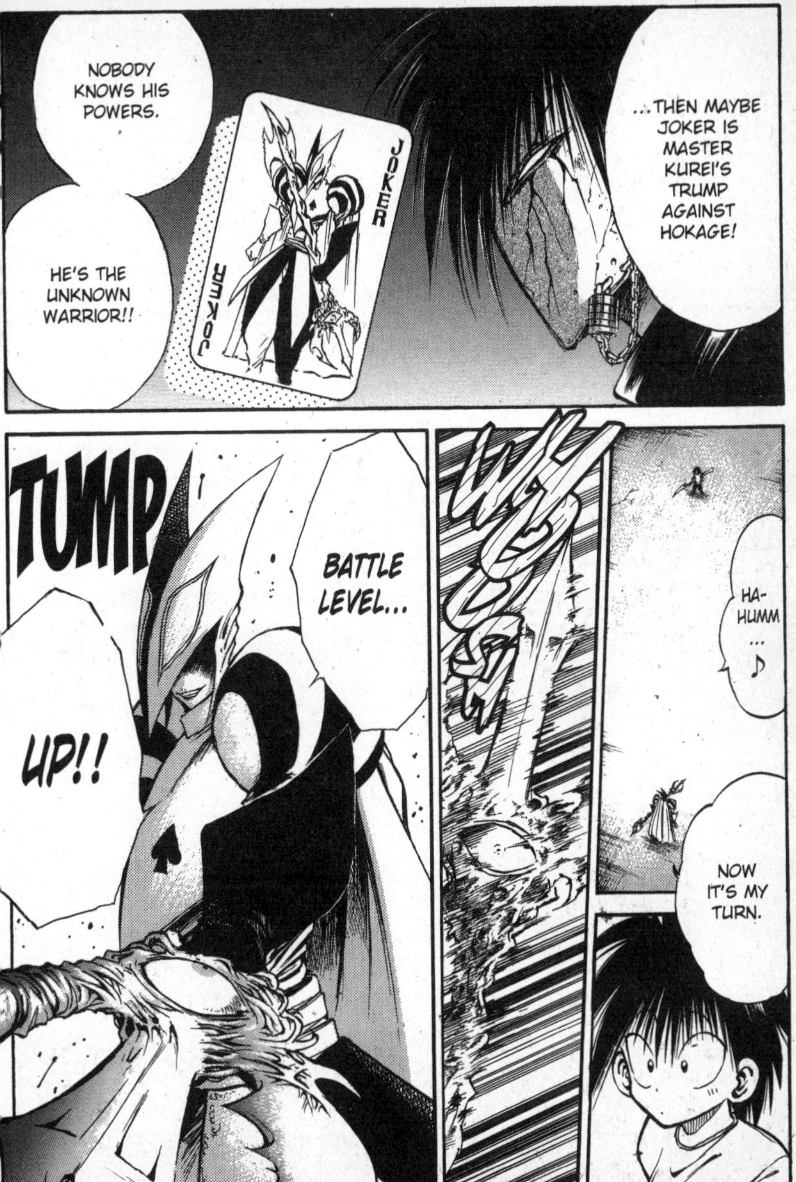
...THEN MAYBE JOKER IS MASTER KUREI'S TRUMP AGAINST HOKAGE!
NOBODY KNOWS HIS POWERS.
JOKER
HE'S THE UNKNOWN WARRIOR!!
HA-HUMM ...♪
NOW IT'S MY TURN.
BATTLE LEVEL...
TUMP
UP!!

Part 134: Joker's Special Power

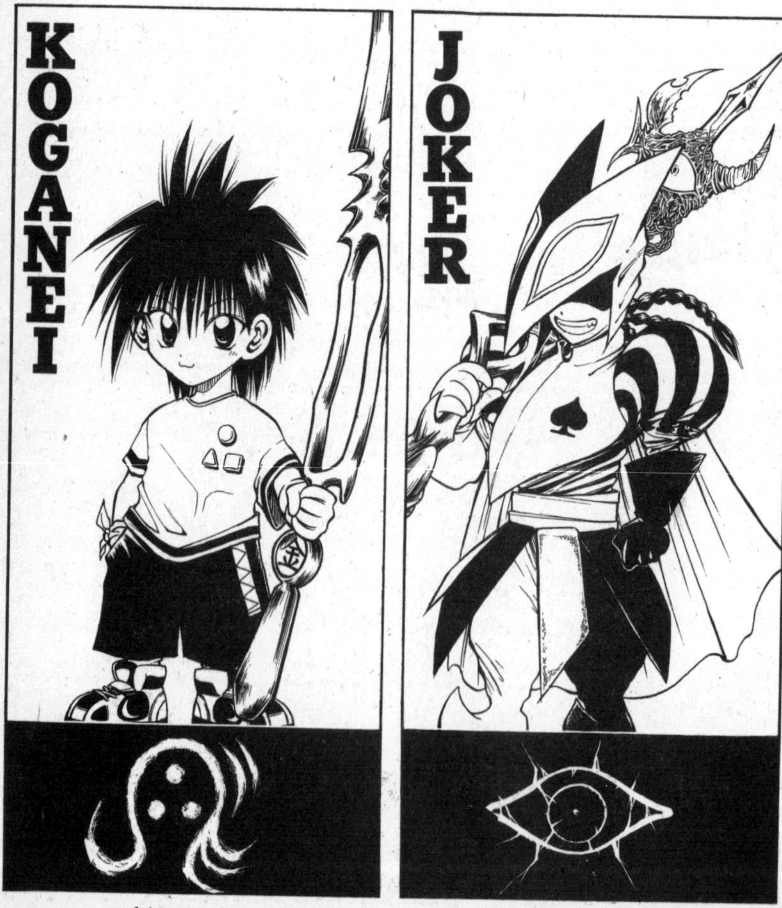
JOKER
KOGANEI

(URUHA-KURENAI)

(HOKAGE)

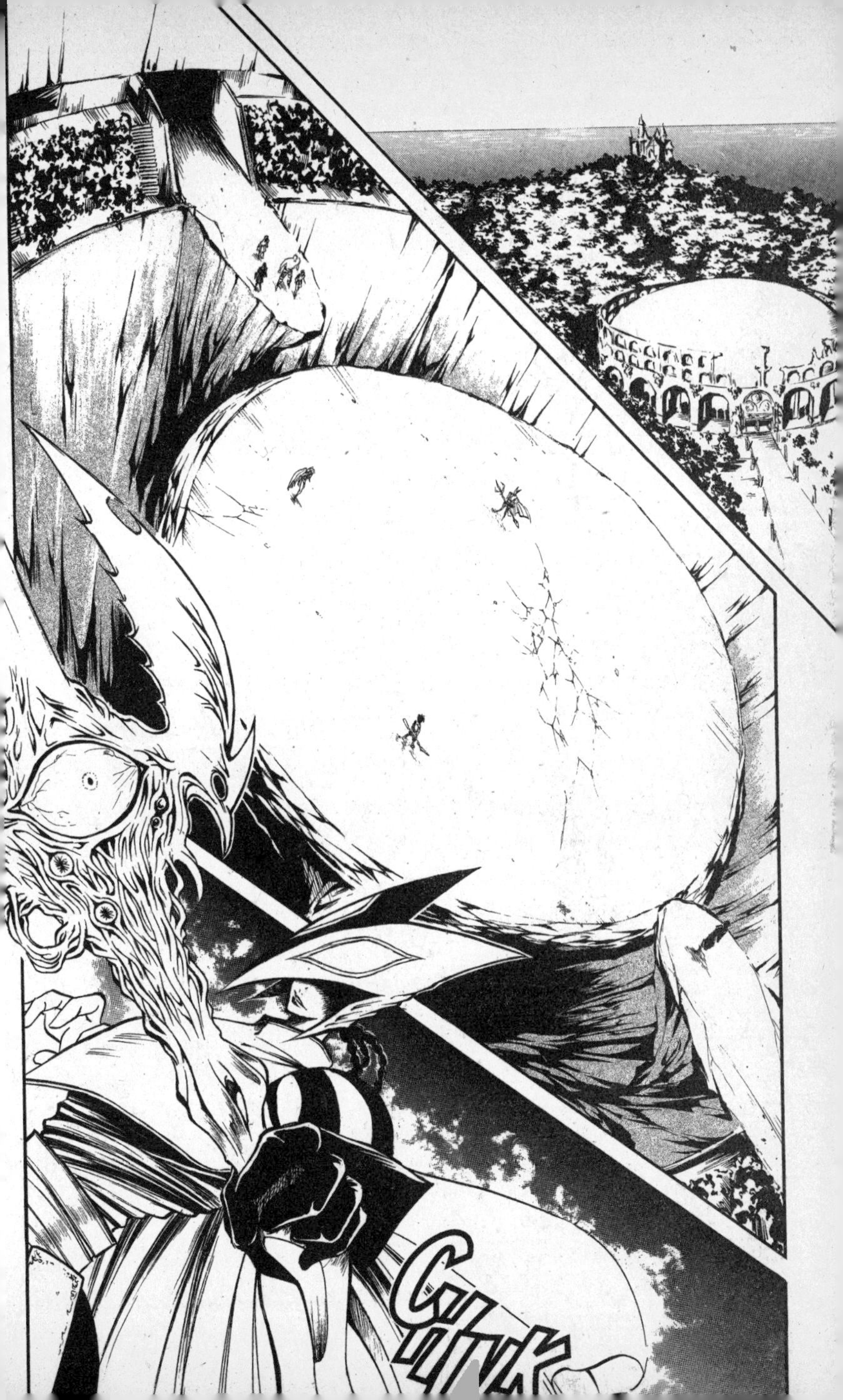
Clunk

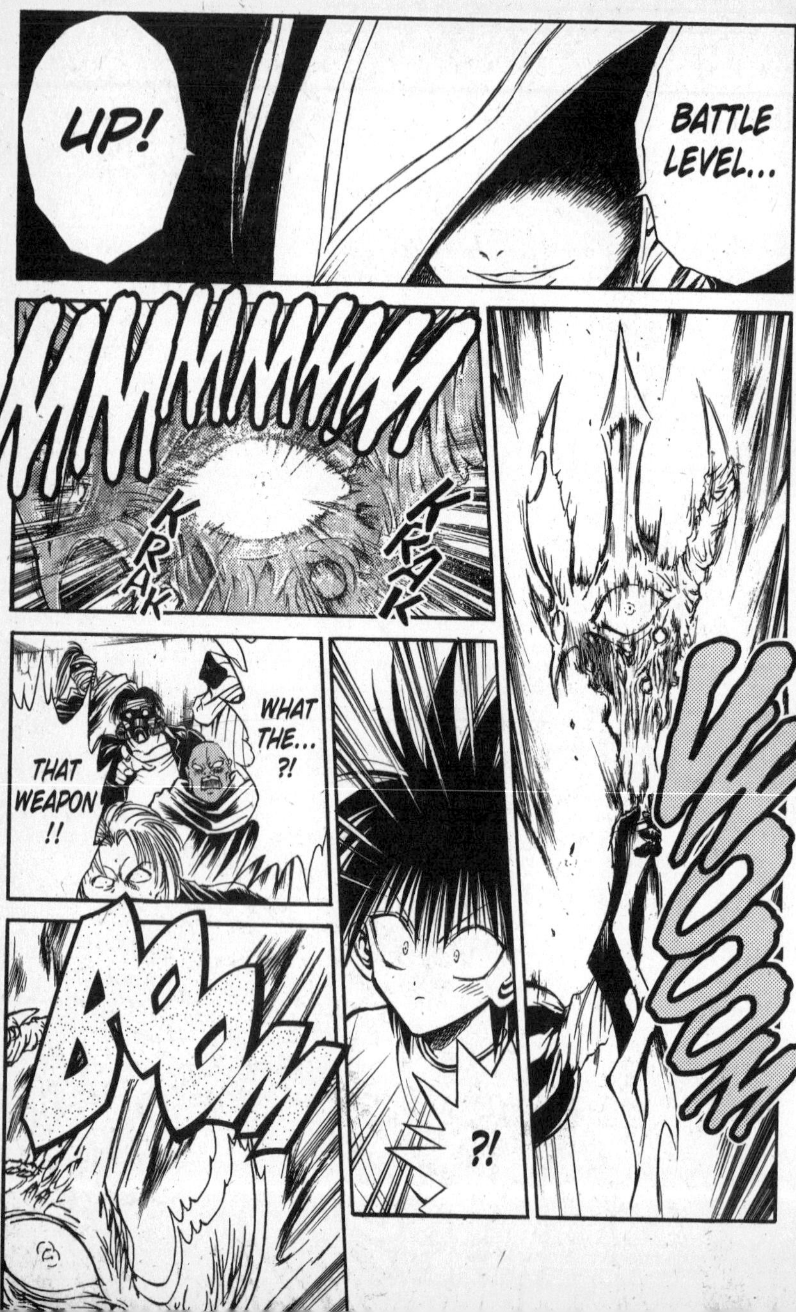
BATTLE LEVEL...
UP!
KRAK
KRAK
?!
WHAT THE...?!
THAT WEAPON!!
BOOM

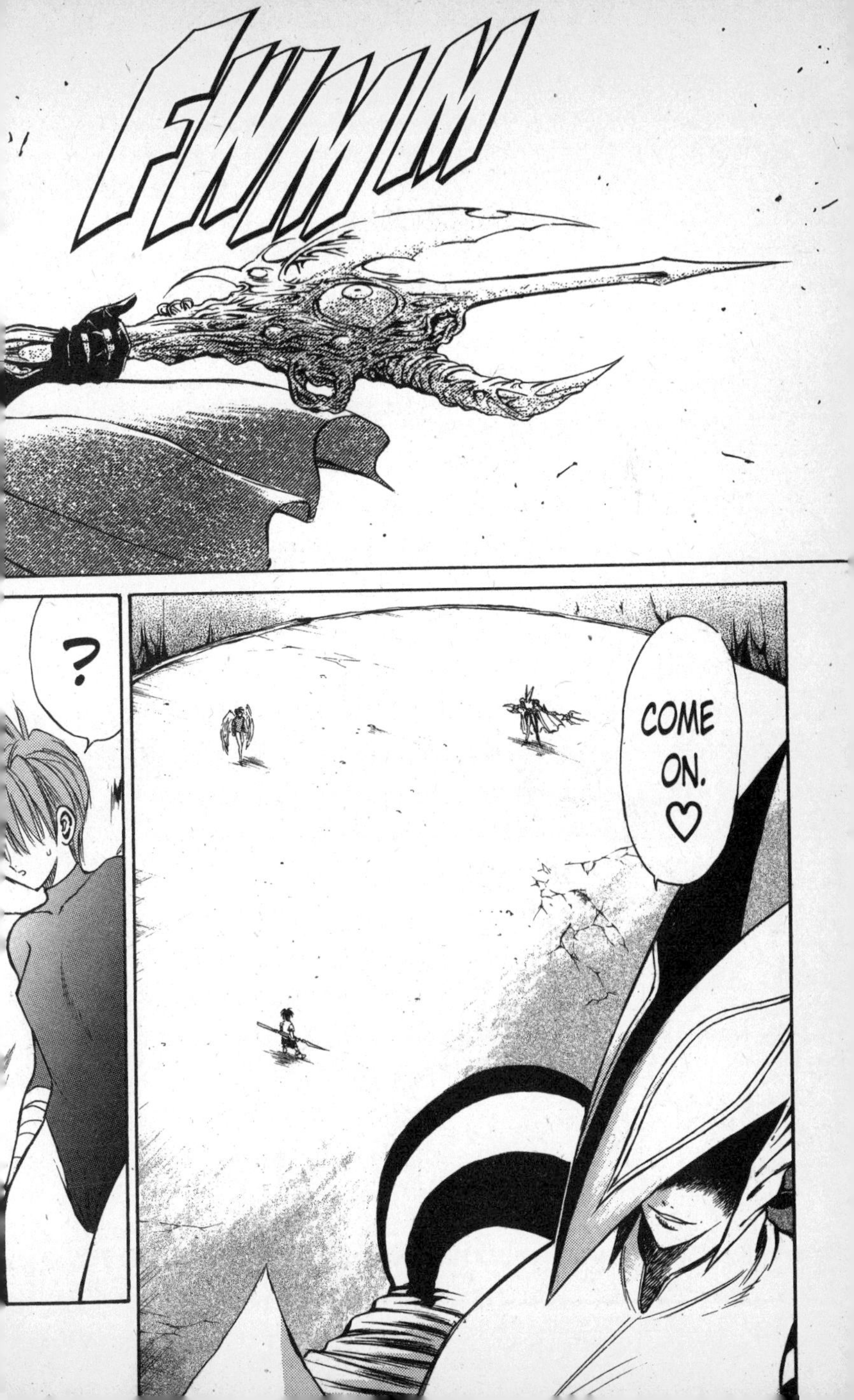
FWMM
COME ON. ♡
?

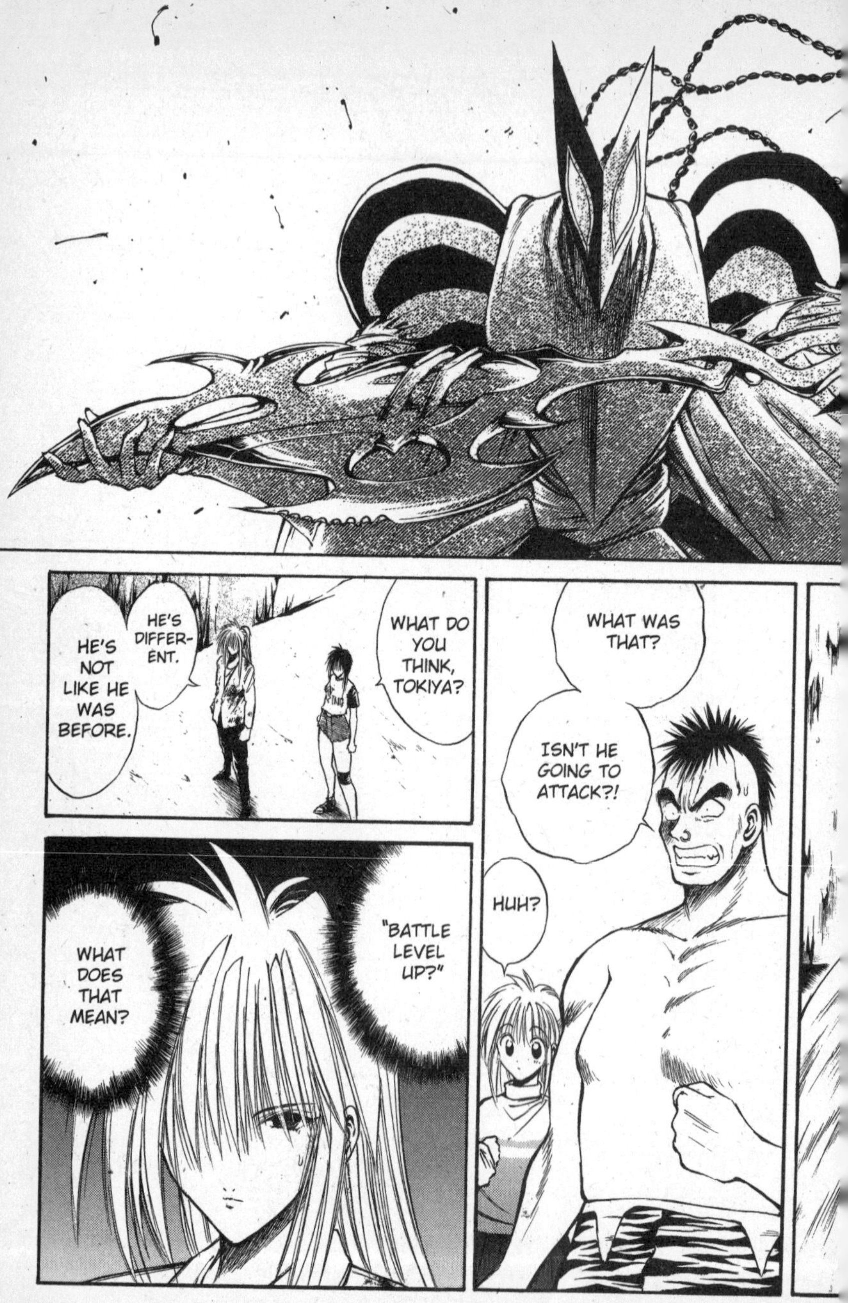
WHAT WAS THAT?
ISN'T HE GOING TO ATTACK?!
HUH?
WHAT DO YOU THINK, TOKIYA?
HE'S DIFFER-ENT.
HE'S NOT LIKE HE WAS BEFORE.
"BATTLE LEVEL UP?"
WHAT DOES THAT MEAN?

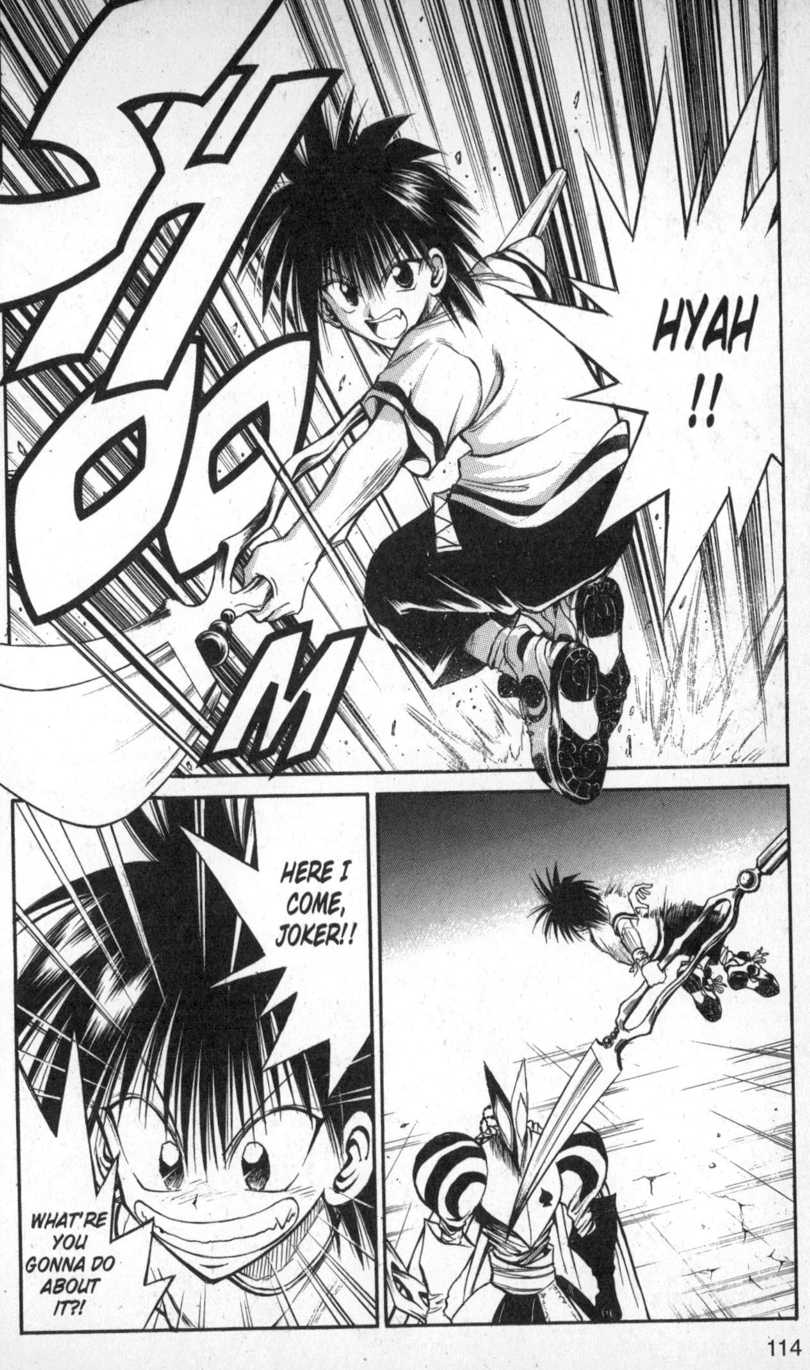
HYAH!!
HERE I COME, JOKER!!
WHAT'RE YOU GONNA DO ABOUT IT?!

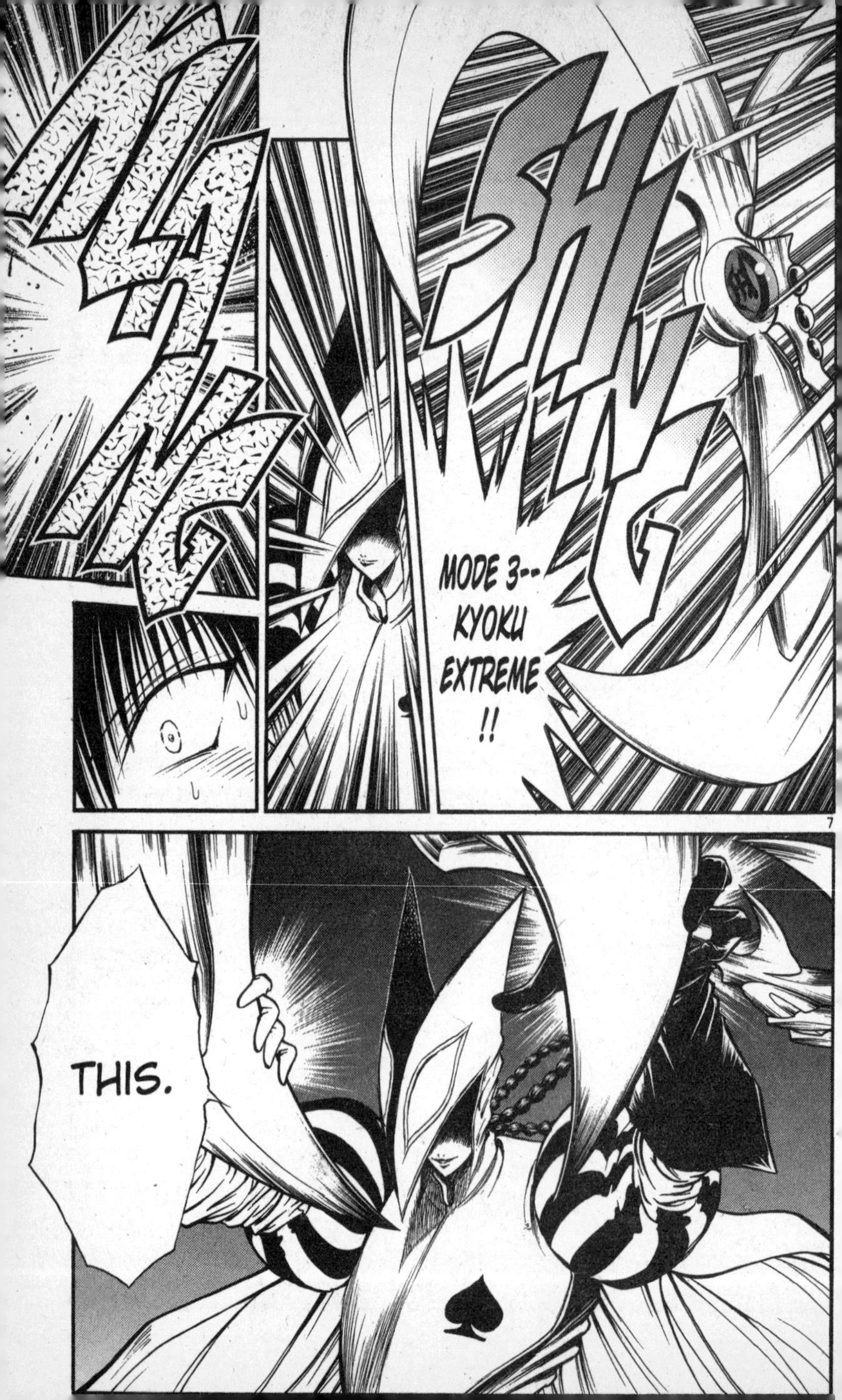
SHING
MODE 3-- KYOKU EXTREME !!
THIS.

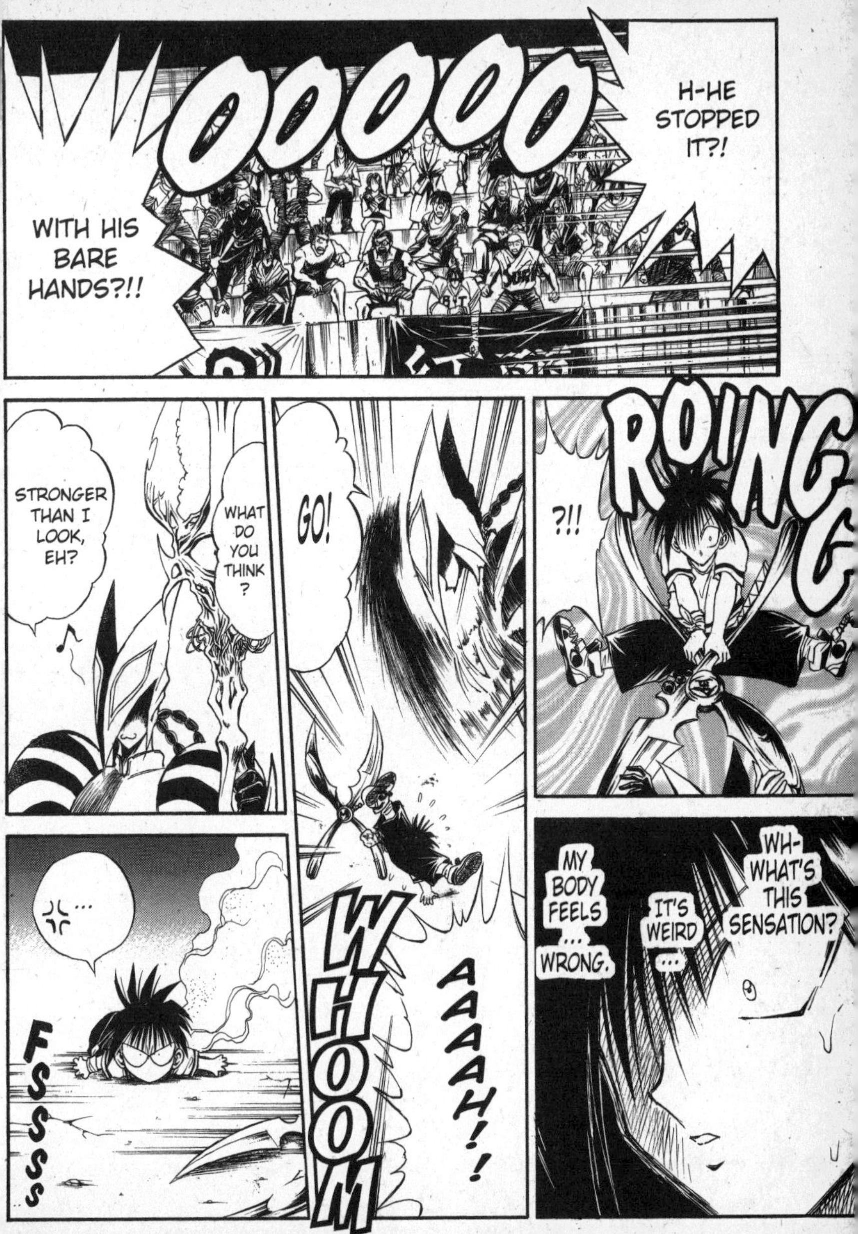
H-HE STOPPED IT?!
OOOOO
WITH HIS BARE HANDS?!!
ROING
?!!
WH- WHAT'S THIS SENSATION?
IT'S WEIRD...
MY BODY FEELS... WRONG.
GO!
AAAAH!!
WHOOM
WHAT DO YOU THINK?
STRONGER THAN I LOOK, EH?
...
FSSSS

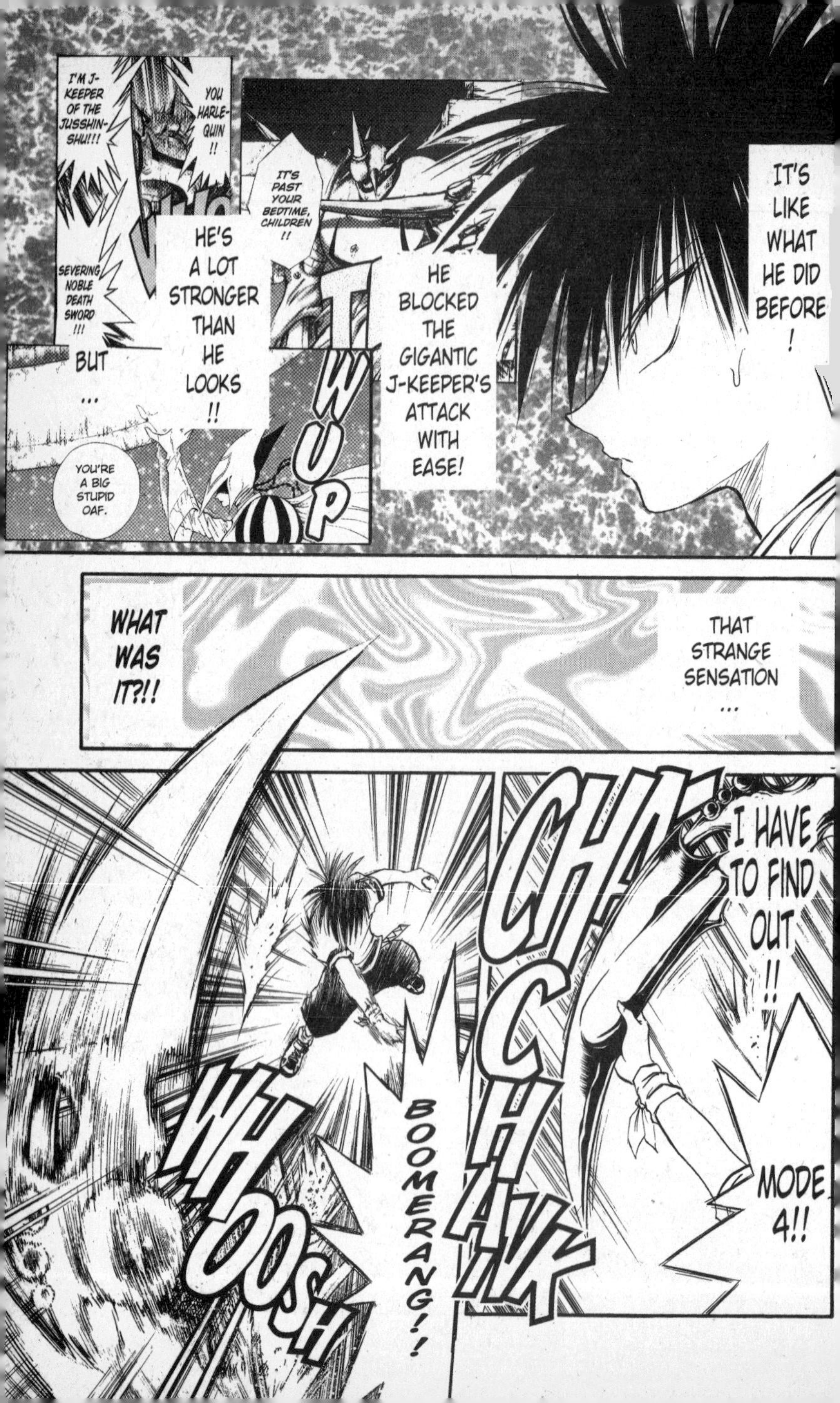
IT'S LIKE WHAT HE DID BEFORE!
HE BLOCKED THE GIGANTIC J-KEEPER'S ATTACK WITH EASE!
IT'S PAST YOUR BEDTIME, CHILDREN!!
YOU HARLEQUIN!!
I'M J-KEEPER OF THE JUSSHIN-SHU!!!
SEVERING NOBLE DEATH SWORD!!!
TWUP
HE'S A LOT STRONGER THAN HE LOOKS!!
BUT...
YOU'RE A BIG STUPID OAF.
THAT STRANGE SENSATION...
WHAT WAS IT?!!
I HAVE TO FIND OUT!!
CHA CHAK
MODE 4!!
BOOMERANG!!
WHOOSH

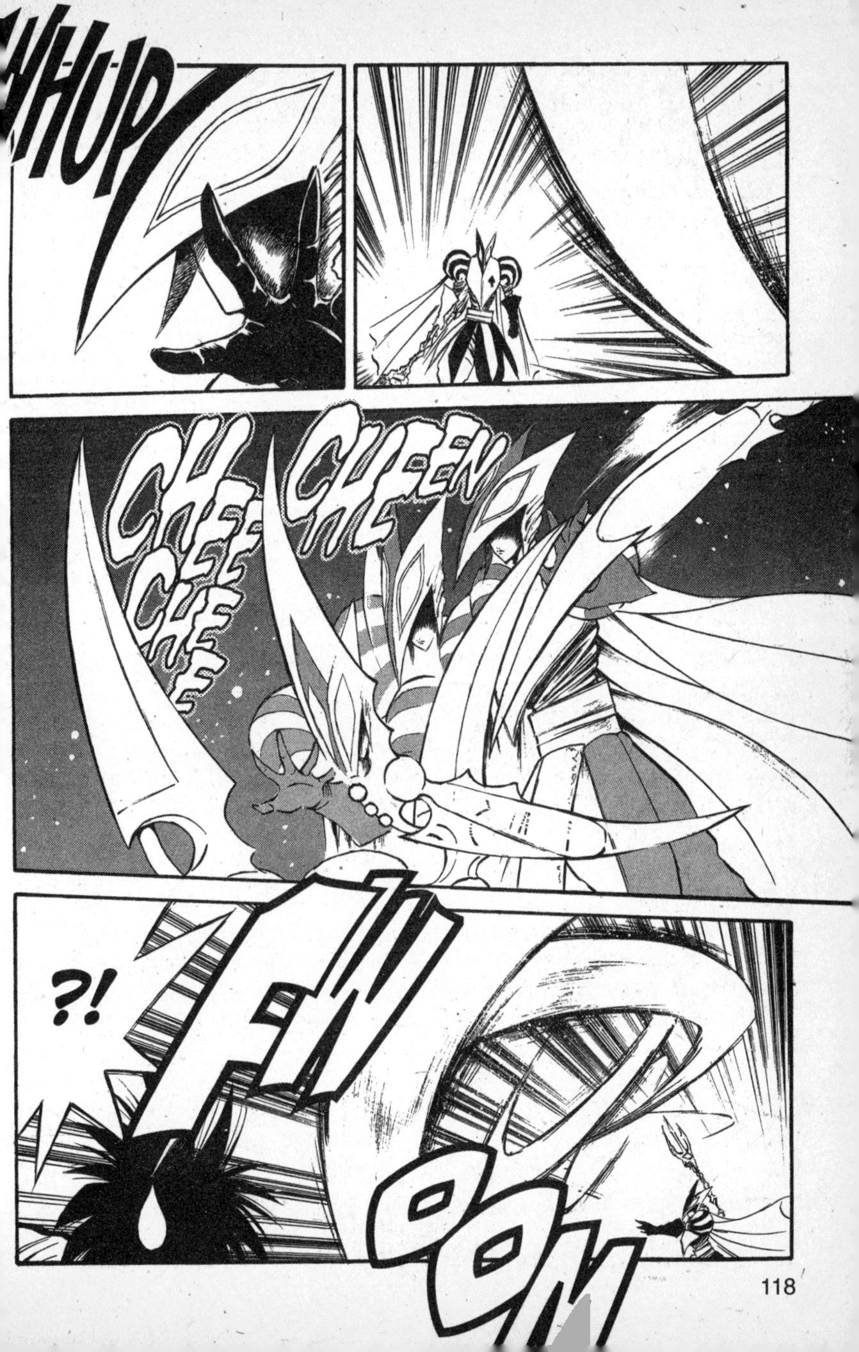
HUP
CHEEN
CHE-CHE-CHE
?!
FOOM

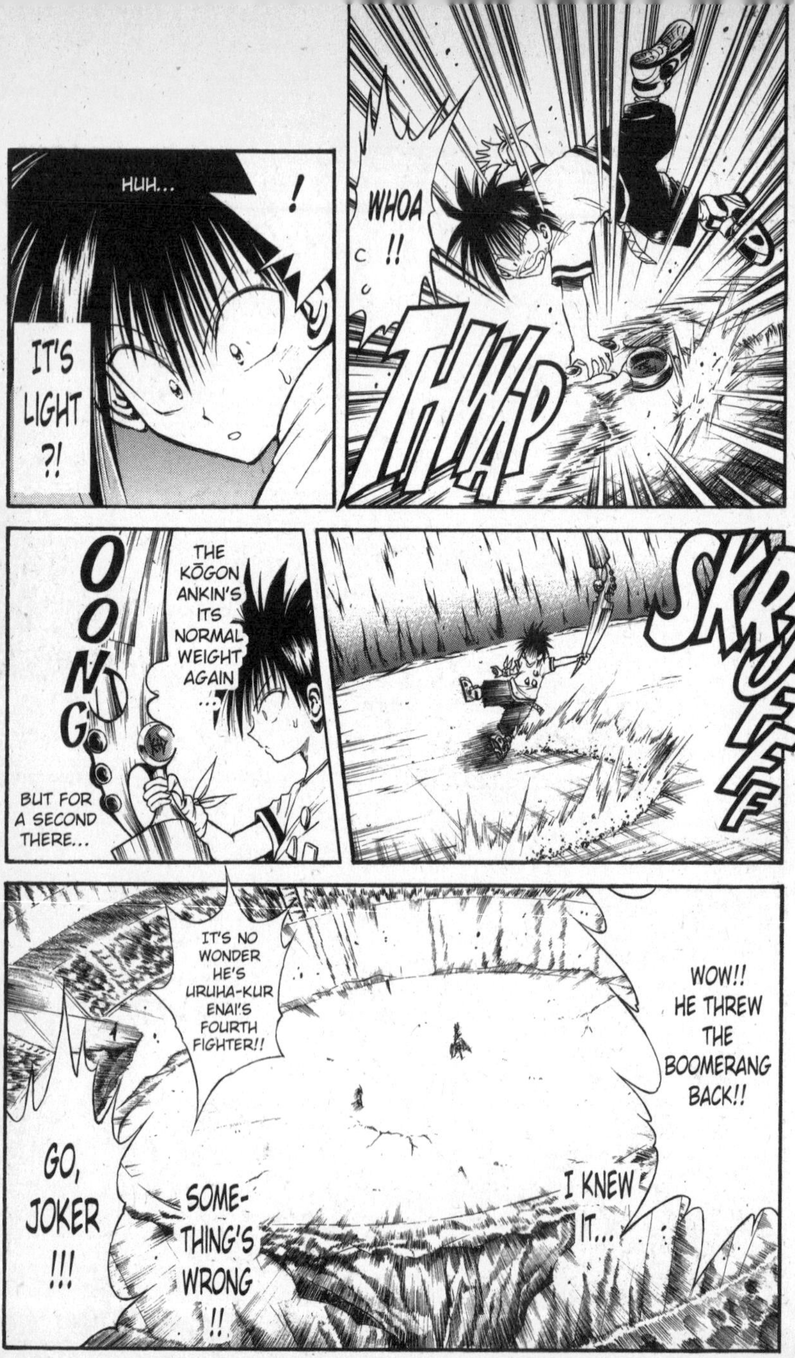
WHOA!!
THWAP
HUH...
!
IT'S LIGHT?!
SKRUFFFFF
THE KŌGON ANKIN'S ITS NORMAL WEIGHT AGAIN...
OOONG
BUT FOR A SECOND THERE...
WOW!! HE THREW THE BOOMERANG BACK!!
IT'S NO WONDER HE'S URUHA-KURENAI'S FOURTH FIGHTER!!
I KNEW IT...
SOME-THING'S WRONG!!
GO, JOKER!!!

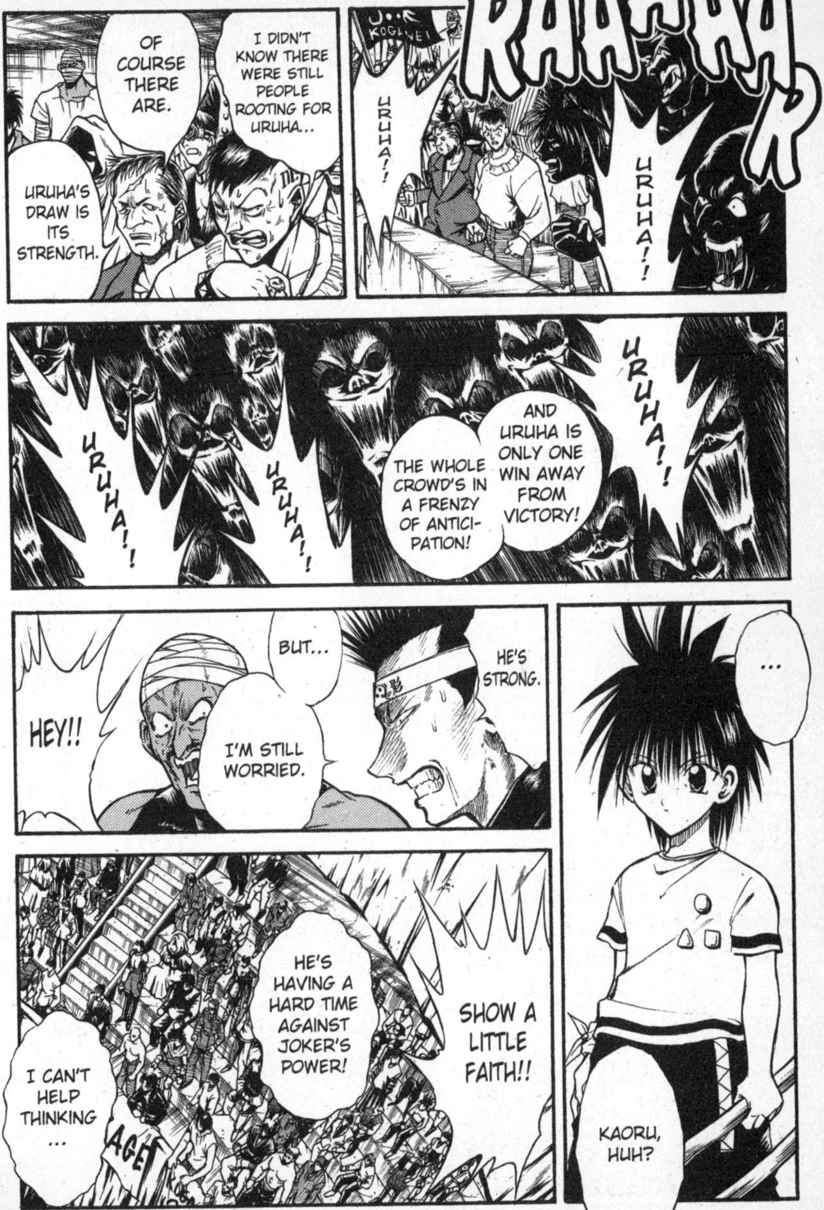
RAAAAAR
URUHA!!
J.O.R KOGANEI
URUHA!!
I DIDN'T KNOW THERE WERE STILL PEOPLE ROOTING FOR URUHA...
OF COURSE THERE ARE.
URUHA'S DRAW IS ITS STRENGTH.
URUHA!!
AND URUHA IS ONLY ONE WIN AWAY FROM VICTORY!
THE WHOLE CROWD'S IN A FRENZY OF ANTICI-PATION!
URUHA!!
URUHA!!
...
KAORU, HUH?
HE'S STRONG.
BUT...
I'M STILL WORRIED.
HEY!!
SHOW A LITTLE FAITH!!
HE'S HAVING A HARD TIME AGAINST JOKER'S POWER!
I CAN'T HELP THINKING ...

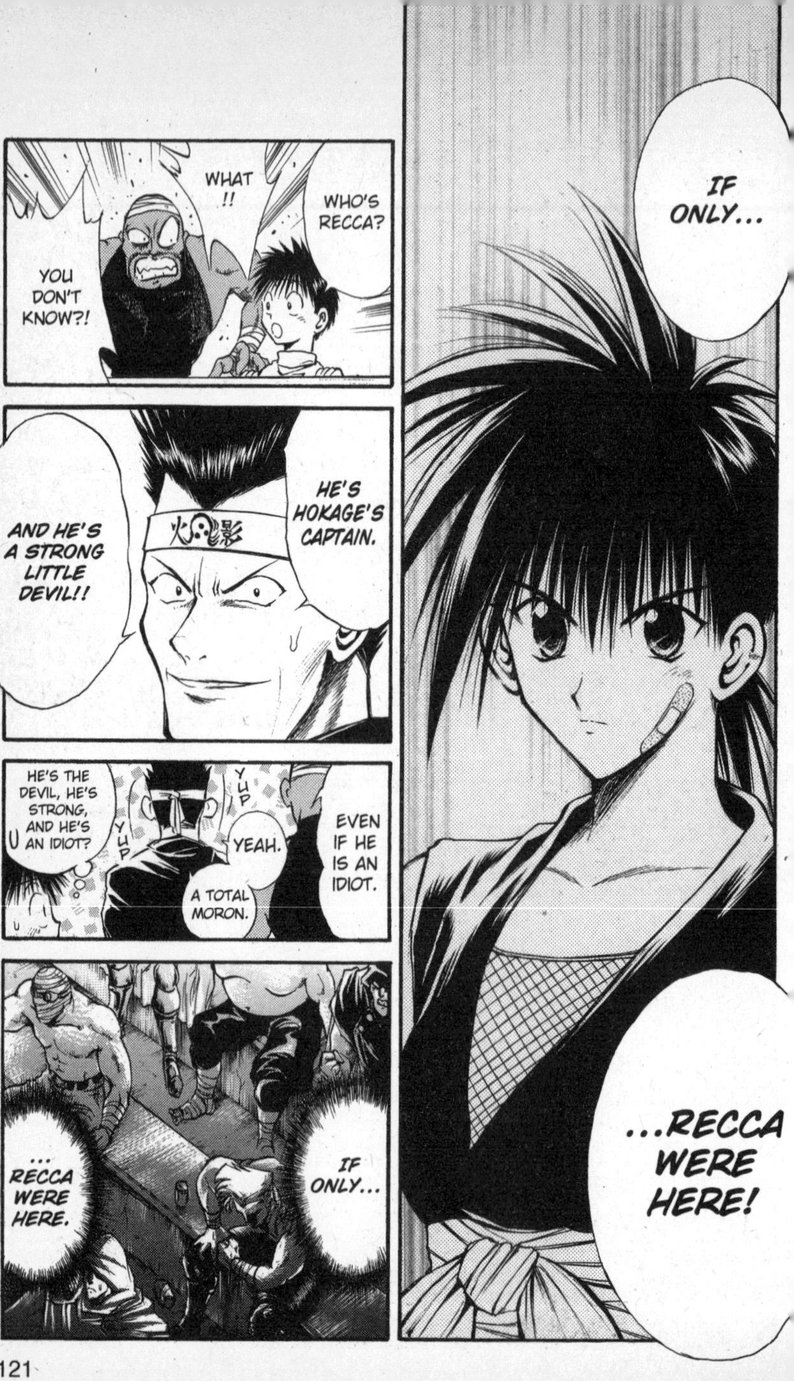
IF ONLY...
...RECCA WERE HERE!
WHO'S RECCA?
WHAT !!
YOU DON'T KNOW?!
HE'S HOKAGE'S CAPTAIN.
AND HE'S A STRONG LITTLE DEVIL!!
EVEN IF HE IS AN IDIOT.
YUP
YEAH.
A TOTAL MORON.
YUP
HE'S THE DEVIL, HE'S STRONG, AND HE'S AN IDIOT?
IF ONLY...
...RECCA WERE HERE.

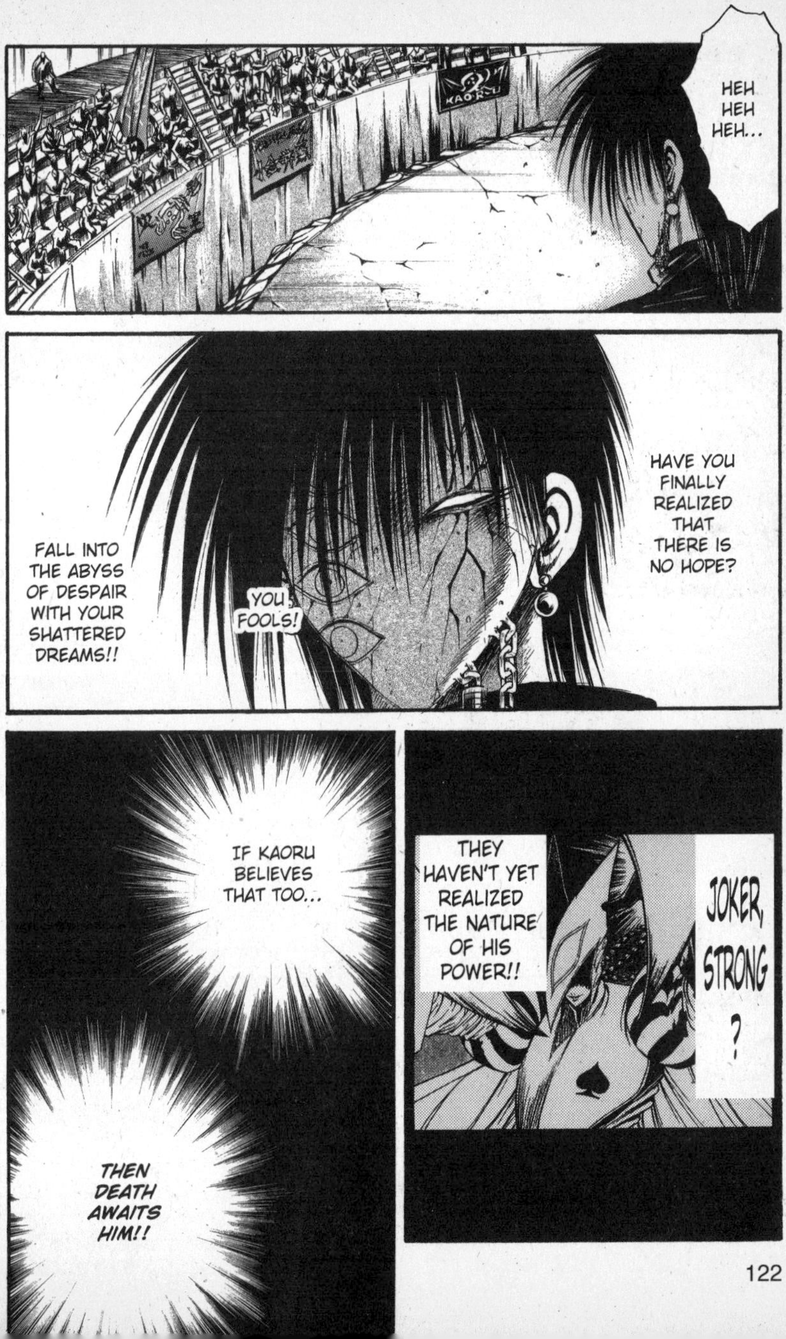
HEH HEH HEH...
HAVE YOU FINALLY REALIZED THAT THERE IS NO HOPE?
YOU FOOLS!
FALL INTO THE ABYSS OF DESPAIR WITH YOUR SHATTERED DREAMS!!
JOKER, STRONG?
THEY HAVEN'T YET REALIZED THE NATURE OF HIS POWER!!
IF KAORU BELIEVES THAT TOO...
THEN DEATH AWAITS HIM!!

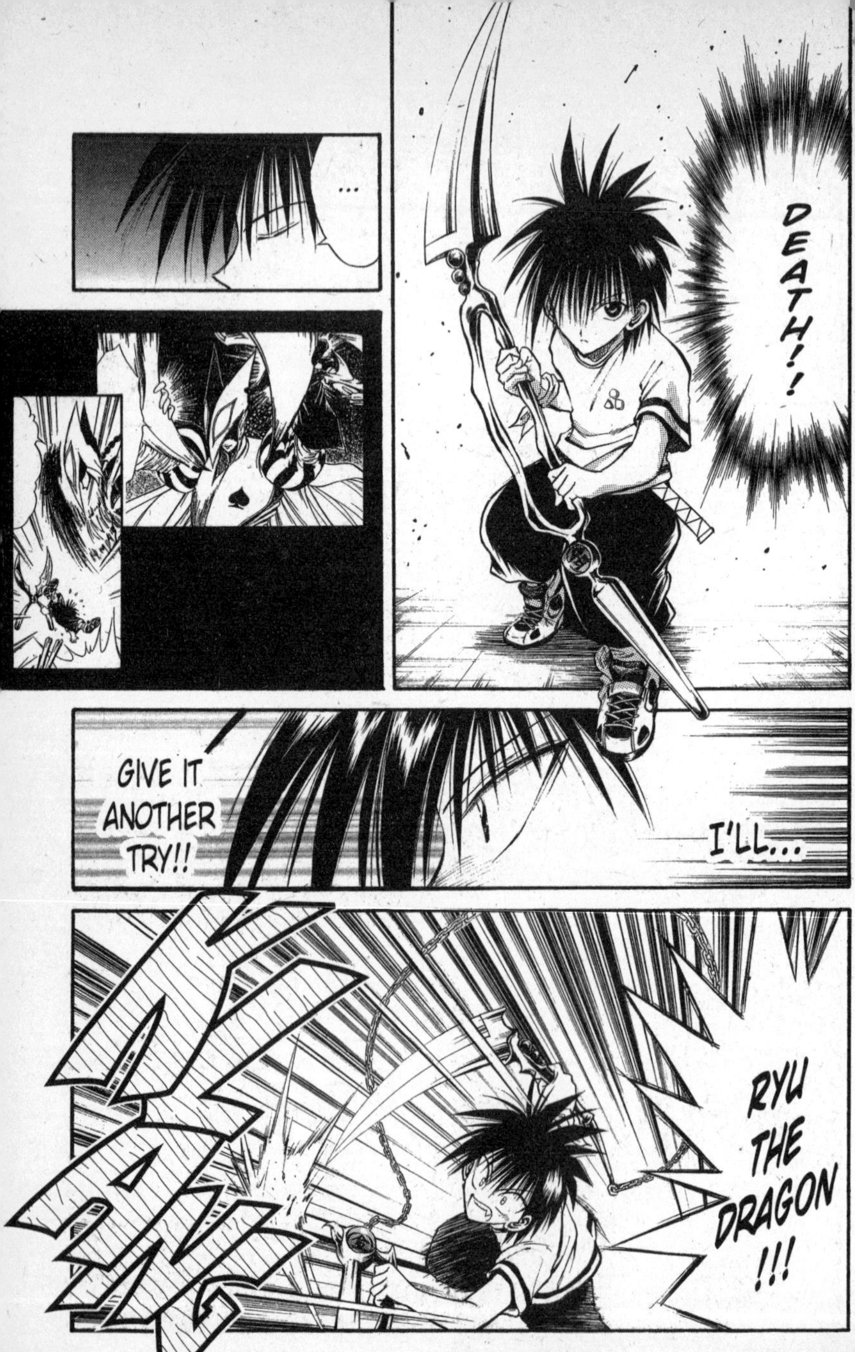
DEATH!!
...
I'LL...
GIVE IT ANOTHER TRY!!
RYU THE DRAGON!!!

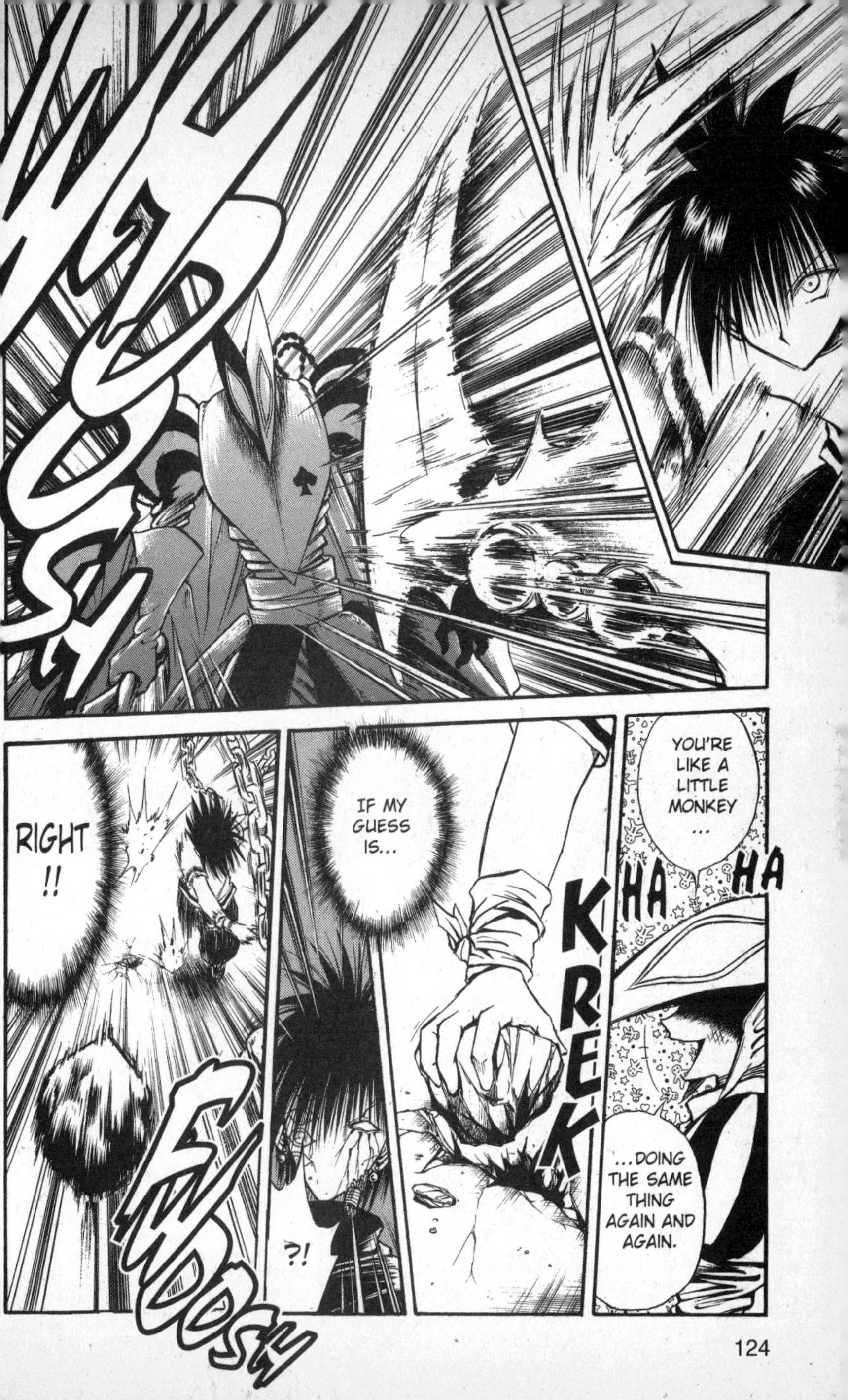
YOU'RE LIKE A LITTLE MONKEY ...
HA HA
...DOING THE SAME THING AGAIN AND AGAIN.
KREK
IF MY GUESS IS...
?!
RIGHT !!
WHOOSH

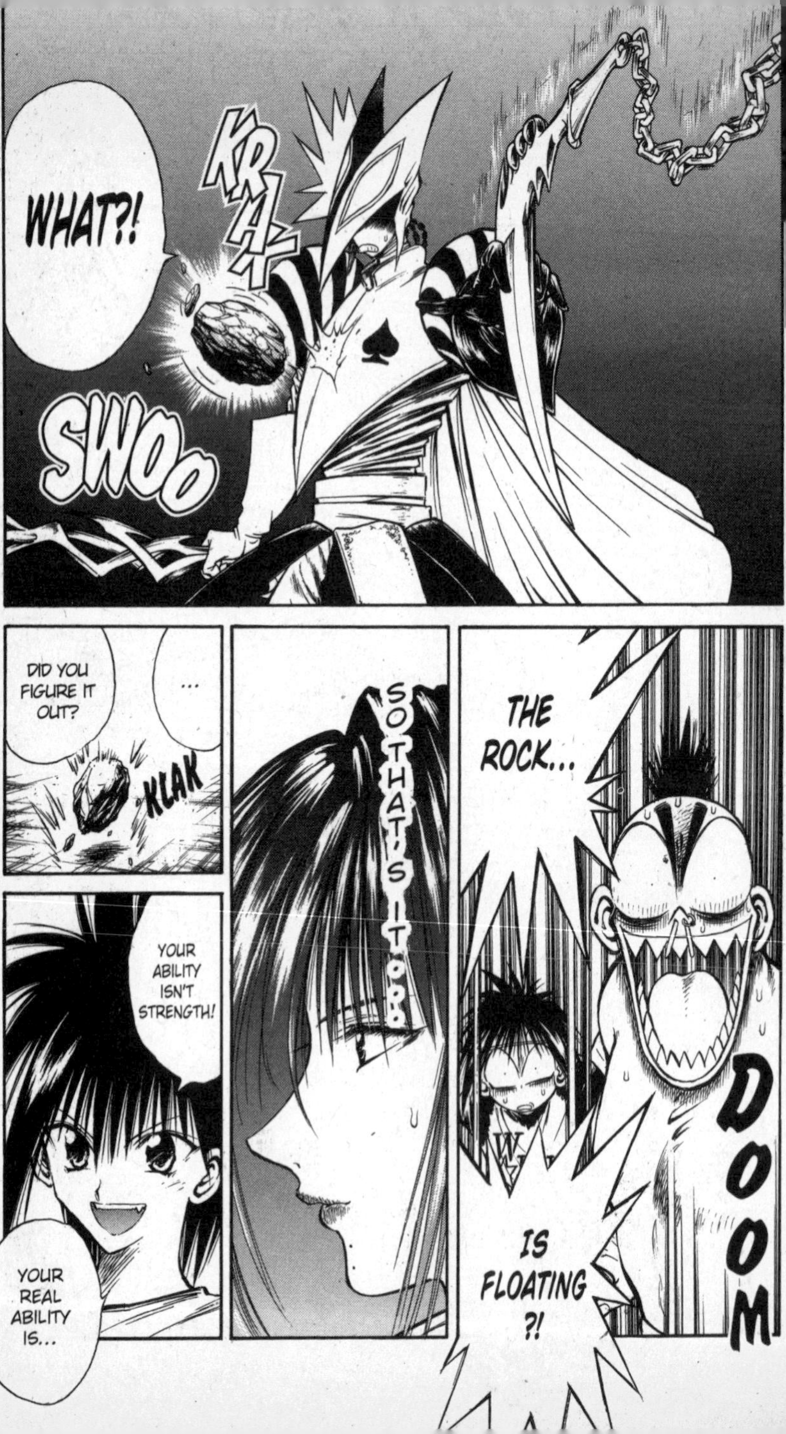
KRAK
WHAT?!
SWOO
THE ROCK...
DOOM
IS FLOATING ?!
SO THAT'S IT...
...
DID YOU FIGURE IT OUT?
KLAK
YOUR ABILITY ISN'T STRENGTH!
YOUR REAL ABILITY IS...

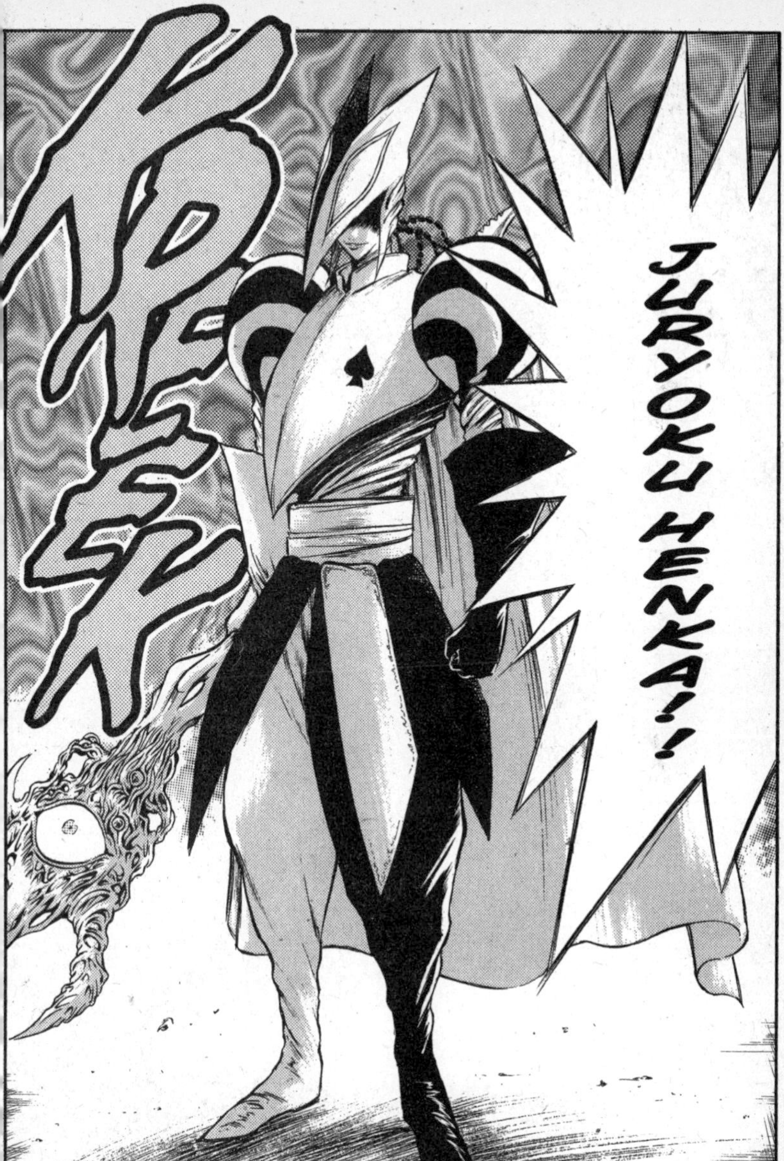
JURYOKU HENKA!!

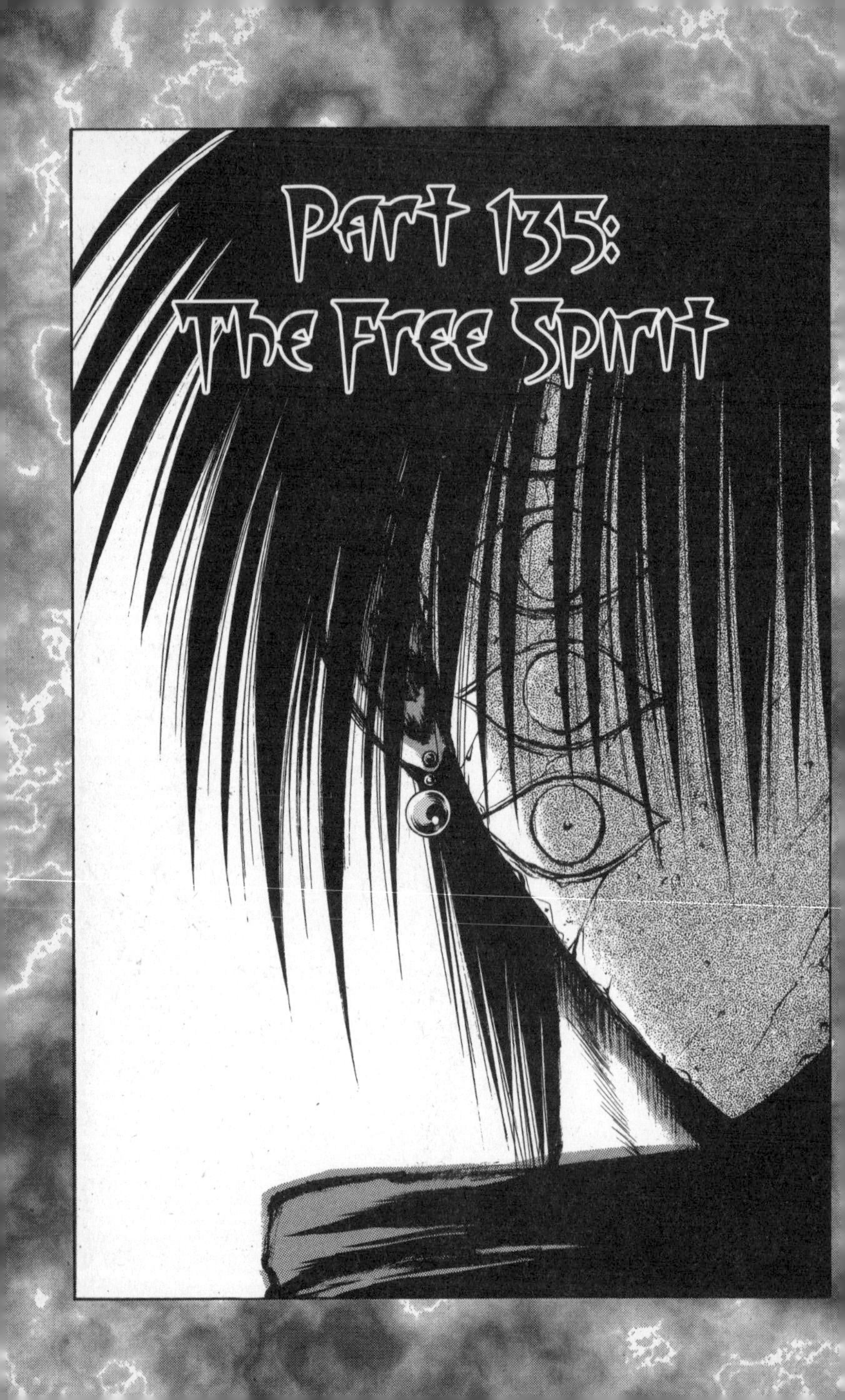
Part 135:
The Free Spirit

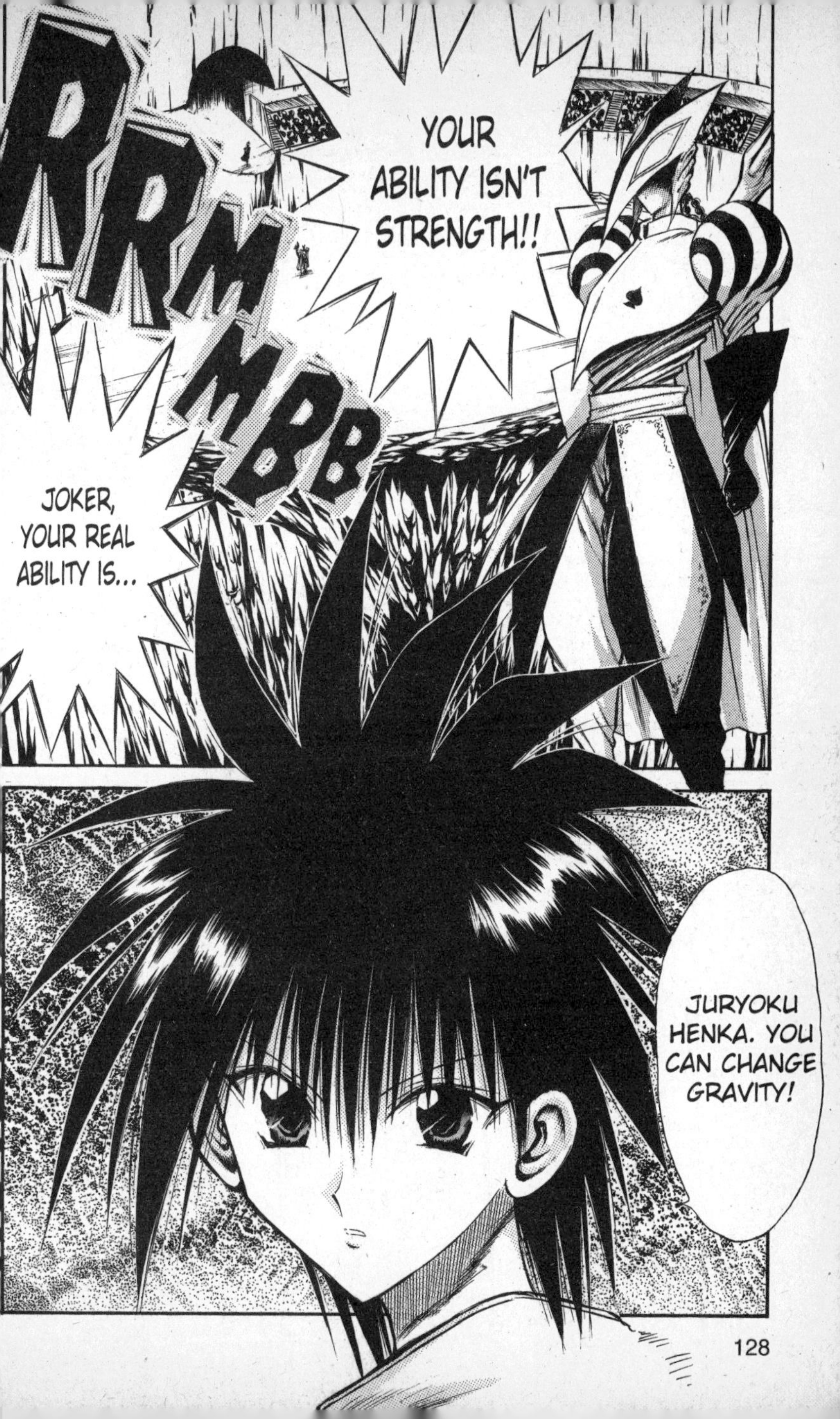
YOUR ABILITY ISN'T STRENGTH!!
RRMMBB
JOKER, YOUR REAL ABILITY IS...
JURYOKU HENKA. YOU CAN CHANGE GRAVITY!

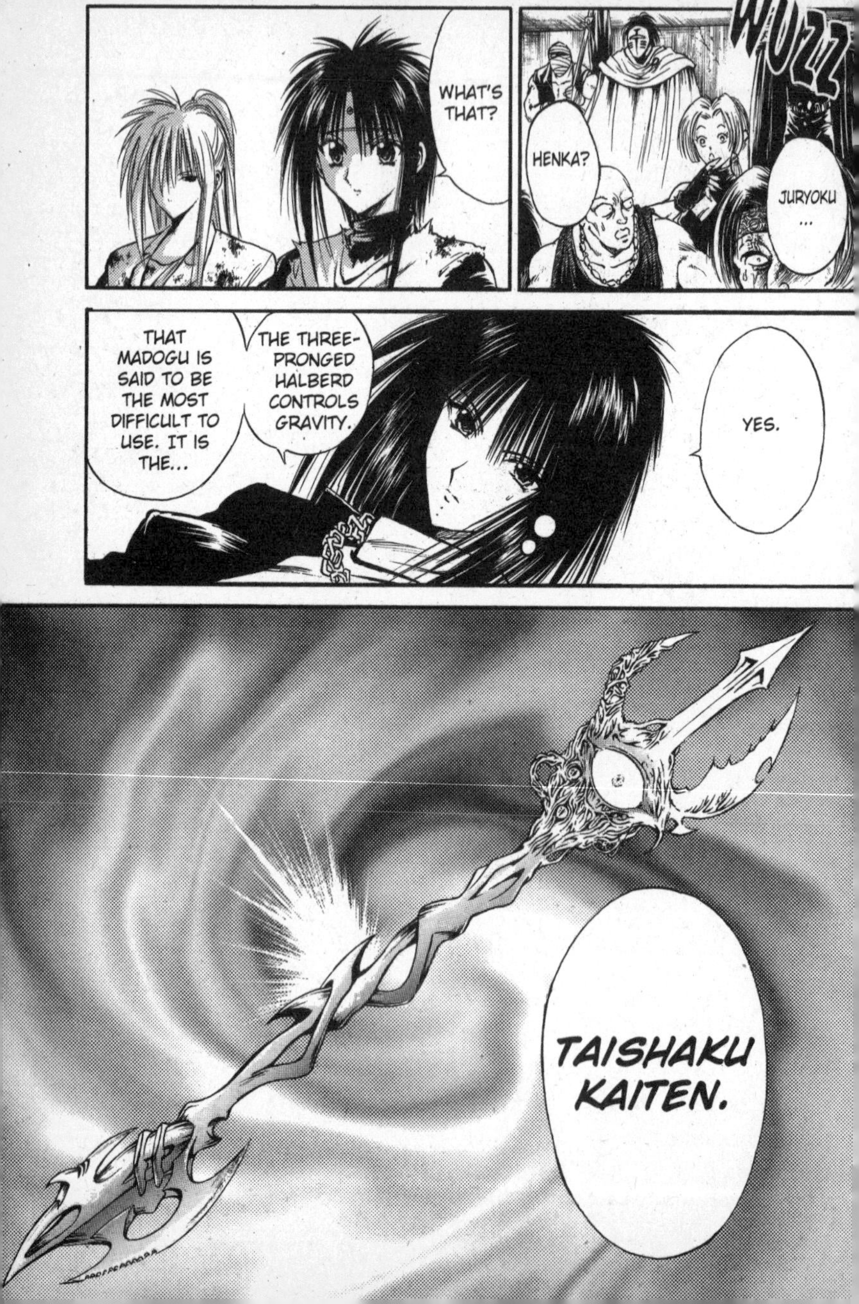
WUZZ
JURYOKU ...
HENKA?
WHAT'S THAT?
YES.
THE THREE-PRONGED HALBERD CONTROLS GRAVITY.
THAT MADOGU IS SAID TO BE THE MOST DIFFICULT TO USE. IT IS THE...
TAISHAKU KAITEN.

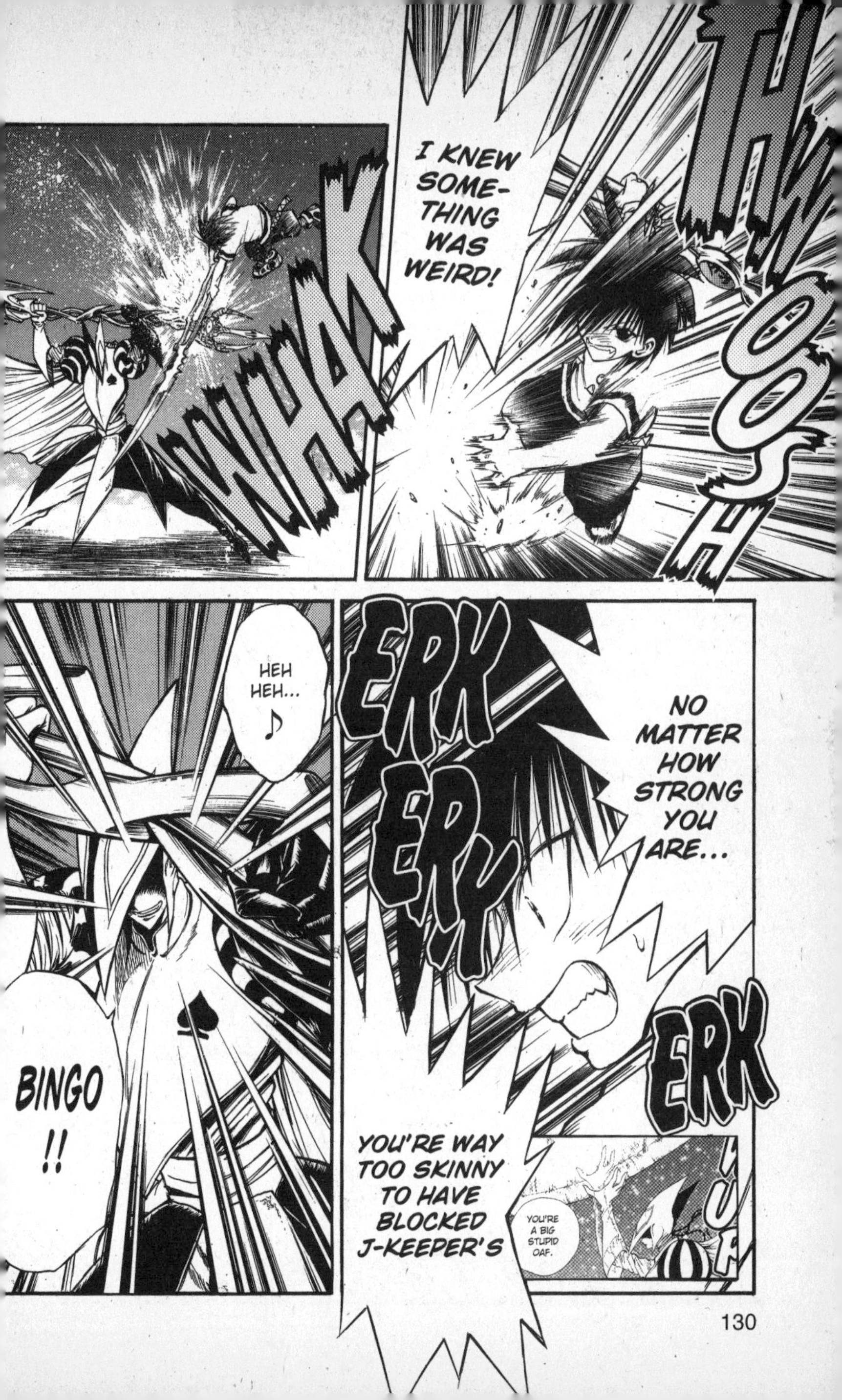
OOOSH
I KNEW SOME-THING WAS WEIRD!
WHAK
ERK
ERK
NO MATTER HOW STRONG YOU ARE...
ERK
YOU'RE WAY TOO SKINNY TO HAVE BLOCKED J-KEEPER'S
YOU'RE A BIG STUPID OAF.
HEH HEH... ♪
BINGO!!

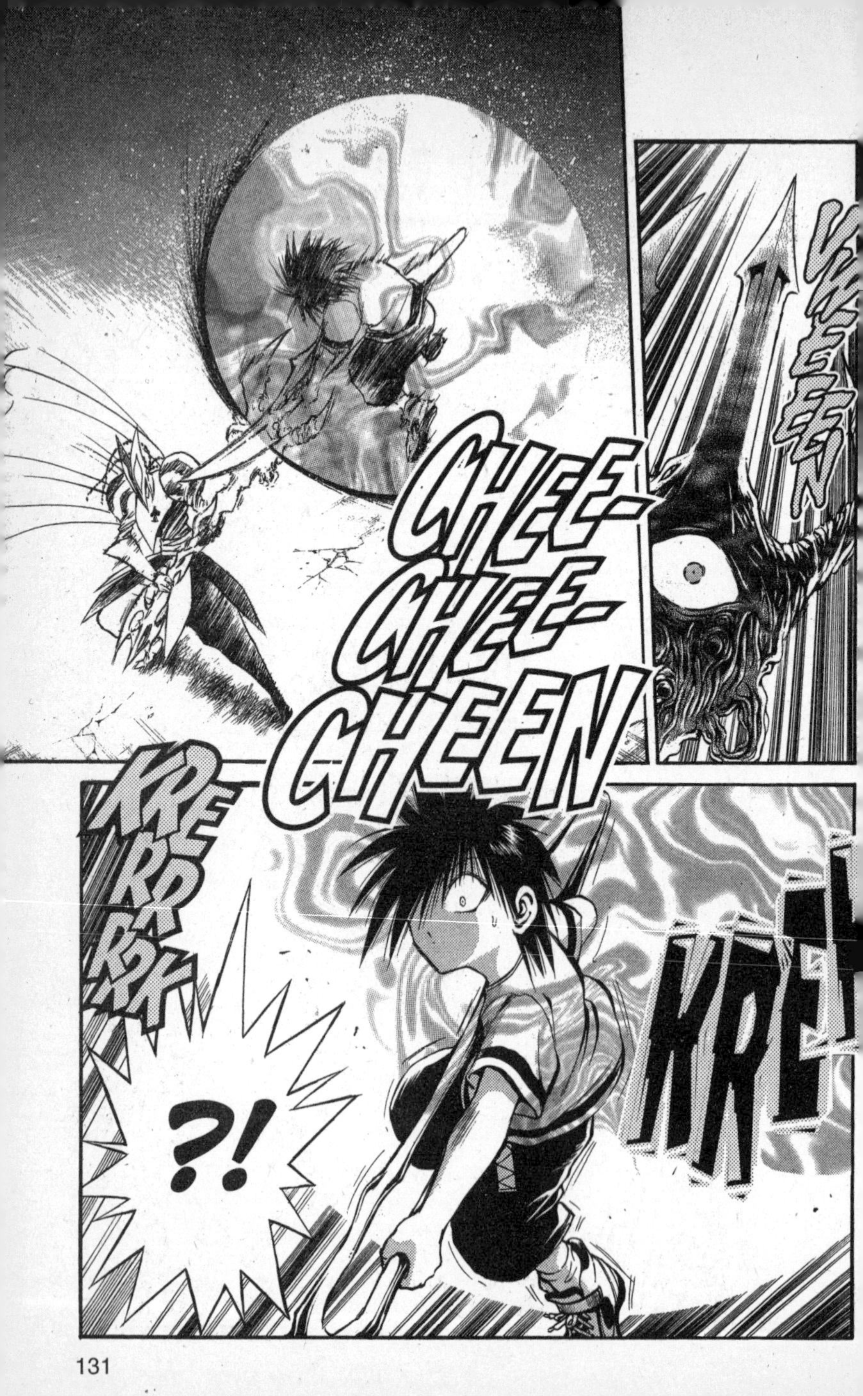
VWEEEEN
CHEE-CHEE-CHEEN
KRE
KRERRRRK
?!

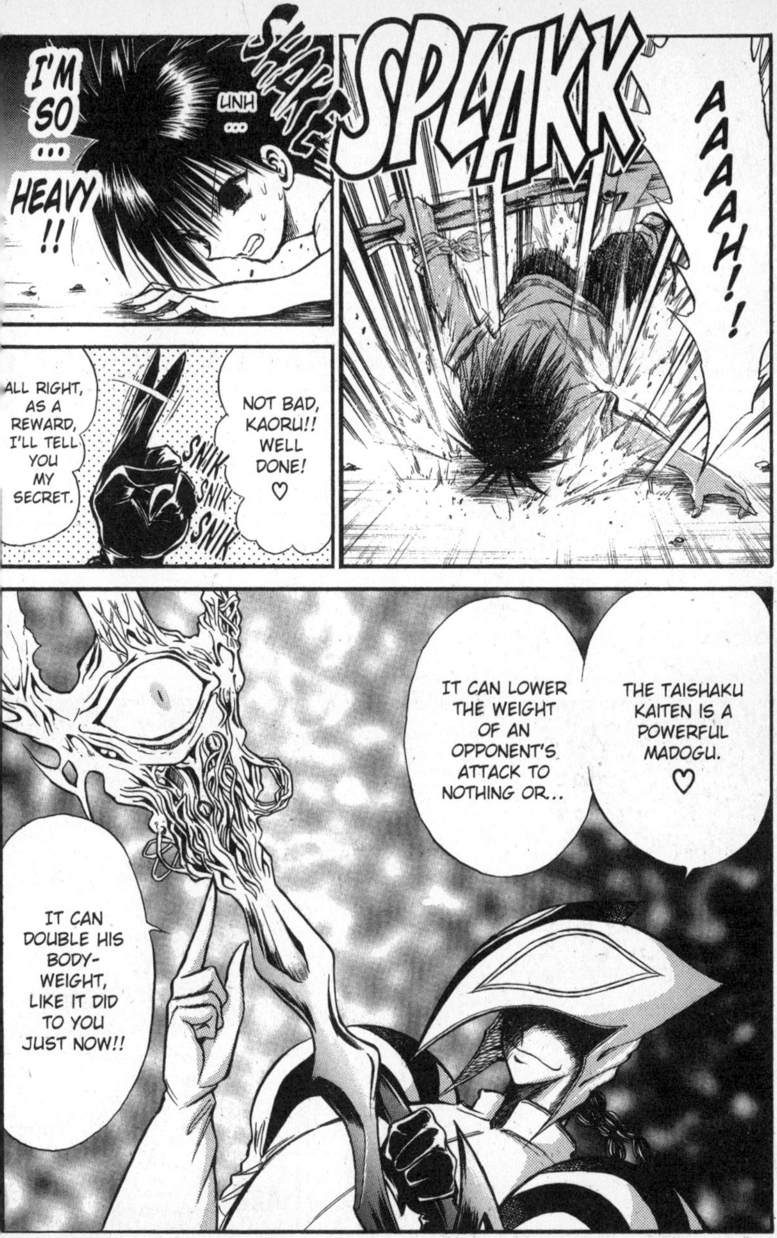
SPLAKK
AAAAAH!!
SHAKE
UNH...
I'M SO... HEAVY!!
NOT BAD, KAORU!! WELL DONE! ♡
SNIK SNIK SNIK
ALL RIGHT, AS A REWARD, I'LL TELL YOU MY SECRET.
THE TAISHAKU KAITEN IS A POWERFUL MADOGU. ♡
IT CAN LOWER THE WEIGHT OF AN OPPONENT'S ATTACK TO NOTHING OR...
IT CAN DOUBLE HIS BODY-WEIGHT, LIKE IT DID TO YOU JUST NOW!!

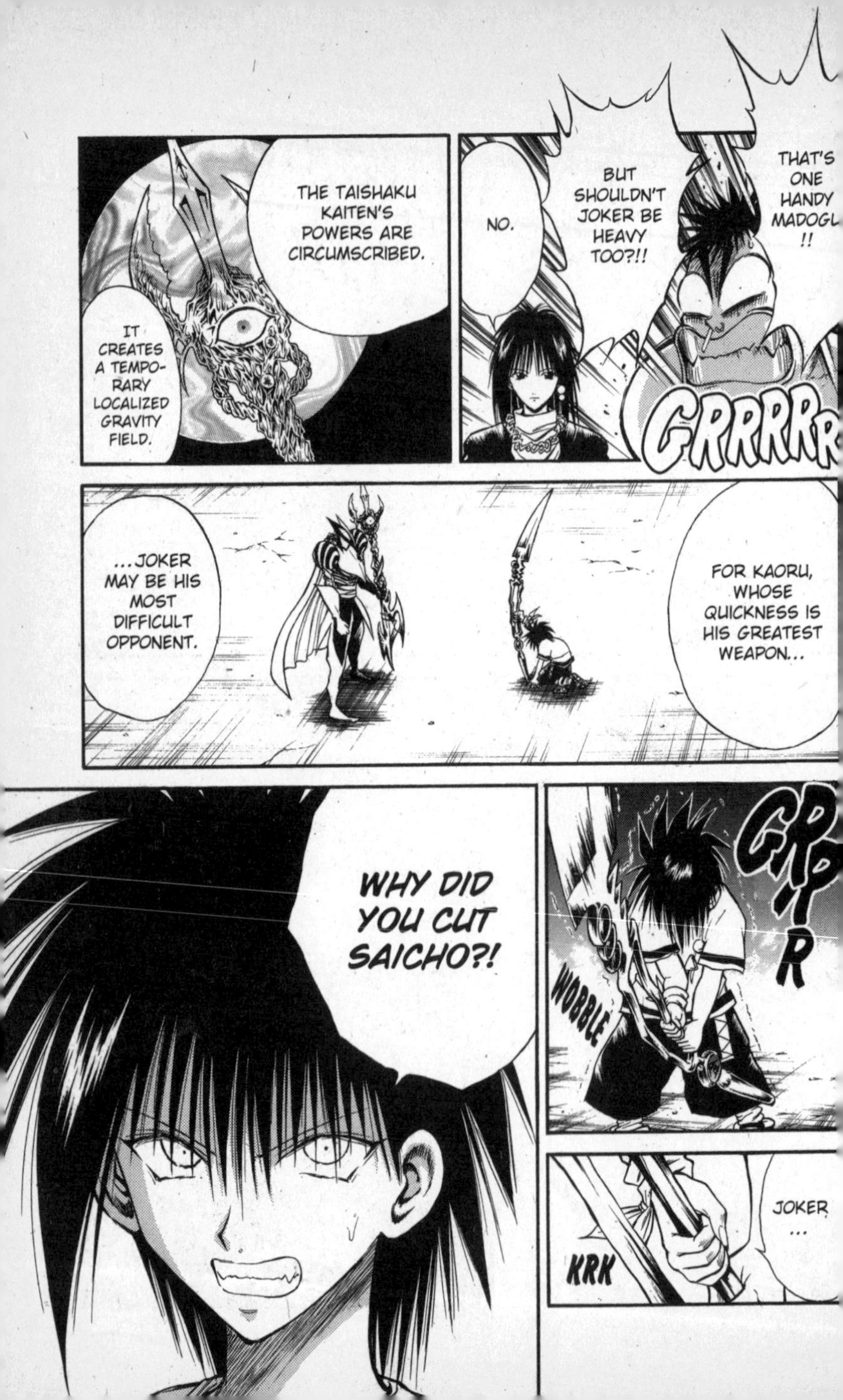
THAT'S ONE HANDY MADOGL !!
BUT SHOULDN'T JOKER BE HEAVY TOO?!!
NO.
GRRRRR
THE TAISHAKU KAITEN'S POWERS ARE CIRCUMSCRIBED.
IT CREATES A TEMPORARY LOCALIZED GRAVITY FIELD.
FOR KAORU, WHOSE QUICKNESS IS HIS GREATEST WEAPON...
...JOKER MAY BE HIS MOST DIFFICULT OPPONENT.
GRRR
WOBBLE
JOKER ...
KRK
WHY DID YOU CUT SAICHO?!

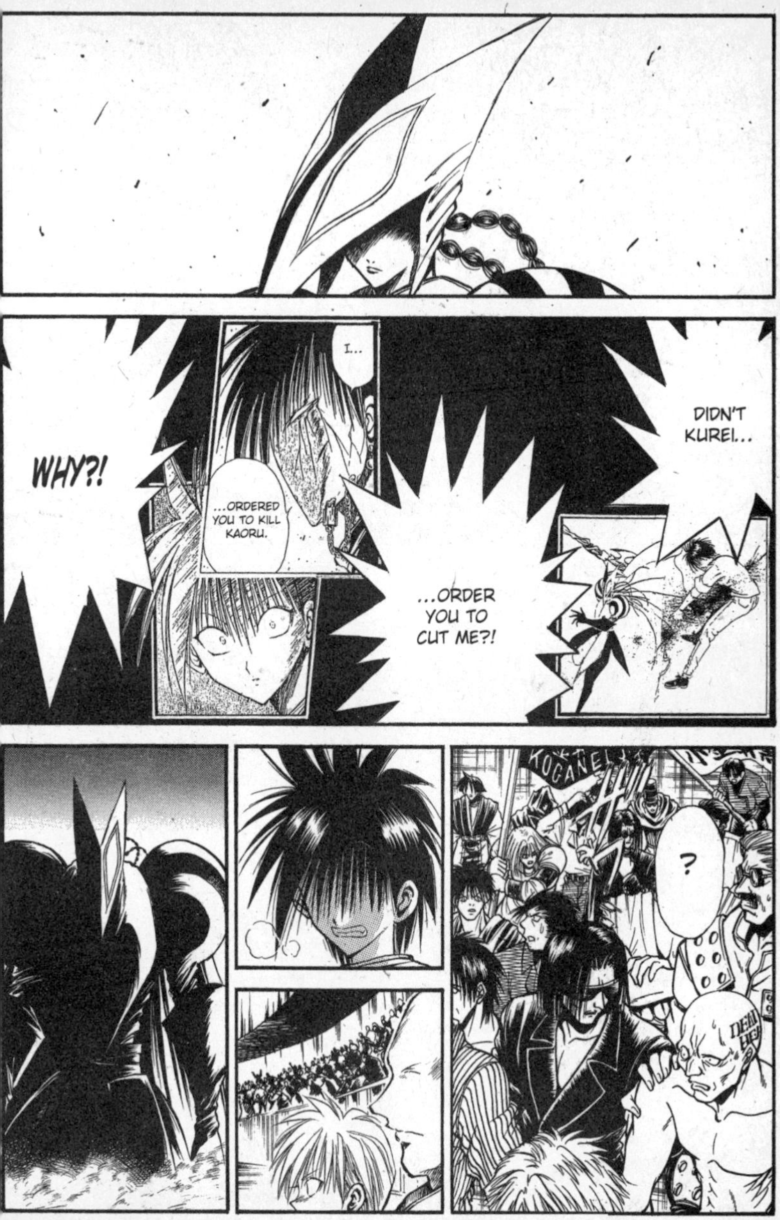
DIDN'T KUREI...
...ORDER YOU TO CUT ME?!
I...
...ORDERED YOU TO KILL KAORU.
WHY?!
KOGANEI
?

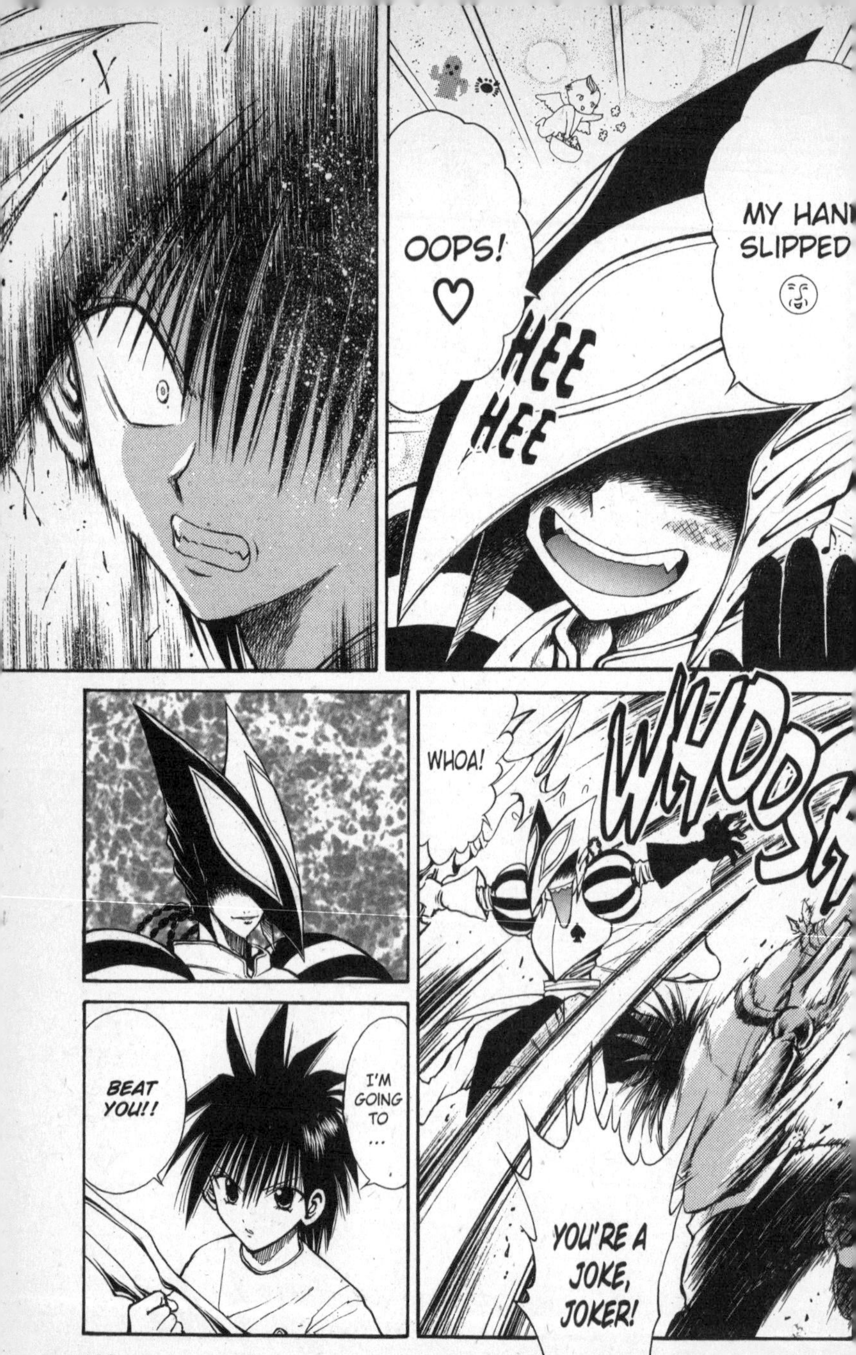

MY HAN
SLIPPED
OOPS! ♡
HEE HEE
WHOOS
WHOA!
YOU'RE A JOKE, JOKER!
I'M GOING TO ...
BEAT YOU!!

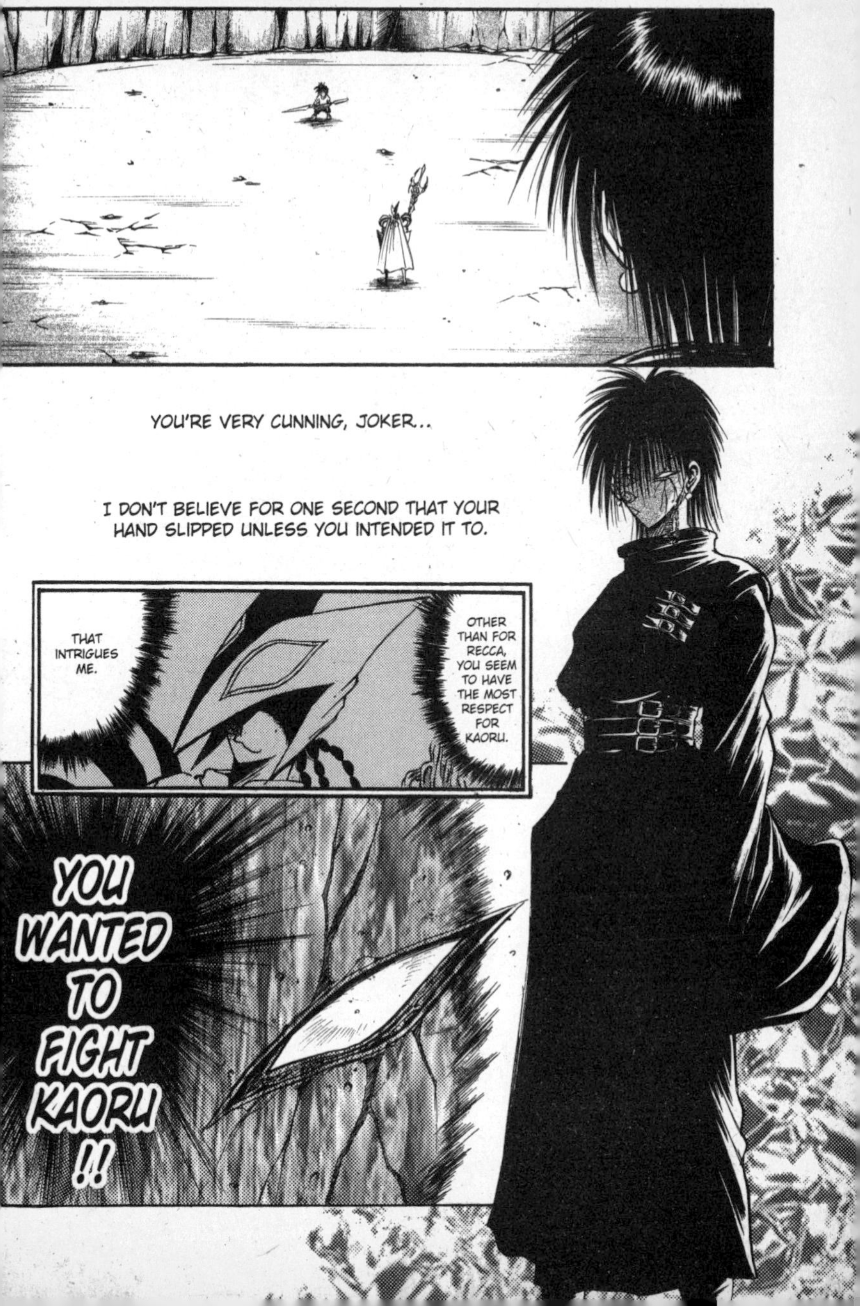
YOU'RE VERY CUNNING, JOKER...
I DON'T BELIEVE FOR ONE SECOND THAT YOUR HAND SLIPPED UNLESS YOU INTENDED IT TO.
OTHER THAN FOR RECCA, YOU SEEM TO HAVE THE MOST RESPECT FOR KAORU.
THAT INTRIGUES ME.
YOU WANTED TO FIGHT KAORU!!

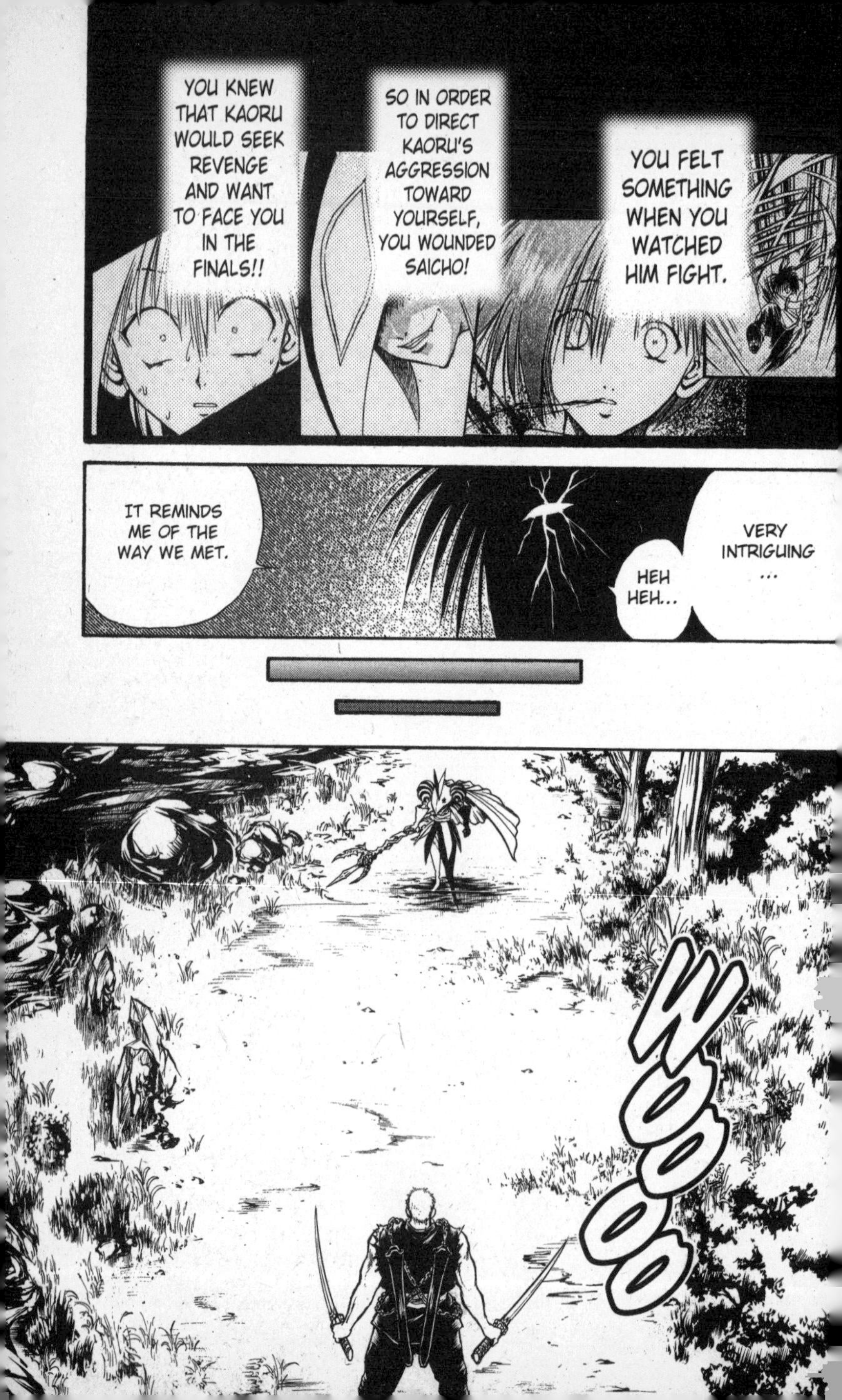
YOU FELT SOMETHING WHEN YOU WATCHED HIM FIGHT.
SO IN ORDER TO DIRECT KAORU'S AGGRESSION TOWARD YOURSELF, YOU WOUNDED SAICHO!
YOU KNEW THAT KAORU WOULD SEEK REVENGE AND WANT TO FACE YOU IN THE FINALS!!
VERY INTRIGUING ...
HEH HEH...
IT REMINDS ME OF THE WAY WE MET.
WHOOOOO

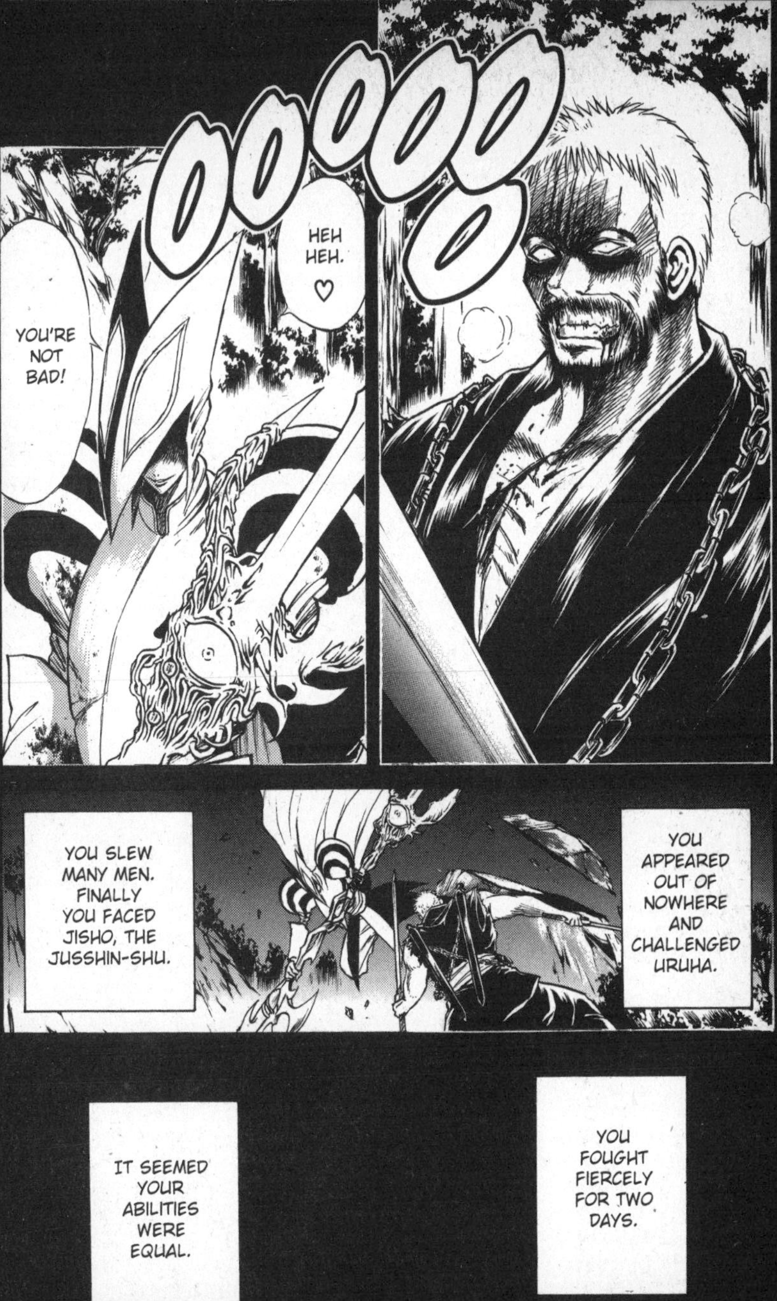
HEH HEH. ♡
YOU'RE NOT BAD!
YOU APPEARED OUT OF NOWHERE AND CHALLENGED URUHA.
YOU SLEW MANY MEN. FINALLY YOU FACED JISHO, THE JUSSHIN-SHU.
YOU FOUGHT FIERCELY FOR TWO DAYS.
IT SEEMED YOUR ABILITIES WERE EQUAL.

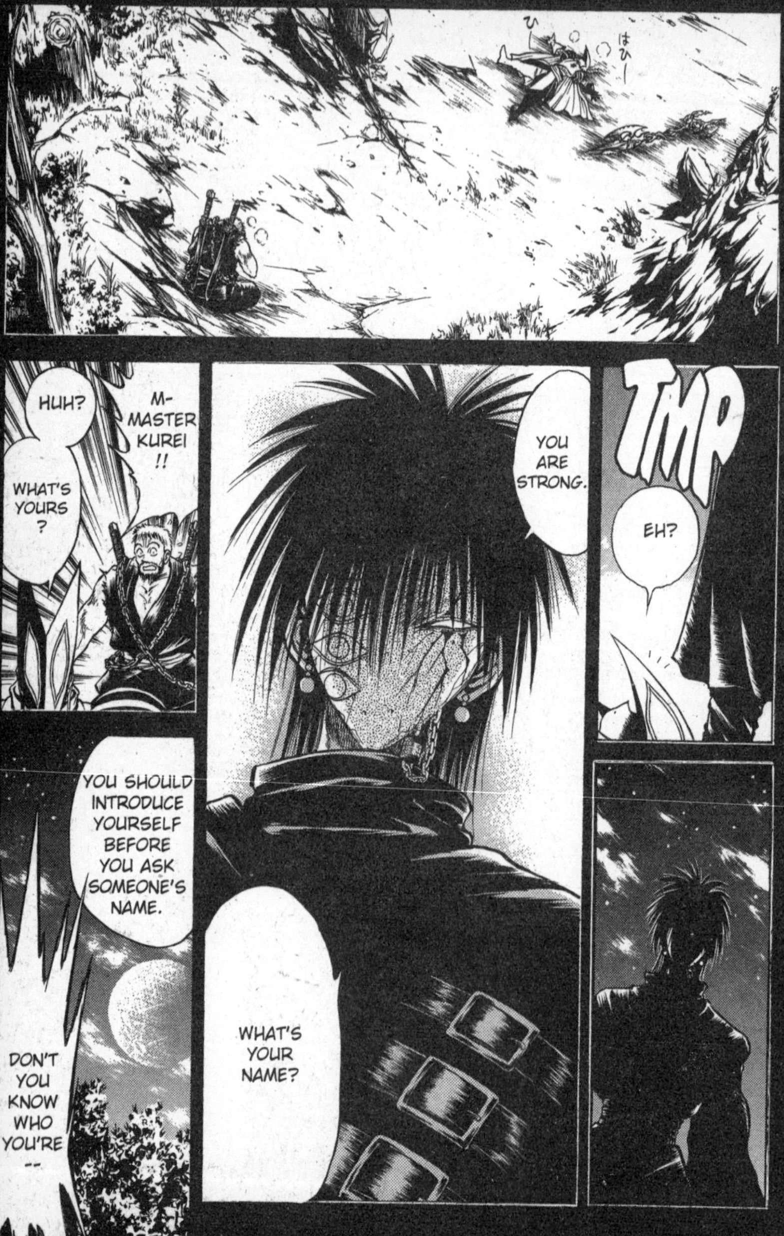
はひー
ひー
TMP
EH?
YOU ARE STRONG.
WHAT'S YOUR NAME?
M-MASTER KUREI !!
HUH?
WHAT'S YOURS ?
YOU SHOULD INTRODUCE YOURSELF BEFORE YOU ASK SOMEONE'S NAME.
DON'T YOU KNOW WHO YOU'RE --

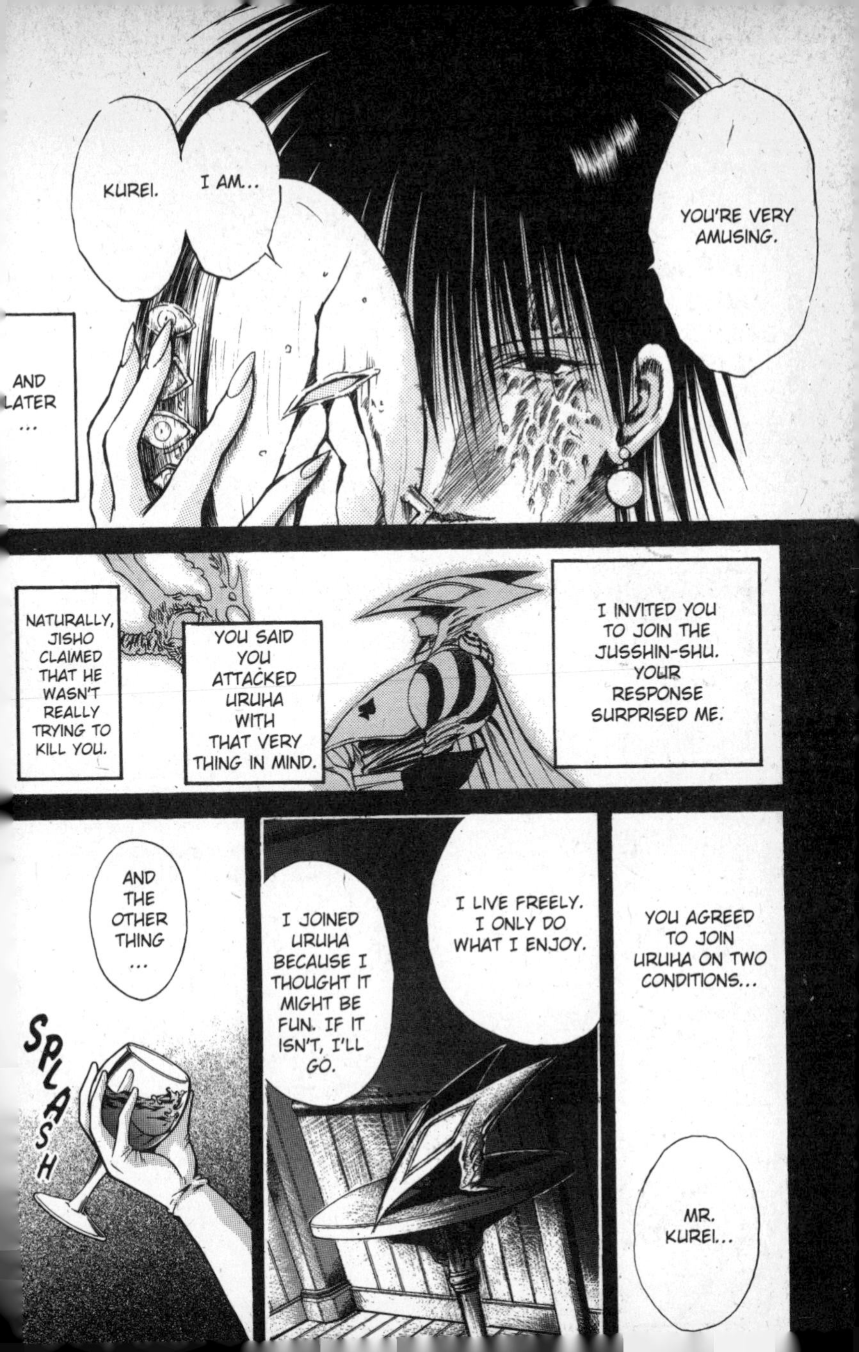
YOU'RE VERY AMUSING.
I AM...
KUREI.
AND LATER ...
I INVITED YOU TO JOIN THE JUSSHIN-SHU. YOUR RESPONSE SURPRISED ME.
YOU SAID YOU ATTACKED URUHA WITH THAT VERY THING IN MIND.
NATURALLY, JISHO CLAIMED THAT HE WASN'T REALLY TRYING TO KILL YOU.
YOU AGREED TO JOIN URUHA ON TWO CONDITIONS...
MR. KUREI...
I LIVE FREELY. I ONLY DO WHAT I ENJOY.
I JOINED URUHA BECAUSE I THOUGHT IT MIGHT BE FUN. IF IT ISN'T, I'LL GO.
AND THE OTHER THING ...
SPLASH

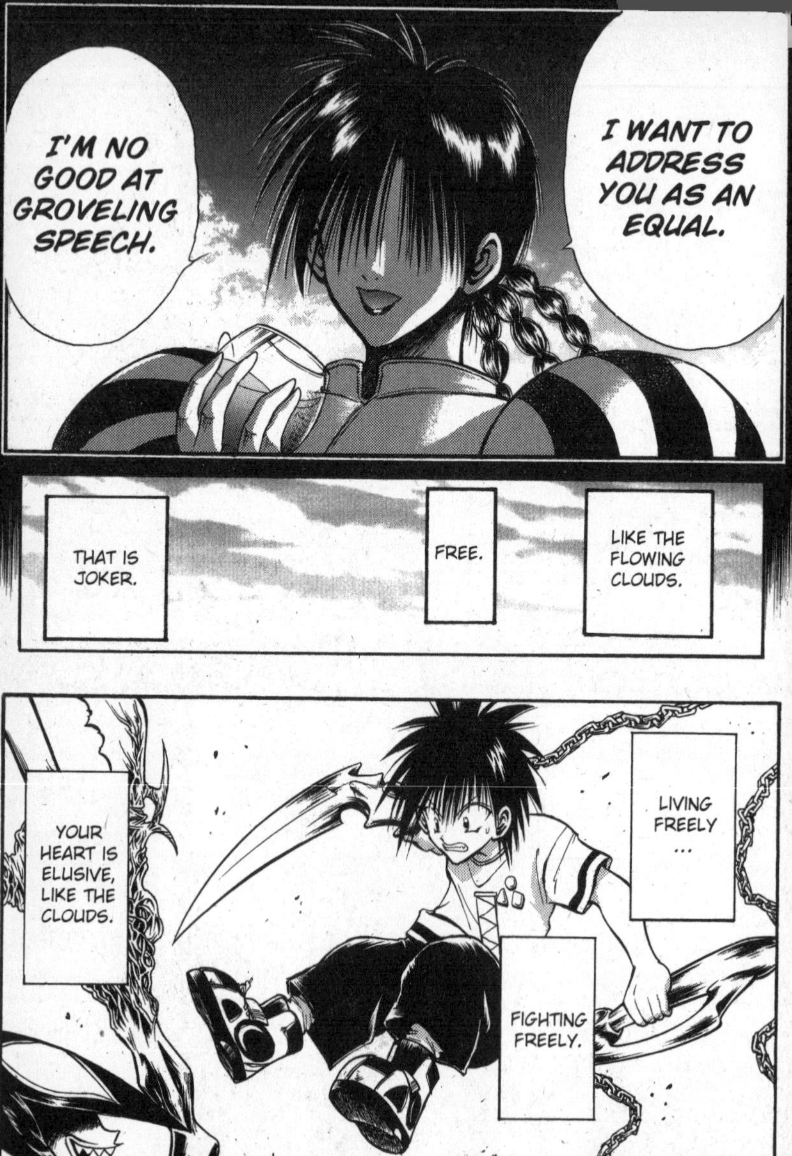

I WANT TO ADDRESS YOU AS AN EQUAL.
I'M NO GOOD AT GROVELING SPEECH.
LIKE THE FLOWING CLOUDS.
FREE.
THAT IS JOKER.
LIVING FREELY ...
FIGHTING FREELY.
YOUR HEART IS ELUSIVE, LIKE THE CLOUDS.

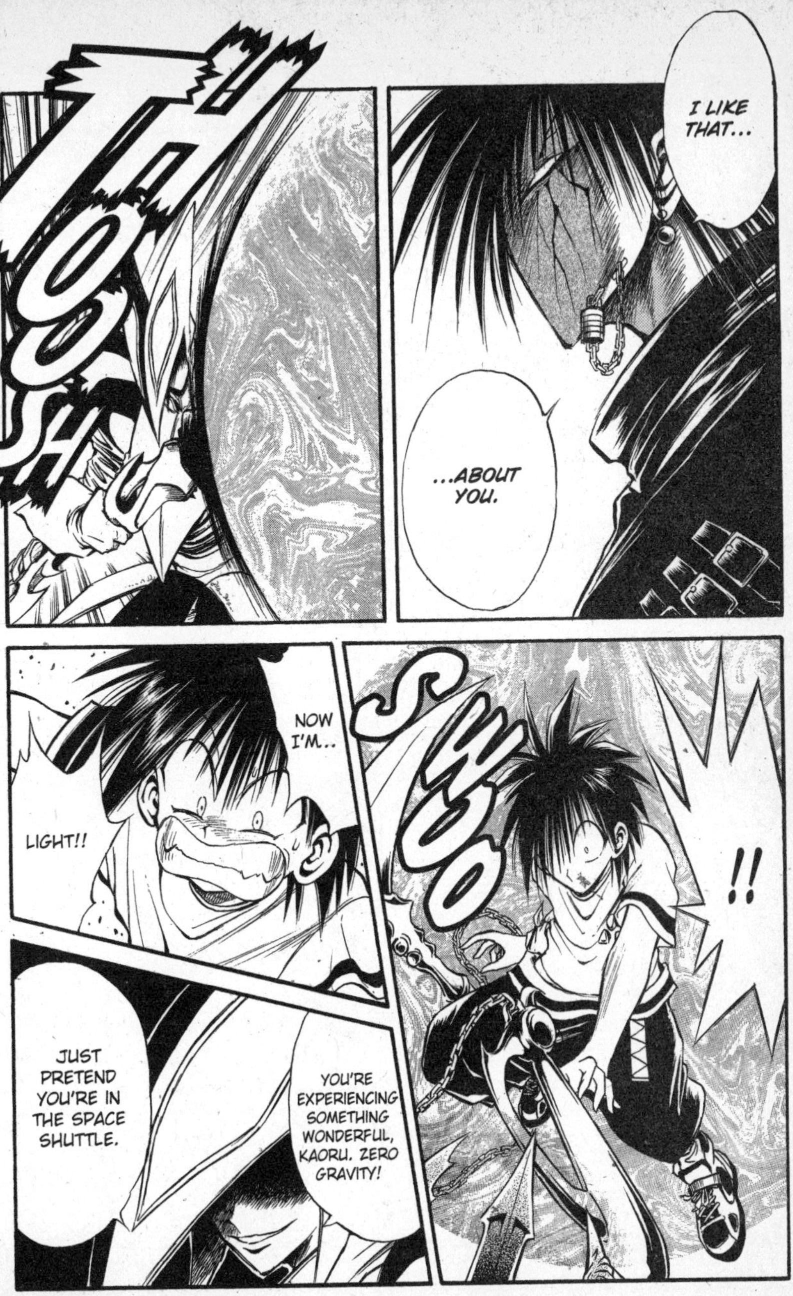
I LIKE THAT...
...ABOUT YOU.
!!
NOW I'M...
LIGHT!!
YOU'RE EXPERIENCING SOMETHING WONDERFUL, KAORU. ZERO GRAVITY!
JUST PRETEND YOU'RE IN THE SPACE SHUTTLE.

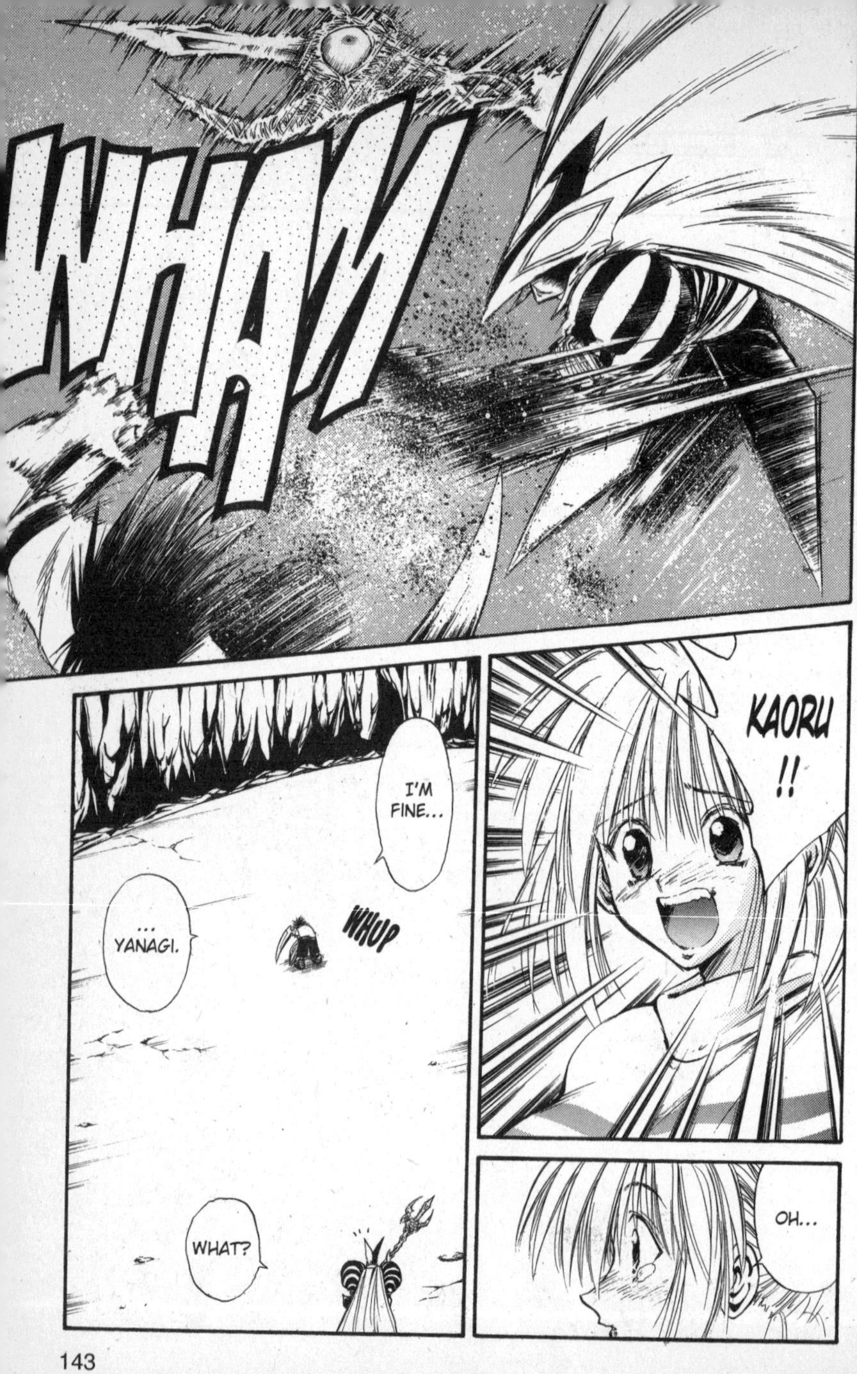
WHAM
KAORU !!
OH...
I'M FINE...
WHUP
... YANAGI.
WHAT?

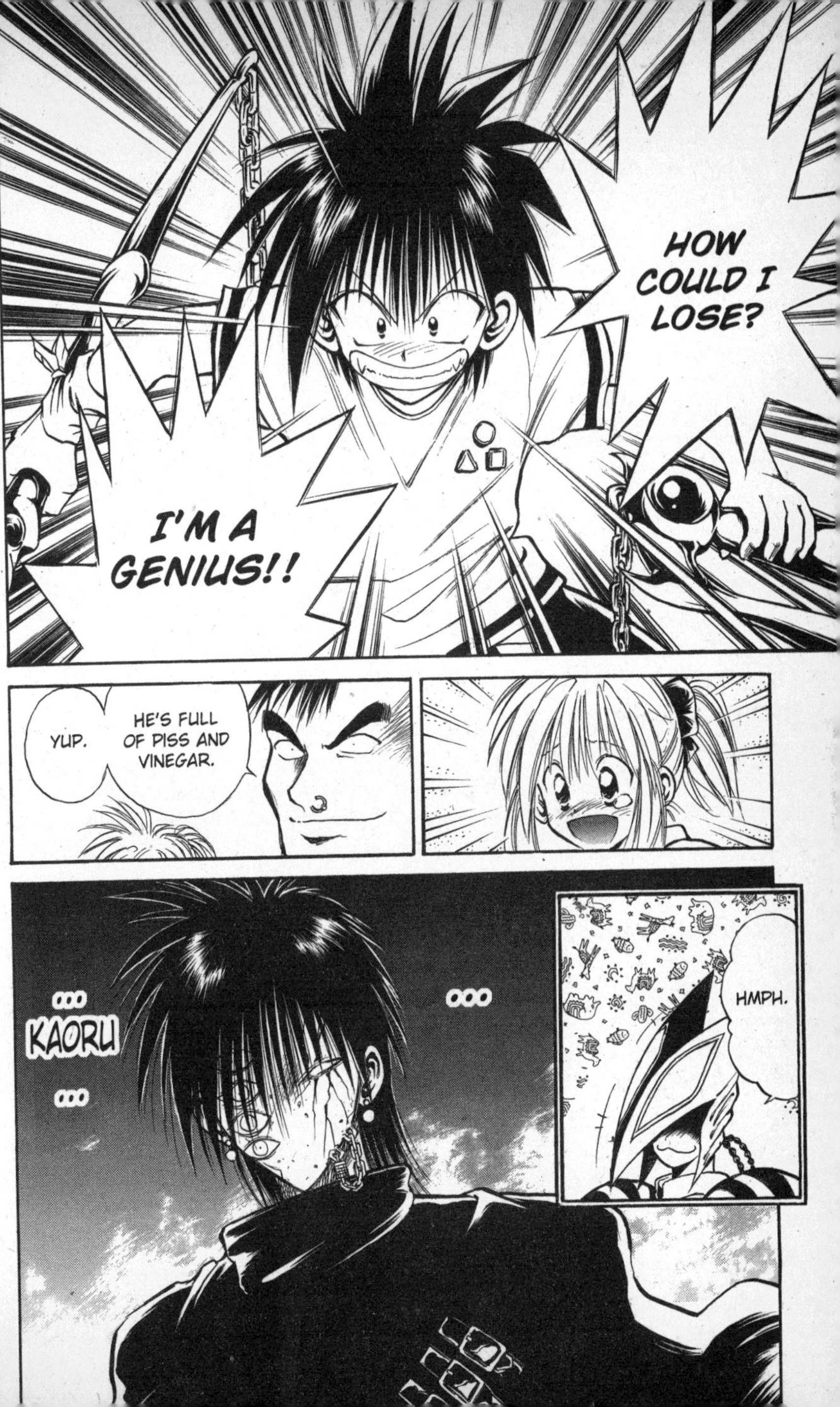
HOW COULD I LOSE?
I'M A GENIUS!!
HE'S FULL OF PISS AND VINEGAR.
YUP.
HMPH.
...
... KAORU ...

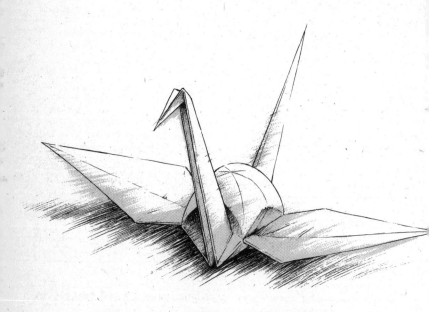

Part 136:
The Savior

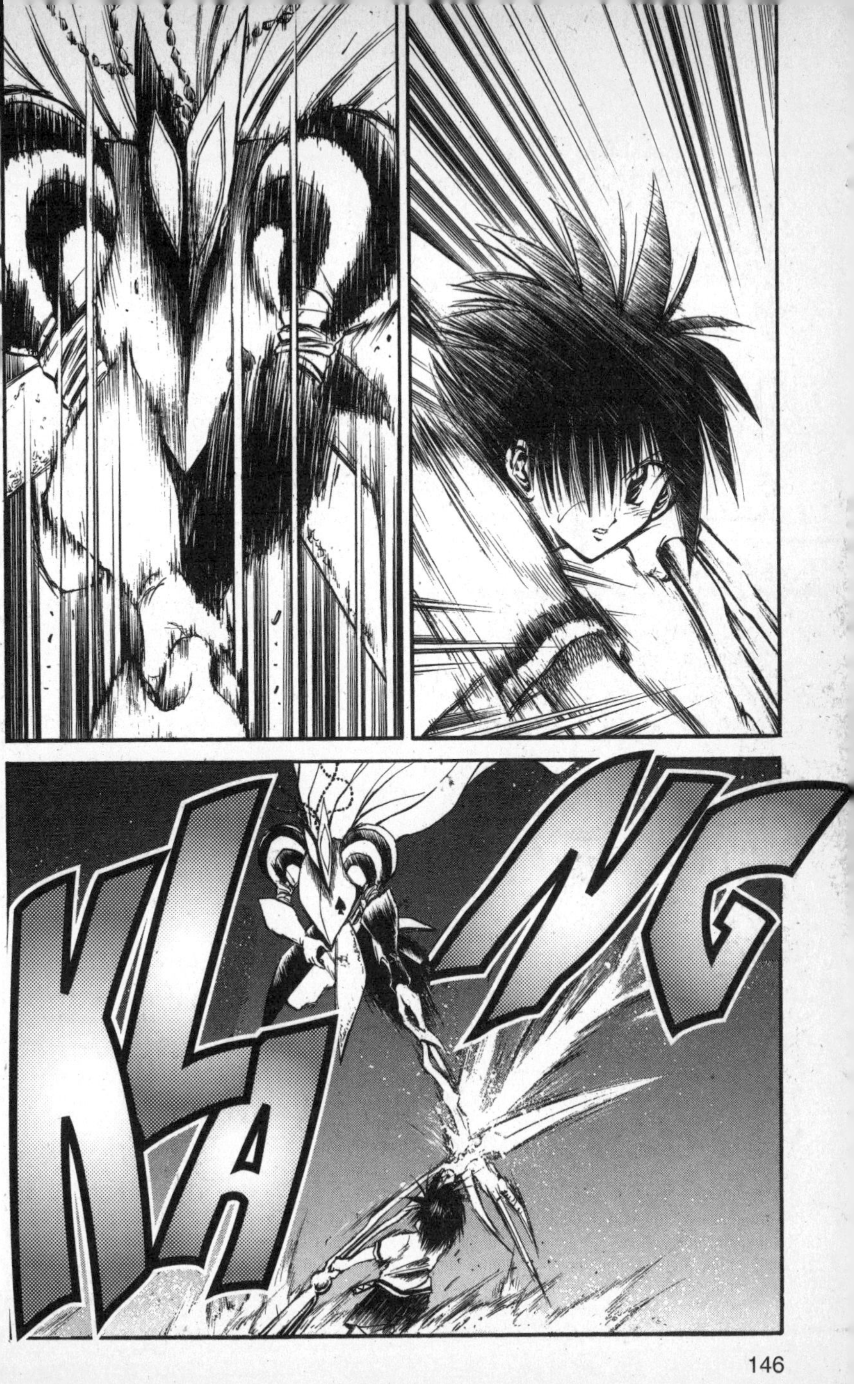
KLANG

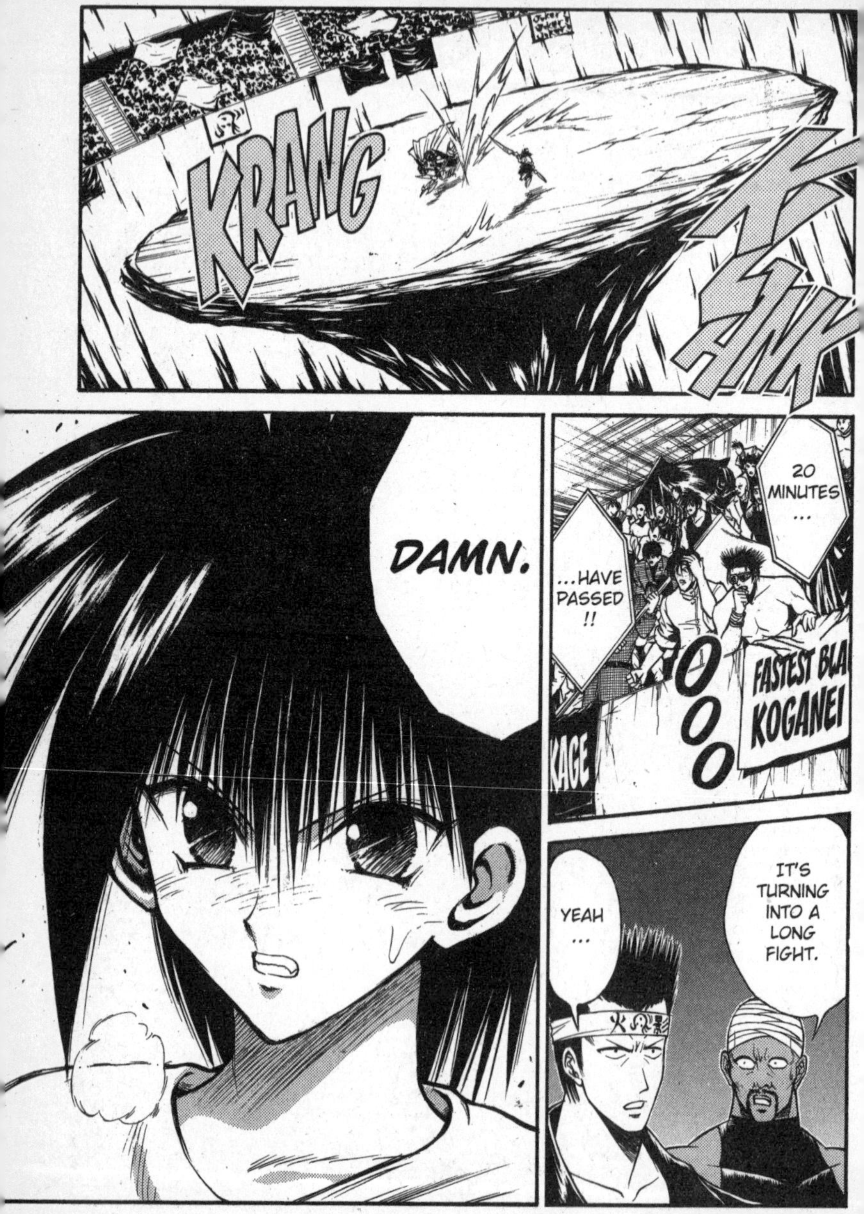
KSHANK
KRANG
20 MINUTES ...
...HAVE PASSED !!
OOOO
FASTEST BLA
KOGANEI
KAGE
IT'S TURNING INTO A LONG FIGHT.
YEAH ...
DAMN.

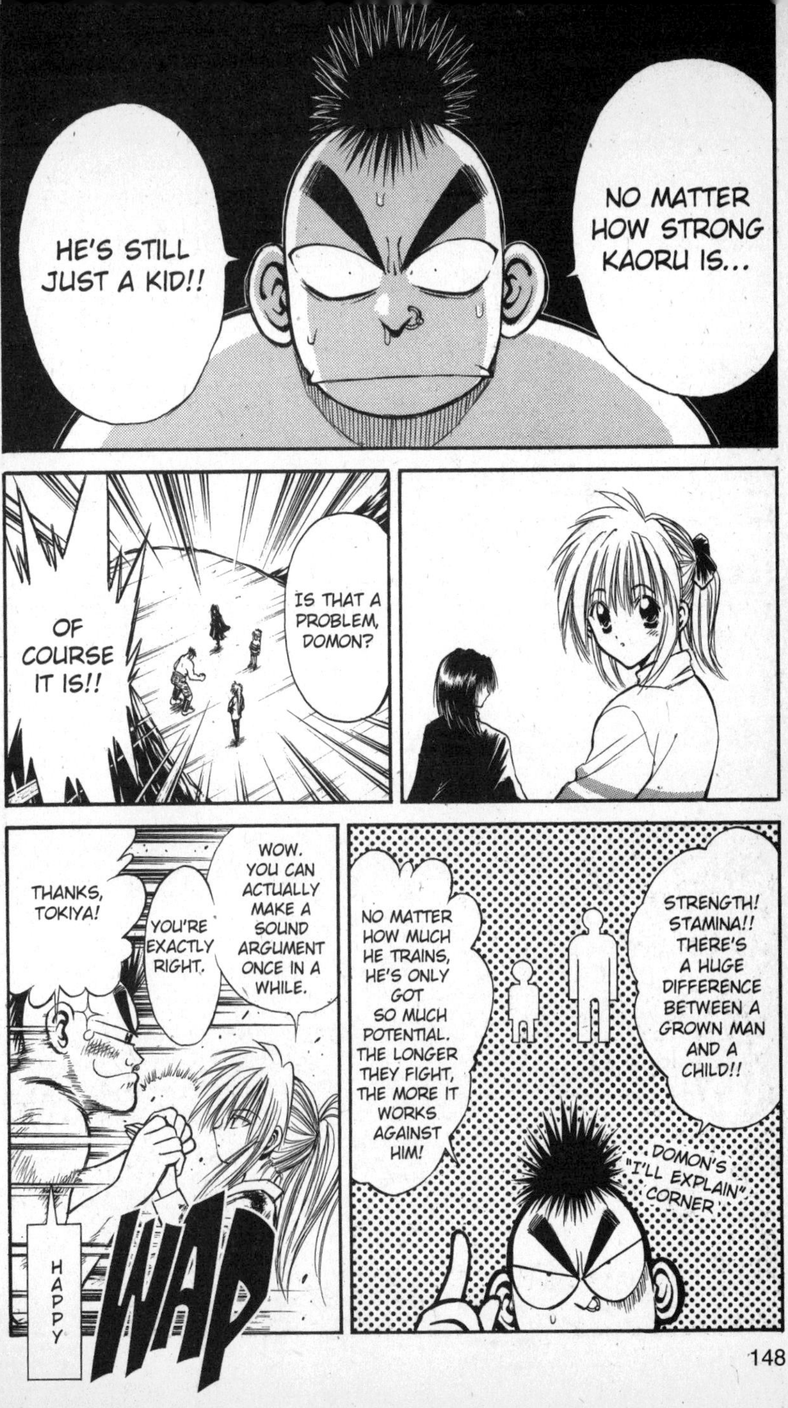
NO MATTER HOW STRONG KAORU IS...
HE'S STILL JUST A KID!!
IS THAT A PROBLEM, DOMON?
OF COURSE IT IS!!
STRENGTH! STAMINA!! THERE'S A HUGE DIFFERENCE BETWEEN A GROWN MAN AND A CHILD!!
NO MATTER HOW MUCH HE TRAINS, HE'S ONLY GOT SO MUCH POTENTIAL. THE LONGER THEY FIGHT, THE MORE IT WORKS AGAINST HIM!
DOMON'S "I'LL EXPLAIN" CORNER
WOW. YOU CAN ACTUALLY MAKE A SOUND ARGUMENT ONCE IN A WHILE.
YOU'RE EXACTLY RIGHT.
THANKS, TOKIYA!
HAPPY
WAP

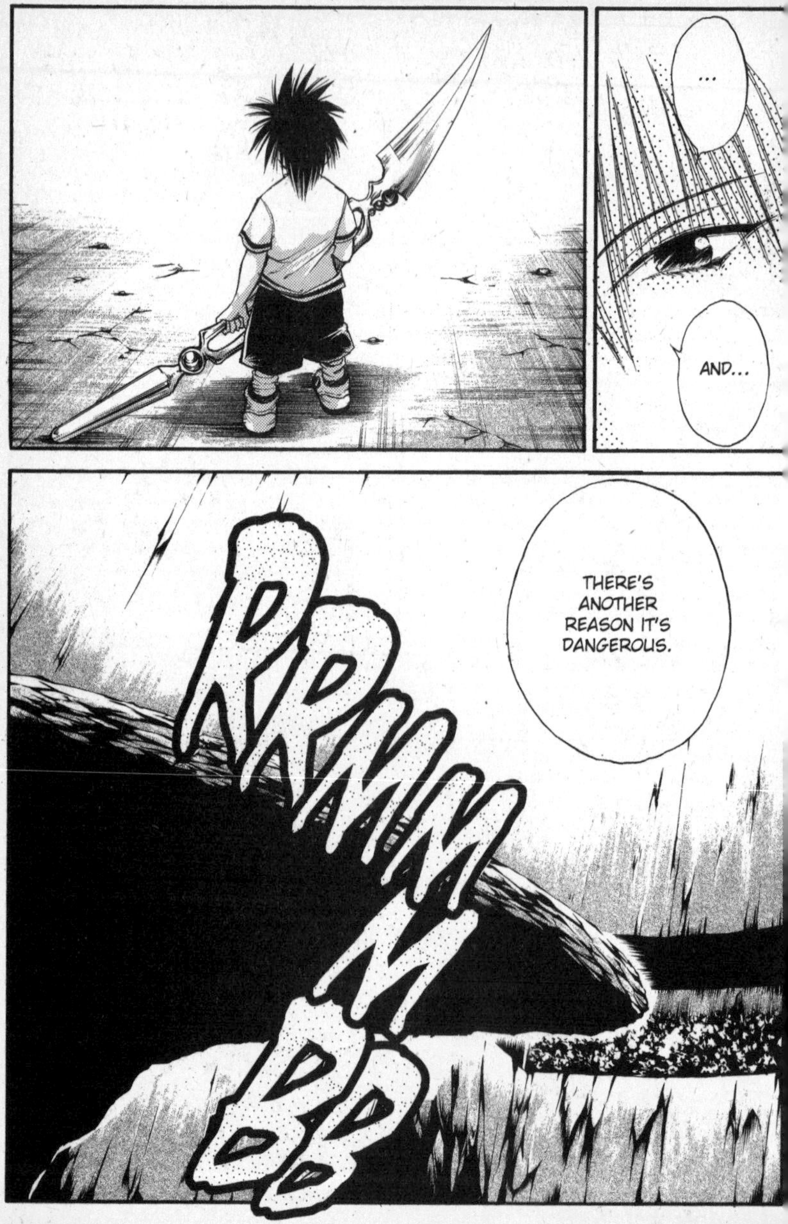
...
AND...
THERE'S ANOTHER REASON IT'S DANGEROUS.
RRMMMBB

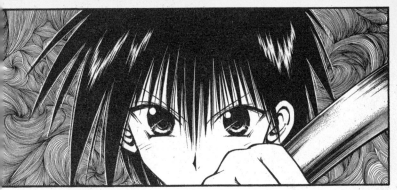

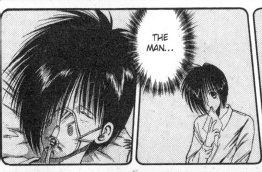

THE MAN...

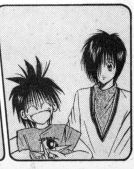

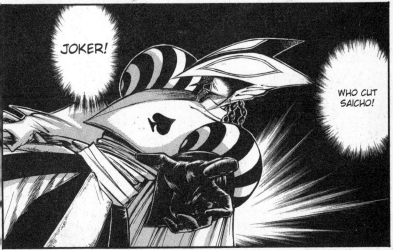

JOKER!

WHO CUT SAICHO!

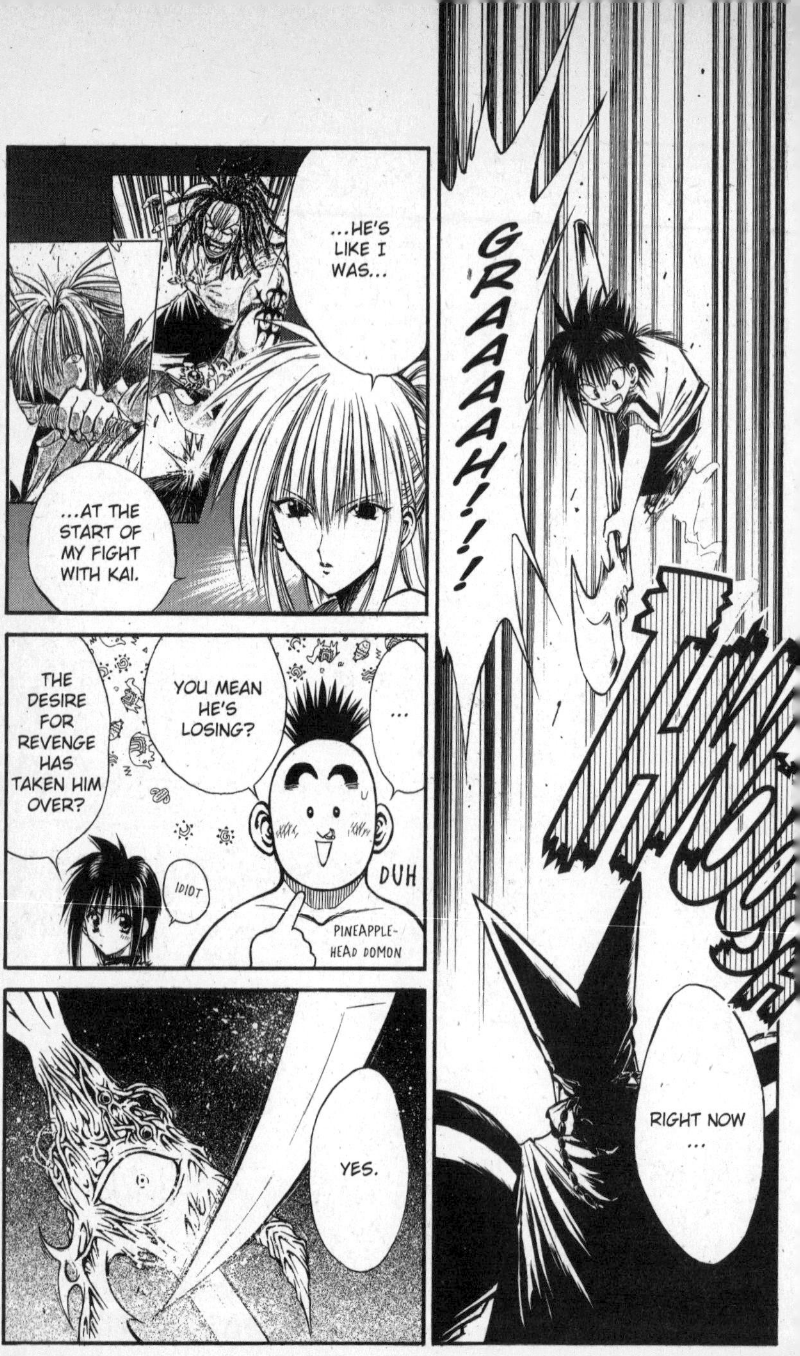
GRAAAAH!!!
RIGHT NOW ...
...HE'S LIKE I WAS...
...AT THE START OF MY FIGHT WITH KAI.
...
YOU MEAN HE'S LOSING?
THE DESIRE FOR REVENGE HAS TAKEN HIM OVER?
DUH
IDIOT
PINEAPPLE-HEAD DOMON
YES.

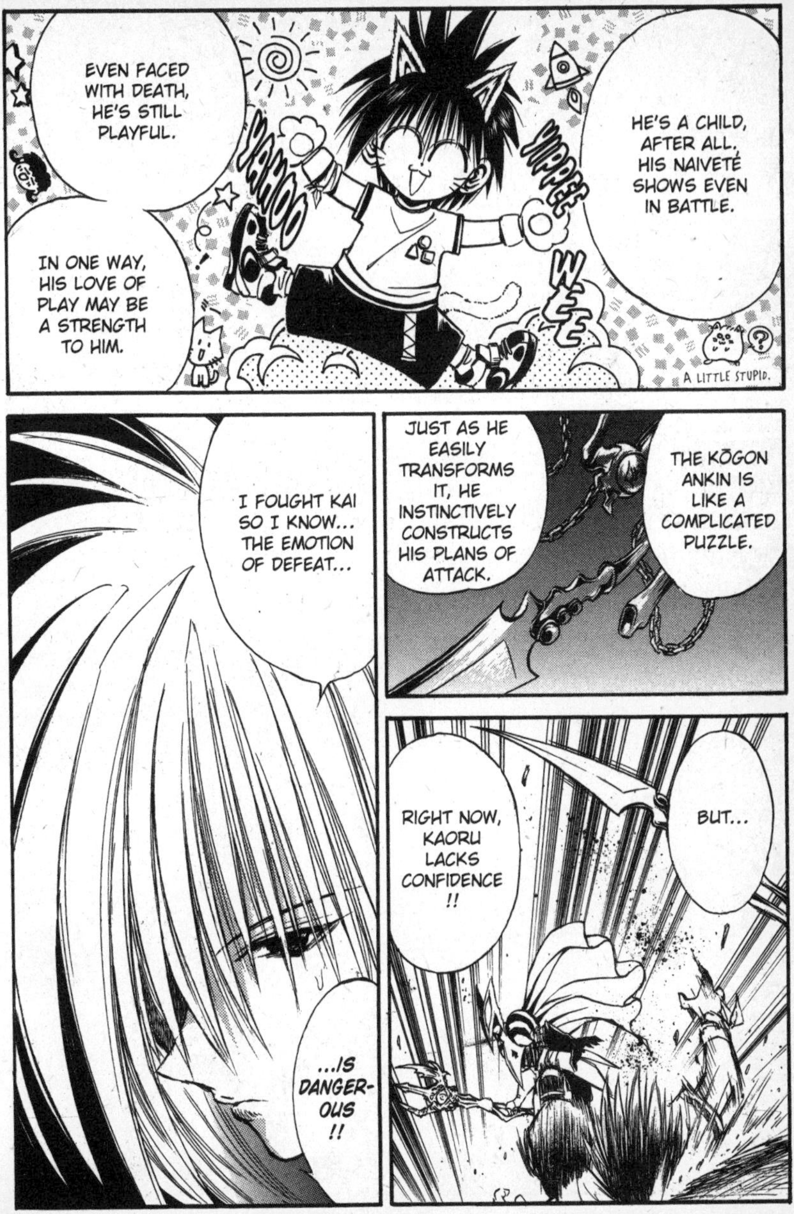
HE'S A CHILD, AFTER ALL. HIS NAIVETÉ SHOWS EVEN IN BATTLE.
YIPPEE
WEE
YAHOO
EVEN FACED WITH DEATH, HE'S STILL PLAYFUL.
IN ONE WAY, HIS LOVE OF PLAY MAY BE A STRENGTH TO HIM.
A LITTLE STUPID.
THE KŌGON ANKIN IS LIKE A COMPLICATED PUZZLE.
JUST AS HE EASILY TRANSFORMS IT, HE INSTINCTIVELY CONSTRUCTS HIS PLANS OF ATTACK.
BUT...
RIGHT NOW, KAORU LACKS CONFIDENCE !!
I FOUGHT KAI SO I KNOW... THE EMOTION OF DEFEAT...
...IS DANGER-OUS !!

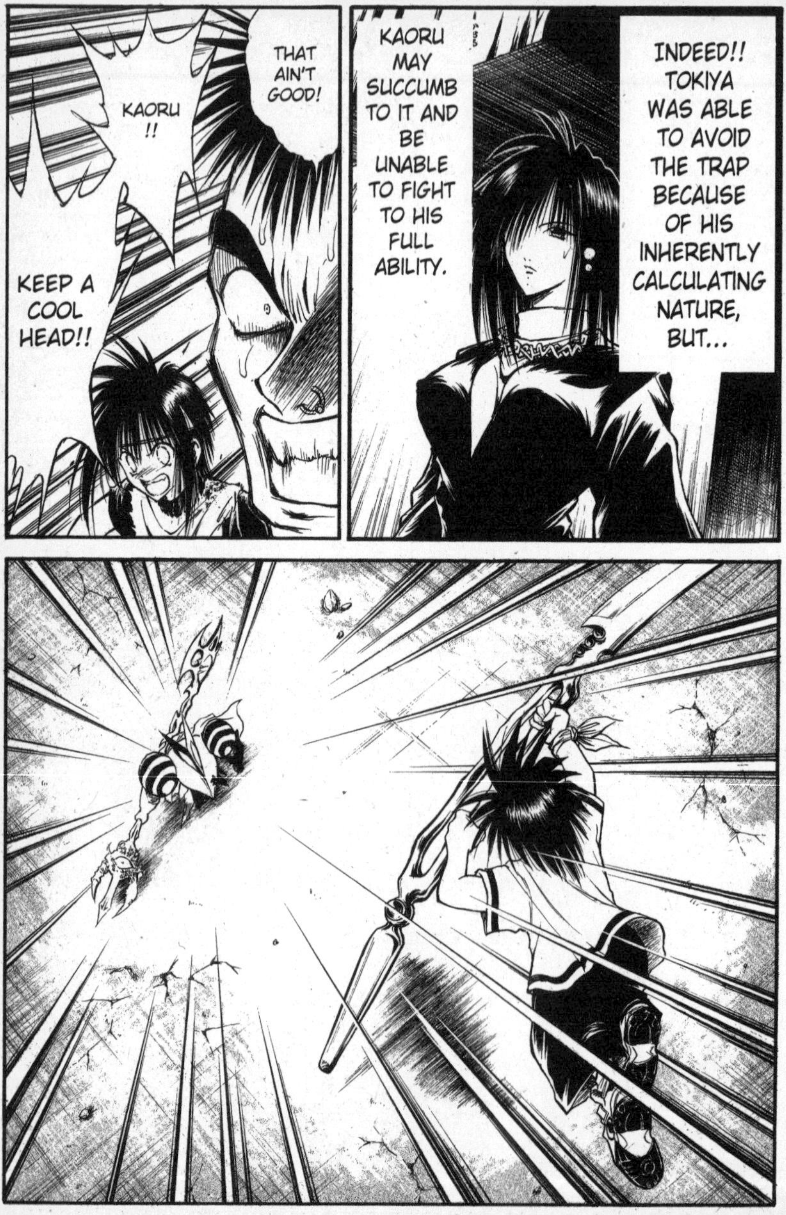
INDEED!! TOKIYA WAS ABLE TO AVOID THE TRAP BECAUSE OF HIS INHERENTLY CALCULATING NATURE, BUT...
KAORU MAY SUCCUMB TO IT AND BE UNABLE TO FIGHT TO HIS FULL ABILITY.
THAT AIN'T GOOD!
KAORU !!
KEEP A COOL HEAD!!

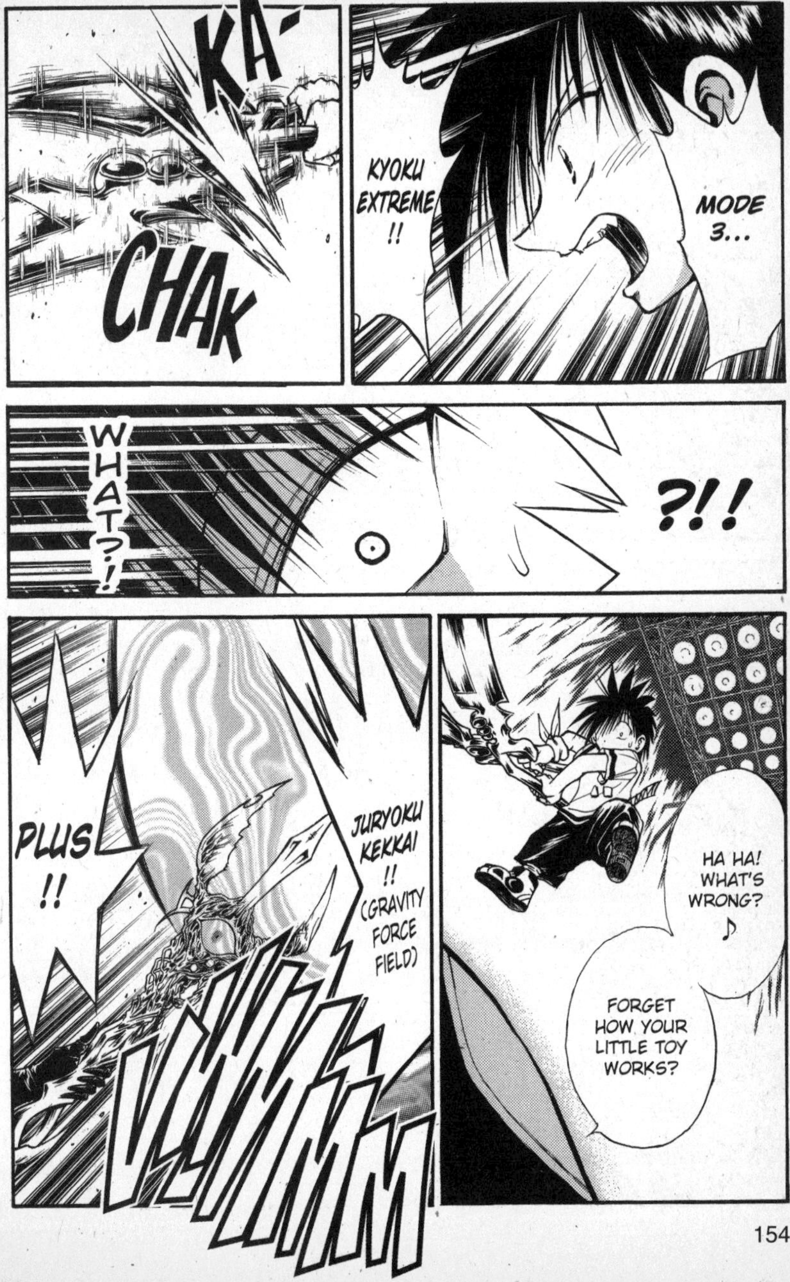
MODE 3...
KYOKU EXTREME !!
KA-
CHAK
?!!
WHAT?!
HA HA! WHAT'S WRONG? ♪
FORGET HOW YOUR LITTLE TOY WORKS?
JURYOKU KEKKAI !! (GRAVITY FORCE FIELD)
PLUS !!

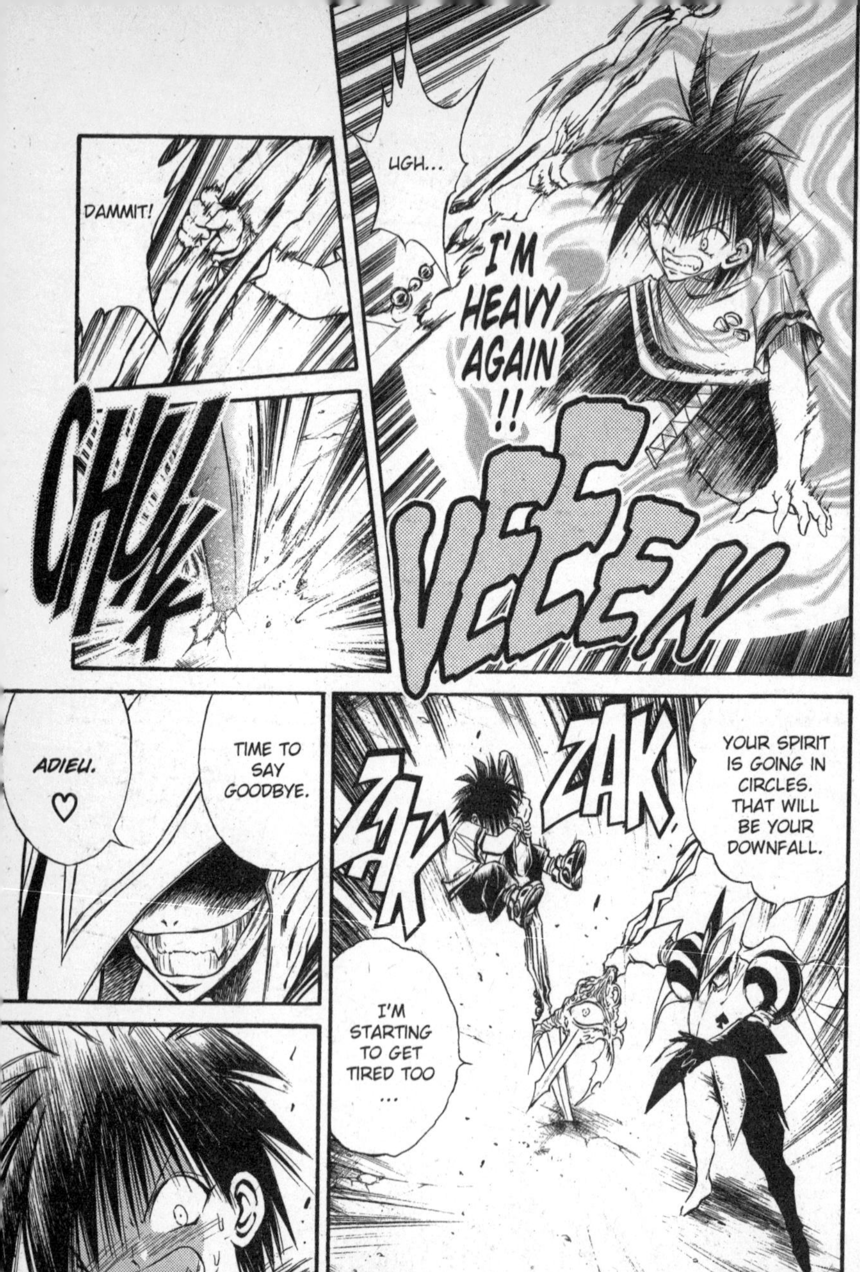
UGH...
I'M HEAVY AGAIN!!
VEEEN
DAMMIT!
CHUNK
YOUR SPIRIT IS GOING IN CIRCLES. THAT WILL BE YOUR DOWNFALL.
ZAK
ZAK
I'M STARTING TO GET TIRED TOO ...
TIME TO SAY GOODBYE.
ADIEU. ♡

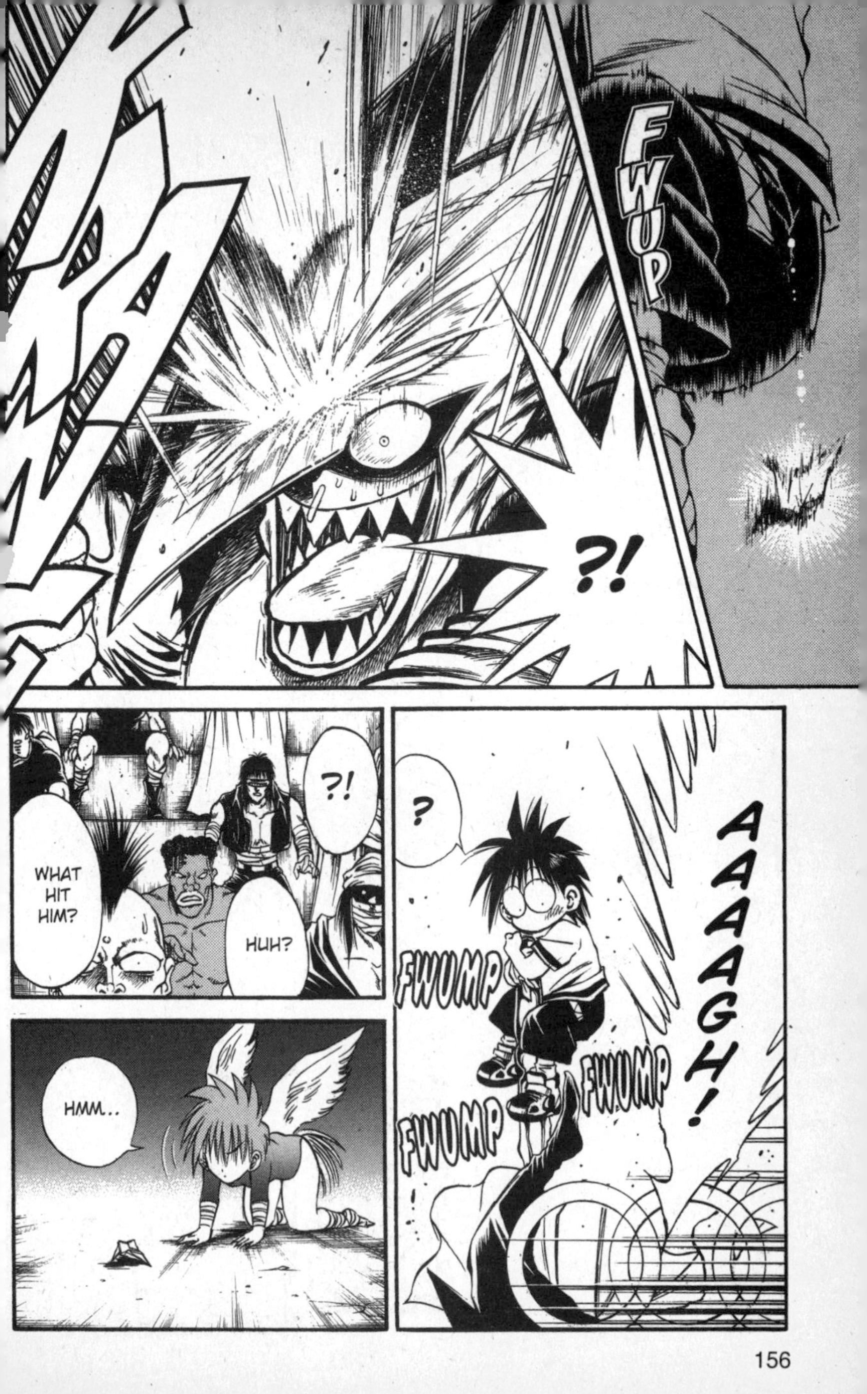
FWUP
?!
?
AAAAAGH!
FWUMP
FWUMP
FWUMP
?!
HUH?
WHAT HIT HIM?
HMM..

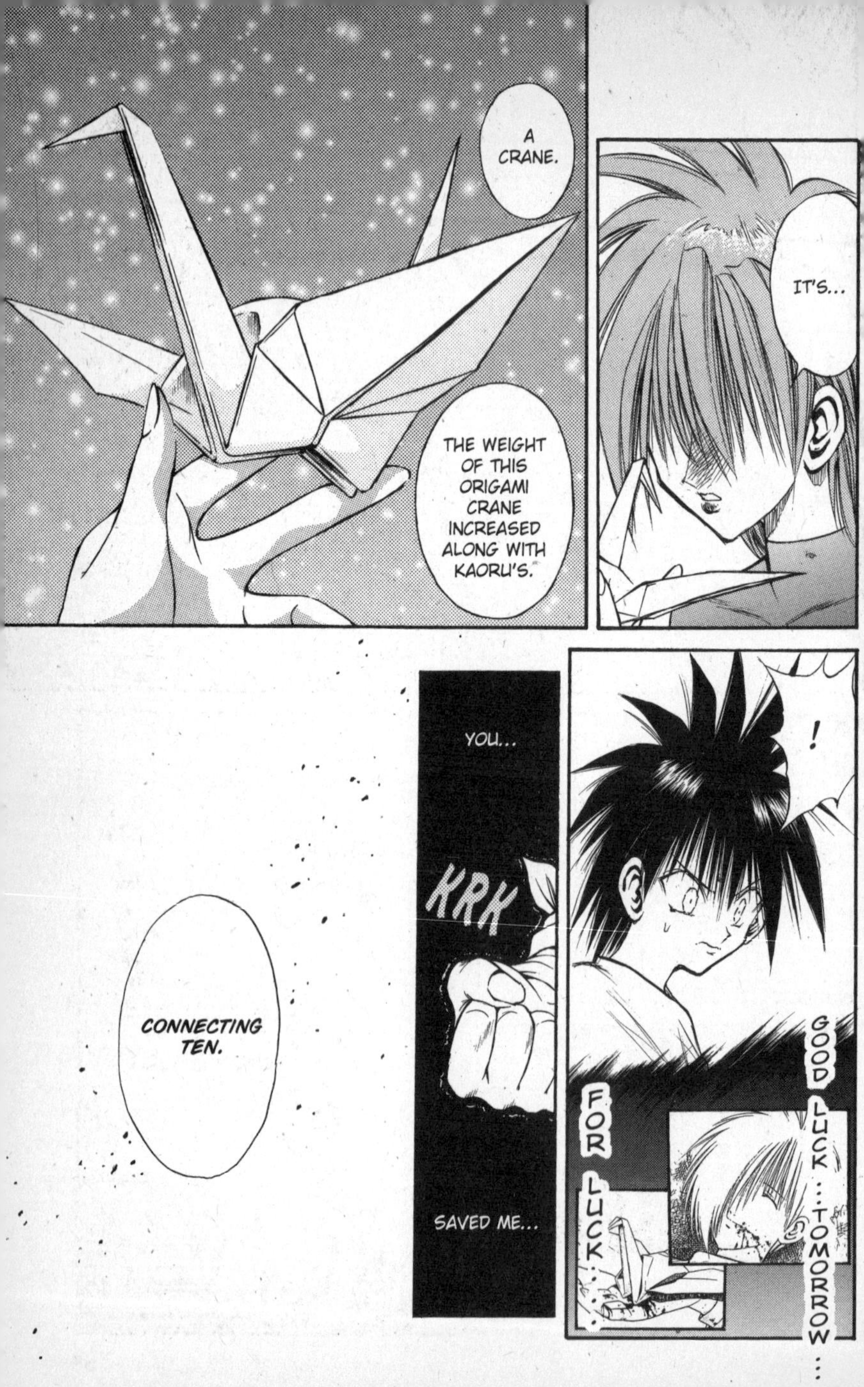
IT'S...
A CRANE.
THE WEIGHT OF THIS ORIGAMI CRANE INCREASED ALONG WITH KAORU'S.
!
GOOD LUCK ...TOMORROW...
FOR LUCK...
YOU...
KRK
SAVED ME...
CONNECTING TEN.

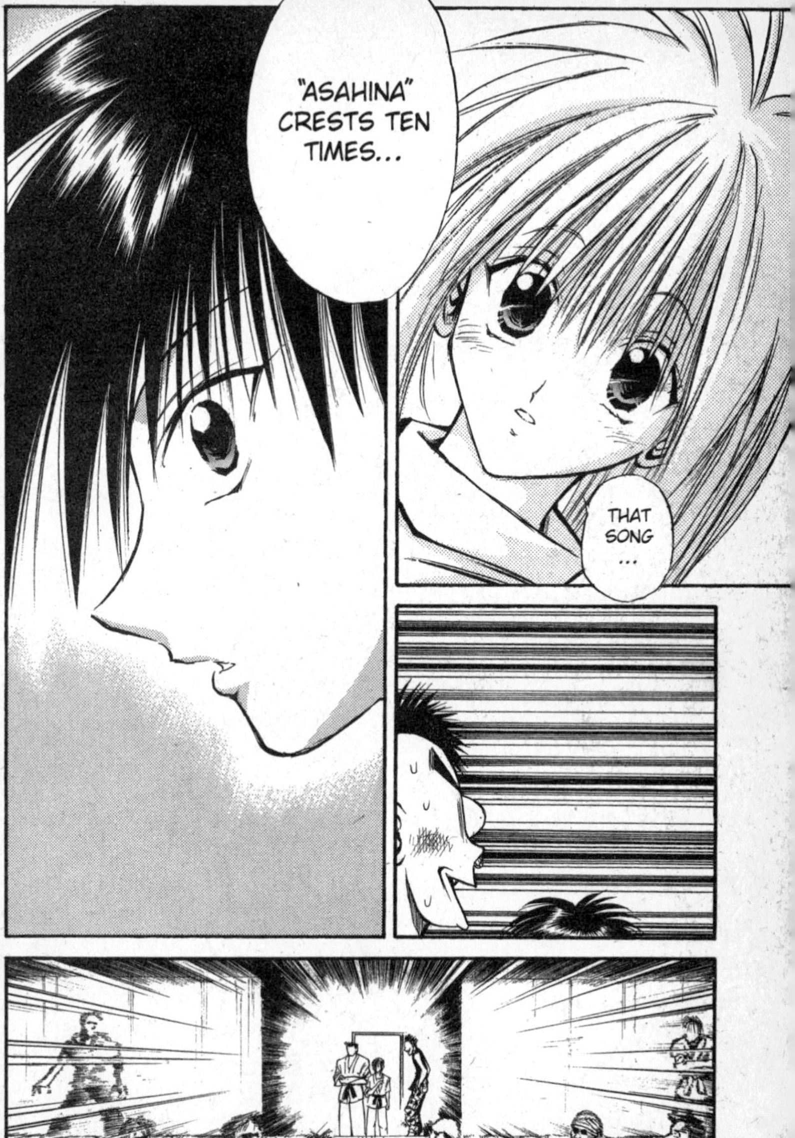
"ASAHINA" CRESTS TEN TIMES...
THAT SONG ...

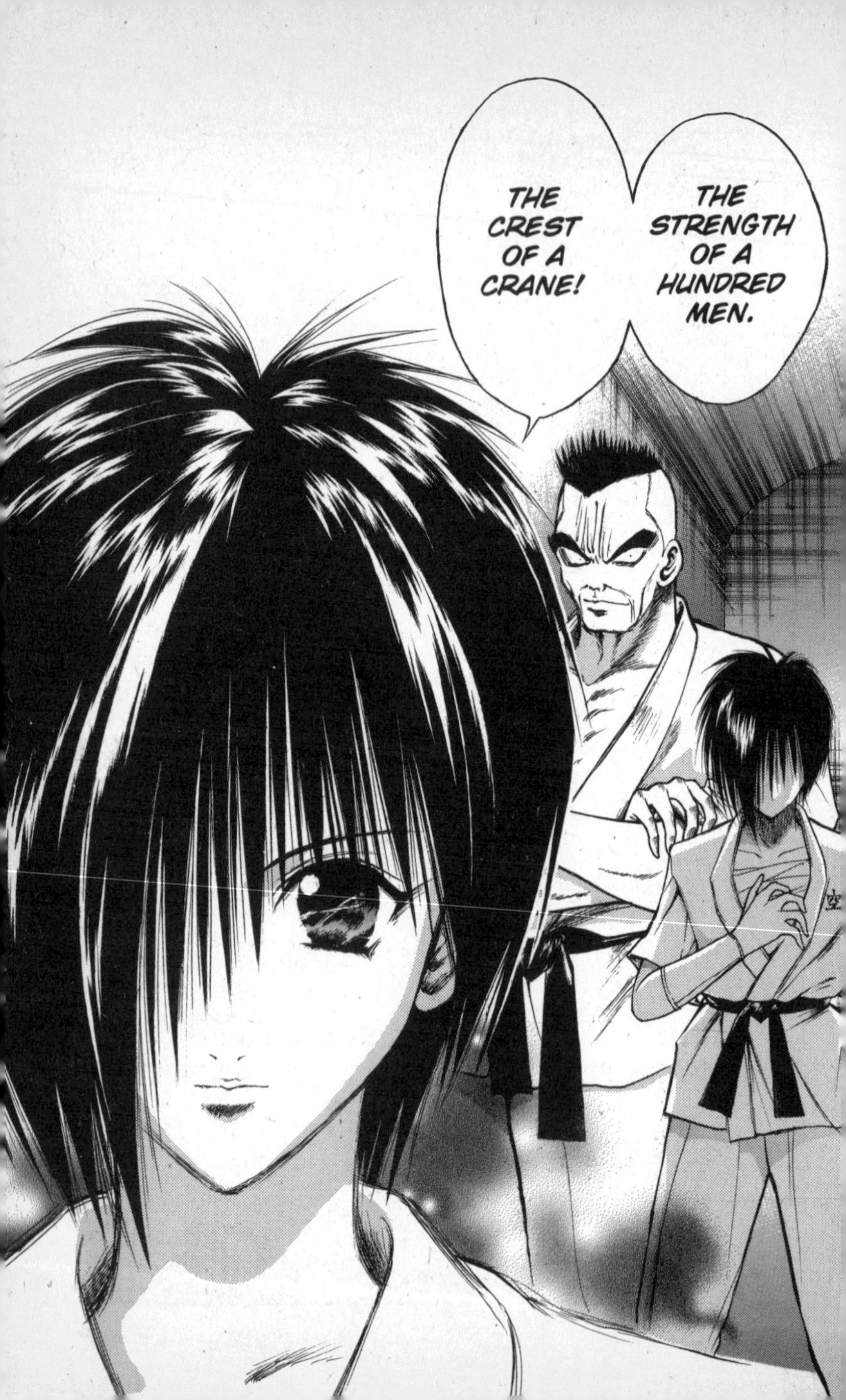
THE STRENGTH OF A HUNDRED MEN.
THE CREST OF A CRANE!

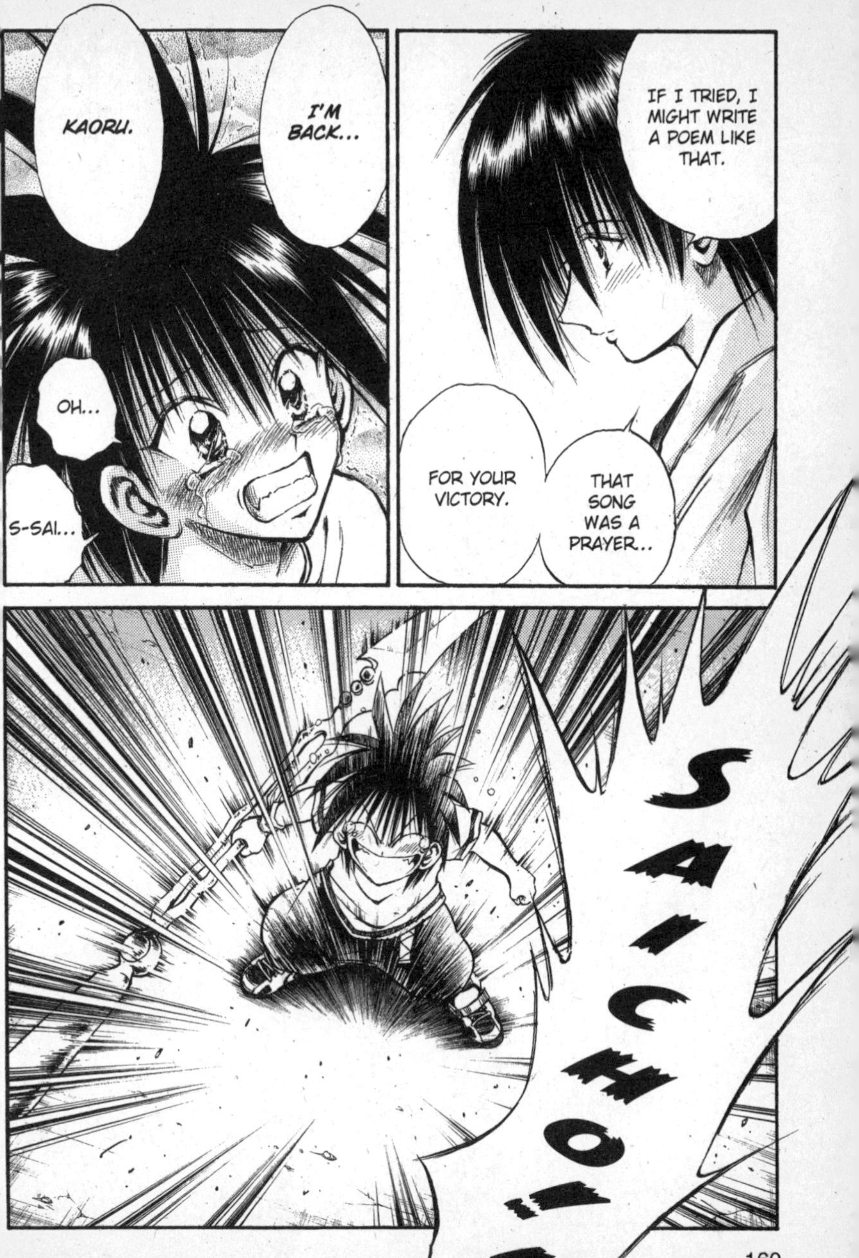
IF I TRIED, I MIGHT WRITE A POEM LIKE THAT.
THAT SONG WAS A PRAYER...
FOR YOUR VICTORY.
I'M BACK...
KAORU.
OH...
S-SAI...
SAICHO!!!

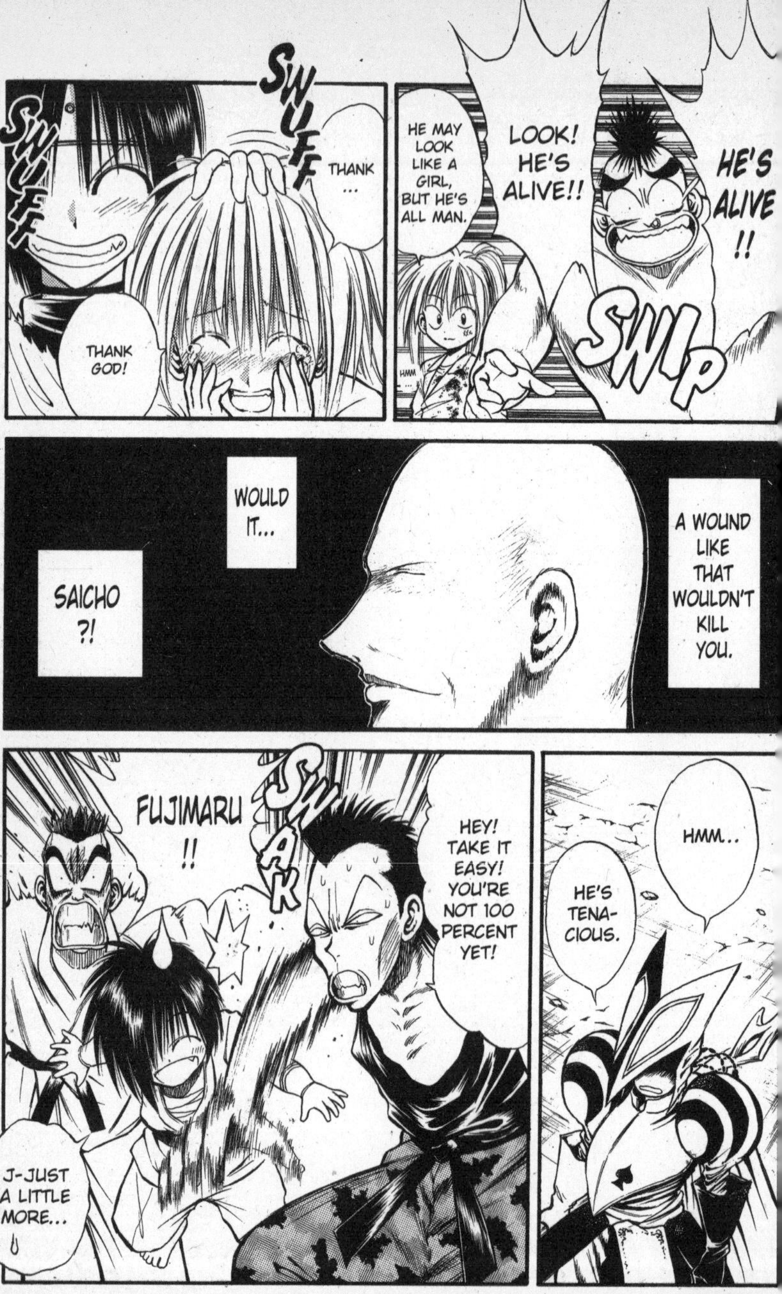
HE'S ALIVE!!
LOOK! HE'S ALIVE!!
HE MAY LOOK LIKE A GIRL, BUT HE'S ALL MAN.
SNIP
HMM...
SNUFF
THANK...
SNUFF
THANK GOD!
A WOUND LIKE THAT WOULDN'T KILL YOU.
WOULD IT...
SAICHO?!
HMM...
HE'S TENACIOUS.
SWAK
HEY! TAKE IT EASY! YOU'RE NOT 100 PERCENT YET!
FUJIMARU!!
J-JUST A LITTLE MORE...

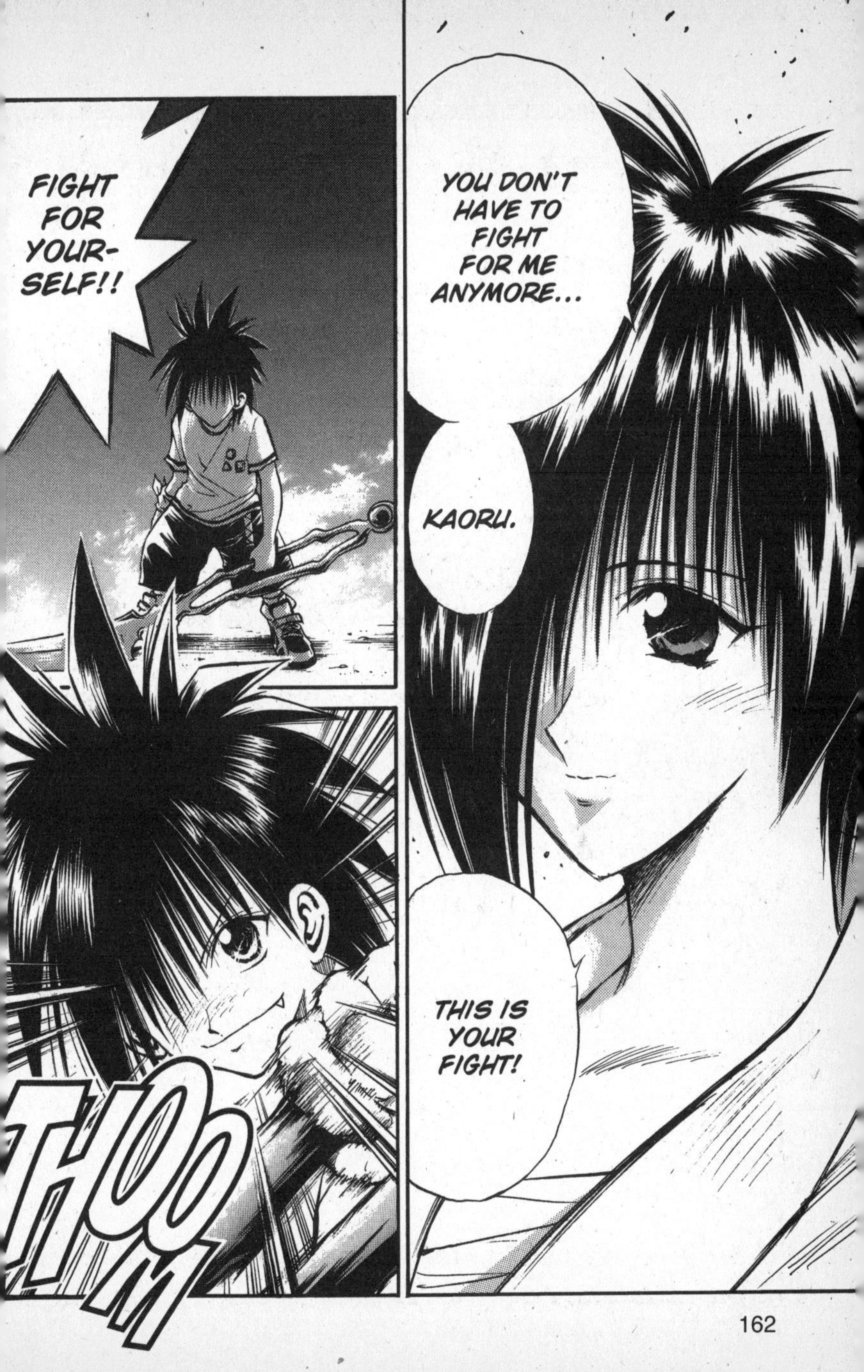
YOU DON'T HAVE TO FIGHT FOR ME ANYMORE...
KAORU.
THIS IS YOUR FIGHT!
FIGHT FOR YOUR-SELF!!
THOOM

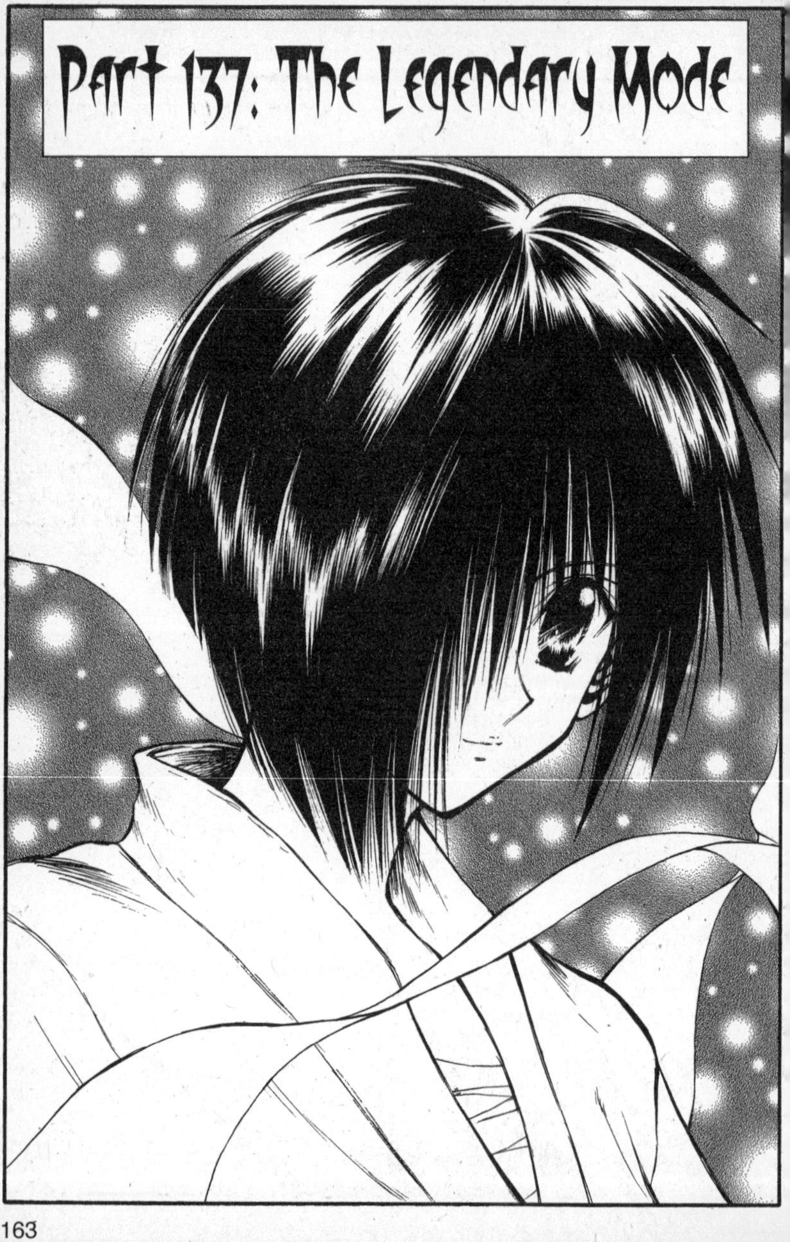
Part 137: The Legendary Mode

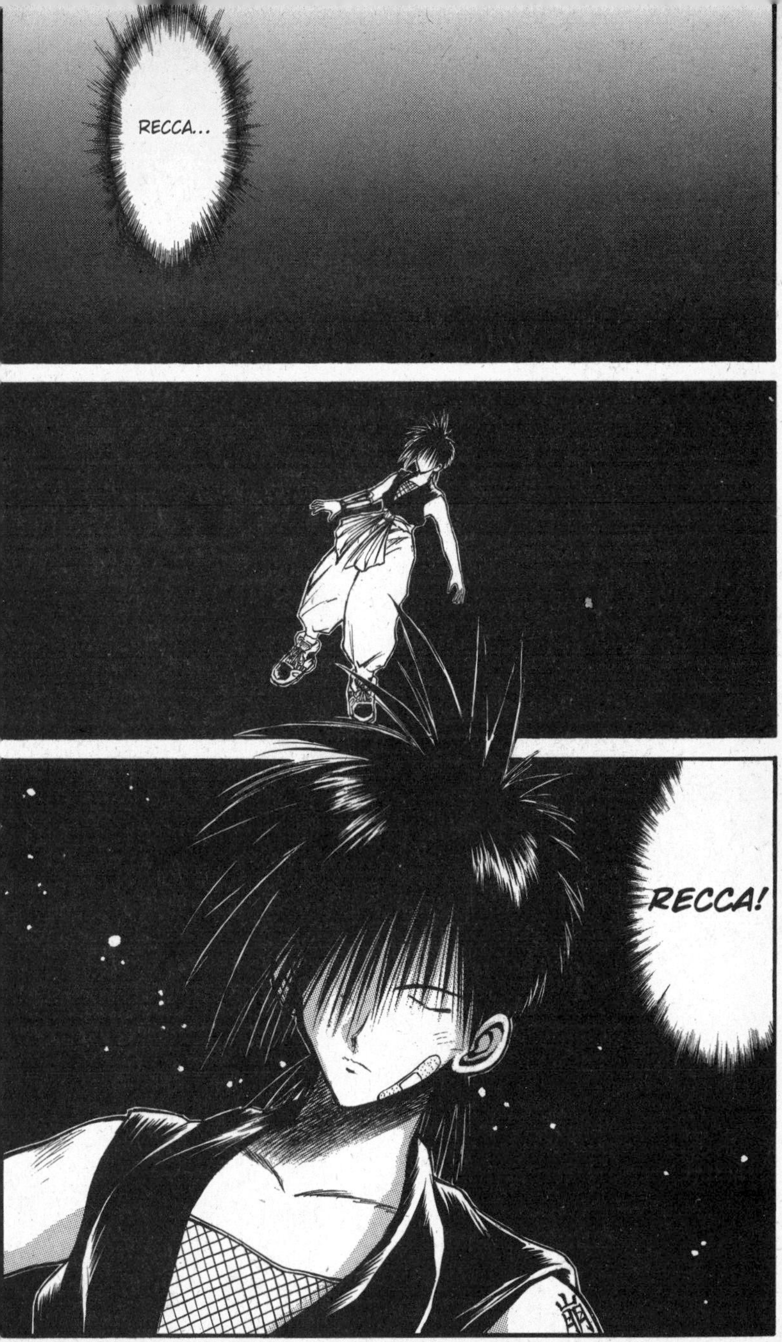
RECCA...
RECCA!

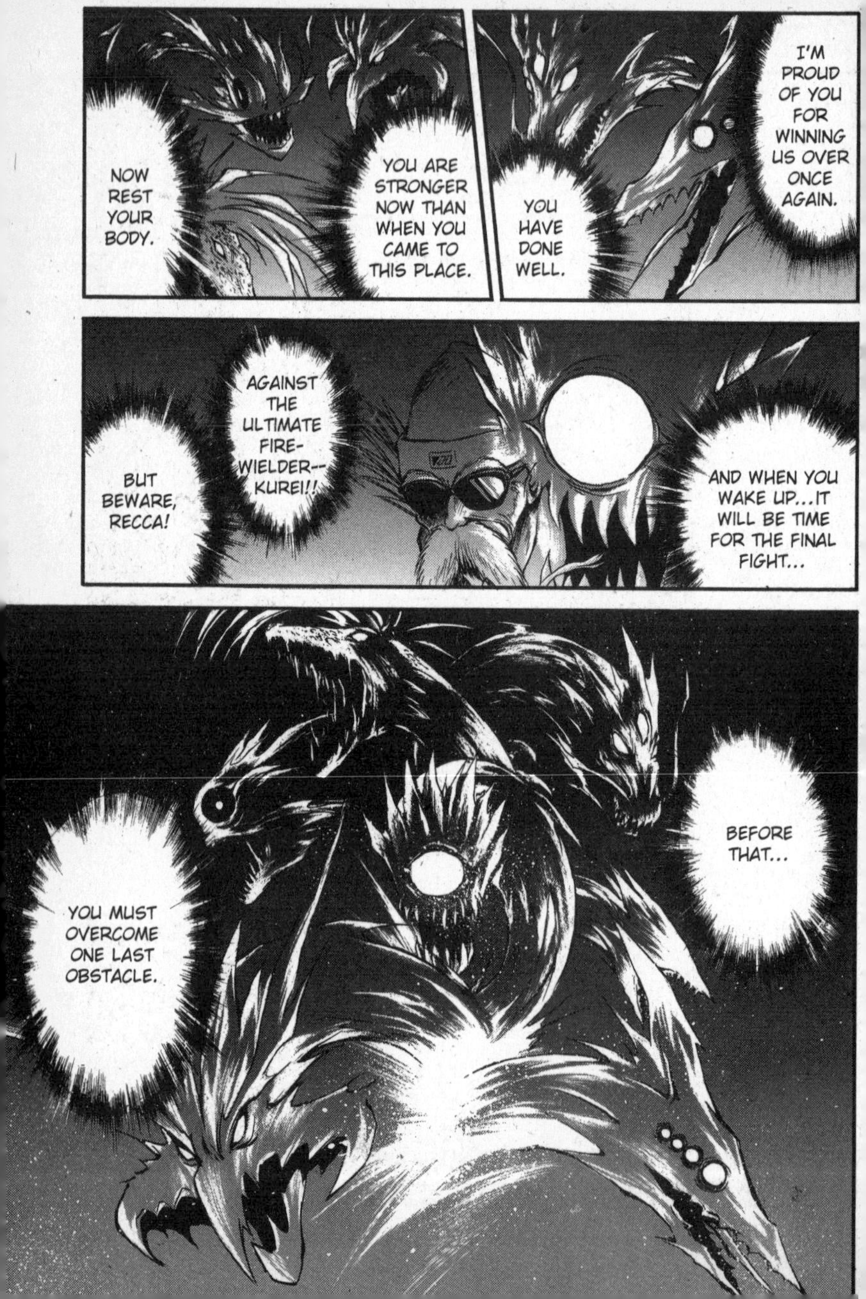
I'M PROUD OF YOU FOR WINNING US OVER ONCE AGAIN.
YOU HAVE DONE WELL.
YOU ARE STRONGER NOW THAN WHEN YOU CAME TO THIS PLACE.
NOW REST YOUR BODY.
AND WHEN YOU WAKE UP...IT WILL BE TIME FOR THE FINAL FIGHT...
BUT BEWARE, RECCA!
AGAINST THE ULTIMATE FIRE-WIELDER--KUREI!!
BEFORE THAT...
YOU MUST OVERCOME ONE LAST OBSTACLE.

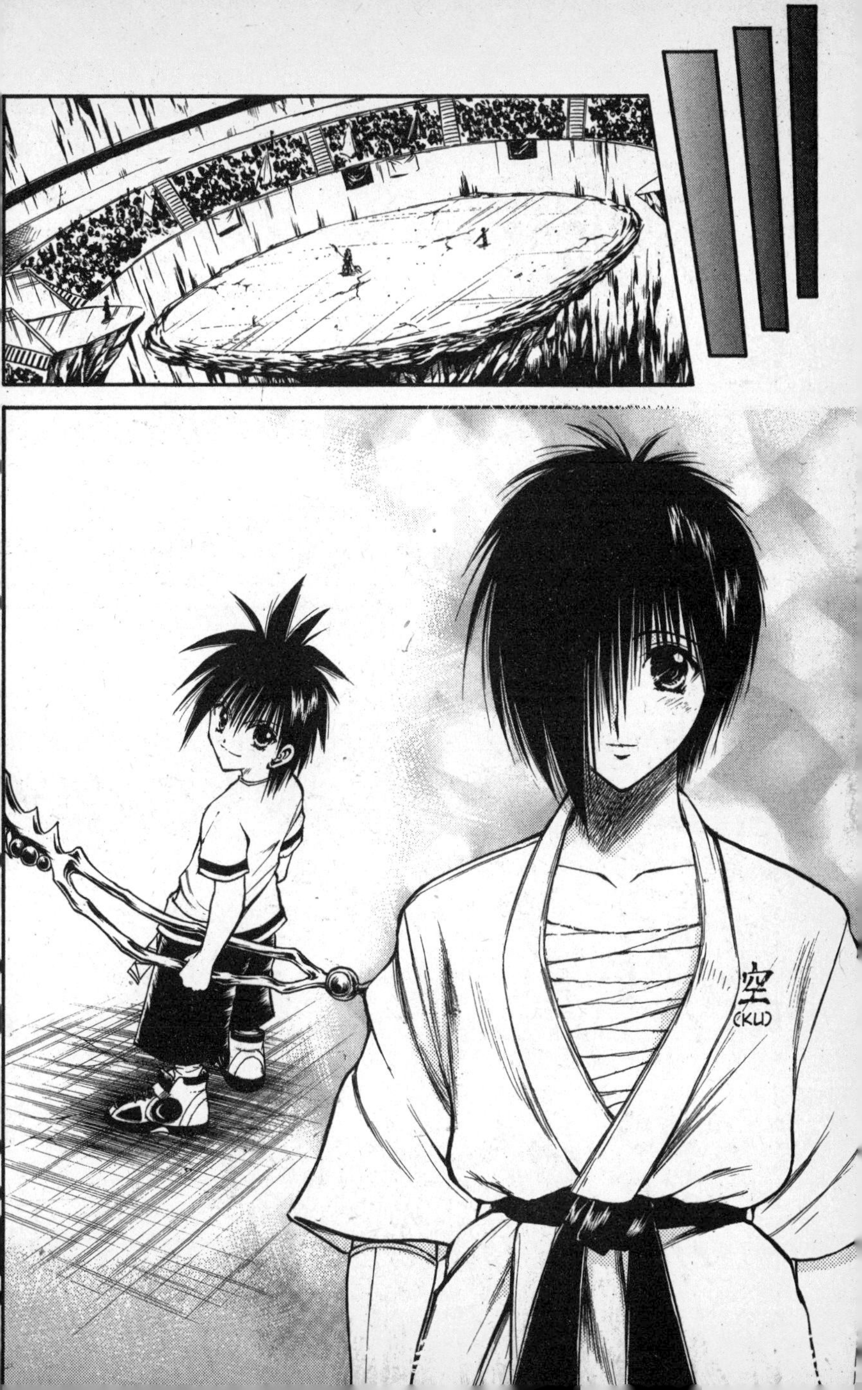
空
(KU)

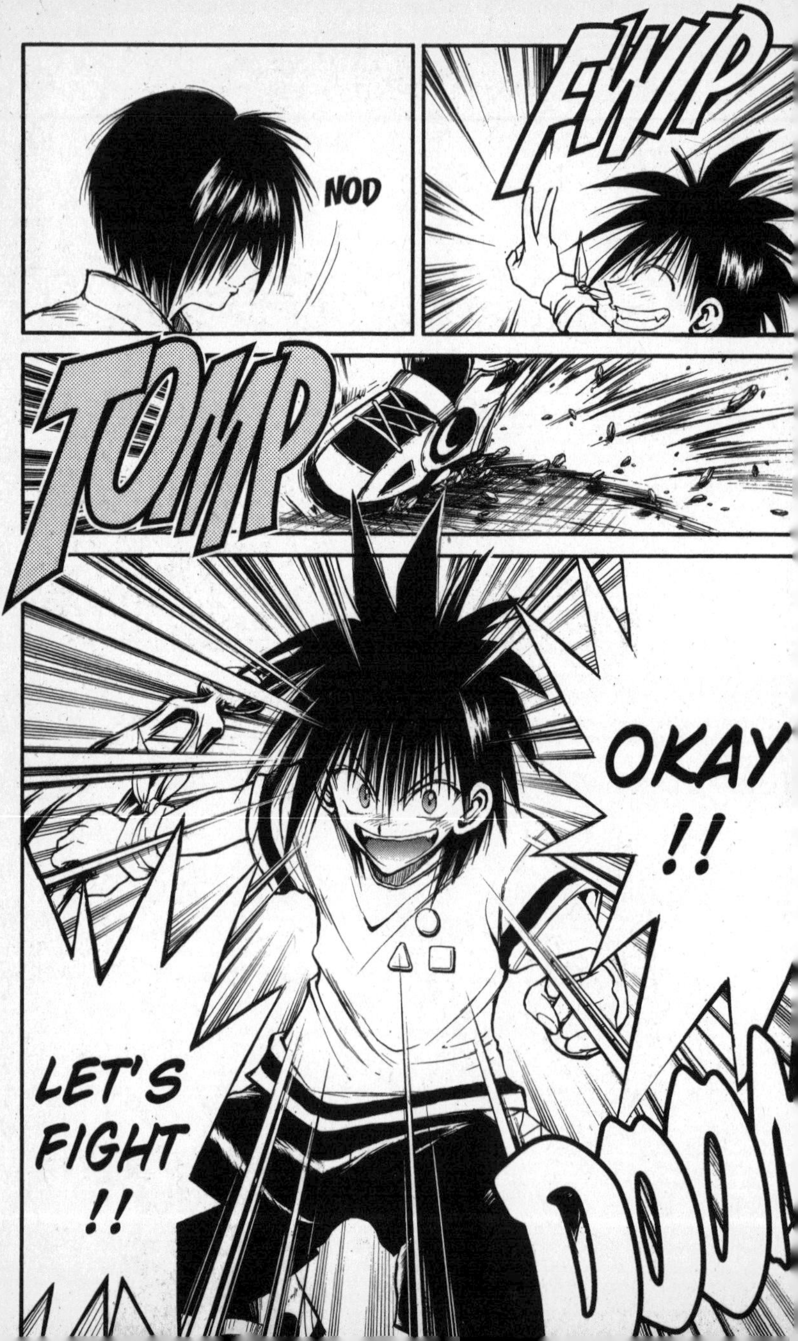
FWIP
NOD
TOMP
OKAY !!
LET'S FIGHT !!

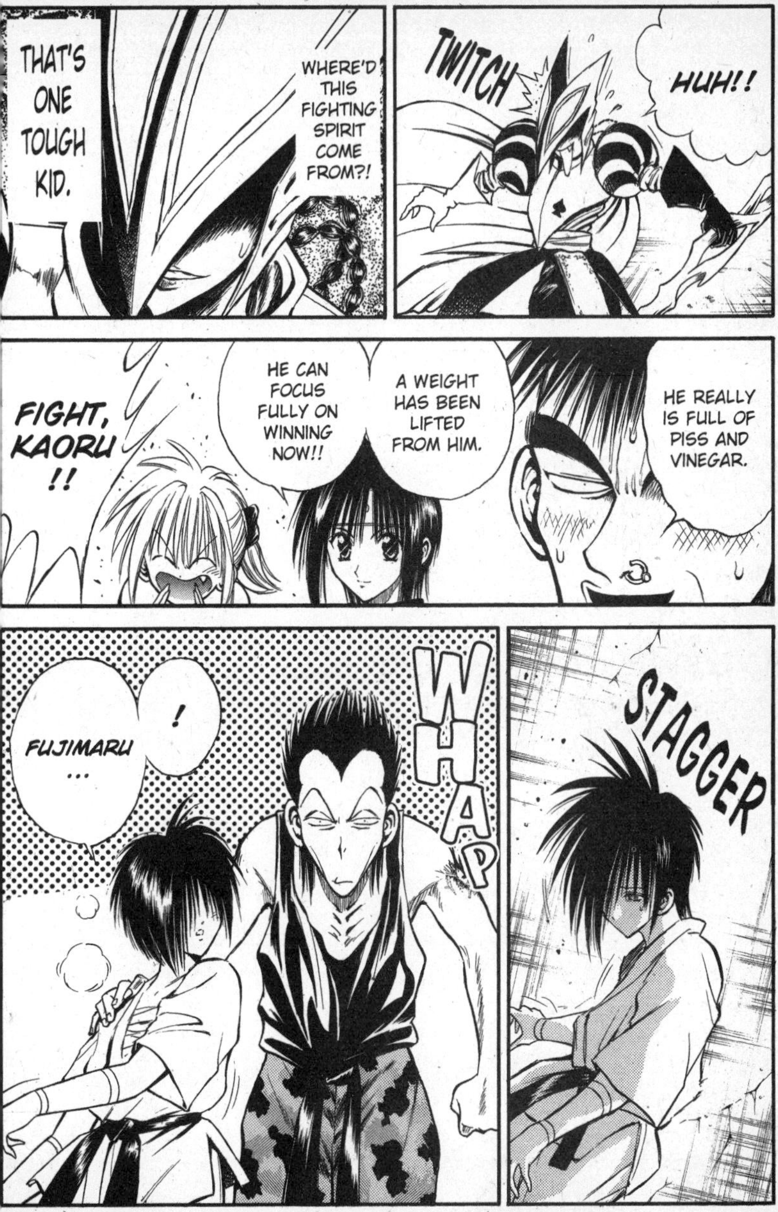
TWITCH
HUH!!
WHERE'D THIS FIGHTING SPIRIT COME FROM?!
THAT'S ONE TOUGH KID.
HE REALLY IS FULL OF PISS AND VINEGAR.
A WEIGHT HAS BEEN LIFTED FROM HIM.
HE CAN FOCUS FULLY ON WINNING NOW!!
FIGHT, KAORU!!
STAGGER
WHAP
!
FUJIMARU...

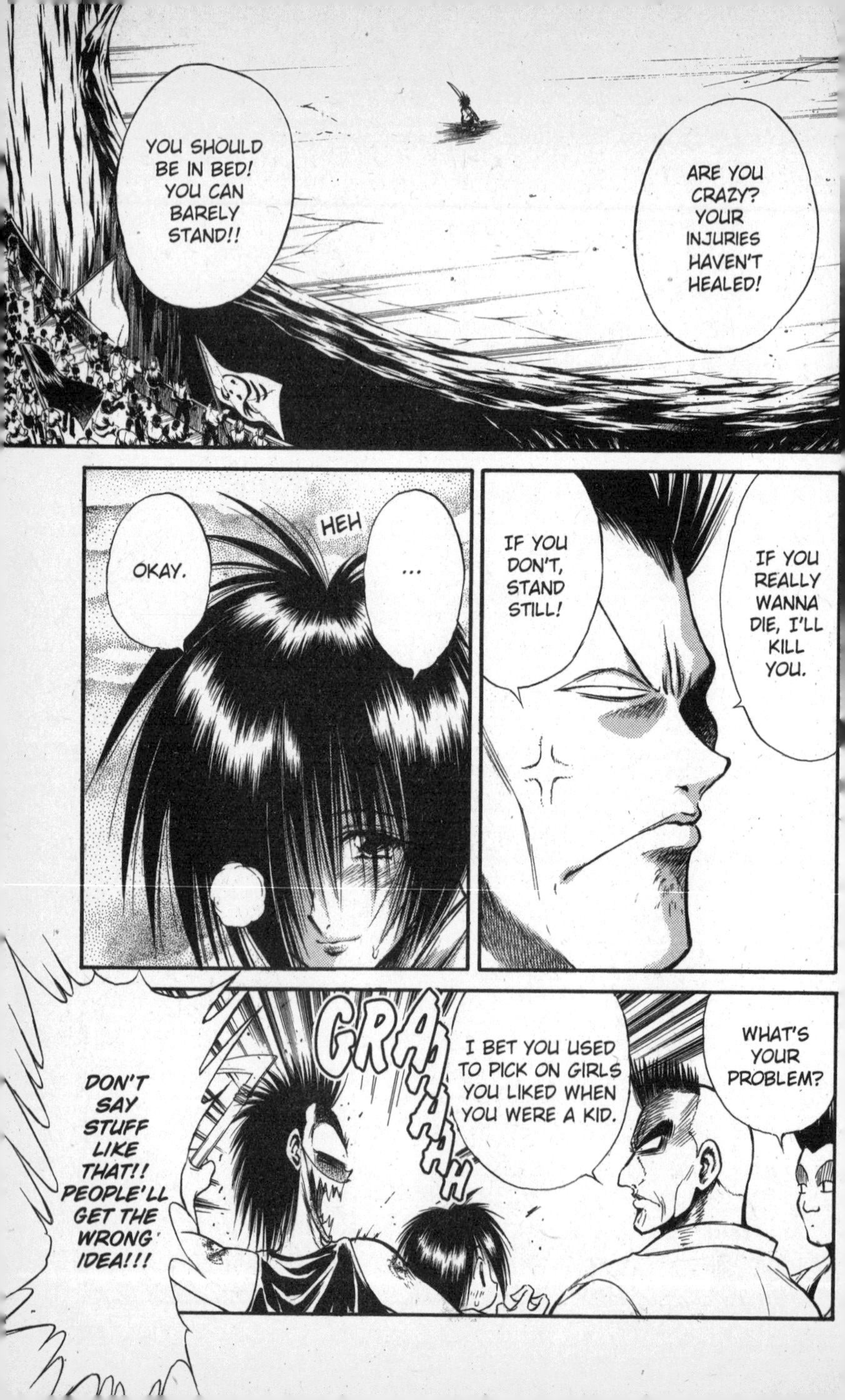
ARE YOU CRAZY? YOUR INJURIES HAVEN'T HEALED!
YOU SHOULD BE IN BED! YOU CAN BARELY STAND!!
IF YOU REALLY WANNA DIE, I'LL KILL YOU.
IF YOU DON'T, STAND STILL!
...
HEH
OKAY.
WHAT'S YOUR PROBLEM?
I BET YOU USED TO PICK ON GIRLS YOU LIKED WHEN YOU WERE A KID.
GRAAAHH
DON'T SAY STUFF LIKE THAT!! PEOPLE'LL GET THE WRONG IDEA!!!

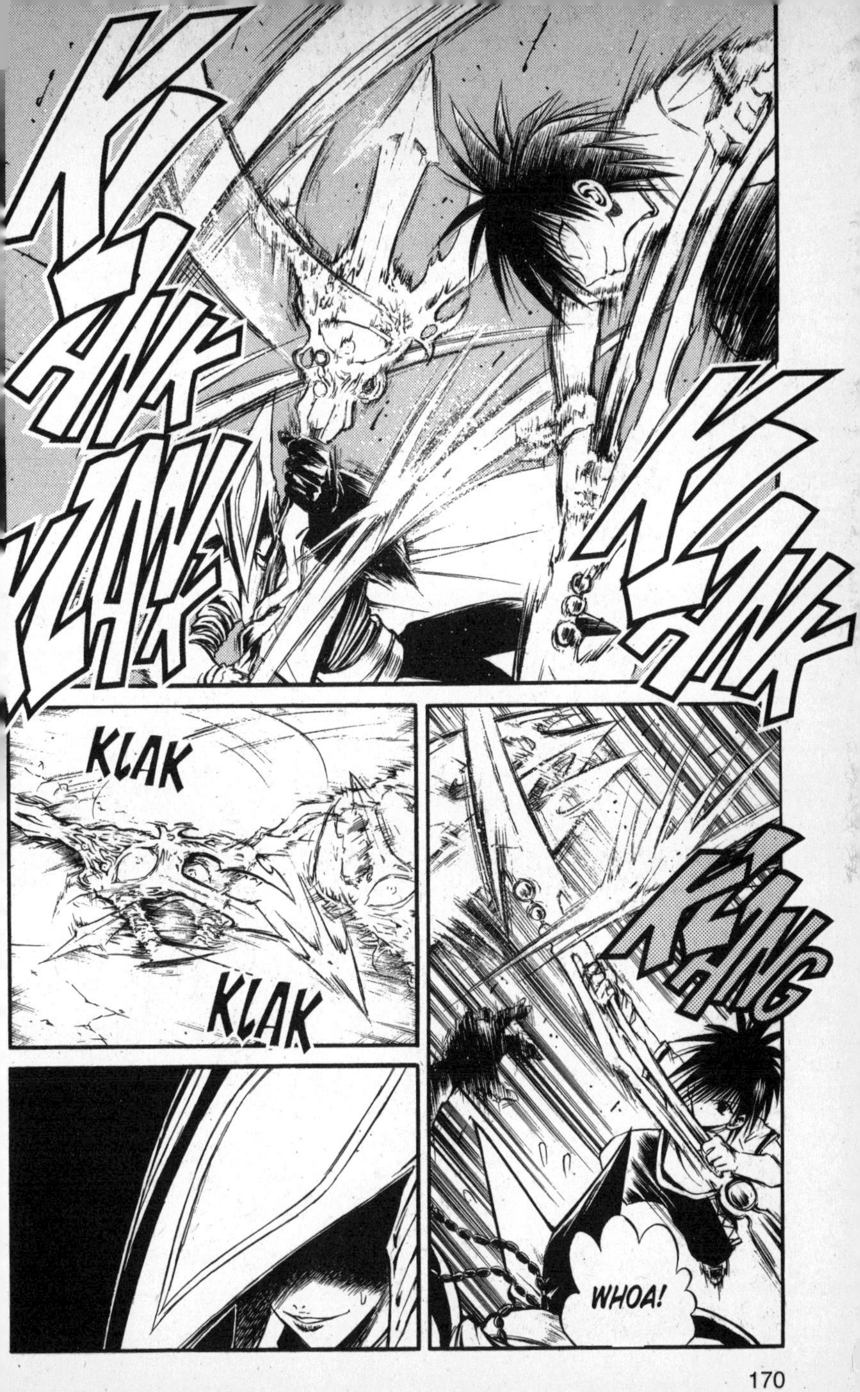
KANK
KANK
KANK
KANG
WHOA!
KLAK
KLAK

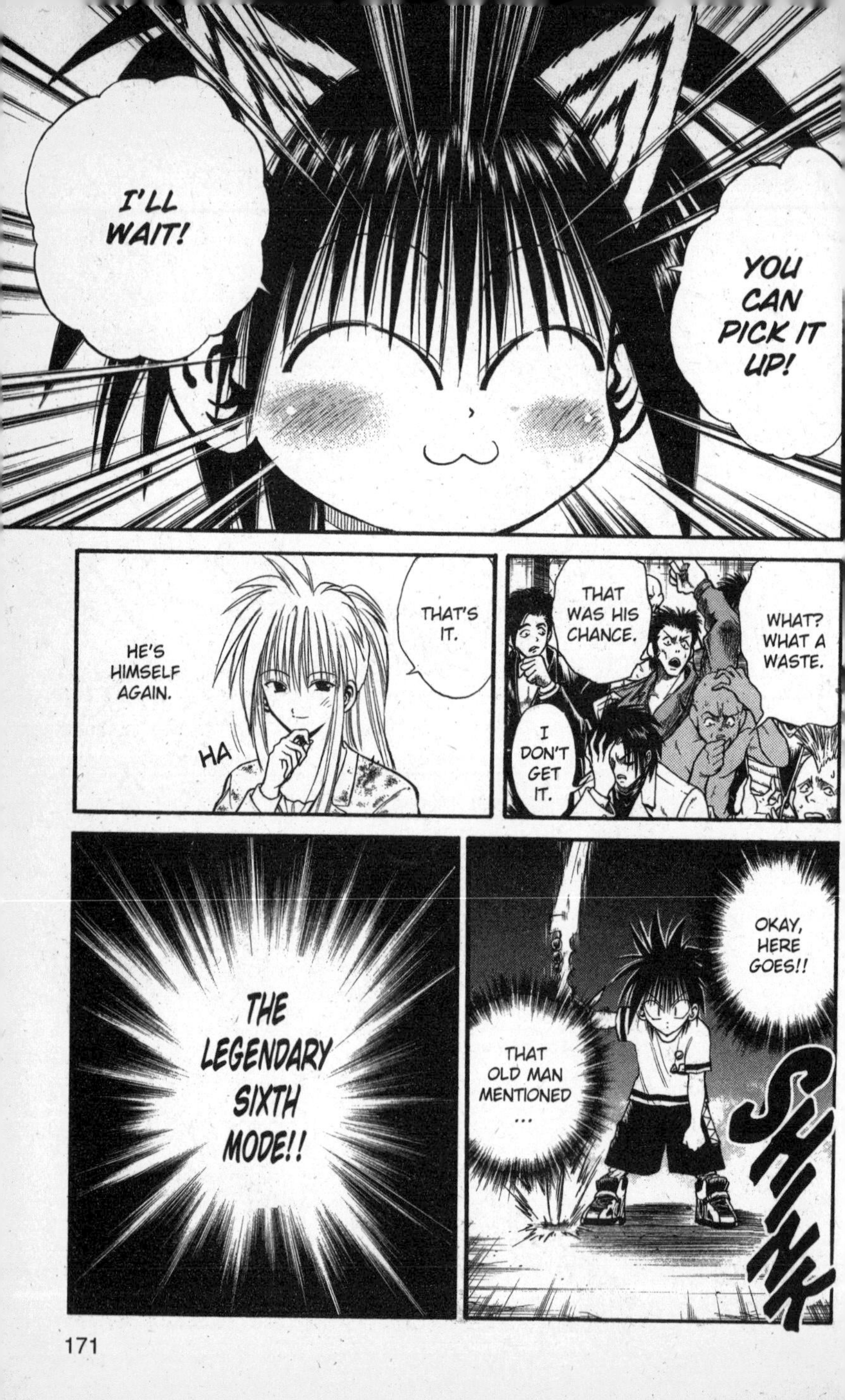
YOU CAN PICK IT UP!
I'LL WAIT!
WHAT? WHAT A WASTE.
THAT WAS HIS CHANCE.
I DON'T GET IT.
THAT'S IT.
HE'S HIMSELF AGAIN.
HA
OKAY, HERE GOES!!
THAT OLD MAN MENTIONED ...
SHINK
THE LEGENDARY SIXTH MODE!!

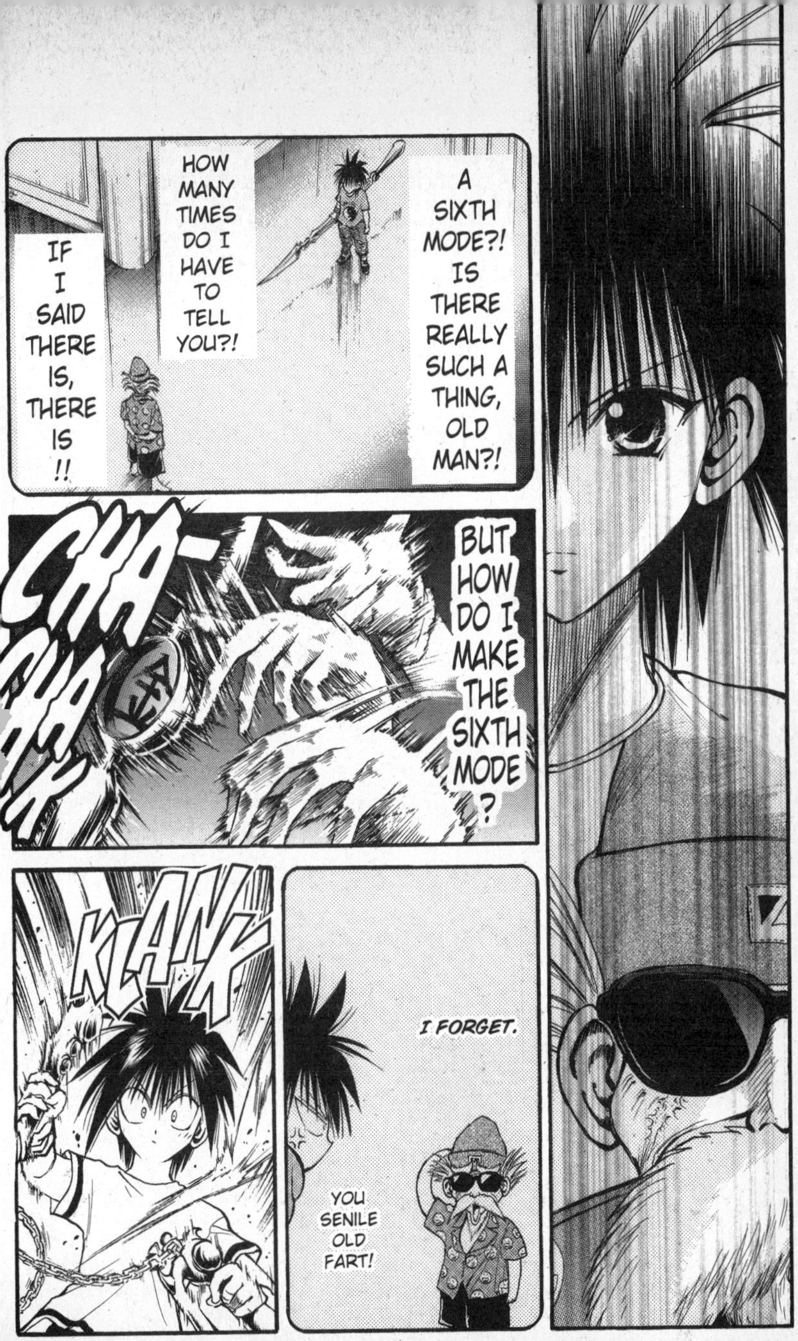
A SIXTH MODE?! IS THERE REALLY SUCH A THING, OLD MAN?!
HOW MANY TIMES DO I HAVE TO TELL YOU?!
IF I SAID THERE IS, THERE IS!!
BUT HOW DO I MAKE THE SIXTH MODE?
CHA-CHAK
I FORGET.
YOU SENILE OLD FART!
KLANK

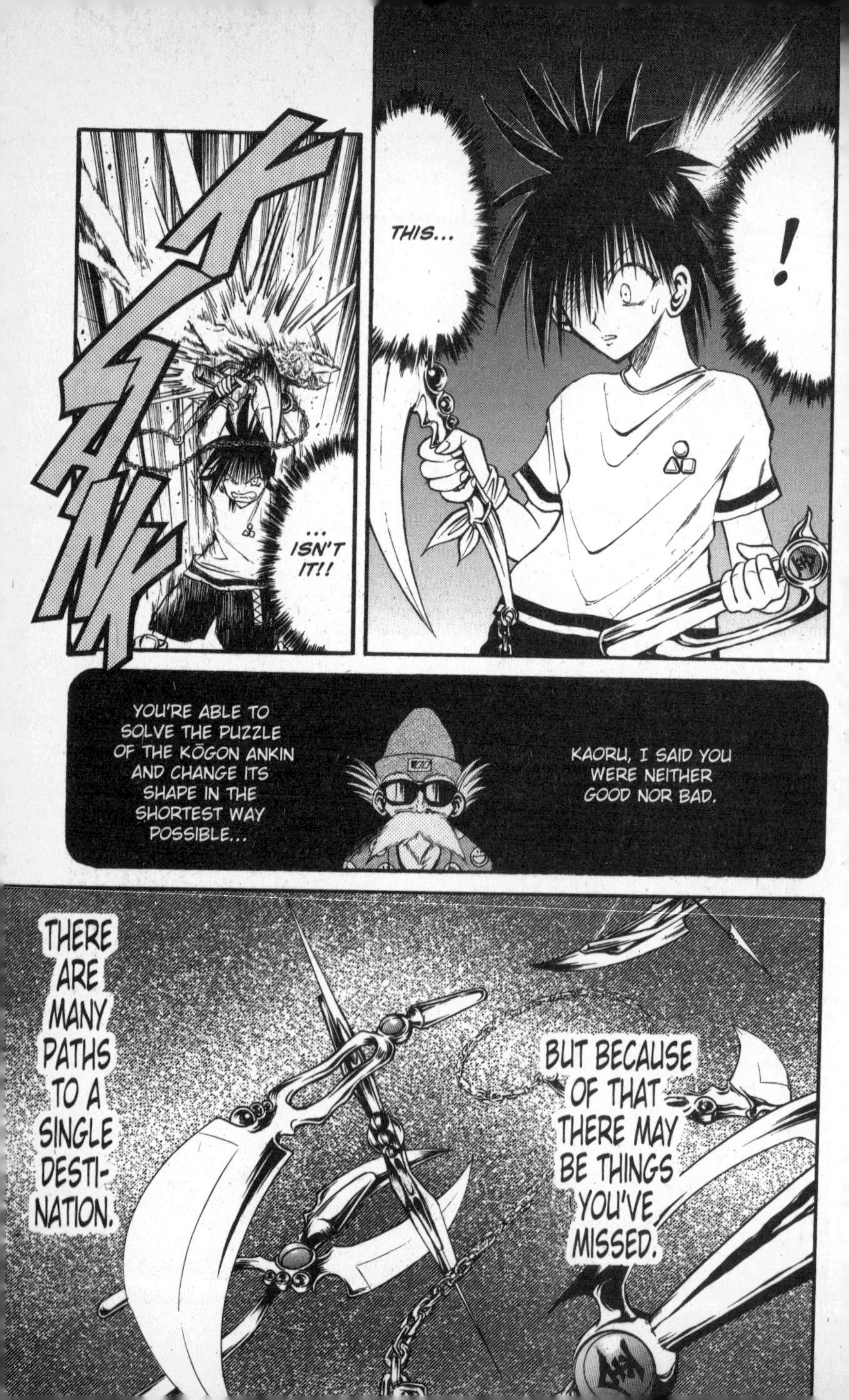
THIS...
!
... ISN'T IT!!
KAORU, I SAID YOU WERE NEITHER GOOD NOR BAD.
YOU'RE ABLE TO SOLVE THE PUZZLE OF THE KŌGON ANKIN AND CHANGE ITS SHAPE IN THE SHORTEST WAY POSSIBLE...
BUT BECAUSE OF THAT THERE MAY BE THINGS YOU'VE MISSED.
THERE ARE MANY PATHS TO A SINGLE DESTI-NATION.

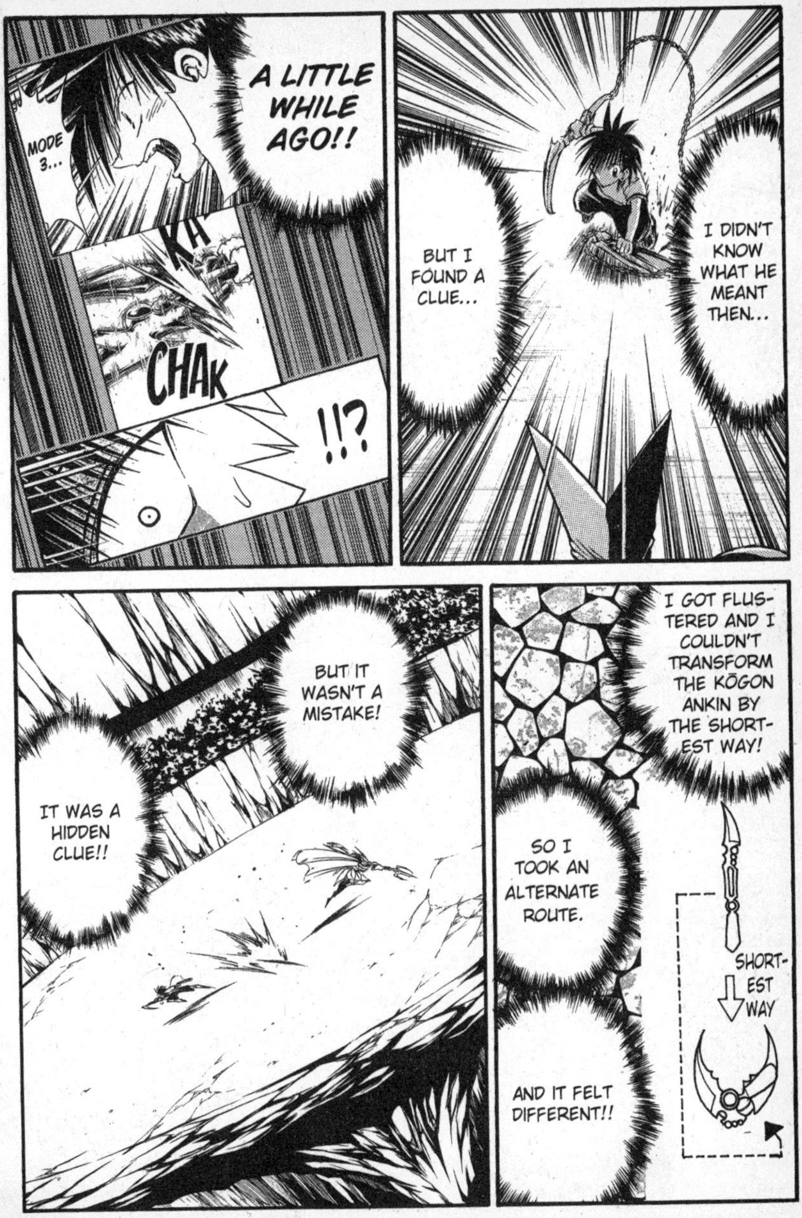
I DIDN'T KNOW WHAT HE MEANT THEN...
BUT I FOUND A CLUE...
A LITTLE WHILE AGO!!
MODE 3...
KA
CHAK
!!?
I GOT FLUSTERED AND I COULDN'T TRANSFORM THE KŌGON ANKIN BY THE SHORTEST WAY!
SO I TOOK AN ALTERNATE ROUTE.
SHORTEST WAY
AND IT FELT DIFFERENT!!
BUT IT WASN'T A MISTAKE!
IT WAS A HIDDEN CLUE!!

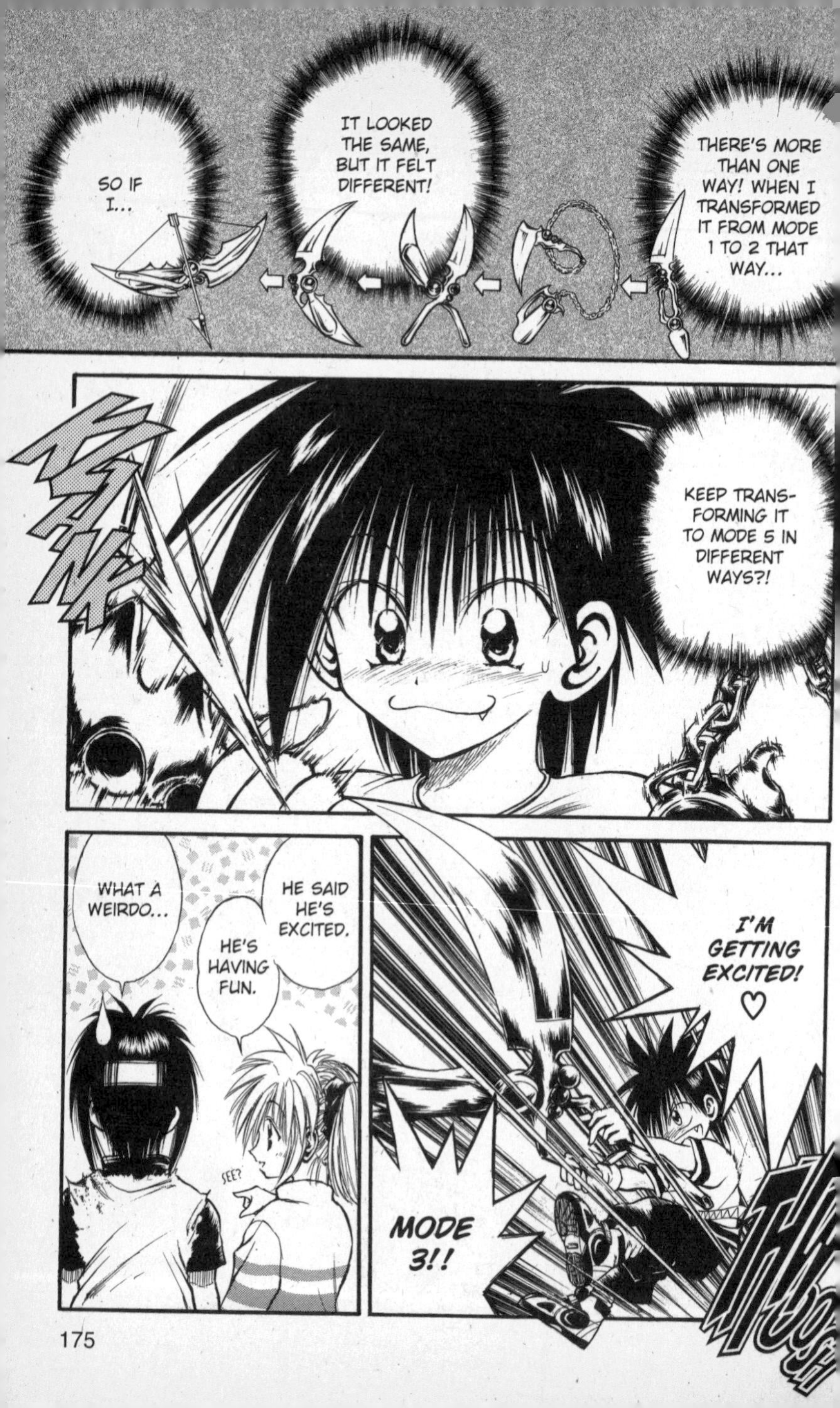
THERE'S MORE THAN ONE WAY! WHEN I TRANSFORMED IT FROM MODE 1 TO 2 THAT WAY...
IT LOOKED THE SAME, BUT IT FELT DIFFERENT!
SO IF I...
KEEP TRANS-FORMING IT TO MODE 5 IN DIFFERENT WAYS?!
KLANK
I'M GETTING EXCITED! ♡
MODE 3!!
HE SAID HE'S EXCITED.
WHAT A WEIRDO...
HE'S HAVING FUN.
SEE?

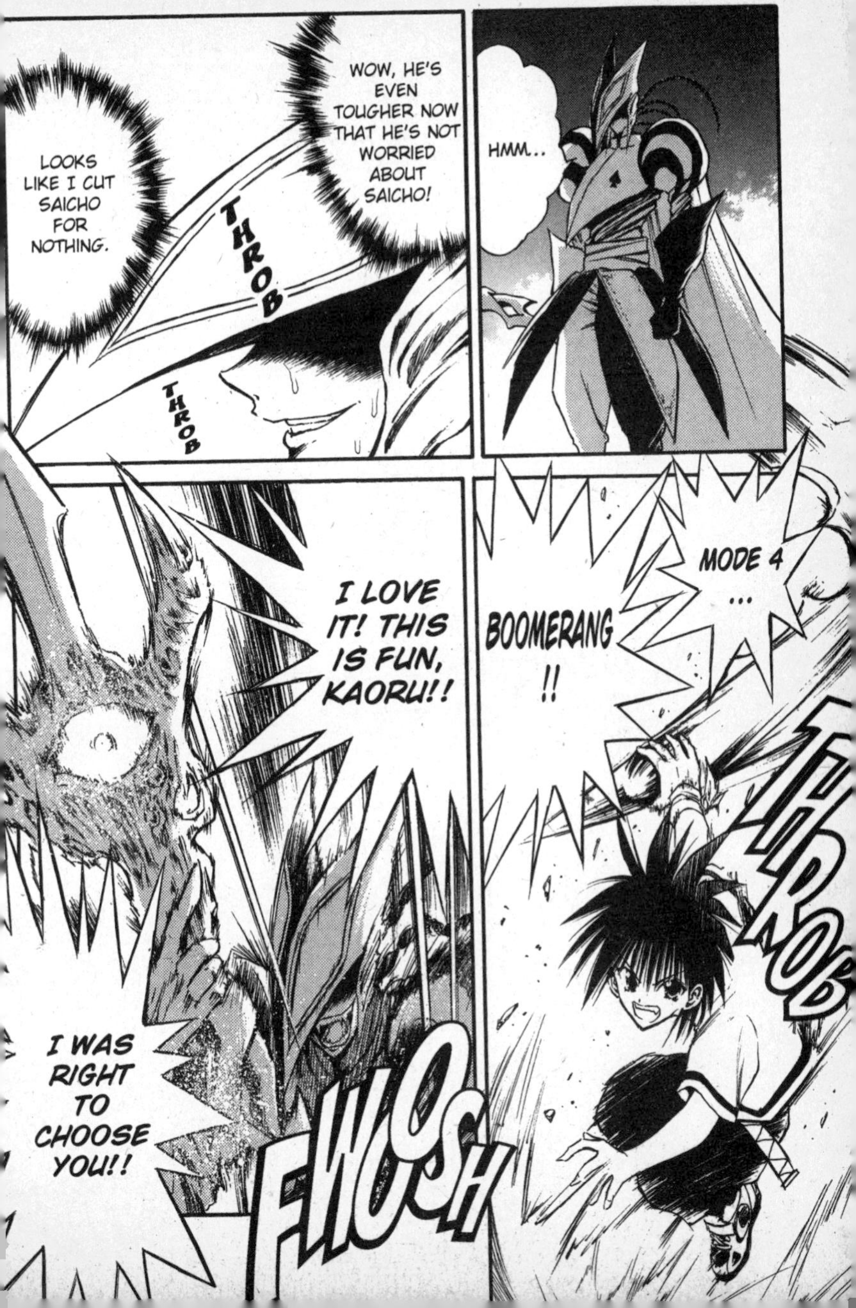
HMM..
WOW, HE'S EVEN TOUGHER NOW THAT HE'S NOT WORRIED ABOUT SAICHO!
THROB
LOOKS LIKE I CUT SAICHO FOR NOTHING.
THROB
MODE 4 ...
BOOMERANG !!
THROB
I LOVE IT! THIS IS FUN, KAORU!!
I WAS RIGHT TO CHOOSE YOU!!
FWOOSH

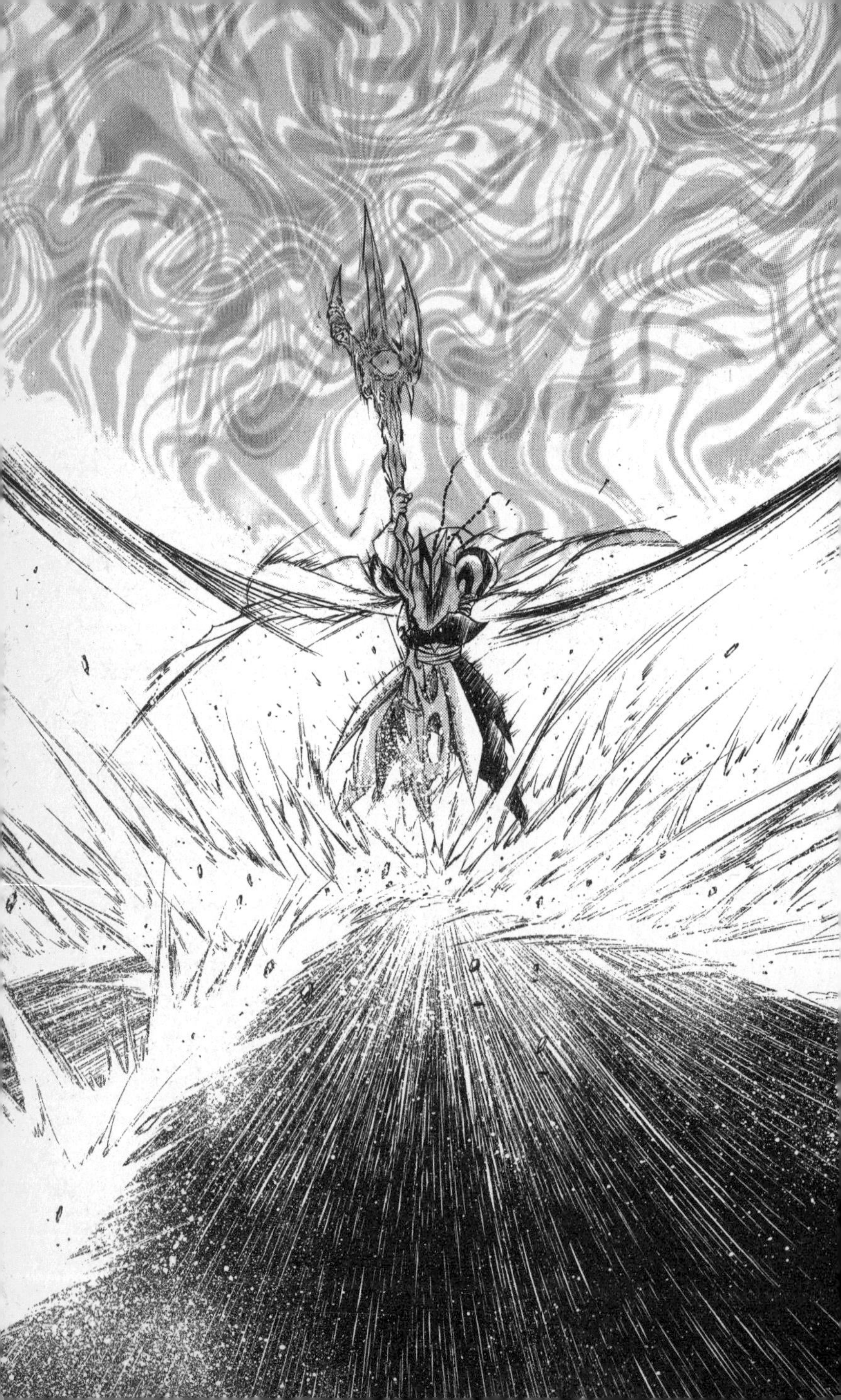

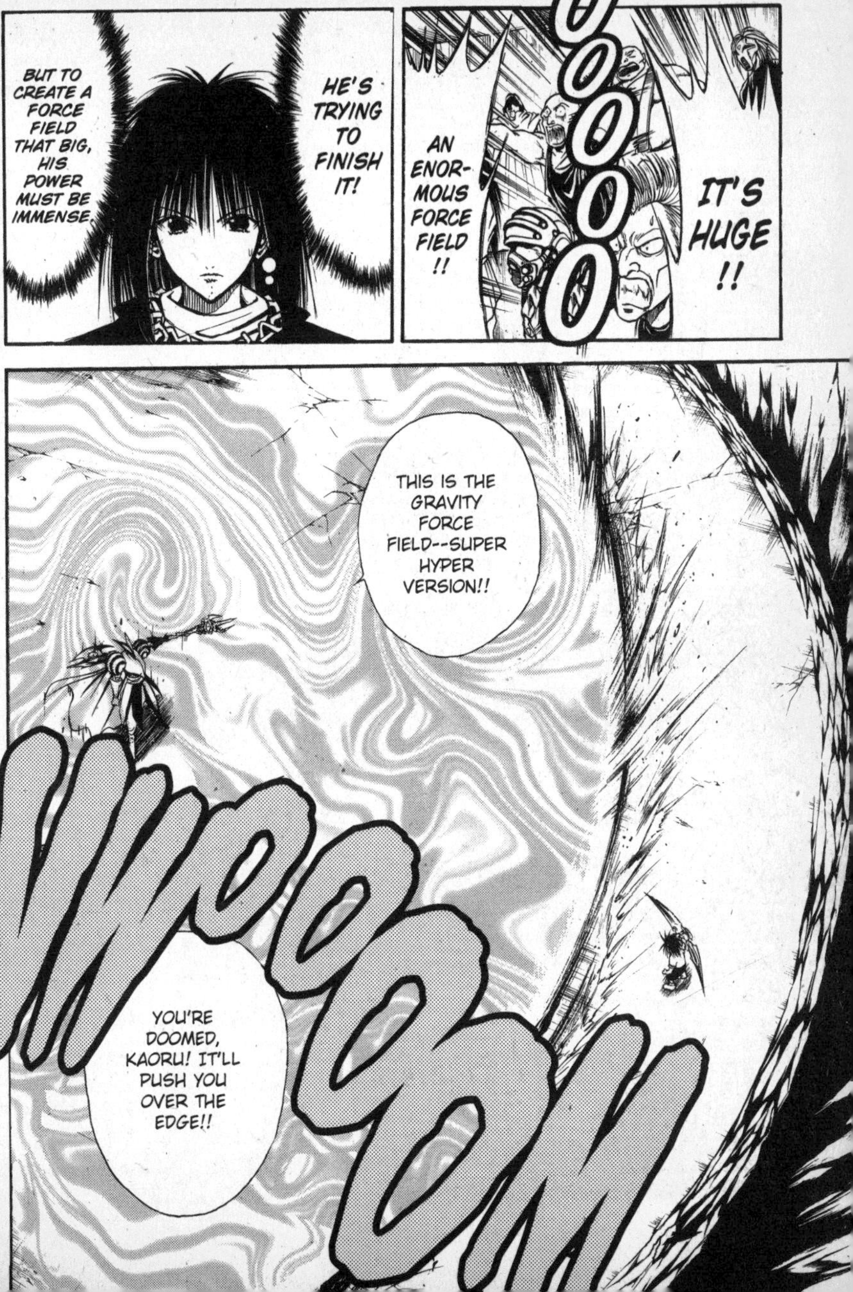
OOOOOO
IT'S HUGE!!
AN ENORMOUS FORCE FIELD!!
HE'S TRYING TO FINISH IT!
BUT TO CREATE A FORCE FIELD THAT BIG, HIS POWER MUST BE IMMENSE.
THIS IS THE GRAVITY FORCE FIELD--SUPER HYPER VERSION!!
WHOOSH
YOU'RE DOOMED, KAORU! IT'LL PUSH YOU OVER THE EDGE!!

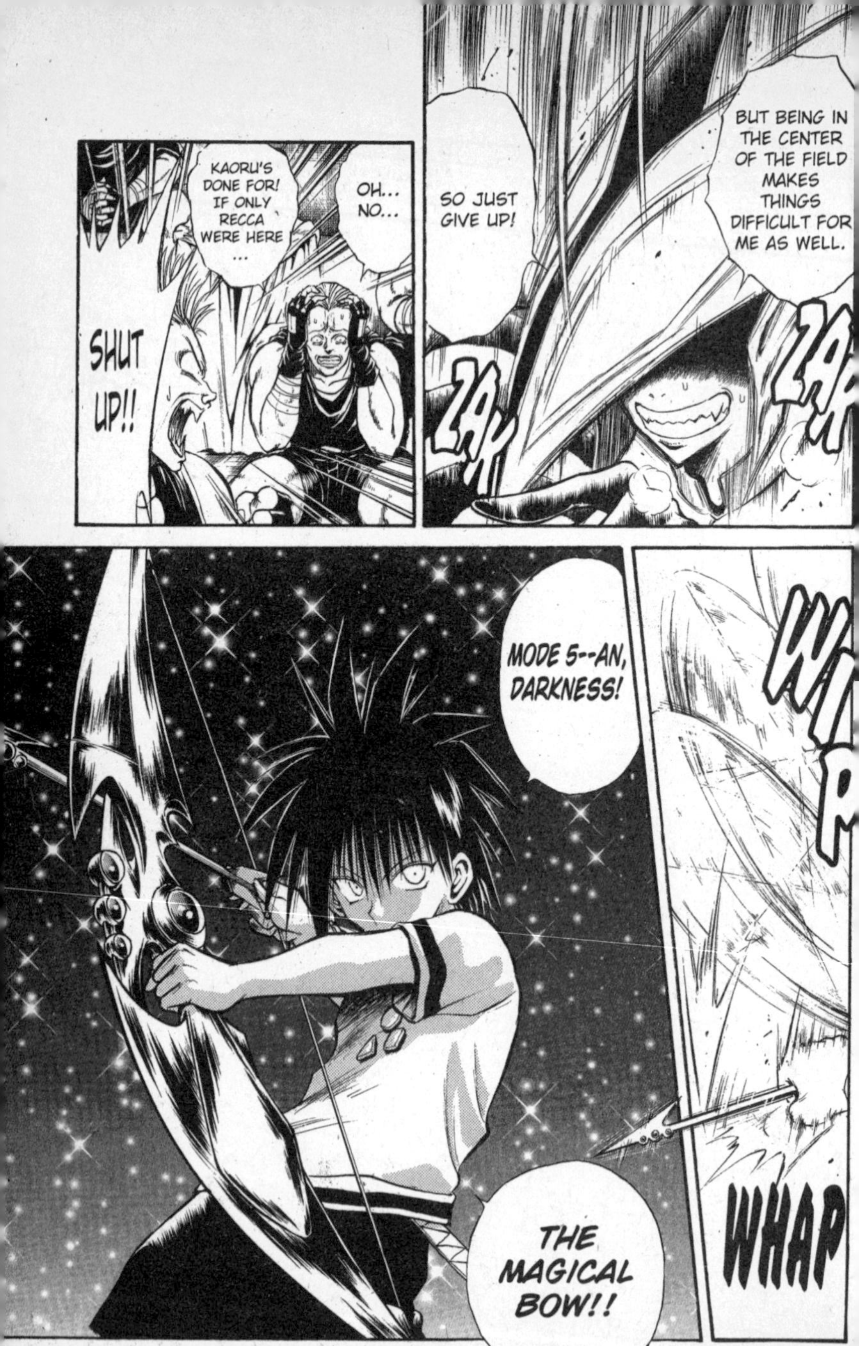
BUT BEING IN THE CENTER OF THE FIELD MAKES THINGS DIFFICULT FOR ME AS WELL.
SO JUST GIVE UP!
ZAK
ZAK
OH... NO...
KAORU'S DONE FOR! IF ONLY RECCA WERE HERE ...
SHUT UP!!
WHIP
WHAP
MODE 5--AN, DARKNESS!
THE MAGICAL BOW!!

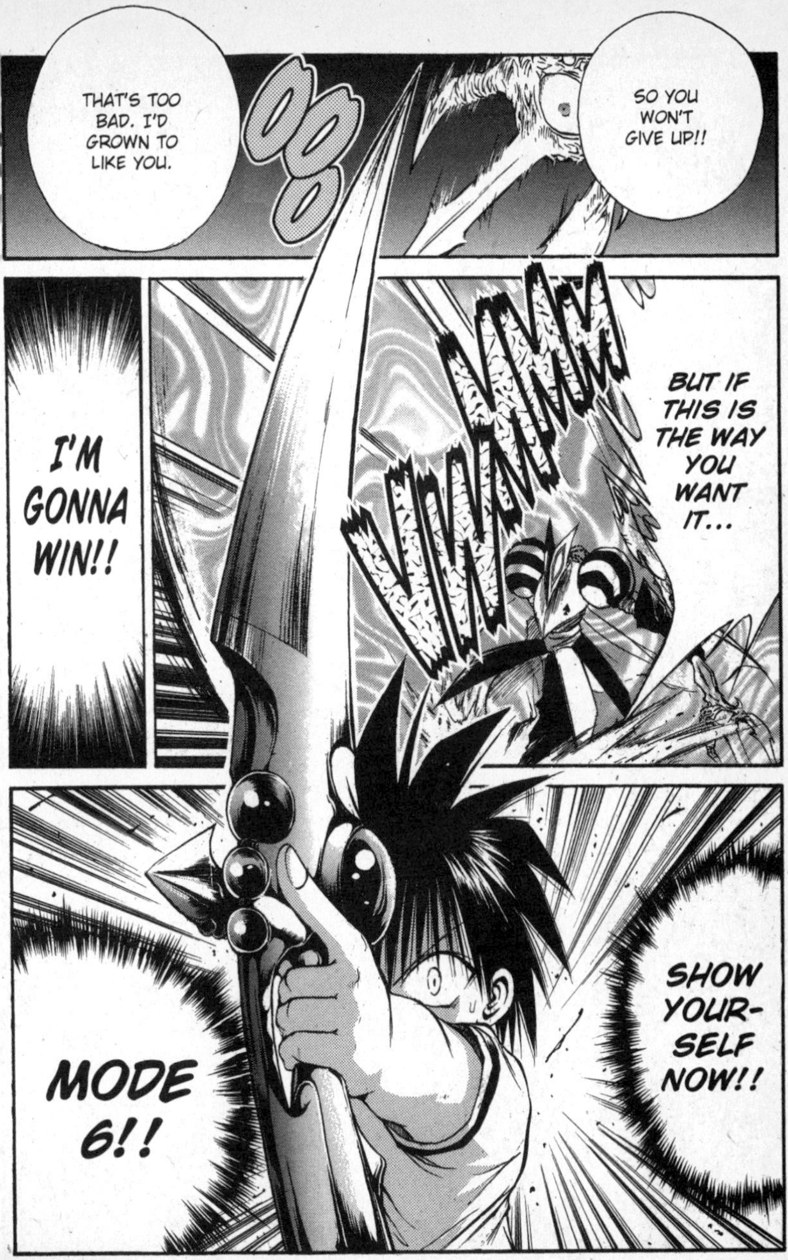
SO YOU WON'T GIVE UP!!
THAT'S TOO BAD. I'D GROWN TO LIKE YOU.
BUT IF THIS IS THE WAY YOU WANT IT...
I'M GONNA WIN!!
SHOW YOUR-SELF NOW!!
MODE 6!!

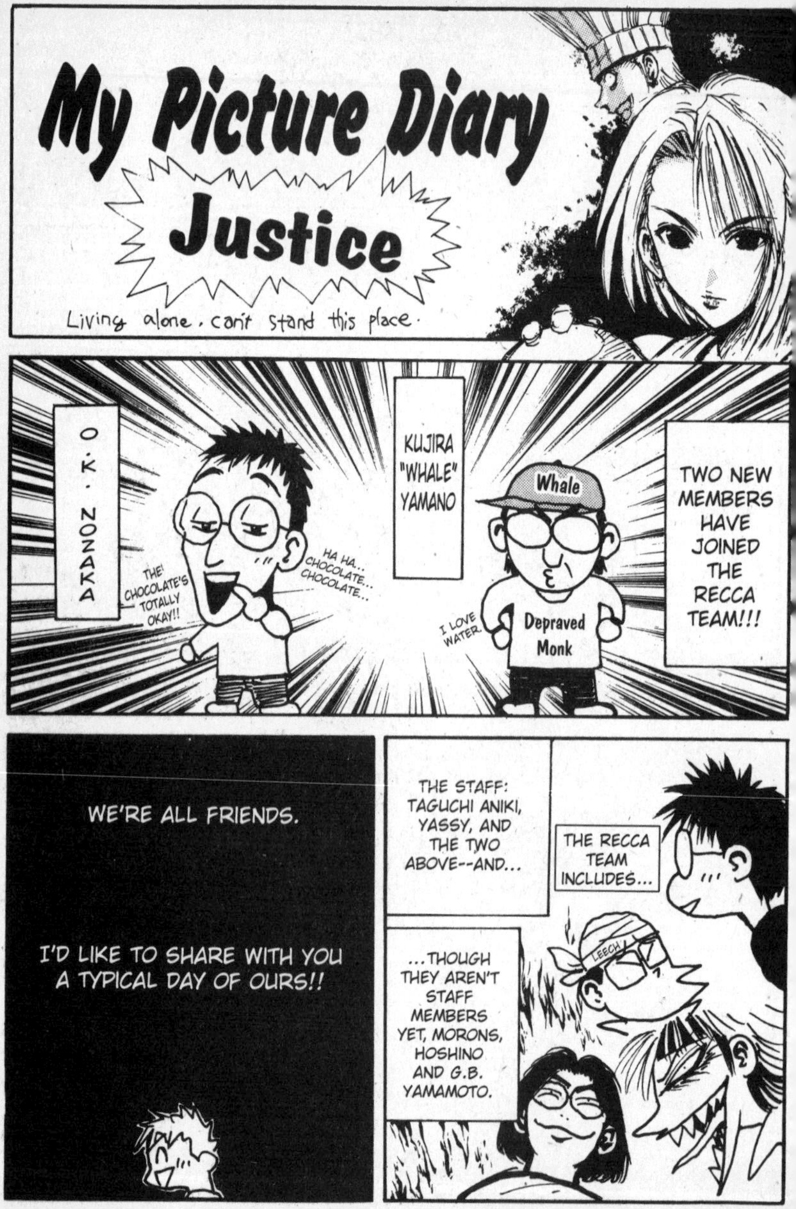
My Picture Diary
Justice
Living alone, can't stand this place.
TWO NEW MEMBERS HAVE JOINED THE RECCA TEAM!!!
KUJIRA "WHALE" YAMANO
Whale
Depraved Monk
I LOVE WATER.
HA HA... CHOCOLATE... CHOCOLATE...
O.K. NOZAKA
THE! CHOCOLATE'S TOTALLY OKAY!!
THE RECCA TEAM INCLUDES...
THE STAFF: TAGUCHI ANIKI, YASSY, AND THE TWO ABOVE--AND...
LEECH
...THOUGH THEY AREN'T STAFF MEMBERS YET, MORONS, HOSHINO AND G.B. YAMAMOTO.
WE'RE ALL FRIENDS.
I'D LIKE TO SHARE WITH YOU A TYPICAL DAY OF OURS!!

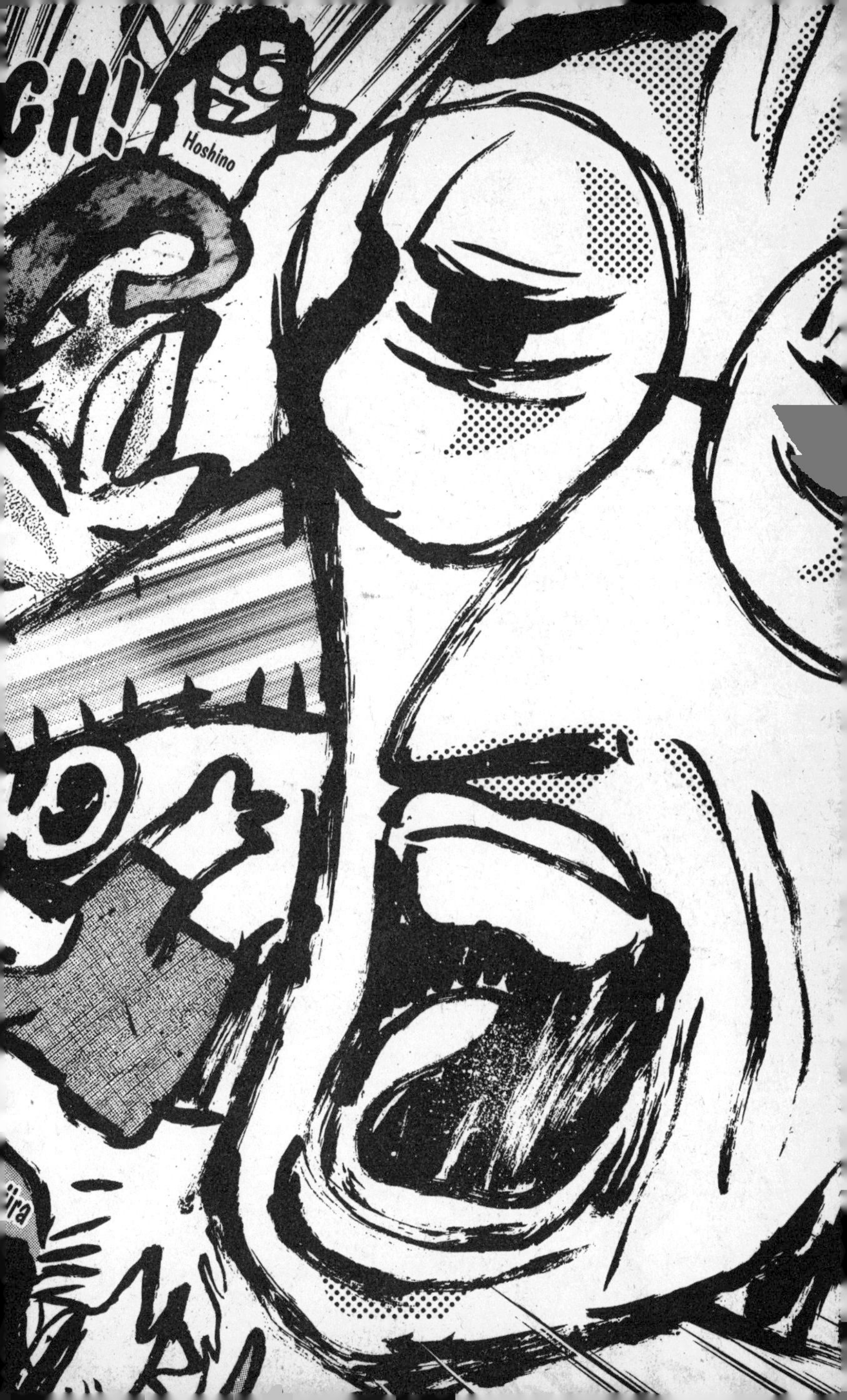
GH!
Hoshino

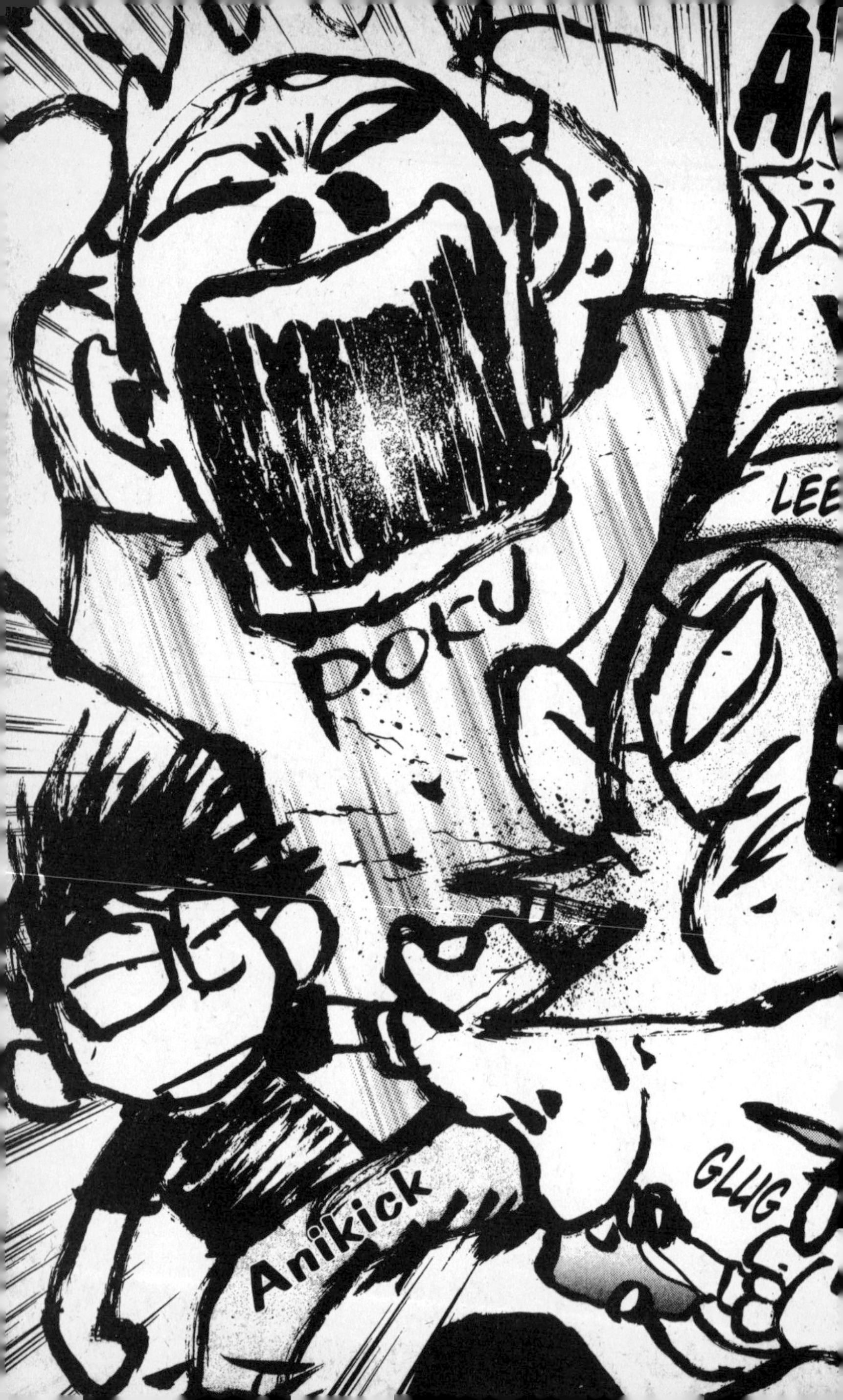
POKU
GLUG
Anikick

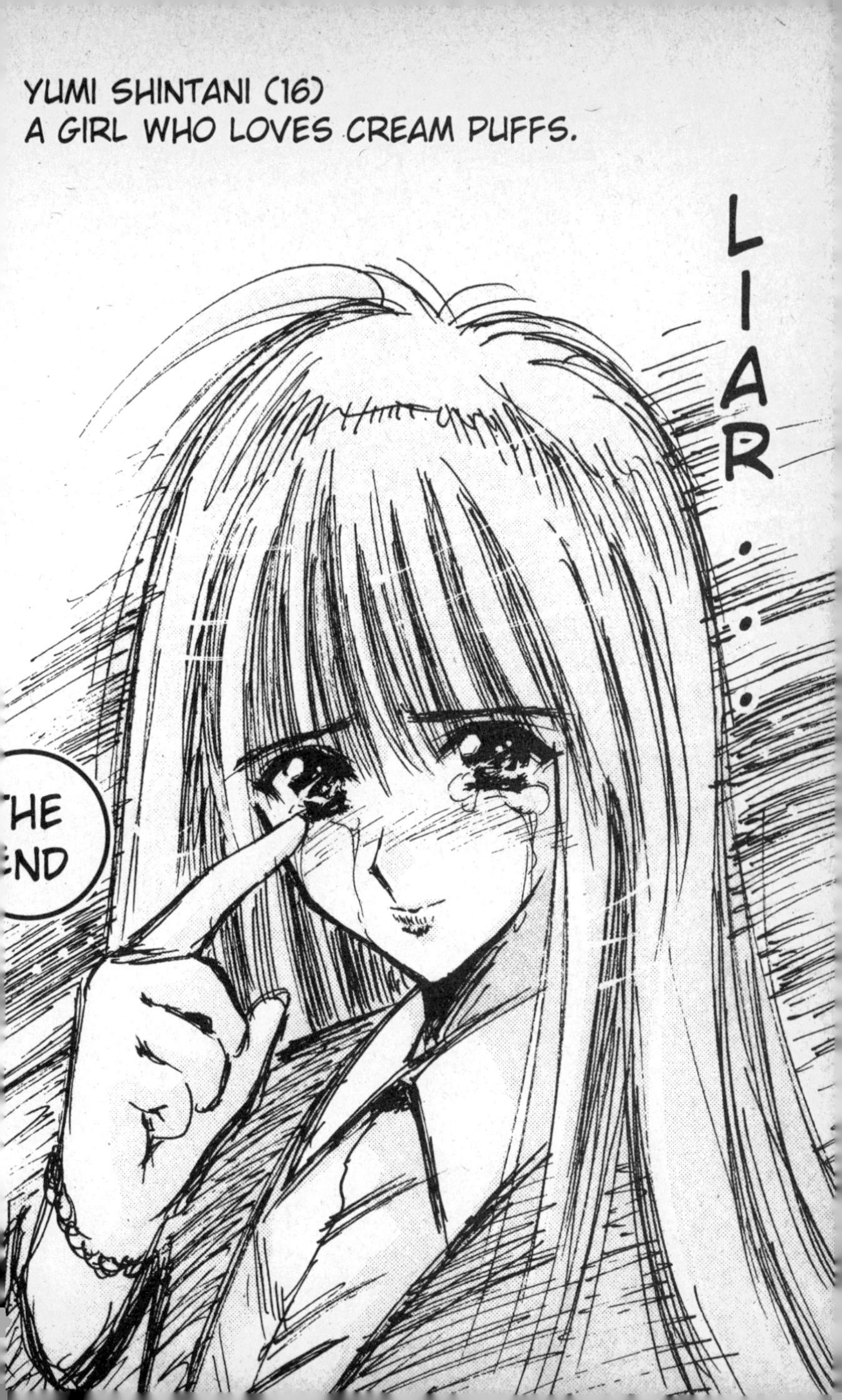
YUMI SHINTANI (16)
A GIRL WHO LOVES CREAM PUFFS.
LIAR...
HE
ND

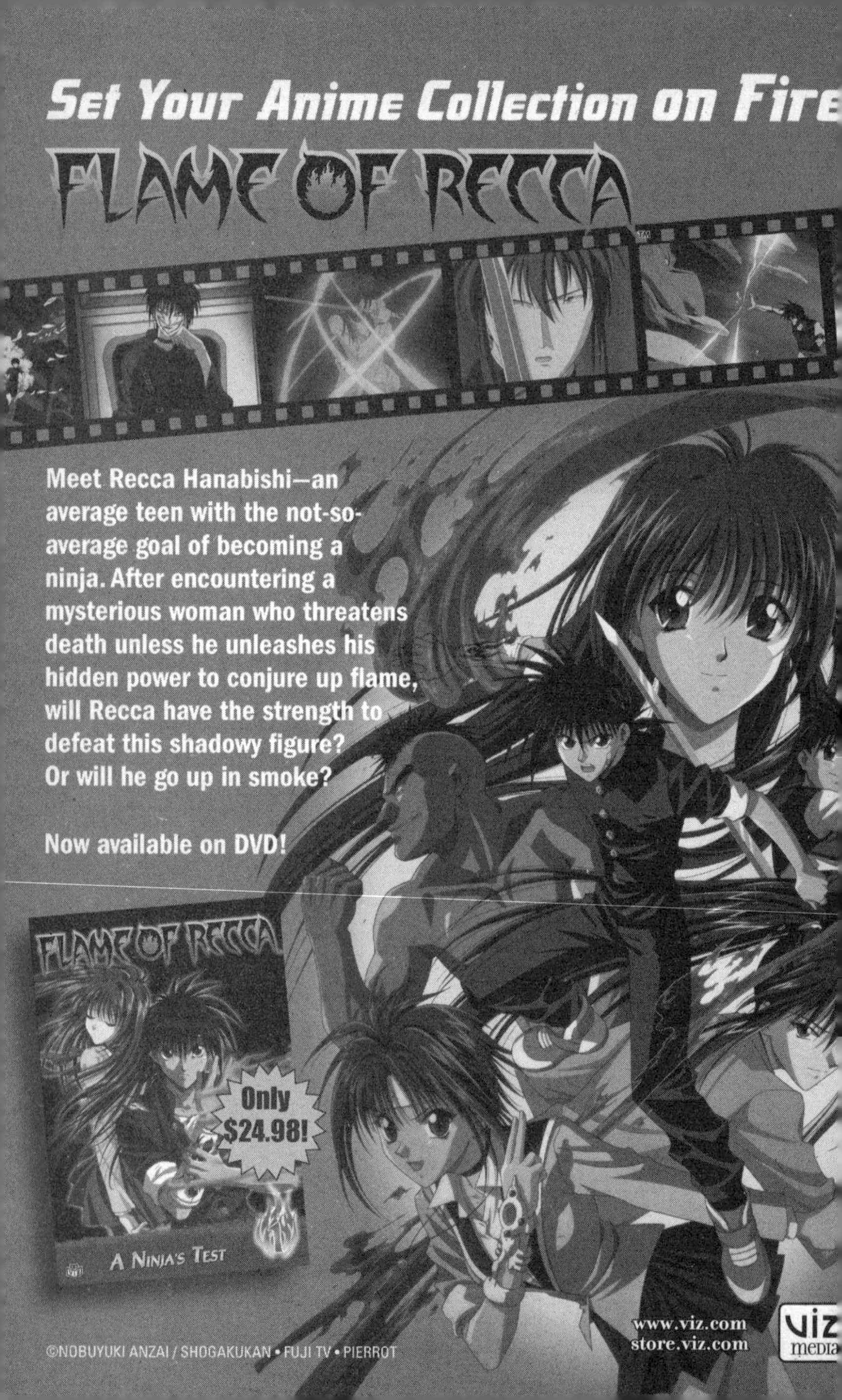
Set Your Anime Collection on Fire
FLAME OF RECCA
Meet Recca Hanabishi—an average teen with the not-so-average goal of becoming a ninja. After encountering a mysterious woman who threatens death unless he unleashes his hidden power to conjure up flame, will Recca have the strength to defeat this shadowy figure? Or will he go up in smoke?
Now available on DVD!
FLAME OF RECCA
Only $24.98!
A NINJA'S TEST
www.viz.com
store.viz.com
VIZ MEDIA
©NOBUYUKI ANZAI / SHOGAKUKAN • FUJI TV • PIERROT

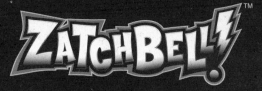

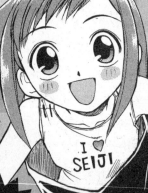
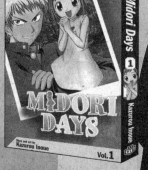

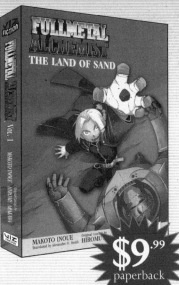
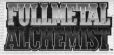
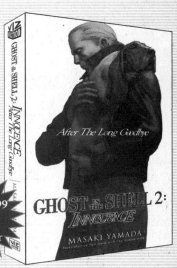

A Novel Concept

Introducing VIZ Media's new fiction line!

When we tell a story, we have the habit of giving you everything—the storyline *and* the visuals. But we're reinventing how you connect to your favorite series through our new line of full-length novels. Follow the characters you've come to love as they embark on new adventures. Except this time, we're just telling the story—we'll let your imagination do the rest.

FICTION
Socrates in Love
Kyoichi Katayama
Socrates in Love
Kyoichi Katayama
Translated by Akemi Wegmüller
VIZ media
FICTION
$17.99
hardcover

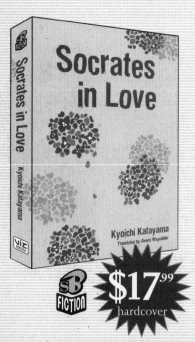

Socrates in Love

by Kyoichi Katayama

The best selling novel of all time in Japan with over 3.2 million copies sold! Finally, U.S. readers can experience the phenomenon that became the inspiration for a blockbuster movie, a hit TV show, and the Shojo Beat manga, also available from VIZ Media.

When an average boy meets a beautiful girl, it's a classic case of young love—instant, all consuming, and enduring. But when a tragedy threatens their romance, they discover just how deep and strong love can be.

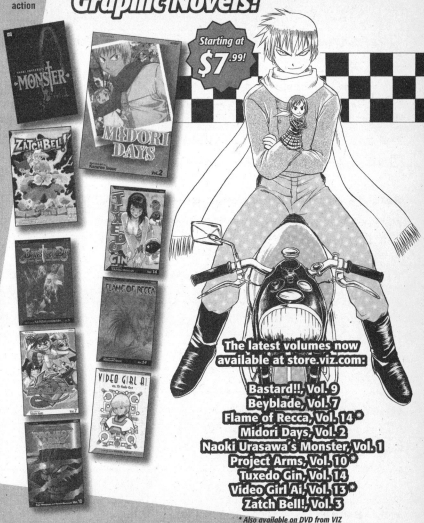